TO

HIS ROYAL HIGHNESS

GEORGE AUGUSTUS FREDERICK,

PRINCE OF WALES, DUKE OF CORNWALL AND
ROTHSAY, &c. &c. &c.

AND

PRINCE REGENT

OF THE

United Kingdom of Great-Britain and Ireland.

SIR,

IMPELLED by a desire of being useful to my
native country and to its parent state, it is
with the utmost deference I most respectfully
offer to your Royal Highness's acceptance a
Topographical Map and Description of the
Province of Lower Canada, completed after
several years of unremitting efforts, and I may
venture to add of unwearied diligence. If it

should obtain the distinguished favour of being honoured by your approval, I shall ever consider such a circumstance as an additional testimony of the readiness with which your Royal Highness patronises any work that may convey information of real utility, however humble, rather than as an indication of superior talent on my part. A servant of our revered Monarch for the greatest part of my life, I have ever believed it incumbent to repay the trust reposed in me, by making the public service a consideration paramount to all others, whenever the performance of my duties or other personal exertions could in any way contribute thereto. This desire, acting as the main spring of my endeavours, has induced me to think, that whatever has a tendency to demonstrate the actual state of the Canadas, and to place their greatly improvable resources in a true point of view, as valuable jewels of the British diadem, would neither be deemed unimportant nor destitute of advantage; I have therefore directed all the abilities at my disposal towards that object. If I have been at all successful, the gracious benevolence of your Royal Highness will cause me to lament the limited capacity displayed in performing the task imposed upon myself. By birth. a Canadian, I have at a distance contemplated with admiration and. heart-felt reverence the unequalled blessings of our constitution, which holds its protecting ægis over the most remote as powerfully as over its domestic subjects, and has so bounti-fully extended its inimitable purity and justice to my fellow countrymen in particular; but this reverence is exalted to the highest degree now that I experience how it endues an in-dividual like myself, from another hemi-sphere, with the privilege freely to approach his Sovereign, and lay the result of a well in-tentioned labour on the steps of the Throne. Scarcely with diminished admiration do I ex-press my acknowledgments for the courtesy that your Royal Highness has so condescend-ingly shewn, by permitting my performance to make its appearance under your auspices ;

such a mark of distinction will increase the grateful impressions with which I feel proud to subscribe myself,

Your Royal Highness's

Most devoted, faithful,

and most obedient servant,

JOSEPH BOUCHETTE.

PREFACE.

THE surrender of Quebec to the army of
General Wolfe, in the year 1759, ultimately
gave England possession of the immense extent
of territory that now forms the provinces of
Upper and Lower Canada. The value of the
conquest was highly rated while the glorious
circumstances of the victory continued to attract universal admiration; but after the ebul-
litions of joy had abated, the magnitude and
importance of the acquisition became less attended to, and in a short time it obtained
scarcely a greater share of consideration than
the other North American provinces. In the
war waged by the colonies against the mother
country, the population of Canada, although
so recently become British subjects, resisted
with fidelity every attempt that was made to
seduce them from their new allegiance, and with
bravery repulsed every endeavour to subdue
them by force. Such devotedness was highly
appreciated, and England, at the termination of that unnatural contest, turned her at-

tention towards giving an increased consequence to her remaining possessions, with the
design of drawing from them some of the supplies she had been accustomed to receive from
the countries just separated from her dominion.
This greatly brightened the prospects of the
colonists, and gave a fresh spur to their industry, whereby both agriculture and commerce were considerably extended. But unfortunately the hopes thus excited were soon
repressed by the great advantages given to the
people just protruded upon the world as an
independent state, and against whom it was
not in the power of the colonies to contend
successfully in the great market, that of supplying the West India islands with provisions
and timber, owing to the commercial regulations being formed so eminently favourable
to their opponents. The importance of these
provinces should be estimated less by their
territorial extent than by the resources they already offer, their capabilities of improvement,
and the great increase that may be given to
their commerce, which even now will be seen,
on an examination of their export and import
returns, to require something more than 300,000
tons of shipping. Ships thus employed and
navigated by British subjects secure the ad-

ditional advantage of furnishing a supply of
hardy and experienced seamen, whenever it
may be necessary to. send forth the warlike
fleets of Britain to repel aggression or defend
her possessions; the nature of the freights too
from these provinces is of first rate consequence,
as they consist of articles of indispensable necessity to the West India islands, and large
quantities of timber for naval uses to England;
and to which could be added, in a very few
years, other naval stores at present supplied by
other countries. The real value of these colonies to the parent state, and the great amelioration they are susceptible of, appears to
have been known hitherto, on this side of the
Atlantic; but by a few persons having some
connection with them: however, it may be
reasonably expected that a more minute in-
vestigation will ere long take place upon this
subject, from seeing the efforts recently made
by the Americans to obtain them; and which
will most assuredly be repeated should a convenient occasion ever again present itself. Towards their permanent security the attention
of government may be profitably turned in several ways; one of the most prominent is the
encouragement of agricultural improvement.
Of the many hundred thousand acres of excel-

lent land now covered by thick forests, much
would be cleared and soon brought into cultivation, were adequate inducements given by
the supreme authority, to promote the introduction of a regular, judicious, and practical
system of husbandry : in fact, to shed prosperity over the province, little more is required
than to subject the soil to the operation of the
plough. If a spring be given to the industry
of the cultivator, amendment in most other
branches of political economy is a matter of
course; the substantial riches and internal
strength of every country are produced by it,
and it is also the cause of wealth flowing in
from other states. Twenty-five years of the
most arduous and expensive warfare that ever
exhausted a country have at length, by England's fortitude, and an achievement in arms
transcending in lustre and heroism all her
former recorded glories, opened upon us the
prospect, and, we are authorised to hope, laid
the foundation of a peace that will be uninterrupted for a long series of years. During such
a protracted time of general exertion and sacrifice, when our country was struggling to maintain its existence as a first rate nation, it will
not greatly excite our wonder, that although
many plans of national improvement have been

adopted, many more should have been unwill-
ingly laid aside until the coming of a more
propitious period for carrying them into effect.
That period, so long sighed for by suffering
millions, is perhaps nearly arrived, when the
talents and attention of statesmen will have no
other view than to diminish the chance of similar calamities recurring, and to give energy
and fresh vigour to industry and the arts of
peace; at such an epoch the wants and claims
of the British North American provinces will undoubtedly obtain the notice they are entitled to.
In what manner their internal situation can be
most beneficially improved, their population
most speedily increased by the encouragement of
industrious settlers, and particularly the cultivation of hemp and flax supported, which may, in
fact, be pursued to almost any extent, belongs
to the sagacity of political economists to point
out; and if the means proposed should receive
the countenance and support of the imperial
government, their safety, welfare and prosperity
will neither be dubious, or, after a short period,
liable to sustain serious injury from casualties.
The interior of Lower Canada being so little
known beyond the limits of the province, a belief that a detailed account of it would not only
be useful by shewing its present state, but by

bringing it under more general notice, might possibly assist in the developement of its vast resources, has led to the construction of a Topographical Map upon a large scale, and to the publication of the following Book to illustrate the same more fully. The result of several years continued labour is now presented to the world, but not without its author's feeling the greatest diffidence in bringing his work before the tribunal of public opinion, of whose decisions even the most scientific and accomplished often feel a dread. The manner and method of the performance must speak for themselves, but of the subject matter it may be worth while to say a few words; and on this point he may perhaps be pardoned for a little self-gratulation, when he notes with confidence the authenticity and correctness of the materials he has had to work upon, which principally consist of the valuable documents and official records, that in his capacity of Surveyor-General of the Lower Province, are lodged with his department, and which he has been permitted the free use of. These, as accurately descriptive of the date and extent of the feudal tenures, and of all the grants made by the English government, may consequently be relied upon; beside this source, a long period of pro-

fessional field service has enabled him to acquire a very critical local knowledge of almost
every part of the province, and to verify the
same by numerous surveys, and careful observations on the nature, quality, and properties of
the best and most valuable tracts; and from
which he ventures to believe he has been able
to present a body of information, relative to this
part of the British Trans-Atlantic dominions,
that has, up to this period, been sought for in
vain from any other work. Nothing has been
admitted into the description without mature
reflection, nor any thing but what he entertains
a well grounded confidence is borne out by the
actual state of the country. What is said of
the province of Upper Canada is the substance
of notes and memoranda made in that country
very recently, as well as a knowledge obtained
of it during an anterior service of six years
as an officer of the provincial navy upon the
lakes; these have been corroborated and enlarged from other sources of undeniable intelligence and veracity. If in the detail of the
work he may be thought prolix, it has arisen
from a desire to display the features, the nature,
and the productions of the country in such a
manner as to point out where it is most susceptible of amelioration, and its agriculture of

being carried beyond the limited science and experience of Canadian farmers, with prospects of success amounting almost to an absolute certainty. Neither on the style or arrangement of his book will he presume to trouble the reader with a single remark, but, sensible as he is of its being defective in both points, he throws himself upon the public candour. His object is to convey information that he feels assured is wanted, and he has to lament the scope of his abilities being incompetent to second his wishes to the utmost extent, by finishing the sketch with a more masterly hand, or as most likely it would have been done by any person whose occupations have permitted him to devote more time to literary pursuits. Three and twenty years of his life have been passed in the service of government, both in its civil and military branches, wherein the duties have almost always been of too active a description to afford much of the quiet and repose, so necessary for the attainment of science, and such a maturity of knowledge as prepares a writer for launching himself upon the ocean of public opinion with a fair chance of acquiring fame. To such a hope, the *ignis fatuus* that has deluded so many, he conscientiously disclaims any pretension, but an honest, though humble zeal to

procure some advantage to the land of his
birth, by impartially giving it that character,
and holding it forth in that true light through
whose medium he firmly believes it ought to be
viewed, has been the cause of intruding himself
upon the public attention ; and if his feeble
endeavours should have the good fortune to
obtain approbation, rather for the attempt than
their real merits, his greatest ambition will be
amply gratified.

LONDON,
November, 1815.

A

· TOPOGRAPHICAL DESCRIPTION,

&c.

Antecedent to the year 1791, the whole extent of country now known as Upper and Lower Canada was denominated the province of Quebec, but as difficulties occurred in managing the concerns of so large a track, it was judged expedient, for better regulating and more effectually providing for its government, that it should be divided into two provinces; which plan was sanctioned by an act of the British parliament.

The province of Lower Canada lies between 45 and 52 degrees of north latitude, and 63 and 81 of west longitude, nearly, from Greenwich. It is bounded on the north by the territory of the Hudson's Bay company or East Maine; on the east by the gulf of St. Lawrence, the river St. John, and that part of

the Labrador coast *, which was, by an act of
the British parliament in 1809, together with the
island of Auticosti at the mouth of the St. Lawrence, finally annexed to the government of
Newfoundland; on the south by New Brunswick
and part of the territories of the United States,
viz. the district of Maine, the province of New
Hampshire, the state of Vermont, and the state
of New York; and on the west by a line which
separates it from Upper Canada, as fixed by
the first mentioned act of parliament, and pro-
mulgated by proclamation in the province on
the 18th day of November 1791, as follows:
" To commence at a stone boundary on the
" north bank of the lake St. Francis, at the
" cove west of Pointe au Baudet, in the limit
" between the township of Lancaster and the
" seigniory of New Longeuil, running along
" the said limit in the direction of north, 34
" degrees west, to the westernmost angle of the
" said seigniory of New Longeuil; then along
" the north-western boundary of the seigniory
" of Vaudreuil, running north, 25 degrees east,
" until it strikes the Ottawa river; to ascend

* Under the French government this portion of the Labrador
coast was deemed within the province of Quebec; in 1764 it
was separated therefrom by act of parliament, and annexed to
the government of Newfoundland; it was afterwards re-incor-
porated with the province of Quebec, and in 1809 finally subjected to the governor of Newfoundland.

" the said river into the lake Temiscaming,
" and from the head of the said lake by a line
" drawn due north, until it strikes the boun-
" dary line of Hudson's Bay, including all the
" territory to the westward and southward of
" the said line to the utmost extent of the
" country commonly called or known by the
" name of Canada *."

* This western boundary, as just recited, must have been founded upon an erroneous map of that part of the country, whereon the westerly angle of the seigniory of New Longeuil, and the south-westerly angle of the seigniory of Vaudreuil are represented as co-incident; when, in reality, they are about nine miles distant from each other: the true intent and meaning of the act appears to be as follows: viz. That the boundary between Upper and Lower Canada shall commence at the stone boundary above Pointe au Baudet, and run along the line which divides the township of Lancaster from the seigniory of New Longeuil, (and this line it is necessary to observe, as well as most of the seignorial lines of the province, ought to run north-west and south-east, reckoning from the astronomical meridian, in conformity to an ancient ordinance of the province, or " Arrêt et reglement du conseil superieur de Quebec, daté 11 de Mai 1676") to the westerly angle of the said seigniory; thence along a line drawn to the south-westerly angle of the seigniory of Rigaud, and continued along the westerly line of Rigaud until it strikes the Ottawa river, as represented on the topographical map by the letters AB, BC, CD. It must be observed that the westerly line of the seigniory of Rigaud, as well as the other lines on the Ottawa, ought to run by the ancient ordinance, nord quart-nord-est, equal to 11 degrees 15 minutes east from the astronomical meridian. There is also a variation between the bearing of the Lancaster township line and the seignorial line of New Longeuil, when, in fact, they ought to be precisely the same; and some grants that have been made by government are supposed to infringe upon the seigniory, from which law-

The etymology of the name of Canada is very uncertain, and whether given by its aboriginal inhabitants, or bestowed by its first European discoverers, there is not sufficient authority to warrant a positive decision; therefore, it must suffice to say, that since the year 1535, when Jacques Cartier, a Frenchman, explored the river St. Lawrence, so called by him from first entering it on St. Lawrence' day, we find the name of Canada applied to the country on both sides of the river as far as he ascended it. Cartier had visited the gulf of St. Lawrence in 1534, but did not attempt any discoveries beyond its shores, although most probably he conceived a design at that time, and sketched a plan of operations, which was put into execution the year following, when he sailed up the river to Montreal, or rather the Indian village, on the spot where that city now stands. Here ended his researches, and Canada has attained its present extension by the various discoveries of indus-

suits between the grantee of the crown and the seignorial tenant have originated; others may, perhaps, frequently recur, as this part of the province is now in a flourishing state of cultivation, unless the governments of both provinces bestow some consideration upon the subject, now that the claims of individuals settled on each side of the line may be more easily adjusted, than after long and undisturbed possession has produced great improvement upon the estates.

trious or adventurous settlers at many different periods. From the time of its being
taken possession of by Europeans, the government and management of the country, under
French dominion, was very irregular, and not
unfrequently disastrous; being entrusted either
to trading companies more eager to extract
present profit than prudent in proposing designs for the future aggrandisement of an infant
colony, or, to daring individuals who had interest enough to procure commissions to con-
quer and settle wherever their arms could
make them masters of the soil. Nor did this
system vary much until the year 1663, when
the court of France, beginning to entertain
more distinct ideas of its importance, thought
proper to bestow attention upon the administration of its concerns, and raised it to the
dignity of a royal government. From this
period its governors were appointed by commission from the king; and the colony, hitherto
but little noticed, became generally known to
Europe as Canada, or La Nouvelle France. At
this time the population very little exceeded
7000 souls: but under the new arrangement
and better management, with the advantages
derived from its trade, now left almost free, an
accelerated progress, from barbarism and poverty towards civilization and prosperity, be-

came visible. If the policy of its governors had been exerted to conciliate the surrounding native tribes, and avoid the destructive wars with them, by which it was continually distressed, it is not unreasonable to presume that its advance to a flourishing state would have been as rapid, or, from its local advantages, probably more so than colonies are in general; but, unhappily, as a conciliatory system was never, or if at all but rarely adopted, the numerous incursions of the Indians, whose movements were always traced by the devastation they committed, paralized its efforts so much, that in 1714 the population could hardly number 20,000 souls. Other and very great disadvantages were felt from the wars carried on between the mother country and England *, which invariably extended their disastrous influence to the colonies, and were indeed waged by the colonists on both sides with a rancour and animosity unknown between the chief belligerents. Under the pressure of such frequent and protracted calamities, any amelioration could scarcely be expected, and the affairs of Canada continued to fluctuate be-

* In 1629 Canada was taken by the English, but was then held in so little estimation, that three years afterwards they again transferred it to its former owners, deeming their conquest not worth the expense of maintaining.

tween partial benefits and positive evils, until, it became the conquest of the English arms, directed by the victorious genius of General Wolfe in 1759; at which period the population of the country may be estimated at 70,000. A new epoch in the history of the province now opens; from this date its prosperity has been progressive, and if not aided by every powerful stimulus that might have been applied, yet it has never been retarded by its new government, either from parsimony or partiality to more ancient possessions. On the termination of the successful enterprize against Quebec, which placed the whole of the French possessions under British dominion, the conquerors lost no time in devising measures which would make the change of allegiance from one sovereign to another as little onerous to the inhabitants as the nature of such a circumstance could permit, and endeavoured to frame them in such a manner as to shew a liberality that might be likely to attract their good-will. This was in some degree effected, by allowing their laws to remain unaltered; securing to them quiet possession of their lands under their ancient tenures; the free and undisturbed use of their religion; the inviolability of all religious property; and by many other concessions of importance, which rendered changes of customs and peculiar habits almost unnecessary. The Canadian was so far fortunate, that he passed from the dominion of one sovereign to that of another professing a different religious faith, without prejudice to his own style of living, his form of worship, his long practised modes of commerce and traffic, or the education of his children. From this period until the commencement of the war between England and her revolted American colonies, the greatest improvement that did take place is to be found in the stability and regularity acquired by the new government in all its branches, and in the strong affectionate attachment evinced by the Canadians towards a constitution that confirmed and protected them in all their natural as well as acquired rights. The strength of this attachment was decidedly and unequivocally shewn by the enthusiasm with which they fled to arms, and in the courage with which they fought to repel every aggression offered to their soil by the inveterate enemies who were so lately their fellow-subjects. Some increase in the population is observable, for in the year 1775 it amounted to something more than 90,000, in which estimate the present province of Upper Canada is included; but as very few settlements had as yet been made there, its inhabitants could form but a very trifling difference in the census. The American army that had entered Canada obtained some successes, but not of such a magnitude as to be enabled to maintain its ground for any considerable period; for in the latter end of the year just mentioned, it was expelled from the territory in a manner that must have conveyed to it but slender hopes of achieving any thing beyond temporary advantages at any future period; so long as the native of the soil remains firm in the loyalty and love of his country which had stimulated him to such vigorous efforts for the expulsion of its enemy *. Invasion so repelled produced security enough for agricultural and commercial pursuits to be carried on without fear of molestation, and which from that time have been continued in a gradual increase to their present conspicuous magnitude, with much benefit to the individuals, but more important

* As one of these natives, I can take upon myself to say in behalf of my countrymen, from the accurate knowledge I possess of their sentiments and feelings, that the services they then rendered, as well as the more brilliant exploits they recently performed against the same enemy, but now become more malignant and implacable, are proofs of an unalterable attachment to their government, as far as that term can be fairly applied to the minds of a grateful people; and they are also indices by no means equivocal, that the energies of such a people, mildly and honorably ruled as they now are, will always rise commensurate with the magnitude of the dangers that menace them.

advantage to the state. With the increase of agriculture, from whence flow the fundamental riches of every state, commerce and all the useful arts usually experience a relative amelioration; an enlarged population is invariably the consequence; and in the course of 39 years a capitation shews an increase to have taken place from 90,000 to no less a number than 335,000 souls, as the whole population of the province of Lower Canada. This aggregate, drawn from sources, and formed upon data that cannot deviate much from the general correctness of round numbers, will be viewed with astonishment by every reflecting person; and must convey to the mind a powerful conviction of the importance of such a colony, whose natural resources, as yet but partially unfolded, have, in so short a space of time, been the means of fostering so vast an increase. Of this total number 275,000 may be called native Canadians, descendants of the original French settlers; the remainder is composed of a mixture of many nations, as English, Scotch, Irish, Americans; in fact, almost of every nation.

At the time this country fell under the English government, the feudal system universally prevailed in the tenure of lands, and which, as before mentioned, still continues with respect to such as were then granted; but the townships and tracts disposed of by the British administration have been granted in free and common soccage; only two or three instances to the contrary being known.

. By the ancient custom of Canada, lands were held immediately from the king *en fief*, or *en roture*, on condition of rendering fealty and homage on accession to the seignorial property; and in the event of a transfer thereof, by sale or otherwise, except in hereditary succession, it was subject to the payment of a *quint*, or the fifth part of the whole purchase money, and which, if paid by the purchaser immediately, entitled him to the *rabat*, or a reduction of two-thirds of the *quint*. This custom still prevails.

The tenanciers, or holders of lands *en roture*, are subject to some particular conditions, but they are not at all burthensome; for instance, they pay a small annual rent, usually between 2*s*. 6*d*. and 5*s*. (though in many seigniories the rents of new concessions have been considerably increased); to this is added some article of provision, such as a couple of fowls, or a goose, or a bushel of wheat, or something else of domestic consumption. They are also bound to grind their corn at the *moulin banal*, or the lord's mill, where one-fourteenth part of it is

taken for his use as *mouture*, or payment for
grinding; to repair the highways and by
roads passing through their lands, and to make
new ones, which, when opened, must be surveyed and approved by the grand voyeur of
the district, and established by proces verbal.
Lands are sometimes held by *bail amphiteotique*,
or long lease of 20, 30, 50, or any number of
years, subject to a very small rent only. *Franc
alleu* is a freehold, under which lands are exempt from all rights or duties to seigneurs,
acknowledging no lord but the king. *Censive*
is a feudal tenure, subject to an annual rent,
paid either in money or produce.

The *seigneurs*, by the old laws that have not
been repealed, are entitled to constitute courts
and preside as judges therein, in what is denominated *haute et basse justice*, which take
cognizance of all crimes committed within
their jurisdiction, except murder and treason.
This privilege has lain dormant ever since the
conquest, nor is it probable that it will ever be
revived, as such ample provision is made for
the regular administration of the laws. The
lods et vents constitute part of the seigneur's
revenue. It is the right to a twelfth part of the
purchase money of every estate within his
seigniory that changes its owner by sale, or
other means equivalent to a sale. This twelfth

is to be paid by the purchaser, and is exclusive
of the sum agreed upon between him and the
seller; for prompt payment of it a reduction
of a fourth part is usually made. In cases of
a sale of this nature the lord possesses the *droit
de retrait*, which is the privilege of pre-emption
at the highest bidden price within forty days
after the sale has taken place; it is, however,
a privilege but seldom exercised. All the
fisheries within a seigniory contribute to increase the proprietor's revenue, as he receives a
tithe of all the fish caught, or an equivalent
sum. Besides these rights, he is privileged to
fell timber anywhere within his seigniory for
erecting mills, repairing roads, or constructing
new ones, or other works of public and general
utility. Many proprietors of seigniories have
become very wealthy from these revenues, as
the sales and exchanges of estates have been
of late years very numerous. Lands held by
Roman Catholics under any of the aforemen-
tioned tenures are further subject to the payment to their curates of one twenty-sixth part
of all grain produced upon them, and to occasional assessments for building and repairing
churches, parsonage houses, or other works
belonging to the church. The remainder of
the granted lands within the province, not
held under any of these tenures, are in free

and common soccage, from which a reservation of two-sevenths is made; one thereof is appropriated to the crown, and the other set apart for the maintenance and support of the Protestant clergy. Many of the lots thus reserved for both purposes are now leased for twenty-one years on the following conditions: viz. for the first seven years twenty-five shillings, or eight bushels of wheat per annum; the second seven years fifty shillings, or sixteen bushels of wheat; and for the remainder of the period seventy-five shillings, or twenty-four bushels of wheat per lot: the lessors having the option of requiring payment to be made in either of the modes stipulated *. These reserves have, for many years past, been exposed to various and very extensive depredations by persons settling thereon and occupying many of the best lots without any title or payment of any rent; and by others felling and carrying away much of the finest

* In 1812 the quantity of land thus reserved amounted to 1,438,872 acres, out of which 363 lots of 200 acres each were let on lease for twenty-one years on the terms above recited. The total value thereof for that period will be found £19,057 10s. currency of the country, or one-ninth part less than sterling; but if the wheat rent be taken, and calculated upon an average price of 6s. 8d. per bushel, a rate rather below the medium price in the province, the amount will be £40,656. In the same year descriptions of 307 lots were made out for different applicants, and a great many of them have since been let.

timber, especially on those situated along the
borders of the rivers; these trespasses, it is
well known, are chiefly committed by natives
of the United States. It cannot be doubted
but that a remedy might be very easily applied
to this evil.

In forming the plan of government for
Canada, the general principles of the English
constitution were introduced wherever it was
practicable: in the upper province no impediments to this course of proceeding were
met with; but in the lower one some small
deviations from them were found necessary, in
order to reconcile it to the genius of a people
so long accustomed to a different regime. The
civil department is administered by a governor,
who is generally a military officer and commander of the forces, a lieutenant governor,
an executive council, a legislative council, and
a house of assembly, or the representatives of
the people. The governor and lieutenant governor naturally exercise their authority under
the royal commission. The members of the
executive council, amounting to seventeen,
derive their appointments from the king, and
this body exercises a direction over the concerns of the province, nearly similar to that of
the privy council in the affairs of England.
The legislative council, by the act of the con-

stitution, consists of fifteen members (although at present that number is increased), all of whom are appointed by mandamus from the king, and may be termed the second estate of the province; and, with the third branch or house of assembly, forms the provincial parliament. The governor is invested with power to prorogue, and in the exercise of his own discretion, to dissolve the parliament; to give the royal assent or refusal to bills passed by it, or to reserve them in cases of doubt or difficulty, until his majesty's pleasure be made known thereon. Such acts as receive the governor's assent are usually put into immediate force, but he is enjoined to have copies of them transmitted to England, that they may receive the approbation of the king in council, and his majesty has the right, with the advice of his council, to cancel any act so passed by the provincial parliament within two years from the date of its arrival in England; but hitherto its wisdom has been so well directed in the arduous task of legislating, that there is no instance on record of this prerogative ever having been exercised. The acts that emanate from the provincial parliament are all of a local nature, such, for instance, as providing for the internal regulations of the country through the various departments; for its defence as far as

relates to enrolling and embodying the militia,
and imposing taxes for raising the necessary
supplies to defray the expenses of government.
But any acts having for their object the alteration or repeal of any laws existing antecedent to the constitution granted in 1791;
the tithes; grants of land for the maintenance
of the Protestant clergy; the rights of presenta-
tion to rectories or the endowments of par-
sonages; whatever relates to the exercise of
religious worship, or disqualification on account
of religious tenets; the rights of the clergy; to
changes or modifications of the discipline of
the church of England; or of the royal prerogative on the subject of waste crown lands,
must, after having passed the provincial parliament, be submitted to the British parliament,
and receive the royal assent before they can
pass into laws. The house of assembly is composed of fifty-two members, and is a model on
a small scale of the house of commons of the
imperial parliament; the representatives are
extensive proprietors of land, and are elected
for the districts and counties by the votes
of persons being actual possessors of landed
property of at least forty shillings clear annual value: for the city of Quebec and the
towns, they are chosen by voters who must be
possessed of a dwelling-house and piece of

ground of not less annual value than five pounds sterling, or else have been domiciliated in the place for one year previous to the writ of summons issuing, and have paid one year's rent, not under ten pounds sterling, for a house or lodging. There exists no disqualification either for the electors or the elected on account of religious tenets, for, in this country, where toleration reigns in its plenitude, every one, whatever may be his faith, is eligible to fill any office or employ, provided the other qualifications required by law are not wanting. The sittings of the house begin in January, and all the public and private business is usually gone through by the latter end of March, about which time it is prorogued, so that the session never exceeds the term of three months between January and April. Should parliament not be dissolved by the governor, a circumstance that, indeed, very seldom occurs, its duration is limited by the act of the constitution to the period of four years; when its functions expire; and writs are immediately issued for the election of another: at such a crisis the independence and energy of the various voters, the professions and humility of the candidates, are as strikingly pourtrayed as in the more turbulent contests that take place on similar occasions in the mother country. The criminal code of the united kingdom extends to Canada, and is carried into effect without the slightest variation. For the administration of civil justice there is a court of appeal, in which the governor presides, assisted by the lieutenant governor, not less than five members of the executive council, and such of the principal law officers as have not had cognizance of the previous trial; against the decisions of this court, as a final resource, an appeal may be made to the king in council. A court of king's bench, a court of common pleas, with each a chief justice and three puisne judges. Quarter sessions of the peace held four times a year, besides a police and subordinate magistrature for determining affairs of minor importance.

From its having been already mentioned that by far the largest portion of inhabitants are descended from French ancestors, the reader will readily surmise that the prevailing religion is Roman Catholic; of this persuasion there is a Bishop of Quebec, a co-adjutor with the title of Bishop of Saldé, nine vicars general, and about 200 curates and missionaries spread over the different districts of the province, by whom the tenets of their religion are inculcated with assiduity and devotion, but little tinctured with bigotry or intolerance, unhappily

so frequently characteristic of the same faith
in the old world. Exercising their sacred functions under the auspices of a Protestant government, they feel the value of mildness in
their own conduct, and strenuously endeavour
to repay its protecting power by a zealous performance of their duties, and by instilling into
the minds of their flock a grateful obedience to
the laws, with a reverence for the constitution,
as well as the obligations imposed upon them in
their character of good citizens. They are also
chiefly employed in the important cares of education, of which they acquit themselves in a .
manner that reflects the highest credit upon their
exertions. To this fact the seminaries of Quebec
and Montreal, and the college of Nicolet, bear
a powerful testimony. In these establishments,
where the higher and abstruse sciences yield to
those of more extended and primary utility,
professors are employed to teach the various
branches of the classics, mathematics, and
belles-lettres, whose learning would acquire
them reputation in any country. In communicating their instructions the French idiom
is in general use, but in the college there is
a professor for the English tongue, an example
worthy of being followed by the two former, as
this language now becomes an essential part
of youthful studies. The revenues of the

Catholic clergy are derived from grants of land made to them under the ancient regime, and the usual contributions ordained by their ecclesiastical government, which are, perhaps, more cheerfully paid by the Canadians, and collected in a manner much freer from vexatious exactions than in any country whatever. The spiritual concerns of the Protestant part of the community are under the guidance of the Lord Bishop of Quebec, nine rectors, and a competent number of other clergymen, who are supported by annual stipends from the government, by the appropriation of one-seventh of all granted lands as provided for in the act of the constitution, and the other sources of revenue peculiar to the church of England, in a degree of moderate affluence, exempt on the one hand from inordinate impropriation, and on the other free from penurious parsimony; thereby giving to the clerical order the degree of consequence in the superior ranks of society that is due to its ministry. In the unrestrained exercise of two systems of divine worship, so widely differing in their tenets, it is a pleasing fact, that the discipline of the two churches never encounters the smallest obstruction from each other; on the contrary, the greatest good-will and harmony is observed to prevail, as well between the pastors as the flocks committed to their charge.

For the defence of the two Canadas a regular military establishment is maintained by the British government, which, in time of peace, may amount to about six or seven thousand men, including artillery, engineers, commissariat, &c.; but when we are at war with the United States, this force is increased as the pressure of circumstances demands; and at this period (1815) I may venture to compute it, although without official documents to fix the precise numerical strength, at from twenty-seven to thirty thousand men in both provinces. In aid of the regular troops, and in order that, under any exigency, the government may be enabled to bring an efficient force into the field, the lower province is apportioned into fifty-two divisions, wherein all males from sixteen to sixty years of age are bound by law to enrol their names every year with the captains of companies appointed for their parish, within the month of April. After the enrolment is completed, they are mustered four times in a year, either on Sundays or holidays, when they are instructed in as much of the rudiments of military exercise as the occasion will allow; beside these four muster days, they are, once in each year, reviewed by the commander in chief, or the officer commanding the division. This is denominated the sedentary militia; and as the average strength of each division so enrolled may be computed about a thousand, it makes the aggregate amount upwards of fifty-two thousand men *. The incorporated militia, by an act passed in the provincial parliament on the 19th May 1812, is fixed, during the war, at two thousand men; but by virtue of authority vested in the governor, it is at present increased to five battalions, or nearly double the number, which, on the re-establishment of peace with the United States, will be again reduced to the standard named in the act. This body is chosen by ballot from the unmarried men of the sedentary militia; its term of service is two years. It is also provided that one-half of each regiment may be discharged annually, and the vacancies filled up by a fresh ballot; a plan that will have the good effect of extending gradually a certain degree of military discipline over the greater part of the population capable of bearing arms. The battalions thus formed of single men, renders the military service less obnoxious to the individual, and less expensive to the state, by saving the provision otherwise necessary to be made for wives and children of militiamen actually embodied. By the same act, the sum of twelve thousand pounds annually is raised for the maintenance

* The adjutant-general's report gives 52,500.

of this constitutional force. The incorporated militia is well equipped, and in a state of discipline that merits the highest commendations, by which it has been enabled to brigade with the regular troops during the existing contest, and take so distinguished a part in some of the actions fought, that it must press upon the consideration of government a firm reliance upon its future exertions and devotedness in the cause of its country. In the upper province the same system, with some trifling modification, prevails, but from the more scanty population the force is proportionably much less; however, the militia of Upper Canada has had its full share of the hardships of the war, as well as many opportunities of distinguishing itself in presence of the enemy; and the real magnitude of its service may be estimated, when it is considered, that, by availing himself of it, the governor general, Sir George Prevost, was enabled with a number of troops of the line, inadequate according to usual military calculations, not only to repel every attempt of the American commanders to invade the British territory in the years 1813 and 1814, but to overwhelm the assailants with defeats, that for a long time will leave an indelible stain upon their military reputation.

To convey a general idea of the face and outline of the province previous to entering on a more minute description, I will assume Quebec as a central point, where the Saint Lawrence is about fifteen hundred yards broad; from the high banks opposite the city the land rises in a gradual ascent for a distance of probably ten leagues towards the first range of mountains; pursuing then a north-easterly course, this chain ends upon the river in the neighbourhood of River du Loup, bounding between it and the two rivers a level well cultivated and fertile space, singularly marked with several extraordinary isolated hills, or rather large rocks, thinly covered with small trees about their summits. Returning again opposite to Quebec for a new departure, the same chain is found to take nearly a south-west direction, crossing the line which separates the province from the United States to the west of Lake Memphremagog, and continuing the same course until it meets with the Hudson river, leaving the extent between its direction and the Saint Lawrence, excepting two or three of the afore-mentioned isolated hills, nearly level, and which, from the richness of its soil, is very thickly settled and populous. Beyond this range, at about fifty miles distance, is the ridge, generally deno-

minated the Land's-Height, dividing the waters
that fall into the Saint Lawrence from those
taking a direction towards the Atlantic ocean,
and along whose summit is supposed to run
the boundary line between the territories of
Great Britain and the United States of America. This chain commences upon the eastern
branch of the Connecticut river, takes a north-
easterly course, and terminates near Cape
Rosier in the gulf of Saint Lawrence. The
extent of country lying between these two
ridges varies very much in quality and fruit-
fulness according to its peculiar situation, but,
perhaps, a tolerable idea may be formed by
the following division of it. From the boundary
on the 45th degree of north latitude as far as
the river Chaudiere, is a district of excellent
and fertile land, divided mostly into townships,
many parts thereof settled and under cultivation; offering generally facilities for agricultural speculations, which, in the hands of
enterprising settlers, would not fail to afford
ample returns for capital applied to such pursuits. In fact, this track bounded by the Saint
Lawrence, the Chaudiere, and the province
line in shape of a triangle, whose western extremity is St. Regis, holds out the flattering
prospect, if due encouragement be given, of
becoming, at no very distant period, the most

flourishing part of Lower Canada, not from its,
luxuriant soil alone, but also from its lying
contiguous to the United States, and comprehending the main roads and principal points,
of communication between the two territories,
both by land and water, by which an uninterrupted intercourse can be at all times, and in
defiance of prohibition, so easily maintained.
From the Chaudiere to Lake Temiscouata the
land is much broken, irregular, and of an indifferent quality; but here and there are interspersed some good and productive tracks,
that would soon repay the expense of clearing
and cultivating.

From Lake Temiscouata, near where it enters the district of Gaspé, to Cape Rosier, the
interior has been but partially explored; however, such parts of it as are known bear an
appearance of sterility that encourages but
slender hopes of remunerating the labours of
the husbandman, even with a scanty crop,
being generally of a rugged and mountainous
character. This description must be understood as applicable in its full extent to the interior only, because, on the banks of the Saint
Lawrence, some good spots are frequently met
with, but hitherto none of them have been
settled upon. On the south side of the ridge
down to the shores of Gaspé and Chaleur bay,

the general description of the country is also mountainous ; notwithstanding which, in many parts of the district, particularly the latter, there is a considerable portion of excellent land, well settled, and containing a population of 3000 inhabitants, most of whom being employed in fisheries, unfortunately pay but little attention to the important duties of cultivation, that, from situation and other advantages, would soon become as productive to them, at all events, as the labours they now pursue. On the north side of the Saint Lawrence, and from the river St. John, the eastern extremity of Lower Canada, a ridge of heights takes a course parallel with and close to it, or rather, in most parts forms its shores as far up as Cape Tourment, where, taking a direction west south-west, it ends upon the Ottawa river about 38 leagues above its confluence with the St. Lawrence, enclosing within it and the two rivers a beautifully picturesque country, well watered and level, particularly so from Deschambault westward, which, in respect to population, good cultivation, and a generous soil, especially along the course of the river, must be considered as the best part of the province. On the north side of the ridge just described lies the remaining part of Lower Canada, yet unnoticed, and which is contained

within the Ottawa river, the 81 degree of west
longitude, and the 52 parallel of north latitude,
intersected laterally by another and higher
range of mountains that forms the Land's
Height, and divides the waters that empty into
the St. Lawrence from those that descend
into Hudson's Bay. Of this great space, so
little has been explored, that it is only known
to be covered with immense forests, whose
dreary solitudes are interrupted only by the
wandering tribes of natives who occasionally
resort thither in their hunting parties to procure furs for traffic with the nearest posts of
the north-west company. It is in America
that nature has displayed her powerful hand in
forming objects of sublimity and grandeur,
more imposing than what are to be met with
in other parts of the world; the mountains
there rise to an elevation but rarely equalled,
and range to a distance unexampled on the
old continent. The rivers roll their gigantic
streams to the ocean, unparalleled for length
of course, and affording facilities for intercourse
with the most remote parts that are quite unknown in other countries; the forests spread
out to an extent, and abound with trees of
a variety, magnitude, and utility that defies
comparison with the most enormous of the
other hemisphere. But, perhaps, of all the

stupendous efforts that unfold so wide a field
for the inquisitive researches of human wisdom
to investigate the effects of her creative power,
none are more calculated to excite admiration,
and baffle the progress of philosophic enquiry,
than the vast collections of fresh waters forming
the chain of lakes, that through the channel of
the Saint Lawrence descend like another sea
to swell the bosom of the Atlantic. To trace
the means, and lay open the secret agency by
which these magnificent objects are produced,
is left to the abler hand of science; my design
is to relate, with the humble ability I am possessed of, the actual state of some of these extraordinary features of a country, even now
but little known, comparatively speaking, to
the rest of the world, as they have appeared to
me, and as they are connected with the work
I have undertaken. In this relation, the majestic river Saint Lawrence, from its importance to the British dominions on this continent,
and, in fact, to the general interests of the British
empire, will claim the first place in whatever way
it can be examined. Embracing an inland navigation of little less than 1000 miles up to
Niagara upon its own stream only, and which
distance, with the exception of about 300 miles,
is entirely within British territory * ; it confers

* From the mouth of the St. Lawrence up to St. Regis, a

benefits of no ordinary kind upon the country through which it flows, benefits that would be increased to a value almost inestimable, upon judicious means being adopted by the administration of the mother country to secure to Canada all, or even some, of the great advantages that its natural resources will ensure to it. Its real consequence to the general interests of the empire will never be questioned, when it is viewed as the outlet by which produce, the property of British subjects, and of vital importance to the state, can be exported in British shipping to the mother country, and render her independent of political chances, by which continental confederacy might again attempt to exclude her from the ports of Europe. That these advantages are not ideal, a comparison of exports from the colony for the last ten years will abundantly prove; and although they have been neglected or overlooked during a long and eventful period of almost universal war, there remain hopes that, with the return of peace, the views of statesmen will be turned towards the arts of industry and commerce, and that this subject will be

distance of about 660 miles, the river is wholly within the British dominions; but, from the latter place, the boundary between the Canadas and the United States is considered to pass along the middle of it and the lakes.

examined with as great a degree of attention as its magnitude lays claim to. The river St. Lawrence, (which, from its first discovery in 1535, has been called by the inhabitants of the country, to mark its pre-eminence, the Great River,) receives nearly all the rivers that have their sources in the extensive range of mountains to the northwards, called the Land's Height, that separates the waters falling into Hudson's Bay still further to the north, from those that descend into the Atlantic; and all those that rise in the ridge which commences on its southern bank, and runs nearly south-westerly until it falls upon Lake Champlain. Of these, the principal ones are the Ottawa, Masquinongé, Saint Maurice, Saint Anne, Jacques Cartier, Saguenay, Betsiamites, and Manicouagan on the north; and the Salmon river, Chateaugay, Chambly or Richelieu, Yamaska, St. Francis, Becancour, Du Chene, Chaudiere, and du Loup on the south. In different parts of its course it is known under different appellations; thus, as high up from the sea as Montreal, it is called St. Lawrence; from Montreal to Kingston in Upper Canada, it is called the Cataraqui, or Iroquois; between Lake Ontario and Lake Erie it is called Niagara river; between Lake Erie and Lake St. Clair, the Detroit; between Lake St. Clair and

Lake Huron, the river St. Clair; and between
Lake Huron and Lake Superior, the distance
is called the Narrows, or the Falls of St. Mary,
forming thus an uninterrupted connection of
2000 miles. Lake Superior, without the aid
of any great effort of imagination, may be considered as the inexhaustible spring from whence,
through unnumbered ages, the St. Lawrence
has continued to derive its ample stream. I am
not aware that the source of this river has thus
been defined before; but examining the usual
mode of tracing large rivers from their heads
to their estuaries, I venture to believe that I
am warranted in adopting the hypothesis.
This immense lake, unequalled in magnitude
by any collection of fresh water upon the
globe, is almost of a triangular form; its
greatest length is 381, its breadth 161, and
its circumference little less than 1152 miles;
and as remarkable for the unrivalled trans-
parency of its waters, as for its extraordinary
depth. Its northern coast, indented with
many extensive bays, is high and rocky; but
on the southern shore the land is generally
low and level; a sea almost of itself, it is
subject to many vicissitudes of that element,
for here the storm rages, and the billows
break with a violence scarcely surpassed by
the tempests of the ocean. In the distant

D

range of mountains that form the Land's Height beyond its northern and western shores, several considerable rivers, and numerous small ones, have their rise, which being increased in their course by many small lakes, finally discharge themselves into Lake Superior. To the southward also there is another lofty range dividing the waters that find their way to the gulf of. Mexico through the channel of the Mississippi, from those that take a northern course into the great lake; so that its vastness is increased by the tributary streams of more than thirty rivers. On its north and north-east sides there are several islands, of which one, called Isle Royale, is the largest, being one hundred miles long and forty broad. Out of Lake Superior a very rapid current is interrupted and broken by many small islands, or rather huge masses of rock, through a channel of twenty-seven miles in length, at the end of which it flows into Lake Huron. The Falls of Saint Mary are nearly midway between the two lakes : this denomination, though generally given, but little accords with the usual appellation of Falls, as applied to the descent of large bodies of water precipitated from great heights, that so frequently occur on the rivers of America ; for, in this place, it is only the impetuous stream of the enormous discharge

from Lake Superior, forcing its way through
a confined channel, and breaking with proportionate violence among the impediments
that nature has thrown in its way; yet this
scene of tumultuous and unceasing agitation of the waters, combined with the noise
and dazzling whiteness of the surge, is not deficient either in grandeur or magnificence. Lake
Huron, in point of extent, yields but little to
Lake Superior; its greatest length from west
to east is two hundred and eighteen statute
miles; at the western extremity it is less
than one hundred, and at about one hundred miles from its eastern shore barely sixty
miles broad; but near the centre it suddenly
trends away southward to the breadth of one
hundred and eighty miles; measuring the circumference through all its curvatures, will
give a distance of little less than eight hundred
and twelve miles: in shape it is exceedingly irregular, yet, with a little assistance from fancy,
may be fashioned into something like a triangular form. From its western side an extensive series, called the Manatoulin islands,
stretches in an easterly direction for one hundred and sixty miles, many of them measuring
from twenty to thirty miles in length, by ten,
twelve, and fifteen in breadth, on some of which
the land rises into elevations of considerable

neight: besides this great chain, there are
many others of inferior dimensions, numerously
grouped in various parts, rendering the navigation intricate, and in some places, particularly towards the west end, dangerous. On
this lake also, the navigator is often assailed by
violent storms, attended with thunder and light-
ning, more terrific than in any other part of
North America. At the western angle of Lake
Huron is Lake Michigan, which, although distinguished by a separate name, can only be
considered as a part of the former, deepening
into a bay of two hundred and sixty-two miles
in length by fifty-five in breadth, and whose entire circumference is 731 miles. Between it
and Lake Huron there is a peninsula that, at the
widest part, is one hundred and fifty miles,
along which, and round the bottom of Michigan,
runs part of the chain forming the Land's
Height to the southward ; from whence descend
many large and numerous inferior streams that
discharge into it. On the north side of Lake
Huron many rivers of considerable size run
from the Land's Height down to it. One
of them, called French river, communicates
with Lake Nipissing, from whence a succession
of smaller ones, connected by short portages,
opens an intercourse with the Ottawa river that
joins the St. Lawrence near Montreal. On

the eastern extremity of the lake is the Matchedash river, which, through another succession,
of lakes, separated only by one short portage,
establishes a communication by Lake Simcoe,
Holland river, and Yonge-street, with the town
of York, now called the capital of Upper
Canada; this route would most materially
shorten the distance between the upper and
lower lakes, and is capable of such improvement, as would render it highly beneficial to
Upper Canada, a subject that will be hereafter
adverted to. From the extremity of Lake
Huron to the southward, the course of the
waters is contracted into a river (called St.
Clair's) that flows between moderately high
banks, adorned by many natural beauties, for
a distance of sixty miles, nearly due south,
when it again expands into the small Lake St.
Clair, almost circular in form, its diameter about
30 miles, and about 90 in circuit, too diminutive
when compared with the preceding ones, (and
not being otherwise remarkable) to demand a
further description. Out of this lake the waters
again assume the form of a river (called Detroit)
continuing the same southerly course for 40
miles into Lake Erie; its stream is divided
into two channels from space to space by islands
of various sizes, the largest being about ten
miles long. On the east side of this river the

prospect is diversified and agreeable, displaying
some of the beauties of an exuberant soil, aided
by a very respectable state of cultivation, and
enlivened by the cheerful appearance of settlements, and villages gradually rising into consequence by the industry of an increasing population. The Detroit opens into the south-west
end of Lake Erie. This lake extends from south-
west to north-east two hundred and thirty-one
miles, in its broadest part it is $63\frac{1}{2}$, and in circumference 658 miles; near the Detroit it is
adorned by many pleasing and picturesque
islands, while its shores on both sides have
many indications of settlement and cultivation.
Gales of wind frequently occur, and bring with
them a heavy swell, with every characteristic of
a gale of wind at sea; but there are many good
harbours, particularly on the northern side,
that afford protection to the numerous vessels
that navigate it; its greatest depth of water is
between 40 and 45 fathoms, its bottom generally rocky, which renders the anchorage
precarious, particularly in blowing weather.
From the north-east end of Lake Erie, the
communication to Lake Ontario is by the
Niagara river, 36 miles in length, and varying
from half a mile to a league in breadth, its
course nearly north; the stream in some places
is divided into two channels by islands, the

largest of which is seven miles in length. The current is impetuous, and being broken in many places by the uneven rocky bottom, is very much agitated : the banks on each side of the river are almost perpendicular, and considerably more than one hundred yards high. On the western side the road passes along its summit, and delights the traveller with many interesting views both of the river and the country, which is thickly inhabited and under excellent culture. Here also his mind will be lost in wonder at viewing the stupendous Falls of Niagara, unquestionably one of the most extraordinary spectacles in nature, that presents to the imagination as powerful a combination of sublimity and grandeur, magnificence and terror, as it can well experience. Any description, however animated, whether pourtrayed by the glowing pencil of art, guided by the liveliest fancy, or flowing from the most eloquent pen that embellishes the page of narrative, would, most probably, fall short of doing adequate justice to the reality. The attempt, however, has been so frequently made, and in some few instances with tolerable success, as to conveying an idea of its immensity, that " a description of the falls of Niagara" has become familiar to almost every general reader. For this reason, and also because in any new

endeavour I should certainly feel but little confident of either reaching the merit of the subject, or contributing to the stock of knowledge
already obtained thereon, I will excuse myself
from repeating what has been so often related
before; and proceed in describing, with my
best means, the general outlines of this majestic
river. Five miles from the great Falls is another, and scarcely less tremendous natural curiosity, called the Whirlpool; it is occasioned by
the stream as it passes from the cataract, sweeping with impetuous violence round a natural
bason enclosed between some rocky promontories, wherein it forms a vortex that ensures
inevitable destruction to whatever comes within
its attraction. By thus diverging from its forward direction, and being as it were embayed
for a time, the velocity of the current is checked,
and subdued to a more tranquil course towards
Lake Ontario. Four miles from hence is
Queen's Town, a neat well built place, deserving of notice, as being the depot for all
merchandize and stores brought from Montréal
and Quebec for the use of the upper province;
but not less so for the romantic beauty and
local grandeur of its situation. For seven miles
further on, to the town of Newark or Niagara;
the river forms an excellent capacious harbonr
for vessels of any size, exceedingly well shel-

tered by high and bold banks on each side, with good anchorage in every part. The river of Niagara communicates with the west end of Lake Ontario, rendered memorable by events recently passed, and most probably destined to become the scene of contests that will be pregnant with momentous import to North America in future ages. In length it is 171 miles, at its greatest breadth 59½, and 467 in circumference; the depth of water varies very much, but is seldom less than three or more than 50 fathoms, except in the middle, where attempts have been made with 300 fathoms without striking soundings; its position is nearly east and west; the appearance of the shores exhibits great diversity; towards the north-east part they are low, with many marshy places; to the north and north-west they assume a lofty character, but subside again to a very moderate height on the south. Bordering the lake the country is every where covered with woods, through whose numerous openings frequent patches of settlements are seen that give it a pleasing effect, which is greatly heightened by the white cliffs of Toronto, and the remarkable high land over Presqu'ile, called the Devil's Nose, on the north; the view on the south is well relieved with a back ground produced by the ridge of hills that, after forming the precipice for the cataract, stretches away to the eastward; the finishing object of the prospect in this direction is a conical eminence towering above the chain of heights, called Fifty Mile Hill, as denoting its distance from the town of Niagara. Of the many rivers flowing into Lake Ontario, if the Genesee and Oswego be excepted, there are none that lay claim to particular notice, unless it be for the peculiarity of all of them having a sandy bar across the entrance. There are some fine bays and inlets, wherein vessels of every description may find protection against bad weather. Burlington Bay is both spacious and secure; but these advantages are rendered of little importance by its narrow entrance being so shallow as to admit nothing larger than boats. Hungry Bay, on the contrary, is conspicuous, as affording good anchorage and safe shelter among the islands to ships of the largest size at all seasons. York and Kingston harbours, belonging to the English, and Sacket's harbour to the Americans, are unquestionably the best upon the lake, as they possess every natural requisite; the two latter are strongly fortified, being the arsenals where ships of war, even of the first rate, have been constructed by both powers, and from whence have been fitted out those powerful hostile squadrons that have conferred so much consequence upon the naval operations in this quarter. Very heavy squalls of wind frequently occur, but they are unattended either with difficulty or danger, if met by the usual precautions every seaman is acquainted with. Of the many islands at the east end of Ontario, the Grand Isle, lying abreast of Kingston, is the most extensive, and, by being placed at the commencement of the Cataraqui river, forms two channels leading into it, that bear the names of the North, or Kingston Channel, and the South, or Carleton Island Channel. The Cataraqui, from its entrance to the place called Petit Detroit, about 39 miles, is almost filled with one continued cluster of small islands, so numerous, as to have occasioned the general denomination of Milles Isles. The distance between Kingston and Montreal is about 190 miles; the banks of the river display a scene that cannot fail to excite surprise, when the years which have elapsed since the first settlement of this part of the country (in 1783) are considered; they embrace all the embellishments of a numerous population, fertility, and good cultivation. Well constructed high roads, leading close to each side, with others branching from them into the interior, render communication both easy and expeditious, while the numerous loaded batteaux and rafts incessantly passing up and down from the beginning of spring until the latter end of autumn, demonstrate, un-. equivocally, a very extensive commercial inter- course. The islands, the shoals, the rapids, with contrivances for passing them, form al- together a succession of novelties that gives pleasure while it creates astonishment. Before reaching Montreal, the lakes St. Francis, St. Louis, and des Deux Montagnes, present them- selves: they do not admit of comparison with those already noticed, and can, indeed, only be considered as so many widenings of the river; they are of no great depth, but form an agree- able variety by having many pretty islands scat- tered about them. St. Francis is 25 miles long by five and a half broad; the shores in some places are marshy, as they do not rise much above the level of the water. St. Louis and Deux Mon- tagnes are formed at the junction of the Ottawa with the St. Lawrence; the first is 12 miles long by six broad; the latter is very irregular, and in its whole length is 24 miles, but varying in breadth from one mile to six. At the con- fluence of the two rivers are the islands of Montreal, Isle Jesus, Bizarre, and Perrot; the first is probably the most beautiful spot of all Lower Canada, and will, in the course of this work, be described with particular attention.

On the south side of this island is the city of the same name, and its convenient port 580 miles from the gulf of St. Lawrence, to which ships of 600 tons can ascend with very little difficulty. On the north-west lies Isle Jesus, that, by its position, forms two other channels of a moderate breadth, one called La Riviere des Prairies, and the other La Riviere de St. Jean ou Jesus; they are both navigable for boats and rafts, and unite again with the main river at Bout de l'Isle, or the east end of Montreal island. From this city the navigation assumes a character of more consequence than what it does above, being carried on in ships and decked vessels of all classes; in the distance from hence to Quebec (180 miles) the impediments to vessels of large tonnage sailing either up or down are not many, and may be overcome with much ease, if it be judged expedient that their cargoes should be so conveyed in preference to transporting them in small craft. On either side the prospect is worthy of admiration; the different seigniories, all in the very highest state of improvement that the agriculture of the country will admit of, denote both affluence and industry; the views are always pleasing and often beautiful, although the component parts of them do not possess that degree of grandeur which is perceivable below Quebec; numerous villages, for the most part built round a handsome stone church, seem to invite the traveller's attention; while single houses and farms at agreeable distances appear to keep up a regular chain of communication; in fact, whoever passes from one city to the other, whether by water or by land, will not fail to have his senses highly gratified, and to meet with many subjects worthy both of observation and reflection. About 45 miles below Montreal, on the south side, is the town of William Henry or Sorel, built at the entrance of the river Richelieu into the St. Lawrence, not far from which the latter spreads into another lake, the last in its progress towards the sea; it is called St. Peter's, is 25 miles long and nine broad; like most of the others, this has a group of islands covering about nine miles of the western part; between them two distinct channels are formed, the one to the south being the deepest and clearest, is consequently the best for ships; the banks on each side are very low, with shoals stretching from them to a considerable distance, so that only a narrow passage, whose general depth is from 12 to 18 feet, is left unobstructed. About 45 miles from William Henry on the north side, at the mouth of the river St. Maurice, stands the town of Three Rivers, the third in rank

within the province; at this place the tide
ceases entirely, and, indeed, is not much felt
at several miles below it: from hence there is
scarce any variation in the general aspect of
the St. Lawrence until arriving at the Richelieu
rapid (about 52 miles), where its bed is so
much contracted or obstructed by huge masses
of rock, as to leave but a very narrow channel,
wherein at ebb tide there is so great a descent,
that much caution and a proper time of the
ebb is necessary to pass through it; at the end
of the rapid is a good anchorage, where vessels
can wait their convenient opportunity. From
Montreal, thus far, the banks are of a very
moderate elevation, and uniformly level, but
hereabout they are much higher, and gradually
increase in their approach to Quebec, until
they attain the height of Cape Diamond, upon
which the city is built. At this capital of the
province and seat of government there is a
most excellent port and a capacious bason,
wherein the greatest depth of water is 28 fathoms, with a tide rising from 17 to 18, and at
the springs from 23 to 24 feet. From whence,
and from Point Levi on the south shore, one
of the most striking panoramic views perhaps in the whole world offers itself to notice;
the assemblage of objects is so grand, and
though naturally, yet appear so artificially con-

trasted with each other, that they mingle surprise with the gratification of every beholder.
The capital upon the summit of the cape, the
river St. Charles flowing for a great distance
through a fine valley abounding in natural
beauties, the falls of Montmorency, the island
of Orleans, and the well cultivated settlements
on all sides, form together a coup d'œil that
might enter into competition with the most romantic. At the basin the St. Lawrence is two
miles across, and continues increasing in breadth
until it enters the gulf of the same name, where,
from Cape Rosier to the Mingan settlement on
the Labradore shore, it is very near 105 miles
wide. A little below the city is the Isle of
Orleans, placed in the midway, consequently
forming two channels; the one to the south is
always used by ships; the shore on that side is
high, and on the opposite, in some places, it is
even mountainous, but in both extremely well
settled, and the lands in such a high state of
improvement, that a large track in the vicinity
of Riviere du Sud is familiarly called the granary of the province. Beyond the island of
Orleans are several others, as Goose Island,
Crane Island, and many smaller ones; these
two are tolerably well cultivated, but the rest
are neglected. At Riviere du Sud the great
river is increased to eleven miles in width, and

the country that adjoins it cannot be easily rival-
ed in its general appearance; the great number
of churches, telegraph stations, and villages,
whose houses are almost always whitened, are
so well exhibited by the dark contrast of the
thick woods covering the rising grounds behind
them up to their very summits, and the termination so completely defined by the distant
range of lofty mountains forming the boundary
before noticed, that very few landscapes will
be found actually superior to it. Beyond
Riviere du Sud is a channel named the Traverse,
which deserves mention from the circumstance
of the river being here 13 miles across; yet
the Isle aux Coudres, the shoal of St. Roch, and
another called the English Bank, interrupt the
fair way so much, that this passage, which is
the usual one the pilots choose, is not more
than from 17 to 1800 yards between the two
buoys that mark the edge of the shoals; it is
the most intricate part of the river below Quebec; the currents are numerous, irregular, and
very strong, on which account large ships must
consult the proper time of the tide to pass it
without accident. On the north shore between
the Isle aux Coudres and the main there is another channel, but the current is so rapid, the
depth of water so great, and the holding ground
so bad in case of being obliged to anchor within

E

it, that pilots always give the preference to
running through the Traverse. Not the smallest
difficulty will ever be found in making this
passage good, if the bearings and directions
laid down upon my Topographical Map be
duly attended to; I can speak with confidence,
from having had the satisfaction to verify
them most completely in August, 1814, when
I passed it on board H. M. S. Ajax, of 74 guns,
Rear Admiral Otway, to whom I feel happy in
acknowledging my obligations for the polite-
ness with which he facilitated, by all the means
in his power, my wish to make such additional
remarks as appeared to me to be necessary.
Passing the Traverse, a very agreeable view of
the settlements of the bay of St. Paul, enclosed
within an amphitheatre of very high hills, and
the well cultivated Isle aux Coudres at its entrance, presents itself. Continuing down the
river, the next in succession are the islands of
Kamourasca, the Pilgrims, Hare Island, and
the cluster of small ones near it, named the
Brandy Pots; these are reckoned 103 miles
from Quebec, and well known as the general
rendezvous where the merchant ships collect to
sail with convoy. From hence, at no great
distance, is Green Island, on which is a light-
house, where a light is shewn from sun-set until
sun-rise, between the 15th April and the 10th

December. Near Green Island is Red Island, and abreast of it on the northern shore is the mouth of the river Saguenay, remarkable even in America for the immense volume of water it pours into the St. Lawrence. Proceeding onwards is Bic Island, 153 miles from Quebec, a point that ships always endeavour to make on account of its good anchorage, as well as being the place where men of war usually wait the coming down of the merchantmen; next to Bic is the Isle St. Barnabé, and a little further on the Pointe aux Peres. From this point the river is perfectly clear to the gulf, and the pilots being unnecessary any longer, here give up their charge of such as are bound outwards, and receive those destined upwards. Below Pointe aux Peres are two very extraordinary mountains close to each other, called the Paps of Matane, and nearly opposite them is the bold and lofty promontory of Mont Pelée, where the river is little more than 25 miles wide, but the coast suddenly stretches almost northerly, so much, that at the Seven Islands it is increased to 73 miles. The settlements on the south side reach down thus far, but hereabouts they may be considered to terminate, as to the eastward of Cape Chat the progress of industry is no longer visible; on the north side the cultivated lands extend only to Mallbay. In the river itself nothing claims our attention except the separation of its shores to the distance already mentioned, from Cape Rosier to the Mingan settlement *. In the mouth of the St. Lawrence is the large island of Anticosti, 125 miles long, and in its widest part 30, dividing it into two channels. As it is of importance to mariners in making the river, the geographical position has been ascertained with exactness, and is thus laid down : the east point lat. 49. 5. long. 62. 0. ; the west point lat. 49. 48. long. 64. 35 ; and the south-west point lat. 49. 23. long. 63. 44. Through its whole extent it has neither bay nor harbour sufficiently safe to afford shelter to ships; it is uncultivated, being generally of an unpropitious soil, upon which any attempted improvements have met with very unpromising results ; yet, rude and unhospitable as its aspect may be, it is not absolutely unprovided with the means of succouring the distress of such as suffer shipwreck on its coasts, there being two persons who reside upon it at two different stations all the year as government agents, furnished with provisions for the use of those who have the misfortune to need them. Boards are placed in different parts,

* In describing the course of the river, and wherever distances are given in miles, they always imply the statute mile of 69½ to a degree, unless otherwise specified.

describing the distance and direction to these friendly spots: these establishments were made in the year 1809, the humane intention of which will be honoured wherever it is made known, because the crews of vessels driven on shore here have, sometimes, at the utmost peril of their lives, forsaken them to make their escape to Gaspé. Anticosti forms no part of the province of Canada, but is at present within the government of Newfoundland. With the powerful conviction upon my mind of the great estimation the river St. Lawrence ought to be held in, from presenting itself as the outlet, designed as it were by nature to be the most convenient one for exporting the produce of these two extensive and improving provinces, the country stretching to the north-west nearly to the Pacific ocean, and even the adjacent parts of the United States, which, in defiance of prohibitory decrees, will find an exit by this channel, I have, it is feared, exposed myself to a charge of being prolix in wishing to convey to others a clear conception of its importance; yet I must still trespass upon the patience of my readers long enough to mention that the observations hitherto made apply only to one part of the year; and also to notice, that from the beginning of December until the middle of April, the water communication is

totally suspended by the frost. During this
period, the river from Quebec to Kingston, and
between the great lakes, except the Niagara
and the Rapids, is wholly frozen over; the lakes
themselves are never entirely covered with ice,
but it usually shuts up all the bays and inlets,
and extends many miles towards their centres;
below Quebec it is not frozen over, but the force
of the tides incessantly detaches the ice from
the shores, and such immense masses are kept
in continual agitation by the flux and reflux,
that navigation is totally impracticable in these
months. But though for this length of winter
the land and water are so nearly identified, the
utility of the river, if it be diminished, is far
from being wholly destroyed, for its surface
still offers the best route for land carriage (if
the metaphor can be excused); and tracks are
soon marked out by which a more expeditious
intercourse is maintained by vehicles of transport of all descriptions than it would be possible to do on the established roads, at this season so deeply covered with snow, and which
are available until the approach of spring makes
the ice porous, and warm springs, occasioning
large flaws, render it unsafe. When this alteration takes place it soon breaks up, and by
the beginning of May is either dissolved or
carried off by the current. The gulf of St.

Lawrence, that receives the waters of this gigantic river, is formed between the western part of Newfoundland, the eastern shores of Labradore, the eastern extremity of the province of New Brunswick, part of the province of Nova Scotia, and the island of Cape Breton. It communicates with the Atlantic ocean by three different passages, viz. on the north by the straits of Belleisle between Labrador and Newfoundland; on the south-east by the passage between Cape Ray, the south-west extremity of the latter island, and the north cape of Breton island; and lastly by the narrow channel, named the Gut of Canso, that divides Cape Breton from Nova Scotia. The distance from Cape Rosier to Cape Ray is 79 leagues; and from Nova Scotia to Labrador 106. On its south side is the island of St. John, otherwise called Prince Edward's island, something in shape of a crescent, about 123 miles long, in its widest part 32, and in its narrowest, at the extremities of two deep bays, less than four: it possesses a good soil, fit for all general purposes, though, from its exposure to frequent thick fogs, the produce of grain is precarious; it is well settled, and can boast at present of a population of 10,000 souls at least; the chief place is Charlotte Town, where the governor resides, it being a distinct government,

though subordinate to the commander in chief
in North America. To the northward of St.
John's are the Magdalen islands, seven in
number, thinly inhabited by a few hundred
persons chiefly employed in the fisheries; from
some anomalous cause or other these islands
are considered within the district of Quebec.
Islands of ice are sometimes met with in crossing the gulf during the summer months: the
ice that drifts out of the St. Lawrence all dis-
appears by the latter end of May, but these
masses make no part of it. The conjecture is,
that they are not formed on any of the neighbouring coasts, but descend from the more
northerly regions of Hudson's Bay and Davis's
Straits, where it is presumed they are severed
by the violence of storms from the vast accu-
mulations of arctic winter, and passing near
the coast of Labrador, are drawn by the in-
draught of the current into the straits of Belle-
isle; they often exceed an hundred feet in
height, with a circumference of many thousands; the temperature of the atmosphere is
very sensibly affected by them, which, even
in foggy weather when they are not visible,
sufficiently indicates their neighbourhood; by
day from the dazzling reflection of the sun's
rays, also by moon-light their appearance is
brilliant and agreeable.

America possesses a climate peculiar to itself; the quantity and prevalence of heat and
cold seems to be governed by laws materially
differing from those that regulate the temperature of other parts of the earth. It is
certain that a person would be materially led
astray were he to form an opinion of the temperature of Canada from the analogy of local
situation; it lies, for instance, in the same
parallel of latitude as France, but instead of
exhaling the exquisite fragrance of flowers, and
ripening delicate fruits into delicious excellence,
as is the case in that country, its surface is covered with accumulated snows for nearly one-
half of the year, and vegetation is suspended
for the same period by continued frost. Yet this
circumstance is unattended with so much rigour.
as any one would be disposed to suspect, and
notwithstanding the apparent severity, Canada
enjoys a climate that is congenial to health in
an eminent degree, and highly conduces to
fertilize its soil. Heat and cold are certainly
felt to extremes; the latter, both for duration
and intensity by far the most predominant, is
supposed to derive much of its force from the
following cause, viz. the land stretches from the
St. Lawrence towards the north pole, which it
approaches much nearer to, and with a less intervention of sea than that on the old continent;

it expands also an immense distance to the westward; therefore the winds between the north-east and north-west, passing over a less surface of water than in the same portion of the other hemisphere, are consequently divested of a smaller quantity of their intense frigor, and afterwards sweeping across the immense chain of mountains covered with perpetual snows and ice that intersects the whole of these cheerless regions, they acquire a penetrating severity by traversing so vast a track of frozen ground, that even their progress into lower latitudes cannot disarm them of. Of these winds the north-west is the most rigorous; and even in summer, as soon as it prevails, the transition from heat to cold is so sudden, that the thermometer has been known to fall nearly thirty degrees in a very few hours. The highest range of the summer heat is usually between 96 and 102 degrees of Fahrenheit; but an atmosphere, always particularly pure, abates the oppressive fervor felt in other parts at the same point. In winter the mercury sometimes sinks to 31 degrees below zero, but this must be considered its very greatest depression, and as happening only once or twice in a season, or perhaps not more than thrice in two seasons, and then its continuance rarely exceeds 48 hours; but the general range of cold in medium years may be estimated from twenty degrees above, to twenty-five degrees below 0. The frost, which is seldom interrupted during the winter, is almost always accompanied with a cloudless sky and pure dry air that makes it both pleasant and healthy, and considerably diminishes the piercing quality it possesses when the atmosphere is loaded with vapours. At the eastern extremity of the province, from its vicinity to the sea, fogs are brought on by an easterly wind, but to the westward they seldom prevail, and even at Quebec are almost unknown. The snow usually lies on the ground until the latter end of April, when it is melted by the powerful rays of the sun, rather than dissolved by the progress of thaw, the air continuing still pure and frosty; when it has disappeared, the spring may be said to commence; and as the ground, being protected by so thick a covering during winter, is seldom frozen many inches deep, the powers of vegetation almost immediately resume their activity, and bring on the fine season with a rapidity that would excite in a stranger to the country the greatest degree of astonishment. Rain prevails most in the spring and fall of the year, but is seldom violent or of long duration in the level parts of the province: towards the mountains, however, their frequency

and duration are both increased. Bordering
on the gulf of St. Lawrence, as the face of the
soil is rugged and mountainous, the climate,
somewhat influenced thereby, participates in its
ungenial nature; but advancing to the westward, it becomes more mild, and encourages
the resumption of agricultural labours at a
much earlier period, particularly in the western
district of the lower, and all the settled parts of
the upper province; at Montreal for instance,
only 79 geographical miles southward and 145
due west from the meridian of Quebec, the
spring is reckoned to commence from five to six
weeks earlier than at the latter place. Vegetation is proportionately more luxuriant and
vigorous, producing crops of greater increase,
by seldom experiencing checks in their early
stages from the hoar frost, so injurious to the
rising growth wherever it prevails. In a comparison between the climates of Great Britain
and the Canadas, some advantages result to the
latter, because the prevalence of fine clear
weather and a pure atmosphere greatly exceeds
that in the former; besides, the degree of cold
is proved by actual experiment not to be proportionate to the indication of the thermometer;
as a corroborating instance, it is remarked, at
its utmost severity, which is in the months of

January and February, the labour of artisans in out-door employments is rarely suspended many days in succession.

From the climate of a country, its soil comes under notice by a sort of natural transition. On making a calculation of the superficial contents of the area enclosed between the two principal ranges of mountains before spoken of, about 16,028,000 square acres may be computed to include the greater part of the land in the lower province yet surveyed that is capable of being turned to any favourable account in an agricultural point of view. In so great an extent undoubtedly every gradation of quality between very bad and very good is to be found; but it would be attended with some difficulty to state with tolerable correctness the relative proportion of each kind. Sensible that, in thus generalising the whole, only an imperfect sketch can be given, it is my intention that as much care as possible shall be used to render the subject more clear and familiar when treating the different districts and divisions topographically. For the present then it may suffice to say, that with respect to goodness, the eastern parts are inferior to the western, being of a more irregular and uneven surface, in many places consisting of a light soil of a sandy nature laid upon a stratum of perfect sand or gravel; in others it

is varied with mixtures of clay, loam, and sometimes a good vegetable mould upon a reddish
argillaceous bottom, constituting a medium
between the two extremes; this latter species
is supposed rather to exceed the inferior classes
in quantity, and with a moderate degree of
careful husbandry will yield the farmer pretty
fair returns. In the western part of the province, although the variety is nearly as great as
in the other, in its nature it is very superior;
the sort most esteemed is a composition of fine
rich loams, both a yellow and a bluish colour,
with a good black earth, forming a soil, that in
the country is supposed to be endued with the
greatest share of fertilizing properties of any of
the natural classes; and of this sort consists the
chief portion of land in the western division;
the remaining part is always above mediocrity;
in fact, it may be fairly asserted, that through
the whole of North America, or indeed in many
other countries, it will be difficult to meet with
land more inviting to form new settlements
upon, or where it is already cultivated, capable
of being made more generous and productive
by the introduction of an improved system of
husbandry. Its superiority over the contiguous
districts of the United States is fully manifest
by the readiness with which American families
in considerable numbers have, for years past,

abandoned the less fertile fields of their nativity, to settle upon a soil that they are certain will abundantly repay the industry and art bestowed upon it. Undoubtedly the burthen of the taxes and peculiar laws will have had some share in causing these migrations across the borders into a country where neither would be felt. But be that as it may, many farmers'thus changing the scene of their labours, have, either by purchase or by lease, obtained extensive estates and endenizened themselves under the British government; whilst others, as eager to enjoy the same advantages, but less honest in their manner of obtaining them, have selected convenient situations among the reserved lands, wherein they have unceremoniously domiciliated without licence or title; and even without the acknowledgment of rent have continued to cultivate and improve their favourite spots thus chosen. This species of tenure certainly ought not to be allowed by the crown, and means should undoubtedly be taken to eject such tenants, because their prior occupancy, the irregularity of it being generally unknown, deprives the natural subject of taking the lots upon the terms before recited in page 14. It is also desirable not to permit the pernicious example of such unauthorized possession of valuable property to communicate its influence, or, indeed, to exist at all. It is much to be wished that the system of management in Lower Canada was as good as the land upon which it is exercised; agricultural riches would then flow in a copious and inexhaustible stream; for if the natural excellence of soil and goodness of climate, contending against the disadvantages of a very inferior, not to say bad mode of husbandry, be capable of yielding crops of 15 to 18 for one, what might not be expected from it, were the modern improvements in implements as well as culture, that have been introduced with so much benefit in England, to be applied to it? The Canadian farmer unfortunately, and it is a circumstance much to be lamented, has hitherto had no means of acquiring instruction in the many new and beneficial methods by which modern science has so greatly assisted the labours of the husbandman. Unskilled in any other mode, he continues to till his fields by the same rule that his forefathers followed for many generations, which long habit and an unprofitable partiality engrafted thereon, seems to have endeared to him; knowing the natural bounty of his land, he places his greatest reliance upon it, and feels satisfied when he reaps a crop not inferior to the one of the year gone by, apparently without a wish to increase his stores by the adoption of untried means. Apprehensions of failure and consequent loss operate more strongly than disinclination ; for a desire to enlarge his profits is full as lively in him as in other men, which, aided by a genius active in imitating, would certainly impel him to try his success at any innovation, productive of corresponding advantages, that might be introduced by another. Example is the only stimulus required, and it is well worth the attention of those to whom the welfare of the British colonies is confided, and who must be sensible of the importance of this one in particular, to consider of means by which this stimulus could be most effectually excited: Whatever encouragement might be given as an incentive to the industry of the native, or the alien settler, to persevere in an approved plan of clearing, draining, and getting under cultivation the new lands, or of improvement upon such as are already under management, by a reform of the present system, a judicious variation of crops, and the introduction of new articles suitable to the climate, of which there are many, would be attended with so much benefit that in a very few years these provinces must become one of the most valuable of all the exterior possessions of Great Britain.

The practice of husbandry in Canada is defective in some very principal points : in the

F

first place the use of the plough, which ought
to be viewed as the basis of all agrarian improvement, is not enough attended to, and
where it is applied, it is done in a manner so
inadequate to the purpose, that the good intended to be derived from it is powerfully coun-
teracted; generally speaking, this operation is
performed so lightly, that scarcely more than
the surface of the ground is broken by it; the
weeds that ought to be extirpated are only cut
off, they consequently shoot out again and ab-
sorb much of the vigour of the soil that otherwise would nourish the seed and plants committed to it. If the Canadian husbandman
could witness the difference between the style
of ploughing in England and his own, I am certain that he would readily be convinced of its
utility, and willing to adopt a method so much
in favour of his autumnal expectations. Another main object in farming improvements
is the judicious application of the various ma-
nures to different soils, in which essential particular it must be admitted the Canadian
practice is much in arrear, as it is only within
a few years, and in the neighbourhood of the
large towns, that it has been in some degree
attended to by a few farmers more intelligent
than their brethren; this neglect, added to the
pernicious practice of sowing the same sort of

grain year after year upon the same land without other means of renovation than letting it lie
fallow for a season, must excite wonder that it
should produce such crops as it actually does.
When the heart of the land is supposed to be
gone or greatly deteriorated, the remedy is,
after taking a crop of wheat from it, to allow a
natural layer of clover and grass, which serves
as summer feed for cattle; in the autumn it
receives a ploughing in the usual way, and in
the ensuing spring is again put under wheat or
oats. This plan is unprofitable and injudicious,
the stock derives but little advantage from the
herbage, while with a little more care the
grounds might be turned to much better account. The introduction of different kinds of
grasses and other succulents, regulated by a
moderate degree of skill, could not fail being
attended with complete success; among the
various sorts, the English red and Dutch
white clover are worthy of notice, being calculated as well for summer feed as excellent
winter store; to these might be added the yellow Swedish-turnip, a species perhaps superior
to any other of its class, as it will endure the
most violent frost, and maintains its goodness
until the spring, as well as in autumn: that the
acquisition of such a plant to a country always
subject to a long winter would soon become

valuable does not admit of a question ; it is entitled to the farmer's attention as being a profitable article : from 20 to 25 tons per acre may
be raised by careful management, which, if
housed before the winter sets in, would furnish
an undeniable food for cattle during that season ; by its means he would obtain a beneficial
employment in fattening his stock intended for
market, and also a large quantity of valuable
manure from his farm-yard, ready to be applied
to the poor and exhausted lands at the breaking up of the frost. Many other advantages
would be the result, if a systematic arrangement
in the change of crops were to take place of the
undeviating practice at present existing ; by it
a great progress would be made in the science
of agriculture, and a long catalogue of hereditary errors would no more remain unopposed by any radical improvement. I must
again repeat, that example only is wanting to
induce the Canadian farmers to explode the
unproductive methods they have so long followed, and yield to the admission of profitable
innovations. There is yet another article or
two of culture of the very first importance to
the mother country, which would most certainly
prove highly beneficial to these provinces if
sufficient attention were to be paid to them.
The first of these is hemp, well known to be a

native plant of the country, with climate and soil peculiarly well adapted to its growth; in small quantities it has been raised on many farms, though as an object of commerce, the cultivation of it has not been attended with success, notwithstanding it has been tried under the sanction of government, that held out the encouragement of premiums, with the additional inducement of a certain good price per ton for all such as might be produced fit for its purposes; as so desirable an object hath not been accomplished under these circumstances, it would seem to imply that some insurmountable obstacle opposes it. In reality there is none such; both soil and climate are favourable as nature could form them, and the extensive demand of Great Britain must ever ensure an undoubted market at prices high enough to remunerate the growers very handsomely; the cause of failure in the attempt must be sought for somewhere else than in any natural deficiencies. That time and considerable sums of money have been wasted is unquestionably true, but it is equally a fact, that the good intentions of administration have been defeated by the inadequate measures pursued in the execution of the plans, and not a little impeded by a want of general agricultural knowledge in the persons to whom its management was con-

fided. It is not to be denied but there are some
existing difficulties to be removed before the
cultivation of hemp can be made generally
agreeable to all persons interested in the agricultural produce of the province; but as the
chief of these arise from the discountenance the
clergy might shew to its introduction on an extensive scale, from a supposition that it would
interfere with raising wheat and other grain
upon the lands now in tillage, and thereby
somewhat diminish their revenues, may they
not be surmounted by making it a tythable
article, and fixing the rate to be paid as it is
in England, namely, five shillings per acre, or
otherwise in the same proportion as the con-
tribution of grain is at present taken by them,
a 26th part? Under such a regulation the ecclesiastical body would consult its own interest by
promoting the increase of this production, a
measure which could be easily accomplished
by the powerful influence that body possesses
in all the concerns of the country people, whether temporal or spiritual. I have been unequivocally assured by a gentleman who has
devoted the greatest part of his life to the improvements of growing and dressing both hemp
and flax, that he has carefully examined several
parcels of the former, sent some time ago from
Canada to London, and is decidedly of opinion

the *growth* is much superior to what is in general imported from Russia; but on the other hand, from mismanagement after pulling, and from being steeped in bad water, its quality and colour are greatly inferior to what they would have been had it undergone a proper process. The management of this plant contains nothing of mystery, and is so plain that it may be carried on by the least intelligent husbandman in the colony, if he be but once put into the proper routine. The choice of a soil fit for the purpose is a leading point, and the kind which is considered the best is a rich deep loam, whereon a very good crop may be raised without manure, but it may be grown on almost any species not absolutely of a bad quality, if it be well manured, except where there is a cold subsoil or a very shallow staple. To ensure a good crop, the most careful attention must be paid to ploughing and preparing the land; the tilth should be as fine and as deep as possible, a circumstance hitherto but little noticed by the most part of our Canadian farmers, and in consequence of this neglect their produce has been most materially reduced in quantity. The seed, of which about four bushels should be allowed per acre, ought not to be put in the ground until the weather is become warm; for the young plants when they begin to shoot up are ex-

ceedingly tender, and liable tó be injured if
night frosts happen in the early period óf their
growth. May is generally the best month for
sowing it; but in Canada this time must be
pointed out by a correct knowledge of the climate. After the seed is got in, a light harrow
should be used, and nothing more is required
until it is fit for pulling; this will be in from ten
to fourteen' weeks. In hemp the male and female
plants are more distinctly defined than in almost
any other species; the former bears a light-coloured flower, but never produces any seed;
the latter, on the contrary, yields the seed, but
does not bear a flower. Land is not at all im-
poverished by the growth of hemp, for after a
good crop has been pulled, it cannot possibly
be in better condition to be laid under wheat,
or indeed any thing else. The different soils
both of Upper and Lower Canada are likewise
admirably well calculated for the growth of
flax, an article well deserving the farmer's consideration, from its yielding, with tolerable good
management, a larger as well as more certain
profit than the greater part of other crops.
Loam, loam mixed with clay, gravel, or sand,
or clay alone, indeed any land but such as is
very wet or very shallow, is good for raising it.
On warm dry soils the sowing may commence
in the middle of March, and continue, accord-

ing to the condition and quality of the land, until the first week in May; but with it, as with hemp, the seed time must be guided by a knowledge of the climate. The ground may be prepared by a moderate ploughing, which is not required to be very deep. From two and a half to three bushels of seed per acre may be sown, which must be harrowed in, or bush-harrowed, and afterwards well rolled. When the plants are from four to six inches high, care should be taken to have them well weeded, and then no further attention is required until the season for pulling arrives: it remains on the ground from twelve to sixteen weeks, and is sufficiently hardy not to receive any injury from night frosts. Flax and flax seed, as well as hemp, may be produced in Canada fully equal, to say the least of it, to what is obtained from any other country; but they have always been so injudiciously managed after pulling, that their natural good qualities have been seriously deteriorated; from whence one might deduce, that unless a very different system be resorted to, no reasonable expectation of profit from growing it can be formed, and consequently few endeavours will be made to extend the cultivation of these valuable articles. But to combat such a supposition, I feel infinite pleasure in being able to make known among my countrymen generally, that the process of steeping and dew rotting now in practice, whereby the fruits of their labour have been so seriously injured, may be entirely superseded, and henceforward the culture of these important productions may be pursued with an absolute certainty of deriving an ample profit therefrom. However doubtful this assertion may appear to many, it will nevertheless be realised by the use of machines for threshing out the seed, and separating the woody from the fibrous parts both of hemp and flax, invented by Mr. Lee, to whom a patent has been granted for his highly valuable discovery. From a minute and attentive inspection of this machinery, simple in its construction beyond all conception, as well as completely effectual in its performance, and from the ocular demonstration of the perfect success of its operation I have had the satisfaction to receive from this gentleman at his factory, I am warranted in saying with the utmost confidence, that if it be introduced into the British North American colonies, the greatest benefits will be derived, not only by them, but by Great Britain also; as it will stimulate the occupiers of land to pursue this branch of husbandry more than any premiums offered, or means resorted to by government, would be able to do under the old method. By

the use of this invention, the necessity of steeping and dew rotting being avoided, the farmer,
after having pulled his crop, has nothing to do
but stack it, when sufficiently dry for that purpose, and let it remain until convenient opportunities occur of bringing it into a market-
able state, which may now be performed in a
very few hours. The superiority of this mode
of preparation is very great, and the advantages
obtained by it in equal proportion. All the
labour and attendant expense of steeping,
spreading, drying, &c. as well as the losses in-
cident to these operations, is wholly saved; the
produce of fibre is full one-third greater by this
than by former methods; while the fibre itself
preserves the whole of its natural strength un-
impaired by any destructive process. In cleaning flax the whole of the seed is preserved, and
some parts of the plant that by steeping are
entirely destroyed, are now saved to be turned
to a very profitable account; the chaff, for instance, is an excellent food for horses, cows,
sheep, &c. and the woody part, when separated
from the fibre, is a strong manure, particularly
good as a top dressing for wheat; both of these
have hitherto been wasted. The mode of using
the machines is so easy as to be worked by
women or even children; they may, without
inconvenience to a family, be fixed in cottages

or the outhouses of any description, so as to furnish a constant in door employment through the winter months. Hemp or flax prepared by this invention is found, from experiment, to be greatly superior in strength to any other. The most impartial criterion, namely, that of suspending a weight by a line made from different sorts, of the same length, thickness, and weight, has been had recourse to, when the one prepared in this manner has supported more than double the weight of the other. From many conversations I have had with Mr. Lee on the subject of his patent, besides frequent proofs of its efficacy, I feel the strongest conviction that the value of his invention will be soon appreciated when it is introduced into Canada: with such an impression upon my mind, I am persuaded I shall be aiding to increase both the interest and comfort of my fellow countrymen, by promoting, as far as lies in my power, the general use of so simple and so well contrived an apparatus. To establish, in some degree, the reality of what has been adduced, I will insert the following estimate of the expenses and produce of one acre of flax, which I have been repeatedly assured by the patentee is the result of many years practical experience as a grower, and formed upon such a calculation as any fair average crop, properly attended to, will not fail of realising always, and most frequently somewhat exceed it.

EXPENSE PER ACRE.

	£	s.	d.
Rent of land	5	0	0
Ploughing and harrowing	1	10	0
Sowing, harrowing, and rolling . .	0	7	6
Weeding by hand	0	15	0
Pulling and setting up	1	0	0
Three bushels of seed	1	11	6
Cartage, stacking, &c.	1	0	0
Threshing out the seed and cleaning the flax fit for the market . . .	8	10	0
	19	14	0

PRODUCE PER ACRE.

	£	s.	d.
10 cwt: at 60s.	30	0	0
Nine bushels of seed at 10s. . . .	4	10	0
Chaff	1	11	6
Manure	2	0	0
	38	1	6
Expense . . .	19	14	0
Profit	18	7	6

This account is made out from the ratio of agricultural expenses in England: some of its items are undoubtedly different from what they would

be in the colonies; but the excess in one would
be balanced, or nearly so, by the reduction of
another; and as the prices allowed for the produce are such as the ordinary state of the
market will always afford, and after making a
reasonable allowance for tythes, freight, &c.
the general result is sufficient to induce speculation with tolerable fair prospects of success.
It must be also taken into consideration, that
the expense of the machinery is very moderate;
nor should it escape notice that a steady demand will be found in England both for flax
and seed at fair prices. With respect to hemp,
it can never be doubted but what his majesty's
government will be again ready to lend every
support and encouragement to the production
of an article in our own dominions that we have
long been forced to purchase from strangers;
which cultivation meeting with success, in a
few years may render our country wholly independent of the north of Europe for its supply, or at any rate liberate it from the ap-
prehension of ever being put to serious inconvenience by any change of political sentiments in sovereigns. The welfare of my native
province and its parent state has ever been
with me the strongest incentive to exertion;
and a ray of hope that I may be an humble

instrument towards promoting a pursuit which would redound to the advantage of both, hath occasioned me to enter more largely into this subject than I at first intended. If my expectations are too sanguine to be borne out by the opinions of persons more enlightened thereon than I can pretend to be, I would much rather they may be attributed to an erroneous judgment, than a willingness to commit myself to the chance of misleading a single individual, by hazarding any unguarded or unfounded representations.

To ascertain, in the scale of importance, to what degree the North American colonies rise, their present value, and how much that value is capable of being increased, it is necessary to take a view of their commercial concerns, in order to bring their resources fairly before us. In attempting to introduce this subject, I feel no small degree of diffidence, from the reflexion that it is one much out of the line of my professional pursuits, in the discussion of which erroneous opinions are very liable to intrude, and that by meddling with it I may be blamed by many for the imperfect performance. My object is to attract to this point the attention of men well informed on the intricate questions of mercantile policy, in the hope that some much abler pen than mine may, at no remote period, place it in a more clear and palpable state, rather than to promote decision by any observations of my own; the extent of my endeavours will be limited to conveying some general ideas of the capabilities possessed by these provinces of rising into commercial greatness, if their interests be attended to and protected. The situation both of Upper and Lower Canada is replete with conveniences for trade: the great extent and many ports of the St. Lawrence accessible to ships of considerable burthen; its inland navigation, even to the extremity of the lakes; the numerous rivers and streams that fall into it, by which produce of all kinds may be conveyed from the most distant settlements to Quebec or other places of shipment, open greater facilities to mercantile speculations than perhaps any other country can offer. This river is the only channel by which the commodities of these two provinces find their way to distant countries, and is also by far the most natural, as well as most easily available egress for such productions of the districts of the United States that lie contiguous to its southern bank, as they are able to furnish beyond their own consumption. Prohibitory laws of the American senate have, indeed, of late been passed to bar its subjects from exportation by this route, but they have not obtained so much attention as it was imagined they would. A very large track of fertile country on their side of the border is thickly settled and in high cultivation; the industry of its inhabitants always insures a large disposable stock of the fruits of their labours, which the vigilance and invention of a speculative disposition will not fail to discover means of transferring to the readiest market, in despite of enactments that are no less disagreeable than disadvantageous. By fostering this intercourse, Canada would always secure a vast addition of articles of the first necessity, in aid of its own surplus produce, to meet a great increase of its export trade, were that trade relieved by the British government from some of the impediments thrown in its way by existing regulations that are highly favourable to American commerce.

The principal exports from the Canadas consist of new ships, oak and pine timber, deals, masts, and bowsprits, spars of all denominations, staves, pot and pearl ashes, peltry, wheat, flour, biscuit, Indian corn, pulse, salt provisions, fish, and some other miscellaneous articles, employing generally about 150,000 tons of shipping. In this enumeration, the articles of primary consequence to England are the growth of the forests, whether considered as the source of employment to British ships and native sailors in the carriage of it, if they were able to contend for the freights against the indulgences granted to their opponents; or as to their being of great and continued consumption, therefore of indispensable necessity. Since the year 1806, the timber trade of the colonies, but of the Canadas in particular, increased in an extraordinary degree, until the state of the country at the commencement of hostilities with America not only checked its further progress, but, from very obvious causes, reduced it below the standard of former years. This diminution, however, must be considered only accidental, and totally unconnected with the resources of the trade, which, according to the most discreet methods of calculation, is not only adequate to supply abundantly the demand of the British West India islands with square timber, planks, deals, staves, and whatever comes under the general name of lumber, but to furnish a large proportion of the same for the use of Great Britain. This ability it was, and perhaps with many may be still the fashion to consider problematical; but let the return of exports from 1806 to 1810 be examined, and it will be readily seen, that in these four years they advanced from about 100,000 to nearly 375,000 tons from all the provinces, of which nearly one-half was from Quebec alone. To meet this demand, no difficulties were encountered in procuring the necessary quantities, either with respect to the number of hands to be employed in collecting it, or any thing like a failure in the forests; and had it been as large again, it might have been answered with proportionate facility. Within the period cited, the increase of this trade in the Canadas only was much more than equivalent to the total consumption of the West India islands, estimated at 142,000 tons annually; and in the year 1810, the oak timber shipped from Quebec was 28,165 tons, which is but little less than half the quantity annually required for the service of the royal navy. The export of timber in this year is, perhaps, the greatest of any that has taken place, yet the ease with which it was procured is certainly an argument that weighs strongly against the assertion, that the North American colonies are unable to supply the necessities of the West Indies.

With respect to the exportation of flour and grain, the progress is certainly not so satisfactory as that of timber; yet this circumstance is far from being conclusive of inability to furnish such quantities as are required for the use of the West India islands, whose annual demand for flour, grain, and biscuit, is computed at something more than 1,200,000 bushels. Of this quantity, Canada hitherto has seldom exported, upon an average, but little more than a third part. So great a disparity of numbers is not a sufficient reason to abandon, without some further reflection, the supposition that the supply may be made to equal the demand. Immediately indeed it could not; but after the lapse of a very few years, may not so desirable an object be obtained, when the good effects of an improved system of agricultural management, and to the encouragement of which the most rigid attention ought to be paid, begin to shew themselves, combined with such measures as would make it the interest of the people of the well cultivated countries of the United States that lie contiguous to our frontier, to bring their disposable produce to the ports of the St. Lawrence? The foundation of these advantages would certainly be laid, were the colonial merchants placed in a situation to contend against those of America in supplying the islands. Until the commencement of hostilities with us, the latter enjoyed the profits of supplying our West Indian possessions both with provisions and lumber, and which were, in fact, secured to them by an act that passed the British parliament, 1807, whereby the privy council was authorised to suspend the operations of

the act of 12th Charles the Second, excluding
foreign ships from trading with the English colonies. Under favour of this suspension, they
employed an immense number of ships in this
trade, every ton of which was a manifest detri-
ment both to our provinces and our commercial
navy. The admission of American produce into
the ports of Great Britain upon paying the same
duties only as are charged upon the importation
of similar articles from our own colonies, is another very powerful check upon their prosperity,
which, from these various combinations against
it, will experience much difficulty in rising to
the eminence it would speedily attain, if that
country; so recently ceased to be an inveterate
enemy, be not again placed by the liberality of
the British government in a situation to impede its progress, and be hereafter viewed in
the same light, and put upon a par with other
foreign nations, in respect to restrictions and
countervailing duties; then the North American
provinces will soon greatly improve their internal situation, and the mother country derive
such benefit from them as will render her more
independent of other nations for supplies of the
first importance than she has hitherto been.

With this imperfect notice of the commerce
of Canada, I will close the succinct account
that I have deemed expedient to offer to my
readers, in order that they may have before

them a summary of the present state and government of the Lower Province previous to entering upon a topographical detail. My object has been to present a short sketch, not to write its history; and my wishes have succeeded, if I have been fortunate enough to convey so much information as will help to place this important appendage to his majesty's crown in its true point of view.

DIVISIONS OF LOWER CANADA.

THE province of Lower Canada is divided into the districts of Montreal, Three Rivers, Quebec, and Gaspé, which, by proclamation of the government, dated May 7, 1792, were subdivided into the following twenty-one counties, viz. Bedford, Buckingham, Cornwallis, Devon, Dorchester, Effingham, Gaspé, Hampshire, Hertford, Huntingdon, Kent, Leinster, Montreal, St. Maurice, Northumberland, Orleans, Quebec, Richelieu, Surrey, Warwick, and York. The minor divisions are, 1st, The seigniories, or the original grants of the French government under the feudal system; these are again partitioned out into parishes, whose extents were exactly defined by a regulation made in September, 1721, by Messrs. De Vaudreuil and Bigon, assisted by the Bishop of Quebec, and confirmed by an "*Arret du Conseil Superieur*" of the 3d of May, 1722. These limits however were not strictly adhered to, for as the population increased, and settlements became numerous and extensive, it was found expedient to build many new churches, that the means and accommodations for religious worship might keep pace with the numerical increase of the communicants; for the support of these, portions of ancient parishes have from time to time been constituted into new ones. 2d. The townships or grants of land made by the English government since the year 1796, in free and common soccage.—The general divisions being thus pointed out, we are at liberty to enter upon the details of such parts as lay claim to particular attention; and, commencing our topographical account where the two provinces are separated from each other, the district of Montreal first presents itself.

THE DISTRICT OF MONTREAL

Is bounded on the north-east by the district of Three Rivers, on the south by the states of New York and Vermont, where the boundary-line, running on the parallel of 45 degrees north latitude, divides the territories of the English and

American governments; on the south-west by the province of Upper Canada and the Grand or Ottawa river; and on the north and north-west it may be supposed to run as far as the limits of the province in that direction, which is the 52 degree of north latitude. The perpendicular breadth from St. Regis, along the general course of the river, is $78\frac{1}{2}$ miles. It contains the counties of York, Effingham, Leinster, Warwick, Huntingdon, Kent, Surrey, Bedford, Richelieu, and Montreal; each sending two members to the provincial parliament, except Bedford, which elects but one; 56 seigniories and fiefs; 32 whole townships, and part of eight intersected by the district line of Three Rivers; all of these are already laid out into separate lots, besides 32 others, that have only been projected; and 54 parishes, with a part of that of Yamaska, lying principally within the adjoining district. The lands granted *en fief et seigneurie* amount to 2,786,101 acres, or 3,269,966 superficial French arpents; and of the townships mentioned as being laid out 816,776 acres have been granted. The proportion of these two quantities now under cultivation may be taken at somewhat more than one half for such as are held under the French grants; but in the townships the amount is comparatively small, as must necessarily be the case from the recent date of the patents; some indeed, though completely surveyed and allotted, have scarce any settlers upon them. As the seigniories offer the best criterion whereby to judge of the general improved condition and comfort of the peasantry, as also to what degree of prosperity the province has reached, it may not be amiss to begin our description with them, and notice the townships and other more recent settlements afterwards.

NEW LONGEUIL (the seigniory of)—the most westerly of all the Lower Province, on the north side of the river St. Lawrence, is in the county of York, and runs along the shore of lake St. Francis, two leagues in front, as far as the boundary-line of Upper Canada, which forms its south-west limit, by three leagues in depth; on the north, a location of 1000 acres to the late Lieutenant-Colonel De Longeuil separates it from the township of Newton; and on the north-east it is bounded by the seigniory of Soulange. On the 21st April, 1734, it was granted to Sieur Joseph Lemoine, Chevalier de Longeuil, and is now the property of Saveuse de Beaujeu, Esq. This tract of land lies rather low; on the north-east side part of a great swamp spreads over a large space, which is covered with cedar, spruce fir, and hemlock trees, the sure indicatives of such a soil; but which requires only the operation of draining to be converted into good and profitable land. To the south-west the ground rises much above the level of the opposite side, and abounds with many spots suitable to the production of grain of all sorts, as well as favourable to the cultivation both of hemp and flax, and every other requisite purpose of farming. The woods afford abundance of fine trees, but beech and maple most predominate; there is, however, great plenty of all the other useful sorts, either for timber or fuel. The rivers Delisle and Baudet water it very commodiously: the first crosses it diagonally from Upper-Canada, where it has its source, into the seigniory of Soulange; and the latter at its south-west angle, from the upper part of the township of Lancaster to Pointe au Baudet: neither of them are navigable, though on the latter, whose banks are much the highest and the current strongest, large quantities of staves and other timber felled in its vicinity are floated down to the Saint Lawrence in the spring, when the stream is swelled by the melted snow and ice; they both turn some good grist and saw mills. The front of the seigniory, along the St. Lawrence, between Ance aux Batteaux and Pointe au Baudet, is very low, and overflowed so frequently as to make it impracticable to maintain a road fit to

keep up a communication through this distance;
but in winter, the route upon the ice along this
part, and on the north side of the lake into
Upper Canada, is preferred, as being shorter
than the road leading by the side of the river
Delisle: this road is, however, called the principal one between the two provinces, but it
will require much amendment to render it so
convenient as it ought to be for the increasing
intercourse between these parts. The greatest
part of the concessions *, in New Longeuil, are
about Ance aux Batteaux and Pointe au Baudet,
on each side of the river Delisle, and still further to the rear in the Cotes St. George and St.
André, where a number of Scotch families are
settled, whose industry has so far benefited their
lands, that they are now among the best parts
of the seigniory, although the other conceded
lots are in a very fair state of agricultural improvement. The male inhabitants of this and
three or four other seigniories in this part of the

* By the term *concession* is meant the lots of land usually
about three acres in front by 20, 30, or 40 in depth, which are
let by the seigniors at some trifling rent, either of money or
produce, according to their quality, to such persons as are willing to settle upon and cultivate them. As it is an object
worthy the attention of proprietors to concede as many of these
lots as they can, the conditions are in general favourable to the
tenants, in order to give every encouragement to bringing new
lands into tillage.

district are mostly *voyageurs,* a name given to
the persons employed in the north-west fur
trade, whose wandering mode of life, toilsome
and laborious as it is in the extreme, has superior
charms for them than the more regular and profitable pursuits of husbandry. Such a disinclination to yield to the quiet sameness of a fixed
residence is seriously inimical to the progress of
cultivation on tracks that are but sparingly
peopled; and from such a cause, neither this or
the adjoining grants, that contain many men
who follow this employment, are in so flourishing a state as it is highly presumable they would
be, from their great fertility and numerous natural advantages, were all their inhabitants of a
more domesticated disposition.

Soulange (the seigniory of) stretches four
leagues on the north bank of the Saint Lawrence, from that of New Longeuil to the Pointe
des Cascades: a small part of the township of
Newton and the seigniory of Rigaud bound it
on the south-west, as does the seigniory of Vaudreuil on the north; with the latter it occupies
the whole of the tongue of land that is formed
by the confluence of the Ottawa and the Saint
Lawrence, at the upper extremity of lake Saint
Louis; it was granted October 12th, 1702, to the
Chevalier de Soulange, and is now the property
of Saveuse de Beaujeu, Esq. The general cha-

racter of the soil through the whole of this grant
is good, and so advantageously varied as to be
fit for all the productions natural to the country.
In the south-west corner the same extensive
·swamp that runs into New Longeuil spreads
over a considerable space: elm, ash, oak, beech,
and a great variety of other trees, produce fine
timber and wood for all purposes in abundance.
The rivers à la Graisse, Rouge, and Delisle
conveniently intersect and water it with their
streams; the last is the largest, though no use
·can at present be made of it for conveyance;
it might, however, become navigable for boats
to the distance of several miles, merely by
clearing its bed from the trunks of trees, that,
with gradual decay, have for ages continued to
fall into and obstruct it. The whole extent of
this property, in front of the Saint Lawrence,
is very thickly settled, and were the inhabitants as strongly attached to husbandry, as they
are to the occupation of *voyageurs,* it might be
improved into a most excellent and productive
track; but even now it is far above mediocrity.
At five miles from Pointe des Cascades is the
pleasant village of the Cedars, consisting of
about forty houses and a well-built church:
being the point of rendezvous for all boats passing up or down the river, and having an established ferry to the opposite seigniory of Beau-

harnois, it is a place of great resort both for travellers and traders. There is but one grist mill within the seigniory, which is situated on a point of land about a mile and a half below the village, and well known by the name of Longueil's mill. A short distance from the Pointe des Cascades lies the Isle des Cascades, that, with two or three smaller ones, break the current of the river at its entrance into lake Saint Louis. A sudden declivity in its bed, obstructed by rocks in some places, and scooped into cavities in others, produces the most singular commotion, called the Cascades; it is an extraordinary agitation of the waters precipitated with great velocity between the islands, which being repelled by the rocks and hollows underneath, the waves are thrown up in spherical figures much above the surface, and driven with the utmost violence back again upon the current, exhibiting nearly the same effect as would be produced by the most furious tempest. To avoid the danger of passing this place, a canal usually called the military canal has been constructed across the point of land, and through which all boats now make their way to the locks at Le Buisson; it is 500 yards in length, and furnished with the necessary locks; on each side a space of ground 100 feet deep has been relinquished by the proprietors of Soulange and

Vaudreuil, and is reserved for public purposes; at the entrance to the canal, from the lake St. Louis, is a guard-house, where a small party of military is always stationed. At a place near Longeuil's mill the batteaux going up the St. Lawrence are unloaded, and their freights transported in carts to the village, in order that they may be towed up light through the Grande Batture or Rapide du Coteau des Cedres. On the opposite shore is the Rapid de Bouleau, deeper, but not less difficult to pass; the combined effects of these two make this the most intricate and hazardous place that is met with between Montreal and Lake Ontario. In a military view it is one of the most important spots that can be chosen, if it should ever unfortunately be again necessary to adopt defensive measures, as works thrown up on the projecting points of each side would completely frustrate any attempt to bring down by water a force sufficient to undertake offensive operations against Montreal. At Coteau du Lac, just above river Delisle, boats again enter locks to avoid a very strong rapid, between Prison Island and the point abreast of it, where a duty is collected upon wines, spirits, and many other articles that are carried by them into Upper Canada. This place has been always esteemed a military post of some consequence; works are

here erected and kept in good repair that command the passage on the north side of the river;
and was another thrown up on Prison Island it
would render the pass so difficult as to make it
very improbable that any enemy, however enterprising, would run the hazard of it, or even
venture through the outer channel between
Prison Island and Grande Isle. The stream is
interrupted hereabouts by several islands, between which it rushes with great impetuosity,
and is so much agitated that boats and rafts
encounter great inconvenience in descending;
to go down in safety they must keep close under
the shores of Prison Island. At two miles from
Coteau du Lac is M'Donell's tavern, a very
good house for the accommodation of travellers
towards the upper province, and conveniently
situated for that purpose. The main road, those
between the concessions, and three good bridges
over the rivers, are all kept in excellent repair
throughout this seigniory.

VAUDREUIL (the seigniory of) is very eligibly situated on the south side of the Ottawa
river (or rather that expansion of it called the
Lac des deux Montagnes), in the county of
York. It begins at Pointe des Cascades, and runs
along the river as far as Rigaud, comprising
one half of the large tongue of land mentioned
in the preceding article: it was granted on

the 23d October 1702, to Philippe de Rigaud,
Marquis de Vaudreuil, and now the property
of the Honourable M. E. G. A. Chartier de
Lotbiniere. This seigniory is in a very flourishing state; two-thirds of it is conceded in lots of
three acres in front by twenty and from that to
thirty in depth, forming six different ranges,
parallel to the Ottawa; the whole number of
lots is 377, and of these 290 are actually under
excellent cultivation. The soil is good nearly
throughout, and in many places of the best
quality, producing grain and all the usual crops
of the country. Three small rivers water it,
that in spring are navigable for boats, but after
the freshes have subsided even small canoes
cannot work upon them. Oak, elm, ash, and
beech of a superior quality are found, besides
many other species of woods fit for all purposes.
On the bank of the river, about six miles from
the Pointe des Cascades, is a pleasant little village, containing from 20 to 25 houses, well built
of wood, surrounding the church and parsonage-
house, which are both of stone. The seignorial, or
manor-house, is situated on a well chosen spot,
near a small rapid, about a mile and a half from
the church; surrounded by some groves of elm,
plane, and linden trees, which with avenues
and other plantations in the English style afford

many very pleasing prospects; at a little distance from the house are a grist-mill and a windmill, which serve the whole community. The major part of the men of this seigniory are voyageurs like their neighbours, yet agriculture does not languish, nor is there a want of artisans in any of the useful trades: there are also five manufactories of pot and pearl ash. The ferry-boats from St. Anne on the island of Montreal, which is the general route to Upper Canada, land their passengers on this seigniory, near the manor-house; and from the number of travellers continually passing much interest and variety is conferred upon the neighbourhood. Besides the main road, several others pass through Vaudreuil, and are all kept in very good repair, as well as the bridges. From Point Cavagnal to the house there are several small islands, all of which are appendages to the original grant. Two *arriere fiefs* within the seigniory are both in possession of M. de Lotbiniere.

RIGAUD (the seigniory of) lies on the south side of the Ottawa, in the county of York, and has for its boundaries Vaudreuil on the east, the province line of Upper Canada on the west, and the township of Newton in the rear; its dimensions are three leagues in front by three in depth, and was granted on the 29th October, 1732, to Messrs. de Vaudreuil and Rigaud; the

present proprietor is the Honourable M. E. G. A.
Chartier de Lotbiniere. A very fertile soil runs
through the whole of this grant, and where
cultivated, is found well adapted to grain and
pulse of all sorts. The Rivers à la Graisse and
Raquette run through it; the first, passing about
the middle of the seigniory, is at all times navigable from the Ottawa up to the fall, and
greatly contributes to the advantage of the settlers on each side of it; the other, in the eastern
part, is not navigable. Very good elm, ash,
and some oak, are found among the timber trees,
and some pines of a fine growth are interspersed
through the woods. From the south-east bank
of River à la Graisse, two mountains of great
height penetrate some miles into the interior,
and greatly encroach upon the quantity of cultivable land; however, about one half of this
tract is conceded in 280 lots of three acres
by 20 or 25, and tolerably well improved;
these concessions are situated on each side of
River à la Graisse, where they are the most
numerous, in Nouvelle Lotbiniere, and in the
Cote Ste. Madelaine; near the fall are a grist mill
and a saw mill, and a little below, at the end of
the road leading to Nouvelle Lotbiniere, is a
spacious parsonage-house built of stone, where
on the second floor divine service is performed until a church can be erected, which is al-

ready begun, as well as a village surrounding it.—The men of this seigniory. are chiefly voy-ageurs, active, resolute, and enterprising; the attention of those who follow that employment being diverted from the cares of husbandry, leaves but a comparatively small number to become farmers; but those who do undertake it carry it on with much zeal and commensu-rate success.

ARGENTEUIL (the seigniory of) is on the north bank of the Ottawa, in the county of York. It adjoins the seigniory of the Lac des deux Mon-tagnes on the eastward, the township of Chat-ham on the westward, and a tract of waste crown lands on the northward; its front extends two leagues along the river, by four in depth. It was granted March 7, 1725, to Mons. Dail-lebout. The present proprietor is Sir John John-son, Bart. Perhaps through all the upper part of the district of Montreal, no tract of equal extent will be found of greater fertility, or pos-sessing more capabilities of being converted within a few years into a most valuable proper-ty. The land is luxuriantly rich in nearly every part of it, while the different species of soils are so well varied as to afford undeniable situa-tions for raising abundant crops of every kind. The lower part bordering on the Ottawa is to-lerably well cleared of wood, where are large patches of fine meadow and pastures; from hence the ground rises with a gradual ascent towards the rear. In the back parts the woods run to a great extent, and yield timber of the different kinds of first rate size and goodness, which have hitherto been very little thinned by the labours of the woodman. The Riviere du Nord crosses the upper part of the seigniory in a direction from east to west, discharging itself into the Ottawa, about four miles below the great falls, and nearly half way between the lateral boundaries; it is navigable as high up as the first mill, a distance of three miles. There is a smaller stream called Riviere Rouge, running in the same direction across the lower part of the grant as the Riviere du Nord, and falling into the navigable part of the latter. The settlements that are already formed in Argenteuil hardly amount to a third part of the whole; the remainder however presents many temptations to agricultural speculation. Of the present concessions, some are situated on the bank of the Ottawa, where they seem to be the most numerous as well as rather the best cultivated; others on the Riviere Rouge; in a range between it and Riviere du Nord; and along both banks of the latter: all shewing strong indications of a thriving industry in their occupiers. There are two grist mills, two saw mills, and a paper mill, the only one I believe in the province, where a large manufacture of that article in all its different qualities is carried on with much success, under the direction of the proprietor, Mr. Brown, of Montreal. Not far below this mill is a good bridge, over which the main road to the township of Chatham, and the upper townships upon the Ottawa leads. On the left bank of the Riviere du Nord, upon a point of land near its mouth, is very pleasantly situated the residence of Major Murray, formerly owner of the seigniory: this stream and the bays of the Ottawa that indent the front abound with a great variety of very excellent fish, as do the low lands thereabouts with wild fowl and game of several sorts. The island Carillion, three miles long by three quarters broad, is very good land, but not put to any use; this with a smaller one near it, and another at the entrance of Riviere du Nord, are appendages to the grant. If fertility of soil and easy access to water conveyance be deemed of influence in the choice of situations, wherein to clear and break up new lands, probably it will not be easy to select a tract where these advantages are better combined than in the seigniory of Argenteuil.

LAC DES DEUX MONTAGNES (the seigniory of) lies on the north bank of the Ottawa river, in the county of York, adjoining Argen-

teuil on the west, Mille Isles on the east, and
on the northward is bounded by part of the
augmentation to Mille Isles, and a tract of
waste crown lands. Its dimensions are three
leagues and a half in front by three in depth,
granted on the 17th October, 1717, to the
ecclesiastics of the Seminary at Montreal,
from whom it has never been alienated. The
original grant has been increased by two augmentations, bearing date 26th September, 1732,
and 1st March, 1735, the respective quantities
of which are mentioned among the Extracts
of Original Grants under this title in the Appendix. The figure of this seigniory is irregular on its eastern side by an incision made by
the north-west angle of Mille Isles, about-four
miles deep. Through the whole of this tract
the soil is very favourable, in many parts consisting of a fine strong loam with a mixture of
rich black earth, that is found to contain a
large share of fertile properties. The surface
is uneven, but never varies into prejudicial
extremes : bordering on the lake, in the vicinity
of the Indian village, it is of a moderate height,
from thence westward to the *Eboulis* it gradually sinks into a flat, from which it rises again
near the boundary of Argenteuil ; eastward of
the village, nearly to the seigniory of Mille
Isles, runs a low heath, having a large bay on

one side of it; at a short distance from the front are the two conspicuous mountains that give the name to both seigniory and lake; one of them is called Mount Calvart, on whose summit are the *remains* of some buildings which have long borne the appellation of the Seven Chapels. Towards the interior the ground declines below the level of the front; proceeding further to the rear there are some ranges of heights that assume rather a mountainous character, but in the spaces between them are many excellent situations for settlements. It is very well watered by the Grande and Petite Riviere du Chêne, the Riviere du Nord, and the Riviere au Prince, which in their course work several corn and saw mills. The influence of the reverend proprietors in promoting industry and directing it towards useful labours is strongly exemplified in the flourishing state of their property, as upwards of three-fourths of it is divided into 661 lots or concessions, by much the greatest number of them settled upon and well cultivated, producing grain of all sorts, pulse and other crops, with a sufficient quantity of good meadow and pasture land. Oak and pine timber are found in some places, but beech, maple, birch and other inferior kinds are plentiful in the woods. The Indian village is agreeably seated on a point of land projecting into

the lake, and consists of about 60 houses, a
church, and a parsonage-house, where a mis-.
sionary always resides, for the purpose of superintending and instructing the inhabitants in
the doctrines of the Christian religion. The
Indians of this village are the descendants of
a tribe that formerly inhabited or rather frequented the lands bordering upon Lake Huron,
but being engaged in one of the wars that so
frequently wasted whole nations of these wan-,
derers, they were surprised by the vigilance of
their enemies, and nearly exterminated; the few
who did survive the massacre effected their
escape to the eastward, and their progeny now
occupies two or three small villages in different
parts of the province. Those of the village of
the Two Mountains are become civilized, and
have adopted many of the manners and customs
of the Canadians who reside in their vicinity, and
acquired a knowledge of the French language,
which they make use of fluently enough : they
are quiet and inoffensive in all their modes of
life, preserving the greatest harmony among
themselves, and civility towards the other inhabitants. They place an implicit confidence
in the resident minister, whose influence over
them is unbounded. Some lands are assigned
to them near their village, which they cultivate

with wheat, Indian corn, and other grain; of late years they have also planted potatoes in considerable quantities: from these sources, increased by the produce of the chase, which a part of the men follow during the winter season, a subsistence is derived, that apparently they enjoy with some of the comforts of civilisation.

MILLE ISLES (the seigniory of) is on the north side of the Riviere St. Jean or Jesus, one part of it lying in the county of York, and the other within that of Effingham, four leagues and a half in front by three in depth, bounded south-west by the seigniory of Lac des deux Montagnes, north-east by Terrebonne, and on the rear by the township of Abercrombie. It was granted May 5th, 1714, to M. M: de Langloiserie and Petit. At present it forms two distinct seigniories, called Du Chêne and Blainville. The land within the grant of Mille Isles is for the most part a good, rich and productive soil of different compositions, very eligible for raising all the various sorts of grain and other productions usual in this part of the province. The division called Du Chêne, the property of M. Dumont, joins the seigniory of Lac des deux Montagnes, is nearly two leagues in front by three deep; extremely well watered by the Grande Riviere du Chêne or Belle Riviere, and some smaller streams, upon all of which there are both saw and corn-mills; the prevailing sorts of timber are beech, ash, maple, and some oak. The greatest part of this property is conceded, and most of the lots settled upon by an industrious tenantry. At the mouth of Riviere du Chêne is the pleasant well built village of St. Eustache, containing from 80 to 90 houses, a handsome church, and parsonage-house. The concessions on the Riviere St. Jean and Du Chêne are in a good state of cultivation, that does some credit to the husbandry of their occupiers, and shews the beneficial effects of industry, well directed, upon a generous soil. The prospect from the village of St. Eustache is beautiful; the fine well stocked settlements upon the Isle Jesus, the mill westward of the village, with the numerous and well diversified islands scattered about the river, present altogether a very happy specimen of the picturesque.

BLAINVILLE (the second division of Mille Isles), joins Du Chêne, is nearly three leagues in front by three in depth, and the property of M. La Croix. This seigniory bears a strong affinity to Du Chêne, as far as respects the nature of its soil, local varieties, and species of timber with which it is stocked. Part of the river Mascouche runs through it, and several small rivulets conduce to its fertility by distributing their waters in all parts : all of these streams turn both saw and grist-mills. By much the largest proportion of Blainville is conceded in lots of the usual extent; the greatest number of these are settled, and appear to be under a very beneficial system of management. On the banks of Riviere St. Jean, from Terrebonne to Du Chêne, the whole of the ground is occupied, besides some large ranges of settlements along the banks of the Mascouche, forming together a valuable and highly improved property.

TERREBONNE (the seigniory of), on the north side of Riviere St. Jean or Jesus, is in the county of Effingham, between those of Blainville and La Chenaie, bounded in the rear by the townships of Abercrombie and Kilkenny; was granted 23d December, 1673, two leagues in front by two in depth, to M. Dautier Des Landes ; but on the 10th April, 1731, the grant of the tract called Desplaines, of similar dimensions, was added to it; and on the 12th April, 1753, an augmentation of a like quantity of land was made to Desplaines, together constituting the present seigniory, two leagues in front by six deep. It is now the property of the heirs of the late Simon M'Tavish, Esq. of Montreal. The soil towards the lower part is as rich and luxuriant as any within the province; about Des-

plaines it is generally of a first rate quality, but
the remote parts are mountainous, with a rough
gravelly or stony soil. The rivers Achigan and
Mascouche, with three or four rivulets, water
it most completely. The high lands produce
abundance of beech, maple, birch, and elm
timber; in some few places that lie low and
wet there are cedars and spruce firs: full two-
thirds of this property is conceded, with the
greatest number of the lots in as respectable
a state of cultivation as any in the district, and
extremely productive in wheat, barley, and
other grains. The front along the river is particularly well settled, and in this tract there is
every appearance of comfort, and even affluence,
among the tenantry. The different streams turn
some very good grist and saw-mills, but those distinguished by the name of the Terrebonne mills
are without exception the most complete and
best constructed of any in the country; they
were very much improved by the late proprietor,
who used every exertion and disregarded expense
to render them of general utility to this part of
the district. His desire of promoting the interest
of the labouring part of the community has fully
succeeded. Some of the houses and part of the
machinery were destroyed by fire a few years
ago; but they were immediately rebuilt, and
placed in their former state by the present oc-

cupier, Henry M'Kenzie, Esq. A carding machine and fulling mill have also been introduced, which are found of great service, where the poor people, as is the case in this country, depend much upon the home-made woollen cloths for their common wear. The village of Terrebonne is pleasantly situated on a projecting point of land, having several beautiful islands in front, which by their varied and romantic scenery greatly contribute to embellish the prospect. It contains about 150 well built houses of wood and stone, besides the church and parsonage-house, the seignorial-house, and the mansion of Roderick M'Kenzie, Esq. which is worthy of remark for the elegance of its construction; indeed there are several houses in a very superior style to be found in this village, it being a favoured spot, where many gentlemen, who have realised large fortunes in the north-west company fur trade, retire to enjoy the comforts and luxuries of private life. It is also a place of some traffic, occasioned by the continued influx of persons bringing grain to the mills from distant parts, and by the large exports of flour that annually take place; in consequence many of the residents are traders and artizans, whose commercial concerns impose a degree of consequence upon the village. The population is sufficiently great to give a maintenance to a schoolmaster for educating the youth. Terrebonne is a very valuable property, which for many years has been continually increasing; some idea may be given of it, as well as some other of the seignorial properties in Canada, when it is mentioned that in the year 1803 it was purchased by Simon M'Tavish, Esq. for the sum of £25,100 currency of the province; since that period many large sums of money have been expended in making numerous judicious and beneficial improvements.

BEAUHARNOIS or VILLECHAUVE (the seigniory of) lies on the south side of the river St. Lawrence, in the county of Huntingdon, having its front extending upon the river six leagues by as many in depth; it is bounded in the rear by the township of Hemmingford, on the south-west by the townships of Godmanchester and Hinchinbrook, and on the north-east by the seigniories of Chateauguay, La Salle, and the township of Sherrington. This ample tract was granted on the 12th of April, 1729, to Sieur Claude de Beauharnois de Beaumont, and is now possessed by the heirs of Alexander Ellis, Esq. In the seigniory there are the following interior divisions, viz. Catherine's Town, Helen's Town, Mary's Town, Orme's Town, North and South George Towns, William's Town, James Town, Russel Town, and Edward's Town.—

Whether estimated by the general goodness of
the land, the variety of timber of every description,
among which oak, elm, pine, and beech
are in great quantities; the advantage of water
conveyance at all times from the breaking up of
the frost until the commencement of winter, or
its contiguity and easy access by main roads to
the State of New York, this is a most valuable
tract of land, affording as good a basis for improvement
as perhaps any other in Lower Canada.
On the front or north-west part there are
a few swampy places covered with cedar and
spruce firs, but they are of no very great extent;
and generally, between the banks of the Chateauguay
and the St. Laurence, a mean breadth
of about three leagues, the country is unexceptionable
in point of locality, as well as for
all agricultural purposes, abounding with many
spots particularly congenial to the growth of
hemp and flax. From the Chateauguay to the
township of Hemmingford there is a gradual
rise, with many fine bold eminences covered with
good timber of large dimensions, and where the
land is, perhaps, superior to that lying towards
the St. Lawrence. In the divisions of James
Town and South George Town is a level space
about three miles and a half by two, called
Blueberry Plains, being an horizontal stratum
of rock of the quartz species, from the crevices

of which sprung immense quantities of the shrubs that bear the berries after which it is named.—The rivers Chateauguay and St. Louis run through the seigniory from south-west to north-east: out of the former many, and not inconsiderable, streams branch off to the interior, some of them crossing the province line into the American territory; of these the principal ones are called the English River, Bean River, Riviere aux Outardes and Sturgeon River. The Chateauguay is a fine river, navigable for boats and the usual river-craft : rafts of large quantities of the timber felled in Beauharnois, and the adjacent townships of Godmanchester and Hinchinbrook are brought down by it into the St. Lawrence. There are roads leading along it, from whence others run to the United States. A great number of concessions are made, but as yet not much more than a fourth part of them are cleared and settled; they are dispersed over the seigniory as follows : in Russel Town, 100 lots abutting upon the township of Hemmingford; in South George Town, 17 lots reaching from the south side of the Chateauguay to the English River; in William's Town, 110 lots on the south side of Chateauguay, and on both sides of Bean River; in Ann's Town, 95 lots on the St. Lawrence and the north bank of the

I

Chateauguay; in North Georgetown, 43 lots; and in Orme's Town, 47 lots, all on the Chateauguay: in Mary's Town, 57 lots; in Helen's Town, 61 lots; and in Catharine Town, 20 lots, all on the St. Laurence: at the mouth of the river St. Louis is the domain called St. Louis, where there are some good corn and saw mills; there are also several others in the different concessions; in St. Mary's Town there is another domain called du Buisson. Previous to the commencement of hostilities between Great Britain and the United States, the population of Beauharnois was a mixture of Canadians and Americans, the latter amounting to about 200 families, who, on that event taking place, immediately withdrew into their own country, as did many others who were settled in the townships lying near the province line. The relative position of this property and that of the adjoining townships with the United States must ensure great advantages when the amicable commercial intercourse between the two countries is uninterrupted, from lying, as they do, contiguous to the line of communication to Montreal, with roads in many directions, numerous routes for an expeditious water conveyance, and a soil so fertile, that where it is cultivated produces abundant crops,

are undoubtedly solid reasons for conjecturing
that this part of the district of Montreal will
attract the attention both of traders and cultivators, and vie in a few years with most others
of the province in population, as well as a
flourishing state of agriculture. The Grande
Isle, four miles and a half long, by nearly one
and a half broad, on whose southern side a redoubt was thrown up, and a road made across
it to communicate with Coteau du Lac, by
Colonel de Lotbiniere in 1813, with two or three
smaller ones adjoining, are appendages to Beauharnois. The Grande Isle divides the stream
of the St. Laurence into two channels; that
on the south side is called the Beauharnois
channel, in the course of which are the rapids
Croche, Les Faucilles, and de Bouleau; the
latter both intricate and dangerous to pass.
It was through this channel, with the view of
avoiding the Rapid and Post of Coteau du Lac,
then held by a British detachment, that the
American General Wilkinson intended to conduct the army under his command, with the
avowed object of invading Lower Canada. He
was however prevented from carrying his design
into execution, and the boasted superiority of
his arms greatly diminished by the unexpected
defeat of part of his force by a much inferior

number at a place called Christlers Farm in Upper Canada on the 11th November, 1813, which compelled him to a precipitate retreat, and to abandon the British territory, by recrossing the St. Lawrence, and ascending Salmon River to a place called French Mills, within the American boundary; in which situation, owing to the panic that embarrassed all his operations, he deemed himself so unsafe, as to think it advisable to destroy all the boats and craft he had collected for carrying his plan into effect, and retire to a position more distant, or more secure from attack. This repulse in the attempt at invasion was rendered decisive by the previous retreat, or rather complete defeat of a force amounting to 7000 men under General Hampton, that was intended to make a diversion in favour of Wilkinson, on the south-western frontier. So sanguine were the expectations of success formed by these commanders, that a junction of their forces was contemplated at Montreal, where they promised themselves winter-quarters, and from whence in the next campaign they calculated a victorious career was to be pursued. The battle of La Fourche or Chateauguay, that annihilated this visionary glory, was one of the singular events that cannot be taken into the ordinary calculations of military operations, and the circumstance of such a force being not only stopped in its progress, but obliged to retire by the exertions of a body of men not amounting in numerical strength to a twentieth part of the assailants, must be a matter of admiration whenever it becomes the subject of professional reflection. This exploit, for it well deserves such a name, was achieved by one company of Canadian fencibles, two companies of voltigeurs, some militia forces of different descriptions, with a few Indian auxiliaries, the whole numbering only 300 men, that formed the advanced picquets of Major-General de Watteville's chain of positions established towards the frontiers, and under the command of Lieut.-Colonel de Salaberry of the Canadian voltigeurs. About 10 o'clock A. M. of the 26th October, 1813, this active and spirited officer discovered the enemy's cavalry and light troops advancing in force on both sides of the river Chateauguay, when he immediately formed the resolution to oppose him by every obstacle that invincible courage, and the means at his disposal, could throw in the way. His handful of men were posted on the north bank of the river in the division of South Georgetown, covered in front by a small blockhouse and an abbatis hastily constructed; the right flank supported by a

party of 22 Indians, and the left by the right
flank company of the third battalion of embodied militia (70 men), under Capt. Daly, on the
opposite of the river, about 350 paces distant:
thus in position he waited the enemy's approach.
The American army left its encampment at
FourCorners on the 21st, passed the boundary
line, and obtained a trifling advantage by surprising a small detachment of Indians and
driving in a piquet of sedentary militia posted
at the junction of the Outarde and Chateauguay
rivers, on whose ground it encamped, and without loss of time began to clear a communication
with its former station, so as to be able to advance the artillery. On the 24th these arrangements were complete, and next day General
Hampton made every preparation for his forward movement. On the morning of the 26th he
passed his right column, composed of the fourth,
thirtieth, and thirty-third regiments of infantry
over the river, about three-quarters of a mile
in front of the British piquets, and it soon
afterwards formed in two lines, about 150 yards
from the position occupied by Captain Daly. At
the same time his left column (which he led in
person) consisting of the tenth, thirty-first, and
two other regiments of infantry, with two hundred cavalry, advanced in column, having his
artillery, ten pieces, in the REAR, towards the

abbatis, and commenced the attack; but in spite
of all his efforts to force a passage by repeated
assaults, he was held in check by the vigorous
well-directed fire of Colonel de Salaberry. On
the opposite side of the river, the American
light brigade under Colonel M'Carty, that had
been detached from the right column to turn
the flank of Captain Daly's position, and take it
en reverse, was intercepted in its progress by the
spirited advance of that officer, supported by
a company of Chateauguay chasseurs under
Captain Bruyers : the brisk fire and skilful
manœuvres of these companies frustrated the
attempt; but both officers being wounded,
and having otherwise sustained some loss, they
fell back, when their position was immediately
occupied in the most resolute manner by a flank
company of the first battalion of militia, who
succeeded in maintaining it. On both these
points, although the Americans were several
times repulsed, they repeatedly rallied and re-
sumed the attack with no better success until
the close of day, when their commander, unable to make any impression upon the invincible bravery of a truly Spartan band, thought
proper to withdraw from so unequal a contest,
overwhelmed with defeat and disgrace. The
loss sustained by the enemy from the British
fire was severe, and much increased by the mis-

management of some of his own detached corps, who fired upon each other in the woods with serious execution. From the events of this day, General Hampton derived such small hopes of establishing his winter quarters at Montreal, that he determined to retire within his own frontiers, and depend more upon the resources of his country than his own endeavours to procure them as the reward of conquest. In this action the devotion of the Canadians in defence of their country stands forth most eminently conspicuous. In the absence of regular troops, that a militia embodied and disciplined hastily to meet the pressing emergency of a crisis threatening more than common danger was able to fulfil the important duties assigned to it, by opposing itself as a barrier against an enemy, elate in his own strength, and reckoning upon encountering courage only in proportion to numbers, will ever reflect the greatest honour upon it, and not only secure the admiration of succeeding ages, but spread a confidence over the whole empire, that the colours which the Prince Regent has been graciously pleased to commit to the charge of the incorporated battalions of Canadian militia will ever be defended by the enthusiastic bravery so natural to men, when prompted by the benefits of a mild and liberal government to protect the land of their birth from the pollution of a conqueror's yoke. The Canadian, gratified by so distinguished an honour as the thanks of his prince for meritorious services, will be found willing and even desirous to shed his blood whenever a similar danger may call him to the field of action. At a time when the military resources of the province were so greatly curtailed by the most arduous continental warfare that ever Great Britain was engaged in, it is a matter of surprise that so much could have been effected with such slender means. An enemy emboldened by possessing an ample force, and inspired by the prospect of obtaining a fertile country, long the object of inordinate desire, could only be successfully opposed by a union of the greatest energy with the most active measures; that such was presented to him is incontrovertible, and the credit of having brought them into action by unceasing perseverance will attach to the judicious dispositions of the Governor-General, Sir George Prevost, and for his strenuous efforts in turning the enthusiasm of the people into a bulwark stronger and more impenetrable than entrenchments or fortresses against an invader. After an invasion defeated by the native courage of a population, resolute in maintaining the integrity of its soil, it is to be hoped the dazzling ambition of conquest may not

again excite enmity between two governments,
the mutual interest of whose subjects it is to live
in amity with each other.

CHATEAUGUAY (the seigniory of), on the
south side of the Saint Laurence, in the county,
of Huntingdon, joins that of Beauharnois on
the south-west, Sault St. Louis on the north-
east, and La Salle in the rear; the front stretches
two leagues on the river by three in depth. It,
was granted September 29th, 1673, to Le Moine,
Sieur de Longeuil, and at present belongs to
the community of Grey Sisters at Montreal.
Through the whole of this property there is very,
little variation in the land, which lies every
where nearly upon a level, generally of a good
cultivable quality; the arable part producing
very fair crops of grain of all sorts. The rivers
Chateauguay and St. Regis cross it diagonally;
the former is navigable in the whole of its
course through the seigniory for bateaux and
rafts, but the latter does not possess these. advantages. There are some good ranges of settlements along the borders of the St. Laurence,
on both sides of the Chateauguay and St. Regis
rivers, and in the intermediate spaces, which
may be reckoned about one half of the whole
grant, under pretty good cultivation. This
seigniory cannot boast of a village; but on the
western side of the Chateauguay, near its dis-

charge, stands a church, dedicated to St. John; on its banks there is a corn-mill and a saw-mill. At its mouth is the Isle St. Bernard, sometimes called Nuns Island, about one superficial mile in extent, and very well cultivated, an appendage to the grant. On it there is a house, usually denominated a convent, a term certainly mis-, applied, for it will in no way answer the description of such an establishment, unless the residence of two members of the order to which the property belongs may be allowed to convert it into a mansion of that class.

SAULT ST. LOUIS (the seigniory of) is on the south side of the Saint Lawrence, within the county of Huntingdon, confined by the seigniories of Chateauguay, La Prairie de la Magdelaine, and La Salle: it is a square of two leagues each way, granted May 29th, 1680, to the order of Jesuits. It is now the property of the tribe of domiciliated Indians, who inhabit the Coghnawaga village. The situation of this track, between the seigniories mentioned as its boundaries, will convey a sufficient idea of it without further description, as there is not much variety through the whole of the level country from La Prairie to St. Regis. The rivers La Tortue, St. Regis, and du Portage intersect it so as to water it very completely through all parts. Nearly all that half of the seigniory which lies towards La Salle is well settled and cultivated by Canadian families; but from the river St. Regis towards the St. Lawrence the remaining part is covered with wood of all the ordinary species, except a small portion reserved by the proprietors for their own uses. The village of Coghnawaga is placed on the banks of the St. Lawrence, and consists of a church, a house for the missionary, who resides with them, and about 140 others, principally built of stone, formed into two or three rows, something resembling streets, but not at all to be remarked either for interior or exterior cleanliness or regularity; their occupants may be altogether about 900, who chiefly derive a subsistence from the produce of their corn-fields and rearing some poultry and hogs, sometimes assisted by fishing, and the acquisitions of their hunting parties, which however they do not, as in an uncivilised state, consider their principal employment. This tribe, the most numerous of any that has been brought within the pale of Christianity in Canada, is of the Iroquois nation, and has long been settled within a few miles of their present village; as they are the descendants of some of the earliest converts that were made by the pious zeal of the Jesuit missionaries, and established within the protection of the colony when its own population and

limits were both very circumscribed. Notwithstanding the remote period when their ancestors
were induced to abandon their forests, and the
barbarous customs of savage life, and the present inoffensive demeanour of their offspring,
they have not yet acquired the regularity of
habit and patient industry that are necessary
to the complete formation of civilized society,
nor indeed will the hopes of those who have
had opportunities to observe the peculiarities
of their character, and try them by the opinions
of philosophers and humanists, ever be very
sanguine that longer time or greater exertion
will effect a more radical conversion; to prevent
a falling off from the improvement already made
is perhaps as much as may reasonably be looked
for. That the fierce and restless spirit of the
wandering savage has been tamed into something like docility cannot be denied; as a proof,
it may be adduced, that some of the men of
this village, and also some of those of the village
of the two mountains, have lately been employed
as auxiliaries in the British army, and during
the periods of their service no difficulty has
been found in bringing them under strict sub-
jection, or confining their operations within the
laws of modern warfare. Between the island
of Montreal and the main opposite to Coghnawaga village the breadth of the Saint Lawrence

is contracted to about half a mile; from this spot to the lower extremity of·what is termed the Sault or Rapide St. Louis, a distance of nearly four miles, there is a gradual shelving descent of its rocky bed. In passing through this channel the stream acquires an irresistible impetus, and towards the lower part moves with a velocity of 18 miles an hour, until it is separated by some small islands below into several channels. The incessant roar of the torrent, the inconceivable rapidity with which unwieldy bodies are hurried on as it were to inevitable ruin, and the agitated surface of the water, present a scene at once extraordinary, appalling, and terrific. Boats and rafts coming down the river are compelled to run through this tremendous pass, that is never free from difficulty and imminent hazard, although guided by experienced persons, who are always employed as pilots, to whose skill may be attributed the singular good fortune that an accident has very rarely occurred; they are constrained to keep as close as possible to the southern shore, and should any mismanagement or error in steerage unhappily take place, certain destruction would ensue.

LA SALLE (the seigniory of) consists of two portions of land adjoining the rear boundaries of the seigniories of Chateauguay and Sault St.

Louis, enclosed between the lateral lines of those of Beauharnois and La Prairie de la Magdelaine; both pieces extend a league and a half in depth, bounded in the rear by the township of Sherrington. It was granted April 20th, 1750, to Jean Baptiste Leber de Senneville, and is now the property of Ambroise Sanguinet, Esq. Very little difference is perceptible between this seigniory and those of Chateauguay and the lower part of Sault St. Louis, with respect to the quality of the land, and which for the most part is applicable to the same agricultural purposes: the river La Tortue, La Petite Riviere, and Ruisseau St. Jacques run through the two pieces. That part which lies behind Sault St. Louis is nearly all settled, exhibiting a favourable specimen of husbandry; but what lies in the rear of Chateauguay is still a waste, a very small portion of it only being conceded.

LA PRAIRIE DE LA MAGDELAINE (the seigniory of) is situated on the south side of the Saint Lawrence, in the county of Huntingdon, two leagues in breadth by four deep. It is bounded in front by the river, in the rear by the seigniory of De Lery and the barony of Longeuil, on the north-east by the seigniory of Longeuil, and on the south-west by those of Sault St. Louis, La Salle, and the township of Sherrington. This track was granted on the

1st April, 1647, to the order of Jesuits, whose
possessions were once so large and valuable
within this province. On the demise of the
last of the order settled in Canada, it devolved
to the crown, to whom it now belongs. The
whole of this grant is a fine level of rich and
most excellent soil, where are some of the best
pasture and meadow lands to be found in the
whole district, that always yield most abundant
crops of good hay. The arable part is also of
a superior class, upon which the harvests, generally speaking, exceed a medium produce.
In the part called Cote St. Catherine there is an
extensive bed of limestone. The different ranges
of concessions enumerate altogether about 300
lots of the usual dimensions, whereof the major
part is settled upon, and in a very favourable
degree of cultivation, almost entirely cleared of
wood, or at any rate of timber, very little of good
dimensions being now left standing. Numerous
rivulets cross it in every direction; beside these
it is watered by the three rivers, La Tortue, St.
Lambert, and La Riviere du Portage, all of
which traverse it diagonally from south-west to
north-east; neither of them navigable for boats
to a greater distance than half a league from
their mouths, and that only during the freshes
of the spring; they afford however always sufficient water to work several corn and saw-mills.

In front of the seigniory is the village of La
Nativité de Notre Dame, or La Prairie, formerly
called Fort de la Prairie, from having once had
a rude defence, honoured with that name, thrown
up to protect its few inhabitants from the sur-
prises or open attacks of the five native tribes
of Iroquois, who possessed the country in its
vicinity. Such posts were established at many
places in the early periods of the colony, while
the Indians remained sufficiently powerful to
resist and often repel the encroachments of the
settlers, although at present none of them retain
a vestige of their ancient form, and very few
even the name by which they were originally
known. La Nativité is now a flourishing, handsome village of 100 well-built houses; nearly
one-fourth of them are of stone, in a very good
style, giving an air of neatness and respectability to the whole. Within the parish there is a
school, not very considerable indeed, although
in the centre of a numerous population; yet
as the good effects of such an establishment,
however humble in its rudiments, will not fail
to be experienced, its advantages will undoubtedly be rendered extensively beneficial to the
rising generation. A convent of the sisters of
Notre Dame, missionaries from the community
formerly founded at Montreal by Madame Bourgeois, is in a much better condition, where all

K

the necessary and some ornamental branches of female education are conducted upon a very good system, with a success highly creditable to the undertaking. The position of the seigniory of La Prairie is extremely favourable, from the numerous roads that pass through it in several directions, and particularly from being the point where an established ferry from Montreal communicates with the main road leading to St. John's, and thence by Lake Champlain into the American states; the general route for travellers between the capital of Lower Canada and the city of New York. In a point of view before alluded to, viz. encouraging the transit of produce from the countries bordering on our frontiers to the ports of the Saint Laurence, the seigniories adjoining this line of communication are most eligibly situated, and if measures having that object in contemplation should be encouraged, they would indubitably attain some eminence in commercial importance.— From its contiguity to the line of boundary, this part of the district was fated to bear the brunt of the war against the lower province; and in the year 1812, when the American government formally unmasked its ill concealed project of conquest, a British corps of observation was encamped towards the centre of La Prairie to watch the motions of General Dearborn, who had then assembled a considerable force on the frontiers; but whose enterprise exhausted itself in a few manœuvres, and a display of strength ill calculated to menace danger, or inspire respect for his professional talent: for finding himself anticipated in all his movements, and his designs penetrated, he relinquished his chance of glory in favour of the more adventurous General Wilkinson, who, in the following campaign, attempted to execute the plan, but fortunately with as little success as had attended his predecessor's demonstrations.

The beautiful island of Montreal forms the seigniory of the same name, and also the county of Montreal; it is of a triangular shape, 32 miles long by $10\frac{1}{2}$ broad, and lies at the confluence of the Grand or Ottawa River and the Saint Laurence: the Riviere des Prairies on the north-west side separates it from Isle Jesus. The greatest part of it was granted in 1640 to Messrs. Cherrier and Le Royer; but whether disposed of by them, or forfeited to the crown, does not appear from any official record that has been preserved: it is at present wholly the property of the seminary of St. Sulpice, at Montreal, the superiors of which, in rendering fealty and homage on the 3d February, 1781, produced as their titles, 1st. A deed passed before

K 2

the counsellor to the king at Paris, bearing date 20th April, 1664, by which the seminary of St. Sulpicius in that city, and other persons concerned with them, granted to the seminary in Canada the lands and seigniory of Montreal; 2d. An arret of the council of state of his most Christian Majesty, made at Versailles in the month of March, 1693, by which the king agrees to and accepts the surrender made to him by the ecclesiastics of the seminary of St. Sulpicius, at Paris, of all the property possessed by them in the island of Montreal; and 3dly, Letters patent, in form of an edict, issued by the King of France in July 1714, being a confirmation of all titles to the lands granted to the ecclesiastics of the said seminary, at Paris, by letters patent, dated March 1677, with the right of alienation. As early as the year 1657 a large part of this, even at that period valuable property, was cleared and settled, under the direction of the Abbé Quetus, who had arrived from France with authority from the seminary for that and other purposes. The island is divided into the following nine parishes, St. Ann, St. Genevieve, Point Claire, La Chine, Sault au Recollet, St. Laurent, Riviere des Prairies, Pointe-au-Tremble, and Longue Pointe. There are altogether 1376 concessions, formed into ranges, or as they are termed *cotes*, distinguished

by the names of St. Anne, Point Claire, St. Marie,
St. Genevieve, St. Charles, St. Jean, St. Remi,
St. Francois, de Liesse, St. Luc, St. Paul, de
Vertu, Sault au Recollet, St. Laurent, des Neiges,
de Verdure, St. Michel, Longue Pointe, Pointe-
au-Tremble, Visitation, St. Antoine, Leonor,
Riviere des Prairies, and the Coteau St. Louis,
and St. Pierre, making so many irregular subdivisions, or interior districts: there is also a
domain of great extent between the Cotes St.
Laurent and St. Michel, which is retained for
the use of the seminary. With the exception
of the mountain, the ridge of the Coteau St.
Pierre, and one or two smaller ones of no great
elevation, the island exhibits a level surface,
watered by several little rivers and rivulets, as
La petite Riviere St. Pierre, Riviere Dorval,
Ruisseau de l'Orme, Ruisseau de Notre Dame
des Neiges, La Coulée des Roches, Ruisseau de
la Prairie, Ruisseau Migeon, and a few others
of inferior note. These streams turn numerous
grist and saw-mills in the interior, while many
more around the island are worked by the
great rivers. From the city of Montreal to the
eastward the shores are from 15 to 20 feet
above the level of the St. Laurence; but in the
opposite direction, towards La Chine, they are
low : between the Coteau St. Pierre and the
river the land is so flat, and particularly near

the little lake St. Pierre so marshy, as to induce
a conjecture that it was once covered by water.
Over this place it is intended to cut a canal; by
which a direct communication between the city
and La Chine will be formed, and the difficult
passage of the rapid of St. Louis avoided; for
the commencement of this work the sum of
£25,000 has been recently voted by the provincial parliament. The soil of the whole island,
if a few insignificant tracks be overlooked, can
scarcely be excelled in any country, and is
highly productive in grain of every species,
vegetables, and fruits of various kinds; consequently there is hardly any part of it but what
is in the most flourishing state of cultivation,
and may justly claim the pre-eminence over
any of Lower Canada. Several roads running
from north-east to south-west, nearly parallel to
each other, are crossed by others at convenient
distances, so as to form a complete and easy
communication in every direction. Within a
few years a good turnpike-road has been made
from Montreal, almost in a straight line, to the
village of La Chine, a distance of seven miles;
by which the constant intercourse between these
places is much easier than it was heretofore:
by this route all the commodities intended for
Upper Canada are conveyed to the place of
embarkation. Within this space there is a great

variety,. and some very romantic. prospects : a mile or two from the town, near the tanneries,. the road ascends a steepish hill, and continues along a high ridge for more than three miles,. commanding a beautiful view over the cultivated fields below, the rapid of St. Louis, the islands in the St. Laurence, and the varied woodland scenery on the opposite shore; descending from the height, it passes over a flat country until it reaches La Chine. - This road was formerly so bad, winding, and interrupted by huge masses of rock, that it was nearly a day's journey for the loaded carts to go from one place to the other. Stores and other articles, intended for the king's warehouses, a little beyond the rapid, are sent by another road, which runs by the river side.

La Chine is a place of greater importance than any other village on the island, being the centre of all the commerce between the upper and lower provinces, and the north-west country also : whatever merchandise is sent upwards is brought hither by land carriage from Montreal, and all the imports are here landed. It consists of only about 20 dwelling-houses, but a great number of store-houses belonging to the merchants, besides the warehouses of the Indian department. A dry dock of great extent, for laying up the bateaux, forms a valuable part of the premises of Mr. Grant. During the months between May and November bateaux to and from Kingston and various parts of Upper Canada are continually arriving and departing, which always occasions a great deal of activity and bustle of business. The nature of these craft may be very shortly described: they are flat-bottomed; from 35 to 40 feet in length, terminating in a point at each extremity, with about six feet of beam in the centre; the usual freight is four or four and a half tons; they are worked by oars, a mast and sail, drag-ropes for towing, and long poles for setting them through the strong currents or rapids; four men manage them in summer, but in the fall of the year another is always added, one of whom acts as a guide. In the bateaux of the merchants the cargoes upwards are a general assortment of merchandise, for which they bring down flour, wheat, salt provisions, pot and pearl-ashes, and peltries. The time employed in the voyage to Kingston is from 10 to 12 days; but the return does not take more than three or four. They usually depart in brigades of from four to fifteen boats, in order that their crews may be able to afford mutual assistance in ascending the rapids: each brigade is under the direction of one man, who is called the conductor. From La Chine also the canoes employed by the north-west company in the fur trade take their departure. Of all the numerous contrivances for transporting heavy burthens by water these vessels are perhaps the most extraordinary; scarcely any thing can be conceived so inadequate, from the slightness of their construction, to the purpose they are applied to, and to contend against the impetuous torrent of the many rapids that must be passed through in the course of a voyage. They seldom exceed thirty feet in length and six in breadth, diminishing to a sharp point at each end, without distinction of head or stern: the frame is composed of small pieces of some very light wood; it is then covered with the bark of the birch tree, cut into convenient slips, that are rarely more than the eighth of an inch in thickness; these are sewed together with threads made from the twisted fibres of the roots of a particular tree, and strengthened where necessary by narrow strips of the same materials applied on the inside; the joints in this fragile *planking* are made water tight by being covered with a species of gum that adheres very firmly and becomes perfectly hard. No iron-work of any description, not even nails, are employed in building these slender vessels, which when complete weigh only about five hundred weight each. On being prepared for the voyage they receive their lad-

ing, that for the convenience of carrying across
the portages is made up in packages of about
three-quarters of a hundred weight each, and
amounts altogether to five tons, or a little more,
including provisions and other necessaries for
the men, of whom from eight to ten are employed to each canoe: they usually set out in
brigades like the bateaux, and in the course of
a summer upwards of fifty of these vessels are
thus dispatched. They proceed up the Grand
or Ottawa River as far as the south-west branch,
by which, and a chain of small lakes, they reach
Lake Nipissing; through it, and down the
French River into Lake Huron; along its
northern coast up the narrows of St. Mary
into Lake Superior, and then by its northern
side to the Grand Portage, a distance of about
1100 miles from the place of departure. The
difficulties encountered in this voyage are not
easily conceived; the great number of rapids
in the rivers, the different portages from lake to
lake, which vary from a few yards to three
miles, or more in length, where the canoes must
be unladen, and with their contents carried to
the next water, occasion a succession of labours
and fatigues of which but a poor estimation
can be formed by judging it from the ordinary
occupations of other labouring classes. From
the Grand Portage, that is nine miles across, a

continuation of the same toils takes place in
bark canoes of an inferior size, through the
chain of lakes and streams that run from the
height of land westward to the Lake of the
Woods, Lake Winnepeg, and onwards to more
distant establishments of the company in the
remote regions of the north-west country. The
men employed in this service are called voyageurs; they are robust, hardy, and resolute,
capable of enduring great extremes of fatigue
and privation for a long time with a patience
almost inexhaustible. In the large lakes they
are frequently daring enough to cross the deep
bays, often a distance of several leagues, in their
canoes, to avoid lengthening the route by coasting them; yet notwithstanding all the risks and
hardships attending their employment, they prefer it to every other, and are very seldom induced to relinquish it in favour of any more
settled occupation. The few dollars they receive as the compensation for so many priva-
tions and dangers are in general dissipated with
a most careless indifference to future wants,
and when at an end they very contentedly
renew the same series of toils to obtain a fresh
supply. Three leagues from La Chine is the
village of Pointe Claire, situated on a point
of land of the same name; it contains from 90
to 100 houses, built with regularity, and form-

ing small streets that cross the main road at right angles. There is a neat parish church, a parsonage-house, and one or two tolerable good houses for the accommodation of travellers. The local beauties of this place can boast of many attractions, being surrounded by extensive orchards and excellent gardens. About three leagues eastward of Montreal is Pointe-au-Tremble, a neat village of fifty houses, a church, chapel, and a parsonage-house. The main road to Quebec passes through this place, which always brings to it a constant succession of travellers, for whose reception there are some inns, where accommodation in all the principal requisites is to be obtained. These are the only villages on the island; but in every parish there is a great number of good houses scattered about, though but few are placed close together; they are mostly built of stone, as that material is to be had every where in great abundance. The city of Montreal is within this seigniory; it stands on the south side of the island, in lat. 45°. 31' N. and 73°. 35' W.; the second of the province in point of size, but with respect to situation, local advantages, and superiority of climate, it is undoubtedly unrivalled by Quebec itself: its form is a prolonged square, that, with the suburbs, covers about 1020 acres of ground, although within the walls of the old fortifications the contents of the area did not exceed 100 acres. A few houses, built close together, in the year 1640, was the commencement of the city of Montreal, or as it was first named Villemarie; the situation being well chosen, and possessing many inducements for the colonists to associate themselves for the comforts and convenience of society, it very soon assumed the appearance of being built with some attention to regularity and solidity of the dwellings, containing a population of 4000 inhabitants; its improvement and extension were both rapid. In 1644 the Hotel Dieu was founded by the pious charity of Madame de Bouillon, and six years afterwards the zeal of Mademoiselle Marguerite de Bourgeois established the convent of Notre Dame. The infant town was exposed to, and almost from its very beginning experienced, the animosity of the Iroquois, who made many attacks upon it. As a protection against these repeated hostilities a sort of barrier was drawn round it, consisting merely of palisades; but so slight a defence not inspiring the inhabitants with much confidence in their security, the more powerful safeguard of a wall, fifteen feet high, with battlements, was substituted, and had the desired effect of repelling these formidable enemies to its prosperity; but as the ardour of the French colonists in prosecuting the trade in furs made them more dreaded by their savage neighbours, whom they succeeded in driving to a greater distance, and repressing their incursions by erecting forts and establishing military posts, the necessary repairs of the wall were gradually neglected, and it fell into decay. The last remains of this ancient fortification have been recently removed by an act of the provincial legislature, to make way for the introduction of some improvements, planned with judicious regard to the convenience, comfort, and embellishment of the place. At different periods the city has suffered extensive damage from fire; but from the gradual widening of the streets, as new buildings take place, the better construction of the houses, and other means of precaution now resorted to, this calamity, when it does occur, seldom causes much devastation. In its present state Montreal certainly merits the appellation of a handsome city. It is divided into the upper and lower town, although the elevation of one above the other is scarcely perceptible; these are again subdivided into wards. The streets are airy, and the new ones, particularly, of a commodious width; some of them running the whole length of the town, parallel to the river, intersected by others at right angles. The houses are for the most part built of a

greyish stone, many of them large, handsome,
and in a modern style: sheet-iron or tin is the
universal covering of the roofs. The Rue Notre
Dame, extending from the citadel to the Re-,
collet suburbs, is 1344 yards in length, and 30:
feet broad; it is by much the handsomest street
in the place, and contains a great many of the;
public buildings; but the cathedral is so in-:
judiciously situated, that it occupies the whole
breadth of it at the Place d'Armes, which,
though not an impediment to the passage,
destroys the perspective that otherwise would
be unobstructed from the citadel to the Recollet gate. St. Paul-street is another fine street,
running the whole length of the town, but more
irregular in its course and breadth than the;
former: from its contiguity to the river, the
situation is very convenient for business. Among
the edifices that attract notice, perhaps more
from the value of the establishments than their
beauty, are the Hotel Dieu, the convent of;
Notre Dame, the General Hospital, the French
Cathedral, the Recollet Convent, the convent
of the Grey Sisters, the seminary of St. Sulpice,
the New College or Petit Seminaire, the English and Scotch churches, the Court-house, the
new gaol, the Government-house, Nelson's monument, and the Quebec barracks. The Hotel
Dieu, in St. Paul-street, extending 324 English

feet in front by 468 feet in depth, in St. Joseph-street, is an establishment for the reception of the sick and diseased poor of both sexes; it is conducted by a superior (La Sœur Le Pailleur.) and 36 nuns. The French government formerly supplied medicines and many other necessaries, but now the funds for maintaining the charity are principally derived from some landed property, which (and it is a subject of regret) is not so ample as could be wished, when compared with its utility; however, this as well as every other charitable institution in the province is occasionally assisted with grants of money from the provincial parliament. The whole of the buildings on the space before-mentioned include the hospital, a convent, and a church; attached is a large garden, a cattle-yard, with extensive stables and out-buildings, and a cemetery. The convent of La Congregation de Notre Dame is in Notre Dame-street, and forms a range of buildings 234 feet in front and 433 in depth along St. John Baptist-street, containing, besides the principal edifice, a chapel, numerous detached buildings for domestic uses, and a large garden. The congregation is composed of a superior (La Demoiselle Deroussel, la Sœur Nativité) and sixty sisters; the object of this institution is female instruction in its different branches, wherein the greatest part of the members are employed; boarders are taken into the house on very moderate pensions, and receive a careful education. From this establishment some of the sisters are sent as missionaries to different parts of the district, for the purpose of giving fuller effect to the intentions of the foundation by opening schools in parishes remote from the convent. The general hospital, or convent of the Grey Sisters, situated about 300 yards south-west of Point Calliere, was founded in 1750, by Madame de Youville, as a refuge for the infirm poor and invalids; it occupies a space of 678 feet along the little river St. Pierre by nearly the same depth, containing a convent for the residence of the nuns, a church, wards for patients of both sexes, all requisite offices, and a detached building for the reception of such as labour under mental derangement. It is governed by a superior (Mlle. Therese Coutlée) and 24 sisters: the cares which they bestow upon those whom misfortune obliges to seek their aid, are directed with great kindness and an unremitting zeal in earnest endeavours to alleviate the burthen of human misery. The cathedral church in Notre Dame-street is plain and substantially built, 144 feet long by 94 wide; but its height is not in due proportion to its other dimensions: it is, however, in every

respect rendered convenient and suitable for
the performance of the catholic service, although
not sufficiently large for the increased population of the city, nine-tenths of which profess
that faith. The interior decorations are rather
splendid, and display some taste in the arrangement. The English church, in Notre Dame-
street, is not yet finished; but from the design
and style of building it promises to become
one of the handsomest specimens of modern
architecture in the province: some delay has
been occasioned in its progress by the funds at
first appropriated being found incompetent to
complete it. The seminary of St. Sulpice, or
Montreal, is a large and commodious building
adjoining the cathedral; it occupies three sides
of a square, 132 feet long by 90 deep, with
spacious gardens and ground attached, extending 342 feet in Notre Dame-street, and 444
along that called St. François Xavier. The
purpose of this foundation is the education of
youth through all its various departments to
the higher branches of philosophy and the mathematics. It was founded about the year
1657, by the Abbe Quetus, who, as before mentioned, then arrived from France, commissioned
by the seminary of St. Sulpice at Paris to superintend the settlement and cultivation of their
property on the island of Montreal, and also to

erect a seminary there upon the plan of their
own. His instructions were so well fulfilled
that the establishment he framed has existed
until the present time, modified by many and
great improvements. The superior of this college is M. Roux, assisted by professors of
eminence in the different sciences, and other
subordinate masters, who pursue a judicious
plan of general instruction that reflects distinguished honour upon themselves, while it
ensures a continual advance in knowledge to
a very considerable number of students and
scholars. The New College, or Petit Seminaire,
near the Little River, in the Recollet suburbs,
is most eligibly situated; the body of it is 210
feet long by 45 broad, having at each end a wing
that runs at right angles 186 feet by nearly 45.
-It is a handsome regular edifice, built a few
years ago by the seminary of St. Sulpice, at an
expense of more than £10,000, for the purpose
of extending the benefit of their plan of education beyond what the accommodations of their
original establishment would admit of. On the
exterior, decoration and neatness are so judiciously blended as to carry an air of grandeur,
to which the interior distribution perfectly cor-
responds; the arrangements have been made
with the utmost attention to convenience, utility,
and salubrity, consisting of residences for the

director, professors, and masters ; a chapel, airy
dormitories, apartments for the senior and junior
classes, refectories, and every domestic office.
The intentions of the institution through every
department are promoted with the utmost regularity and good effect, both with respect to
instruction and internal economy. The director,
M. Roque, and chief professors are as eminently
distinguished for their literary acquirements as
for their zeal in diffusing them : the annual
public examinations that take place demonstrate the progress made, not only in useful
learning, but even in the superior walks of
abstruse science, in a manner highly compli-
mentary to their diligence, and far exceeding
any expectations that would be generally entertained from the college of a colony ; but on this
point, as well as on many others, the capabilities of the province have been but little understood or much misrepresented in Europe. In
this college, as well as in the seminary, the
number of pupils is very great, with whom a
very moderate annual stipend is paid ; the
benefits that arise from the dissemination of
useful instruction over so large a space as the
lower province will not fail to be duly appreciated by every feeling mind, and for their endeavours in so beneficent a cause the reverend
Sulpiciens are fairly entitled to the gratitude

of all their Canadian brethren. Besides these principal seats of learning, wherein the French language is the vernacular idiom, there are in Montreal some good English schools, conducted by gentlemen of exemplary morals and talents, who by their exertions supply in some degree the want of an English college. It is certainly a subject of surprise that no such establishment has yet been formed, considering how eminently serviceable it would prove, by contributing to bring the language of the parent country into more general use. I feel a confident hope, however, that such a foundation will not much longer be a desideratum, particularly as a basis has been laid for it by the late Hon. James M'Gill, who died in 1814, and by will bequeathed a very handsome country-house and lands appertaining thereto, at the mountain near Montreal, with the sum of ten thousand pounds, for the purpose of endowing an English college, provided it be applied to that use within ten years after the bequest, or in failure thereof the property is to revert to his family. The first steps towards insuring to the colony the benefits of so munificent a donation have already been taken. In giving full effect to which it cannot be doubted but that the provincial, and, if necessary, the imperial legislature, will aid with its accustomed liberality the testator's praise-

worthy intentions, should his legacy be found
inadequate to the design. The court-house, on
the north side of Notre Dame-street, is a plain
handsome building, lately erected, 144 feet in
front, where the courts of civil and criminal
judicature are held. The interior is distributed
into halls for the sittings of the chief courts,
besides apartments for the business of the police
and courts of inferior decision. Within it is
also a spacious room, allotted to the use of the
public library of the city, that contains several
thousand volumes of the best authors in every
branch of literature: the good regulations under
which it is managed, and the method in which
the books are arranged, reflects great credit
upon the committee that has the superintendance thereof, and greatly contributes to the
amusement of its numerous supporters. The
handsome appearance of this building is heightened by its standing some distance from the
street, with a grass-plot in front, enclosed by iron
railings; its proximity to the Champ de Mars
renders it extremely airy and agreeable. The
gaol of the district stands near the court-house;
it is a substantial, spacious building, erected
about seven years ago, upon the site of the
old one that was destroyed by fire in 1803.
The salubrious situation of this spot is peculiarly
fitted for such an establishment; the interior

plan is disposed with every attention to the
health, cleanliness, and comfort (as far as the
latter is compatible with the nature of such a
place) of its unfortunate inmates, both debtors
and criminals. The government house, usually
classed among the public buildings, is on the
south side of Notre Dame-street; being very
old, and an early specimen of the unpolished
architecture of the province, it is not much entitled to notice; it is however kept in good repair, and furnished as an occasional residence
of the governor in chief, when he visits the
upper district: on the opposite side of the
street, bordering on the Champ de Mars, is an
excellent and extensive garden belonging to it.
The old monastery of the Recollets stands at the
western extremity of Notre Dame-street; it is
a substantial stone building, forming a square
of about 140 feet each way, and more remarkable as being convenient to the purposes for
which it was designed than for its beauty. The
church within it is still used for divine worship;
but the house itself is converted into barracks,
and the extensive ground belonging to it is retained by government for military purposes.
At the upper part of the new market-place,
close to Notre Dame-street, is a handsome monument, erected to commemorate the Hero of
Trafalgar, immortal Nelson: it is composed of

a pyramidal column placed upon a square
pedestal; at the base of the column, on the different angles, are allegorical figures, of very good
workmanship, representing the victor's chief at-
tributes, and on the sides suitable inscriptions;
in compartments, on each face of the pedestal,
are bass reliefs of four of his principal achieve-
ments, executed with great spirit and freedom,
and composed with a chasteness of design guided
by much classical correctness. This highly
ornamental tribute to departed worth was completed in London, and the expenses defrayed
by subscription among the inhabitants of Montreal, and will convey to posterity their public
feelings and their gratitude towards the invincible chief who deserved so much from every part
of the empire he so valorously defended. The
principal streets, both lateral and transverse,
have a direct communication with the suburbs,
which, as will be seen from a preceding computation, occupy a much greater space than
the city itself: they surround it on three sides;
on the south-west are the divisions called the
St. Anne, the Recollet, and the St. Antoine
suburbs; on the north-west the St. Laurent,
St. Louis, and St. Peter's; and on the north-
east the Quebec: in all of them the streets run
in the same direction as those of the city; they
are very regular, and contain a great number of

superior dwelling-houses, built of stone, as several inhabitants of the first rank have fixed their residences there. Between the old walls and the suburbs there is a space upwards of 100 yards in breadth, that has hitherto been reserved by government for the purpose of erecting fortifications and for other military uses; but as the number of inhabitants and dwellings has experienced so great an increase, and the necessity of these defences almost superseded, this ground has been diverted from its original appropriation in favour of some improvements and embellishments that are in contemplation. Montreal, as it is at present, containing a population of 15,000, rivals the capital of Canada in many respects, and as a situation for a commercial town certainly surpasses it : seated near the confluence of several large rivers with the St. Laurence, it receives by their means the productions of the best settled and also the most distant parts of the district, as well as from the United States, besides being the depot of the principal trading company of North America, whose concerns are of great extent and importance. Possessing these combined attractions, it is by no means unreasonable to infer that in the lapse of a few years it will become the most flourishing and prosperous city of the British North American dominions; and Quebec, viewed as a military position, may always be looked upon as an impregnable bulwark to them. When the act that passed the provincial parliament, in 1801, " for removing the old walls and fortifications surrounding the city of Montreal, and otherwise to provide for the salubrity, convenience, and embellishment of the said city," shall have been carried into effect, according to the plan projected, none of the external possessions of England, excepting its easternd ominions, will embrace a town of so much beauty, regularity, extent, and convenience as this. Part of these alterations, as far as the sums hitherto assigned would enable the commissioners to proceed, have already been made, and the remainder will be continued as fast as further funds become applicable. These improvements are intended to be as follows: an elevated terrace, extending from the suburbs on the south-west side of the city, along the river as far as the Quebec suburbs; which, independent of its utility as a road, will be sufficiently high to form an effectual barrier against the floating ice at the breaking up of the frost; it will also impede the communication of fire to the town, should it take place among the large quantities of timber and wood of every description .that are always collected on the beach. The little river.St. Pierre is to be embanked on both sides as far as the new college, forming a canal 20 feet wide, which is to.be continued along the south-west and north-west sides to the Quebec suburbs, with bridges over it at the openings of the principal streets and other convenient places; at the angles ornamental circular basins are to be formed, and a lock near the mouth of the little river, by which the water may be drawn off for the purpose of cleansing it; this work will be so constructed as to raise boats, &c. from the St. Laurence, from whence they may proceed to the further extremity of the canal. The buildings on each side are to be retired thirty feet from the water, thereby forming a street eighty feet wide, having the canal in the centre. To the northward of Notre Dame-street there is to be another parallel to it, sixty feet wide, called St. James's-street, running the whole length of the city, and terminated at the Quebec suburbs by one of the same breadth, leading to the St. Laurence: between St. James's-street and the canal, parallel thereto and running in the same direction, will be a street of 24 feet wide. Where the Quebec gate now stands will be formed a square 174 feet by 208, extending towards the suburbs. The Place d'Armes is to have its dimensions enlarged to 392 feet by 344, which will protract it to the canal; from the south-west side of the canal, towards the St. Antoine suburbs, another square or rather parallelogram will be made, 468 feet by 180. The Champ de Mars, from being very circumscribed, and quite inadequate as a place of military exercise, will be made level, and carried on nearly to the canal, to form a space 227 yards by 114; this has been nearly completed, and it is now an excèllent parade as well as an agreeable promenade for the inhabitants: seats are fixed for the accommodation of the public, and trees planted in various parts of it. From this spot there is a fine view of the well cultivated grounds, beautiful orchards, and country houses towards the mountains. Adjoining the new college a lot of ground, 156 feet by 258, is reserved as the site of a new house of correction. The new market-place, occupying the ground where formerly stood the college, founded by Sieur Charron in 1719, and destroyed by fire a few years back, has been finished according to the proposed plan; it is 36 yards wide, and reaches from Notre Dame-street to St. Paul-street; in the middle of it are ranges of stalls for butchers, covered in by a roof supported on wooden pillars: great care is taken to enforce the regulations to ensure cleanliness in this part. The two principal market-days

in each week are well supplied with every necessary, and nearly every luxury for the table,
in great abundance, at prices extremely moderate. The produce of the upper part of this
fertile district is almost wholly brought hither
for sale, besides a great quantity from the American states, particularly during the winter season, when fish frequently comes from Boston
and the adjacent parts. The whole of the plan
sanctioned by the act of parliament has been
arranged and acted upon by commissioners appointed under it, who have for many years been
indefatigable in their exertions to carry its provisions into effect: as their functions have been
arduous and frequently unpleasing, from the
numerous law-suits they have found it necessary
to institute and defend in cases of disputed
claims, they are entitled to the esteem of their
fellow citizens for the manner in which they
have always performed these duties to the
public *gratuitously.* The harbour of Montreal
is not very large, but always secure for shipping
during the time the navigation of the river is
open. Vessels drawing fifteen feet water can
lie close to the shore, near the Market-gate, to
receive or discharge their cargoes; the general
depth of water is from three to four and a half
fathoms, with very good anchorage every where
between the Market-gate Island and the shore:

in the spring this island is nearly submerged by the rising of the river; but still it is always use-ful in protecting ships anchored within it from the violent currents of that period, and at other times serves as a convenient spot for repairing boats, water-casks, and performing other indis-pensable works. Two small shoals lying off the west end of it, at the entrance of the harbour, and the narrowness of the deep water channel below it, generally make it necessary to warp out large ships, and drop them down the stream by kedge-anchors until they come abreast of the new market-place, as the leading winds for bringing them out cannot always be depended upon: at the east end of the island is a channel of which small craft can always avail themselves. The greatest disadvantage to this harbour is the rapid of St. Mary, about a mile below it, whose current is so powerful, that, without a strong north-easterly wind, ships cannot stem it, and are sometimes detained even for weeks about two miles only from the place where they are to deliver their freight. In pursuing the grand scale of improvements it may probably be found practicable to remedy this evil by the forma-tion of another short canal, or extension of the one already designed to the foot of the rapid; ships might then discharge their cargoes at their anchorage below the current into river craft, which could be by such a communication conveyed immediately to the city. The environs of Montreal exhibit as rich, as fertile, and as finely diversified a country as can well be imagined. At the distance of a mile and a half from the town, in a direction from south-west to north-east, is a very picturesque height, whose most elevated point at the furthest extremity. is about 550 feet above the level of the river; it gains a moderate height at first by a grádual ascent, which lowers again towards the middle, from thence it assumes a broken and uneven form until it is terminated by a sudden elevation in' shape of a cone. The slopes on the lower part are well cultivated, but the upper part is covered with wood; from several springs that rise towards its top the town is plentifully and conveniently supplied with water, which is conveyed to it under ground by means of wooden pipes. The summit, to which there is a good road of very easy ascent, commands a grand and most magnificent prospect, including every variety that can embellish a landscape; the noble river St. Laurence, moving in all its majesty, is seen in many of the windings to an immense distance; on the south side the view is bounded by the long range of mountains in the state of New York, that is gradually lost in the aerial perspective.

The space near the town, and all round the lower part of the mountain, is chiefly occupied by orchards and garden-grounds; the latter producing vegetables of every description, and excellent in quality, affording a profuse supply for the consumption of the city. All the usual garden fruits, as gooseberries, currants, strawberries, raspberries, peaches, apricots, and plums are produced in plenty, and it may be asserted truly, in as much, or even greater perfection than in many southern climates. The orchards afford apples not surpassed in any country; among them the pomme de neige is remarkable for its delicate whiteness and exquisite flavour; the sorts called by the inhabitants the fameuse, pomme gris, bourrassa, and some others, are excellent for the table; the kinds proper for cyder are in such abundance that large quantities of it are annually made, which cannot be excelled in goodness any where. On the skirts of the mountain there are many good country-houses belonging to the inhabitants of the city, delightfully situated, and possessing all the requisites of desirable residences. By the side of the road that passes over the mountain is a stone building, surrounded by a wall that was formerly distinguished by the appellation of the *Chateau des Seigneurs de Montreal,* but now generally called *La Maison des Pretres,* from its belonging to the seminary: there are extensive gardens, orchards, and a farm attached to it, which are retained for the use of the proprietors; it is also a place of recreation, where, during the summer time, all the members of the establishment, superiors and pupils, resort once a week. About a quarter of a mile below this stands the handsome residence and farm of the Hon. Wm. M'Gillivray, member of council. A little more than a quarter of a mile to the northward, most conspicuously situated beneath the abrupt part of the mountain, is a mansion erected by the late Simon M'Tavish, Esq. in a style of much elegance: this gentleman had projected great improvements in the neighbourhood of this agreeable and favourite spot; had he lived to superintend the completion of them, the place would have been made an ornament to the island. Mr. M'Tavish, during his lifetime, was highly respected by all who enjoyed the pleasure of his acquaintance, and as much lamented by them at his decease; his remains were deposited in a tomb placed at a short distance from the house, surrounded by a shrubbery : on a rocky eminence above it his friends have erected a monumental pillar, as a tribute to his worth and a memento of their regret. Both the house and the pillar are very prominent objects, that disclose themselves in almost every direction.

Of ten established ferries from the island, in different directions, the longest is that from the town to La Prairie de la Magdelaine, a distance of six miles; it is also the most frequented, as the passengers are landed on the southern shore, at the main road, leading to Fort St. John's, and into the American States: from the town to Longeuil is the King's Ferry, three miles across, and also much frequented, as many roads branch off in all directions from the village of Longeuil, at which the boats arrive; that from the west end of the island to Vaudreuil is three miles across, in the direct line of communication between Upper and Lower Canada: from the eastern Bout de l'Isle to Repentigny, where the road between Montreal and Quebec crosses, the ferry is about 1300 yards only. The others are of much less distance: at all of them convenient bateaux, canoes, and scows are always ready to convey passengers, horses, carriages, &c. from one side to the other. From Repentigny to Isle Bourdon, in the Riviere des Prairies, and from thence to the island of Montreal, a handsome wooden bridge was constructed, at a very great expense, by Mr. Porteous of Terrebonne, authorised by an act that passed the provincial parliament in 1808; but it was unfortunately destroyed the spring after it was finished, by the pressure of the ice at the break-

ing up of the frost. The same gentleman had
previously obtained an act in 1805, but in the
spring of 1807 the works were carried away
before his undertaking was entirely completed.
Notwithstanding these failures, it is considered
that some plan may yet be devised to erect one,
whose span may be sufficiently high to allow
the masses of ice to drift down the stream without being so lodged as to accumulate an over-
bearing force. In this situation such a work
would be of great public utility, from connecting the most frequented main road of the province. The Isles Bourdon, just mentioned,
were granted, the 3d November, 1672, to Sieur
Repentigny, and are now the property of Mr.
Porteous. At the confluence of Riviere des
Prairies and the St. Laurence is a cluster of
small islands, whose names are Isle St. Therese,
Isle à l'Aigle, Isle au Cerf, Isle au Canard, Isle
au Bois Blanc, Isle aux Asperges, and Isle au
Ver. The first is the largest, being two miles and
a half long and one broad, with a good soil, that is
entirely cultivated ; the number of houses upon
it may amount to 20; there is a road that goes
quite round it, besides others to the interior,
which are kept in very good repair: it is the
property of Mr. Ainse. Captain Cartwright is
proprietor of Isle à l'Aigle, a very picturesque
and pretty spot; mostly good meadow land:

M 2

the owner resides in the only house upon it, which is charmingly situated. The others are of little extent, but furnish excellent pasturage and some good meadow land; they belong to two persons, whose names are Dubreuil and Montreuil, who are also proprietors of the ferries, on each side of the Riviere des Prairies. The Isle St. Paul lies a short distance from that of Montreal, and a little above the town, it is about three miles in circumference, and was granted to the Sieur Le Ber, April 23d, 1700; it now belongs to one of the communities of nuns at Montreal.

Isle Jesus (the seigniory of) is in the county of Effingham, comprehending the whole of the island, in length twenty-one miles, and six at its greatest breadth, lying north-west of that of Montreal, from which it is separated by the Riviere des Prairies, and from the main land by the Riviere St. Jean or Jesus. It was granted, with the Isles aux Vaches adjacent thereto, the 23d October, 1699, to the bishop and ecclesiastics of the seminary of Quebec, by whom it is still possessed. The original name was L'Isle de Montmagny; but soon after its grant the proprietors thought proper to bestow on it the appellative it now bears. The land is every where level, rich, and well cultivated: on the south-east side, bordering the river, there are some excellent pasturages, and very fine meadows; the other parts produce grain, vegetables, and fruits in great perfection and abundance. From almost every corner of it being turned to agricultural uses, there is very little wood remaining, except what is left for ornament on the different farms. There is one road that goes entirely round the island, and one that runs through the middle lengthways; these are connected by others, that open an easy communication between every part of it. There are two parishes, St. Vincent de Paul and St. Rose; the houses, mostly built of stone, are dispersed by the sides of the roads; now and then a few of them are placed close together, but no where in sufficient numbers to be called a village. Around the island are several corn and sawmills on the two large rivers; in the interior there is no stream of sufficient force to work either. About midway of the Riviere des Prairies is the strong rapid called the Sault au Recollet. The rafts of timber that are brought down the Ottawa from the upper townships descend this river into the Saint Laurence at the Bout de L'Isle. The communication between Isle Jesus and the islands of Montreal and Bizare and the main land is kept up by several ferries in convenient situations for maintaining a continual and sure intercourse, The

Isle Bizare is separated from the south-west end of Isle Jesus by the Riviere des Prairies; it is nearly of an oval form, rather more than four miles long by two broad. No records relative to this property have been preserved in the secretariat of the province; but when the present owner, Pierre Foretier, Esq. did fealty and homage, on the 3d February, 1781, he exhibited proof of its having been granted on the 24th and 25th of October, 1678, to the Sieur Bizare. It is a spot of great fertility, wholly cleared and cultivated. A good road passes all round it, near to the river, and another crosses it about the middle; by the sides of these the houses of the inhabitants are pretty numerous, but there is neither village, church, nor mill upon it.

ISLE PERROT (the seigniory of) lies off the south-west end of the island of Montreal, comprising the island after which it is named, and the Isles de la Paix, that lie in front of the seigniories of Chateauguay and Beauharnois; it was granted to Sieur Perrot, October 29, 1672, and is now the property of Amable Dézéry, Esq. The length of the island is seven miles or a little more, and nearly three in breadth at its widest part: of 143 concessions, rather more than one half are settled upon, and tolerably well cultivated; the soil is of a light sandy nature generally, but where this is not the case

it is an uneven surface of rock. The wood is
not entirely cleared from it yet; of what remains, beech and maple constitute the chief
part. The houses of the inhabitants are scattered over the island near the different roads,
but no village upon it; there is one church,
and only one wind-mill. Of two fiefs within
the seigniory one is called Fief Brucy, ten acres
in front by thirty in depth, the property of the
representatives of Ignace Chenier; the other,
named La Framboise, is of an irregular figure,
containing 180 acres superficial measure, and
belongs to François Freinch. There are four
ferries from Isle Perrot: the first to St. Anne, on
the island of Montreal, for which the charge is
two shillings; one to the main land, above the
rapid of Vaudreuil, and another to the foot of
the same, one shilling and eight-pence each;
and the fourth to the canal at Pointe des Cascades, for which the demand is three shillings
and four-pence each person. The Isles de la
Paix serve for pasturage only.

LONGEUIL (the seigniory of) lies on the
south side of the Saint Laurence, in the county
of Kent; bounded by La Prairie de la Magdelaine on the south-west; Fief Tremblay and
Montarville on the north-east; and by the
barony of Longeuil and seigniory of Chambly
in the rear: it is two leagues in breadth by

three deep; granted, 3d November, 1672, to
Sieur Le Moine de Longeuil, and now the property of Madame Grant, Baroness of Longeuil.
This tract from front to rear is quite level, the
soil generally a fine black mould, very congenial
to the growth of grain and most other species
of agricultural produce; towards the middle is
a swampy patch, called *La Grande Savanne*,
and a little distance from the front is another,
called *La Petite Savanne;* but a good system
of drainage has proved so beneficial, that they
are both nearly converted into good fertile land.
Almost the whole of the seigniory is conceded,
and full two-thirds of it in a good state of cultivation; it is more sparingly watered than perhaps any other lying on the banks of the Saint
Laurence, as the little rivulet of St. Antoine,
near its front, and another equally insignificant
that crosses the lower corner into the Montreal
river, are the only streams within its limits.
Many good roads cross it nearly in all directions; but the most public ones are that leading from the village or church of Longeuil to
Fort Chambly and Fort St. John's, the middle
road of Cote Noir to Longeuil ferry, and the
upper road from La Prairie to the same place.
The village, near the rivulet St. Antoine, contains only fifteen houses that surround the old
church, now in ruins; hard by it is the parson-

age-house, and at a short distance a wind-mill, recently, converted into a magazine for gunpowder and ordnance stores. Near this village was the ancient fort of Longeuil, one of the many formerly raised as barriers against the Iroquois nation; but its site is now covered by a very handsome well built church, which stands on the west side of the road to Chambly. The situation of this little place and its vicinity is so pleasant, that many persons of the first respectability reside hereabout; it was long the favourite retreat of the late Catholic Bishop of Quebec, M. Deneaux, who when raised to that dignity would not forsake the spot he so much admired. The Isle St. Helene, lying nearly in front of Montreal, Isle Ronde, several small ones close to it, and Isle au Heron, are appendages to Longeuil. St. Helene being rather high, commands a view of the city in its most favourable point; it is reserved as a domain, very fertile, exceedingly well cultivated, and embellished by some very fine timber. The Baroness Longeuil resides on the south side of it, in a handsome house, surrounded by good gardens and ornamental grounds; on the opposite side are the extensive mills called Grant's mills, belonging to the same family, besides whom there are no other inhabitants on this beautiful little spot.

CHAMBLY (the seigniory of), on the river Richelieu, is in the counties of Kent and Bedford, bounded on the north-west by the seigniories of Longeuil and Montarville; on the south-east by Monnoir; on the north-east by Rouville and Belœl; and on the south-west by the barony of Longeuil: it is three leagues in length by one in depth on each side of the Richelieu, and was granted 29th October, 1672, to M. de Chambly. This valuable property is at present divided into several portions, held by General Christie Burton, Colonel de Rouville, Sir John Johnson, Mr. Jacobs, and Mr. Yule. Throughout the grant the land lies nearly level, of a quality, generally speaking, not excelled by any in the district, and is nearly all under cultivation, in a very favourable style of husbandry. The Richelieu, or River Chambly, that is navigable the whole of its length, contributes, by passing through the middle of the seigniory, many advantages to the local good qualities of the property. Within its boundary also is the beautiful expansion of the river called the Bason of Chambly, nearly circular in form, and about two miles in diameter, embellished by several little islands, covered with fine verdure and natural wood, as ornamentally disposed as if regulated by the power of art. Three of these lie at the mouth of the river Montreal; some smaller ones, called the Islets St. Jean, are spread in a very picturesque way, at the descent of the rapid of Chambly into the basin;

the dark-hued foliage of the wood, that nearly, covers them, forms a pleasing contrast to the brilliant whiteness of the broken current. On the western side of the basin is Fort Chambly, which, when seen from a distance, has some resemblance to an ancient castle: it was built (of stone) by Monsr. de Chambly, some years previous to the conquest of Canada by the English, and is the only one of the kind within the province; its form is nearly square, containing several buildings and all the requisite means of modern defence, which have been recently put into substantial repair; the approaches to it are not protected by any out-works, nor is there a ditch round it... Before the late hostilities with America .only a small detachment of about two companies formed the garrison, but when the war began, the advantageous position and proximity to the enemy's frontier pointed it out as a strong *point d'appui*, where troops might be assembled; and for forming an extensive depôt: during the season for operations, in the years 1812, 1813, and 1814, there was always a considerable force encamped on the plain near it, which in the last mentioned year exceeded 6000 men; during this period also additional storehouses and other buildings were erected on the ground that has always been reserved by government for such purposes. The village of Chambly is

on the west side of the Richelieu, and not far
from the fort: it contains 90 or 100 houses,
chiefly built of wood, forming one principal
street. At the south end of the village are some
large and valuable mills belonging to General
Christie Burton; they are situated close to the
rapid of Chambly; thereby securing the advantage of being able to work at all seasons of
the year: near the mills stands a good manor
house, belonging to the same gentleman. This
place is a great thoroughfare, as the main road
from Montreal to the American States passes
through it, which, with the continual resort to
the mills, occasions a good deal of activity
among the traders and mechanics, and contributes very much to its cheerfulness as a place
of residence; among the inhabitants are reckoned many of the most respectable families of the
district, invited hither by its agreeable situation.
The landscape of the surrounding country is
rich and well diversified, affording several very
beautiful points of view; and there are many
spots from whence they may be seen to great
advantage. The fort, the mills, and the church
of St. Joseph, houses dispersed among well
cultivated fields, all the varieties of woodland
scenery, both near and remote, the distant
church on Point Olivier, with the more distant
mountain of Chambly or Rouville, added to the

continued change of objects on the basin and river, where vessels under sail, bateaux, and canoes are constantly passing up and down, and the singular appearance of unwieldy rafts descending the rapid with incredible velocity will amply gratify the spectator's admiration.

The barony of Longeuil, in the counties of Huntingdon and Kent, is between the seigniories of La Prairie de la Magdelaine and Chambly, bounded in the rear by the seigniory of Longeuil, and in front by the Richelieu, extending three leagues in length by a depth of one league on each side of the river, was granted on the 8th July, 1710, to the Baron de Longeuil, and is now the property of Madame Grant, Baroness of Longeuil. This is a very level and exceeding fertile tract of land, well settled and cultivated, traversed by the great southern road and several others; watered by the Richelieu, and conveniently situated for water carriage. It contains the parishes of St. Luke and Blairfindie, the town of Dorchester and Fort St. John. Dorchester scarcely merits the name of a town, containing at most not above eighty houses, many of which are used as stores; but will probably in a few years rise to some importance, from being so favourably situated as to become an entrepot for merchandise in its transit, either by land or water, between the two countries both in summer and winter: during the latter season a very brisk intercourse takes place by means of sleighs travelling upon the frozen surface of the lakes and rivers. Before the war the timber trade was carried on here to a great extent; and most probably with the return of peace will resume its former activity. A large proportion of the inhabitants resident here are American emigrants, who have sworn allegiance to the British government; some of them keep the best inns of the place, and are proprietors of the stage coaches that travel regularly from hence to La Prairie on one side, and to the states of Vermont and New York on the other. Fort St. John, on the west bank of the Richelieu, is of an irregular figure, and is an old frontier post; but little can be said in favour of its construction, or of the defences that surround it, as they are merely field works strengthened by pallisades and picketings; within the fort are about twenty houses, including public storehouses, magazines, &c. Being so near the frontier, it is a post of much importance; latterly a strong force has been kept at it, and the works placed in a very effective state of defence. The officer who commands here is charged with the superintendance of the more advanced posts on this line, from whence he receives all military reports, and

transmits them to the general officer commanding the district. The British naval force employed on Lake Champlain has its principal
station and arsenal here, where vessels mounting from 20 to 32 guns have been built; by
which our superiority on the lake was maintained until the unfortunate conflict before
Plattsburgh, in 1814, that terminated in the
destruction of the flotilla : this event, although
disastrous, was not dishonourable to the national
flag; and had the war continued, increased
efforts, with the means that had been prepared,
would doubtless soon have regained the accustomed ascendency.

DE LERY (the seigniory of) is in the county
of Huntingdon, bounded by the barony of Longeuil on the north-east, by the township of
Sherrington and the seigniory of La Prairie de
la Magdelaine on the west and north-west, by
the seigniory of La Colle on the south, and by
the river Richelieu on the east : it is two leagues
in front by three in depth; granted 6th April,
1733, to Chaussegros de Lery, and now the
property of General Burton. The whole of this
tract is low, having in many parts cedar swamps
and marshes that spread over a large space :
where the land is dry, a good black soil generally
prevails, that when cultivated proves very fertile; but the proportion yet settled upon is not

near so great as in the adjoining grants; a large part still remains in its natural state of wood-land. The river Montreal runs through, and the Bleuri and Jackson Creek have their sources in it. A small lake near the middle frequently overflows the surrounding low lands, and makes a marsh to a considerable distance round it; but neither the marshes nor swamps are so deep but what the operation of draining, judiciously performed, would in a short time render the land fit for the plough, or convert into excellent pastures: however, while there remains so much of a good quality to be granted, that compara-tively requires so little trouble to clear and im-prove, it is most probable that these tracts will long continue in their present condition. The best settled parts are about L'Acadie, and by the road leading to the state of New York, which, with a few other dispersed settlements, may amount to about one third of the whole seig-niory. The road that passes through the woods of L'Acadie, being the military one to the frontiers, and the line of march for troops mov-ing in that direction, has lately been benefited by some substantial repairs, and in many parts causewayed for the passage of artillery and heavy baggage. Near the boundary of La Colle is a small place called Burtonville, composed of a few houses, distributed without regularity on each side of the main road. In the Richelieu, near where the Bleuri falls into it, is Isle aux Noix, formerly the property of the late General Christie, but now belonging to the Crown; it is a flat, but a little above the level of the river, containing altogether only eighty-five acres, lying ten miles and a half from the boundary-line; in an excellent situation to intercept the whole communication by water from Lake Champlain; consequently a most important military station, that has been fortified with all the care its commanding position deserves. At the west end of it the principal work is an irregular fort, very well constructed, and of great strength, surrounded by a ditch, and mounted with guns of large calibre; in advance of this, at a short distance, are two other forts of less extent, but proportionately strong, with ditches round them also; besides these there are several block-houses at the different points that could be deemed assailable by an enterprising enemy. In 1814 the island was further strengthened by a boom extended across the river, and a line of gunboats moored in a direction that their fire might completely enfilade the whole passage; by these means it was always safe from attack, even if the enemy should have an unopposed force on the lake. At the east end of the fort is a slip for

building ships, and from thence the Confiance
of 32 guns was launched.

BEAUJEU, or LA COLLE (the seigniory of),
on the west side of the river Richelieu, in the
county of Huntingdon, bounded by De Lery
on the north, the state of Vermont on the south,
and the township of Hemmingford in the rear;
extends two leagues along the river in front by
three deep: it was granted March 22, 1743, to
Daniel Lumard de Beaujeu, and is now the property of General Christie Burton. Towards the
front of the seigniory the land is rather low, with
some few swampy patches; yet, with these exceptions, of a general good soil, very well timbered: in the rear it is much higher, and although
partially intersected by strata of rocks and veins
of stone, lying a little below the surface, the soil
is rich, and perhaps superior to that of the low
lands. On these upper grounds there is much
beech, maple, and elm timber; the wet places
afford abundance of cedar, tammarack, spruce
fir, and hemlock. Although the greatest part of
this seigniory is very eligible for all the purposes
of cultivation, and would produce all sorts of
grain abundantly, besides being peculiarly well
suited to the growth of hemp and flax, there is
not more than one third of it settled. The river
La Colle, winding a very sinuous course from west

to east, intersects it and falls into the Richelieu; but is not navigable even for canoes: at the numerous rapids that mark the descent from its source, there are many excellent situations for mills. A number of houses, situated on each side of the road that runs along the ridge from the state of New York, about two miles and a half towards La Colle, have obtained the name of Odell Town, from Captain Odell, who was one of the first and most active settlers in this part: he is an American by birth, and so are the greatest part of the other inhabitants, but they are now in allegiance to the English government. The effect of the activity and good husbandry that are natural to American farmers is much to be admired in this small but rising settlement: fields well tilled and judiciously cropped, gardens planted with economy, and orchards in full bearing; above all, the good roads in almost every direction, but particularly towards the town of Champlain, attest their industry; and it is likely, from its vicinity to the thickly inhabited townships on the American side of the boundary, the small distance from Champlain, Plattsburgh, and Burlington, the easy access to the Richelieu for expeditious water carriage, and especially from the persevering labour of its population, that it will advance in agricultural improve-

N 2

ment, and become a wealthy, flourishing, little
town. The river Richelieu, and the road by
Odell Town, being two principal points of entrance into Lower Canada, made this place lately
the scene of military operations, and it consequently shared some of the usual disasters that
inevitably attend a state of warfare, from the
necessity of defending these passes against the
intrusion of an American army. In 1813 a log
breast-work was thrown up on the north side
of La Colle, sufficiently extensive to cover the
road and blockade the passage; a short distance
in front, and on the left of the road, a redoubt
was constructed to flank the approach to this
defence; to the left of the breast-work, and in
the rear of La Colle mills, was Sydney redoubt,
a strong work, defending the passage of the
river at that point; in support of these positions were different small encampments of
troops, nearly along the whole line of front.
The enemy at various times made several demonstrations against this line, when trifling
skirmishes ensued; but the most worthy of
notice was the affair at La Colle mills, which
took place on the 30th of March, 1813, and
terminated very brilliantly in favour of the
British arms. General Wilkinson had collected
at Burlington and Plattsburg what he calculated
was a sufficient force to ensure success to his

operations; he advanced by the road leading through Odell Town to Burtonville, in the seigniory of De Lery, as far as the road that turns off to La Colle mills, where, leaving a body of troops to mask his design, he hastily made a flank movement towards the mills. The approach of the enemy was somewhat impeded by the advanced piquets, as they retired in good order and fighting against his superior numbers. The attack on the main road, being intended as a feint, was not long persevered in, and the principal one was directed against the post at the mills, which Major Handcock, of the 13th regiment, defended with no less skill than bravery. His piquets, stationed about a mile and a half in front, were driven in, and the enemy shortly afterwards appearing in force, was able to establish a battery of 12 pounders, that was soon opened against the British position. Major Handcock, being advertised of the near approach of two flank companies of the 13th to reinforce him, made a gallant dash against the guns, but was unable to carry them, as the surrounding woods were filled with infantry for their support; and after a smart conflict succeeded in withdrawing his party. Another favourable opportunity occurring soon afterwards, it was seized with eagerness by a company of grenadiers of the Canadian Fenci-

bles, and another of Canadian Voltigeurs, who
had hung upon the enemy's left flank during
the whole of his movement, in order to afford
support to whatever point he might direct his
attack against; but their bravery was unavail-
ing from the same cause as before, yet they
were not impeded from reinforcing the post.
On the first report of the enemy's attempt, a
sloop and some gun-boats were promptly moved
up from Isle aux Noix to the mouth of La Colle
River, which opening a destructive fire upon
the Americans, left them but little chance of
victory; they persevered, however, in their fruit-
less efforts until night, when they moved off their
guns and retreated by Odell Town to Champlain, after sustaining severe loss, but without
the British force being able to molest them in
the retrograde movement. Near the mouth of
the river La Colle is Isle aux Tetes, or Ash
Island, on which there is a redoubt commanding the whole breadth of the Richelieu. This
little spot and the flotilla moored between it
and La Colle, in July 1814, formed the advanced naval position towards Lake Champlain, at which period the American flotilla was
stationed at Pointe au Fer and Isle à la Motte,
about ten miles distant.

BLEURIE (the seigniory of), in the county
of Bedford, on the east side of the Richelieu, is

bounded on the north-east by the seigniories of Chambly and Monnoir, on the south by the seigniory of Sabrevois, and on the west by the river: it was granted, November 30, 1750, to Sieur Sabrevois de Bleurie, and is now the property of General Christie Burton : according to the terms of the original grant it ought to be three leagues in front by three in depth ; but as the grants of the adjoining seigniories are of a prior date, and as such an extent could not be taken without infringement upon others, it now forms a triangular space of much less superficial measurement. Although lying generally low, with large swamps in many places, there are some tracts of very good land, and also some fine timber ; the spots that are cultivated lie chiefly upon the Richelieu, and bear but a small proportion to the whole. A new road, called the Bedford Turnpike, crossing it diagonally to the river, opposite Fort St. John, has been traced and measured in the field, and is now proceeding upon. A joint company has undertaken it, and obtained an act of the provincial parliament for the purpose: when completed it will greatly enhance the value of this and the other properties through which it passes, by opening a shorter communication with Montreal, and rendering the intercourse with distant places much more easy.

SABREVOIS (the seigniory of), in the county of Bedford, on the east side of the Richelieu, bounded on the north by Bleurie, on the east by the townships of Stanbridge and Farnham, on the south by the seigniory of Noyan, and on the west by the river; it was granted, November 1, 1750, to Sieur Sabrevois, two leagues in front by three deep; it is now the property of General Christie Burton. Between this and the preceding seigniory of Bleurie there is a great resemblance in situation and quality of the land; the swamps are perhaps rather more extensive in this one, but here and there some patches of fertile good soil are met with, and many of greater extent might be added by draining, which could in several places be performed with but little labour or expense. At present the quantity of land under cultivation is rather insignificant. The Bedford Turnpike will pass through this seigniory, and may probably be the means of increasing the settlements in it.

NOYAN (the seigniory of), in the county of Bedford, joins Sabrevois on the north, the township of Stanbridge on the east, the seigniory of Foucault on the south, and the river Richelieu on the west; it was granted, July 8, 1743, to Sieur Chavoye de Noyan, and is now possessed by General Christie Burton. The Isle aux

Tetes, or Ash Island, near the mouth of River La Colle, is included in this grant. The same lowness and swampy nature of the soil that marks the two preceding seigniories characterises this one also; but such parts of it as are cultivated, or capable of being so, are of a rich quality and very fertile: it abounds with fine timber of many sorts, among which there is found some pine of large dimensions. The Riviere du Sud, that falls into the Richelieu a little below Isle aux Noix, waters this seigniory very conveniently, and is navigable for boats and canoes about six miles. To it there is a road from Missisqui Bay, by which produce, after being brought from Phillipsburg by the ferry, is conveyed in waggons to be embarked and sent down the Richelieu to St. John's and other places: both here and in the adjoining seigniories, on the boundary, there is a field for improvements of the greatest utility. Were a canal to be cut to connect Missisqui Bay and Riviere du Sud (which would not require more than two miles and a half or three miles), it would be most eminently serviceable, not only to the settlers of the neighbourhood, but likewise to the new townships on the Canadian frontier, containing a population that, in 1812, exceeded seventeen thousand; by such a canal the intercourse with the Richelieu would be totally unobstructed, and it would besides materially contribute towards drawing much of the produce of the populous townships on the American territory into the hands of British traders, for the purposes of exportation by the Saint Laurence, at all times either in war or peace. This route to a certain market would be shorter and much less expensive than to convey the growth of these districts to New York, or other places, for exportation; and whoever is acquainted with the character of an American farmer, will be convinced that he will always continue so keen a speculator as to prefer that market by which he can most speedily convert the produce of his fields into capital without risk: prompted by an insatiable desire of gain, any convenient mode of realising his profits will obtain a much greater share of his attention than the prohibitory laws that deprive him of choosing the persons with whom he would deal. The increasing value and importance of the English townships and settlements on this line will, in a few years, become apparent, and is a subject at this period well entitled to a serious consideration, as they will not only be instrumental in enlarging the prosperity of the province, but mainly contribute to its future safety and protection. If the attention of government could be directed to this point, with

a determination to avail itself fairly and justly
of the ample means it affords for amelioration,
the most important advantage to Lower Canada,
and consequently to the empire, would soon be
the result of its care; but if left merely to the
strength of their own efforts, the period of extensive improvement must of necessity become
much more remote.

There is however one subject on which the
British settlers in this district have a strong
claim to the interference of government in their
behalf, to rescue them from the vexatious de-
lays and arbitrary impositions they have been
forced to submit to for years, from the custom-
houses established on Lake Champlain by the
Americans. The navigation from Phillipsburg,
on the eastern side of Missisqui Bay, to St.
John's on the river Richelieu, by which nearly
all the produce of these townships is conveyed
to a market, for a considerable distance runs
within the American waters; as vessels of all
descriptions must proceed several miles down
the lake before they can double the point of Al-
burg to get into the river. In doing this they are
brought to by the United States revenue boats,
and often detained, under very frivolous pre-
tences or litigious objections, for a long period,
frequently to the injury of their cargoes, and
always detrimental to the proprietors. Against

such proceedings all remonstrances with the local authorities have been hitherto treated with inattention or disrespect, and redress sought for in vain; it is therefore become necessary for government, whose interest it is to watch over the welfare of all its subjects, and protect the most distant of them from injustice, to provide against the continuation of such a practice; otherwise, from the spirit of appropriation natural to the American government, long forbearance will be construed by the opposite side into a natural right.

FOUCAULT (the seigniory of), in the county of Bedford, is bounded on the north by the seigniory of Noyan, on the south by the state of Vermont; on the east by Missisqui Bay, and on the west by the Richelieu; it was granted, May 1st, 1743, to Sieur Foucault; two leagues in front by two and a half in depth, and is now possessed by General Burton. The line of boundary between Lower Canada and the United States runs through this seigniory, whereby great part of it is placed within the state of Vermont. The land hereabout is low, but far superior in quality to the other low lands on the east bank of the Richelieu, and may be cultivated with the greatest success for grain or all other produce; but this superiority, joined to the benefit of having water communica-

tion at its east and west boundaries, has yet
attracted but few settlers, chiefly American
farmers, fixed in different parts of the seigniory:
however, as the neighbouring townships advance in prosperity, the local advantages of
Foucault are likely to procure it an increase of
inhabitants.

St. Armand (the seigniory of), situated on
the east side of Missisqui Bay, in the county of
Bedford, is bounded on the north by the townships of Stanbridge and Dunham, on the south
by the state of Vermont, on the west by Missisqui Bay, and on the east by the township of
Sutton; was granted, September 28, 1748, to
Sieur Nicolas Réné Le Vasseur, and is now the
property of the Honourable Thomas Dunn.
According to the terms of the original grant,
this seigniory ought to have an extent of six
leagues in front by three in depth; but as the
boundary line of the United States intersects
it, there is not now more than one league and
a half of it in that direction within the British
territory. The greater part of the land is of a
superior quality, affording good situations and
choice of soil for every species of cultivation;
the surface is irregular, and in some places,
particularly towards the township of Sutton,
there are ridges that rise a considerable height,
and many large swells that approach almost to

mountains, covered with beech, birch, maple
and pine timber. The shores of the bay, south
of the village, are rather high, with a gentle
slope down to the water's edge; but they subside to the general level on advancing towards
the head of it. It is watered by several streams,
the largest of which is Pike River, that has its
source in the adjoining township of Dunham,
and, after winding a very irregular course through
the seigniory and the township of Stanbridge,
falls into Missisqui Bay. This property is well
located with respect to the means of improvement, as it adjoins the state of Vermont, which
is both a populous and flourishing district,
with good roads leading in every direction, besides the main road that runs through Phillipsburg by Burlington and Vergennes, down
to Albany, and which is the most direct line of
communication with New York; it cannot but
benefit by the advantages to be derived from
so easy an intercourse with a country that has
already made great progress in agricultural
knowledge. The first settlement made within
this seigniory was in the year 1785, by some
Dutch loyalists, whose industry was so well
applied that the increase has been so rapid as
to make it an estate of great value; there are
187 lots of 200 acres each conceded, besides an
extent of nearly three miles in depth from Mis-

sisqui Bay, by the whole breadth, divided into much smaller portions, and now extremely well cultivated. The village of Phillipsburg is conveniently situated on the edge of the bay, about one mile from the province line; it is a handsome place, containing about sixty houses, exceedingly well built of wood, many of them in the peculiar style of neatness common to the Dutch, and the others more in the fashion of the American than the Canadian villages: some regard has been paid to regularity in the formation of the principal street, which has a lively and agreeable appearance; between this street and the bay'are many store-houses, with wharfs for landing goods at a short distance from them. At this place there are many of the inhabitants employed in trade and mercantile pursuits, besides artizans, and perhaps more than a due proportion of tavern-keepers. On the south side of the road, leading from the village to the eastern part of the seigniory, is a handsome church (built of wood) dedicated to St. Paul, and a good parsonage-house; there are also two baptist meeting-houses, a public free school, and several private schools; from the wharfs there is a ferry to the opposite side of the bay, a distance of about four miles. The village of Frelighsburg is on the south side of Pike River, about twelve miles from Phillipsburg, consisting of only seventeen houses, a free school, forge, trip-hammer, mills, and some out-buildings; the church (Trinity) is a short distance from the river, on the north bank. The population of St. Armand has within a few years greatly added to its numbers, being at present 2500 souls : emigration from the United States has been one great occasion of this increase. Among the persons so settled, it should be noticed, that a great proportion of them have not sworn allegiance to the British government, a duty the magistracy of the district ought not to dispense with from those who choose to domiciliate so near the borders ; as in the event of hostilities, and which latterly was the case, many of these people would remove the whole of their property and stock to the American territory. Lands are not granted by the crown to any individual who has not previously sworn allegiance, and the same precautions should be taken with respect to strangers, particularly in the frontier townships, who acquire lands by purchase or otherwise. The different streams work many grist and saw-mills, which about the villages are eight in number. The Pinnacle Mountain, one of the large swells already spoken of, covers a superficies of about 600 acres; and rises in a conical shape to a considerable height; it is seen at a great distance in the surrounding country. Between Phillipsburg and the boundary line is a high ridge of land, on which General Macombe encamped in March, 1813, when he made an incursion into the province, and held possession of the village for some time; he succeeded so far as to spread alarm among the inhabitants, drive off some cattle, and destroy the young orchards, before he received intelligence of a British detachment advancing upon him: on that information being communicated, his orders for a retrograde movement were promptly given, and obeyed with unanimous celerity by his troops.

MONNOIR (the seigniory of), in the county of Bedford, with its augmentation, extends from the rear of the seigniory of Chambly to the township of Farnham and the banks of the river Yamaska; bounded on the south-west by the seigniory of Bleurie, and on the north-east by those of St. Hyacinthe and Rouville: its extent is two leagues in front by three in depth; granted 25th March, 1708, to Sieur de Ramzay: the augmentation, equal in dimensions to the seigniory, was granted June 12, 1739, to Sieur Jean Baptiste Nicolas Roc de Ramsay: the whole is now the property of Sir John Johnson, Bart. Throughout this tract the land, though various in its nature, is of a moderately good quality, and where it is under management raises very good crops of grain; many of the parts not yet broken up, would prove very favourable to the growth of flax: the upper division, adjoining Chambly, is nearly all cultivated, as well as an extensive range on the left bank of the Yamaska, and on both banks of a rivulet near the township of Farnham; towards the western boundary it is somewhat low, and rather inclining to swamp. The upper part is watered by several streams that branch off from the river Huron, and penetrate towards the middle of the seigniory. The uncleared land is pretty thick of wood, mostly of the inferior sorts, though here and there some good timber of large dimensions may be met with. There are many roads, nearly in all directions, some of them principal ones, taking a southerly course towards the frontier townships, and into the United States. Near the middle of the seigniory there is a single hill, called Mount Johnson, of no great circumference, but rising high enough to be conspicuous for many miles round; it is however not so remarkable as several others of the same isolated nature in some of the adjoining seigniories. This property touching, or very nearly so, upon the rivers Richelieu and Yamaska, that are both navigable all the summer season for boats and rafts, offers many inducements to settlers in the ad-vantages of its situation, and possessing in other respects great capabilities of being highly im-proved.

MONTARVILLE (the seigniory of·) lies in the county of Kent, between those of Boucherville and Chambly, bounded on the north-cast by the seigniory of Beloeil and its augmentation, and on the south-west by Fief Tremblay: it extends one league and thirty French arpens in front, by one league and a half in depth; was granted, October 17, 1710, to Sieùr Boucher, and is now the property of Réné Labruere and X. Beaubien, Esqrs. The land in this grant is of a good species, producing grain and vegetables of all the sorts common to the country, in great abundance; about two thirds of it is under a very favourable system of husbandry. What wood remains is chiefly of the inferior sort, used for fuel, with but very little timber among it. Towards the north-eastern angle of the seigniory is the Moun-tain of Boucherville, on whose summit are two small lakes, from whence descends the only rivulet that waters the property, which, in its course down the declivity, turns two grist-mills; the first of them agreeably and singularly enough situated on the brow of the mountain. A road leading from the St. Lawrence to the Richelieu and several others in a transverse direction traverse this seigniory.

TREMBLAY (fief) is on the south side of the St. Laurence, in the county of Kent, between the seigniories of Longeuil and Boucherville, bounded in the rear by Montarville; its front is only twenty-eight French arpens; its depth is two leagues; granted 29th October, 1672, to Sieur de Varennes, and now the property of Joseph Dubai, Esq. and the heirs of Edward William Gray, Esq. In this small tract the land is of an excellent quality, fit for every branch of husbandry, and nearly all under cultivation; it is but sparingly watered.

BOUCHERVILLE (the seigniory of), on the south side of the Saint Laurence, in the county of Kent, having the fief Tremblay on the west, the seigniory of Varennes on the east, and bounded by Montarville in the rear; its dimensions are 114 French arpens (eighty-four of which make a league) in front, by two leagues in depth; was granted 3d November, 1672, to Sieur Boucher, and now belongs to Madame Boucherville. The quality of the land in this grant, if it cannot be rated in the first class, is yet far above mediocrity, being for the most part a lightish mould, inclining something towards sandy, and with careful husbandry is found by no means deficient in fertility; in fact, nearly the whole of it is now under cultivation, and generally produces very good average crops of all sorts. The wood remaining upon it is inconsiderable in quantity, and only of the inferior species. Two small rivulets that fall into the St. Laurence partially water it towards the front, one of which works the seignorial mill in its course; there is no stream whatever in the lower part. There is a main road leading from the village of Boucherville down to the Richelieu, and from thence to Chambly; several other roads that are well kept up, pass through all the settled parts of the seigniory. The village is most agreeably and conveniently seated on the bank of the river; it contains from 90 to 100 houses, a church and parsonage-house, a chapel and a convent, or rather a residence for two or three of the sisters of the congregation of Notre Dame at Montreal, who are sent hither from the chief establishment as missionaries for the education of females. There is likewise a school for boys. In this place many families, who still retain some of the titles of the ancient *noblesse* of the country, have fixed their residence; and formed a society to themselves, wherein much of the ceremony and etiquette that used to characterise the titled circles of the French nation is still observable, diminished indeed in splendour, but unabated in precision. Many of these residents have built some very good looking houses for themselves, that are rendered rather conspicuous by forming a strong contrast with the major part of those belonging to the other inhabitants, which in that respect are by no means calculated to attract notice; for symmetry and proportion seem to have been as much set at defiance in their construction, as regularity has been neglected in the streets. This omission, however, detracts little or nothing from the general amenity of situation.

The Isles Communes, or Isles Percées, a range that extends along the front of nearly the whole seigniory, are included in the grant; the largest is about three quarters of a mile in breadth; they are quite flat and very level; some of them afford good meadow land, and the others are common pasturage for the cattle belonging to the inhabitants of the village.

VARENNES (fief), in the county of Surrey, between the seigniories of Boucherville and Cap St. Michel, or La Trinité, is bounded in the rear by the augmentation to the seigniory of Beloeil; its content is twenty-eight French arpens in front by one league in depth; was granted 29th October, 1672, to Sieur de Varennes, and is at present the property of Paul Lussier, Esq. The whole of this little fief is

good and fertile land, nearly all in cultivation,
and pleasantly watered by two or three little
streams. The church, belonging to this property,
surpasses in beauty all those of the surrounding
seigniories, and merits some notice for the style
both of its outward ornament and interior decoration : in coming down the river its three
spires form a conspicuous object, which may be
seen from Montreal, a distance of five leagues:
a very good parsonage-house stands near it;
there is also a neat chapel within the fief. The
houses of the tenants are, many of them, well
built, and dispersed through every part of it;
but no where in sufficient number to form a
village.

CAP ST. MICHEL, or LA TRINITE' (the
seigniory of), in the county of Surrey, joins
Varennes on the south-west, the fief Guillaudiere
on the north-east, and is bounded by the augmentation to Beloeil in the rear; one league in
front by a league and a half in depth; was
granted 3d November, 1672, to Monsieur de
St. Michel, and is now the property of Jacques
Le Moine Martigny, and Trapui Gautier, Esqrs.
A diversity of soil prevails through this seigniory,
the greater part of which is good, being either
a fine black or a greyish mould, that proves
fertile where it is tolerably well managed; the
quantity under culture amounts to two thirds

of the whole. The rivers St. Charles and Notre
Dame run across it, and are sufficiently deep
to be navigable for boats of burthen. The uncleared lands, that scarcely exceed in extent
half a league square, afford hardly any other
wood than the spruce fir, a species of very
trifling value. On the rivers there are two
grist-mills and one saw-mill. A part of the
seigniory is divided into four small fiefs, that
are the property of Messrs. Delette, Beaubien,
Gautier and Mondelette, containing together
one-fourth of a league broad by half a league
deep. Two islands in the St. Laurence, lying
in front of this grant, are appendages to it;
each of them is nearly three quarters of a mile
long, and from eight to ten arpens broad; cattle are sometimes pastured on them.

GUILLAUDIERE (fief) is in the county of
Surrey, adjoining Cap St. Michel, and contains
thirty arpens in front by a league in depth; was
granted 3d November, 1672, to Sieur de Grandmaison, and now belongs to ——— Hertel,
Esq.

ST. BLAIN (fief), between Guillaudiere and
the seigniory of Vercheres, is twenty-three arpens
broad by two leagues deep; was granted 29th
October, 1672, to Sieur de Vercheres, now the
property of Madame de Boucherville. There
is a strong affinity between the soils of these

two fiefs, which consist principally of a blackish friable mould, that if moderately well managed is very fruitful ; about three-fourths of each are under tillage.

VERCHERES (the seigniory of), on the south side of the Saint Laurence, in the county of Surrey, joins the fief St. Blain on the south-west, the fief Bellevue on the north-east, and is bounded in the rear by Cournoyer ; it extends one league in front by two deep ; was granted October 29, 1672, to Sieur de Vercheres, and now the property of Madame Boucherville. The land is for the most part good, with several varieties of soil ; the largest proportion of which is under a creditable state of culture : it is watered by a small river and two or three rivulets, that turn a grist-mill, and some saw-mills. It has a neat church, a parsonage-house, and a chapel, in the centre of a small village.

BELLEVUE (fief) lies between the seigniories of Verchefes and Contrecoeur, bounded by Cournoyer in the rear, and contains half a league in front by a league in depth ; was granted 3d November, 1672, to Sieur de Vitré, and now belongs to ———— Chicoine, Esq. All this slip is under good cultivation, but is not watered by river or stream.

CONTRECOEUR (the seigniory of), on the south side of the Saint Laurence, in the county of Surrey, is bounded by the fief Bellevue and Cournoyer on the south-west, the seigniory of St. Ours on the north-east, and the seigniory of St. Denis in the rear; is two leagues in front by two in depth; was granted October 29th, 1672, to Sieur de Contrecoeur, and is now the property of the heirs of Monsieur de Laperriere. The land in this seigniory is rich and fertile; in some few places it is flat and low, but is almost every where in a favourable state of cultivation, and produces good crops of grain of excellent quality; so much of it is settled upon, that the tracts of woodland remaining are insignificant in proportion to the whole extent, and in these timber of large dimensions is scarce. The Ruisseau La Prade, that has its source about the middle of the seigniory, and several smaller streams, contribute to the fertility of the soil, and in their course work some mills of both kinds. There are five ranges of concessions of different depths, that are separated by as many public roads, which are again intersected by others running from the Saint Laurence, and also by the main road from St. Denis and St. Antoine on the Richelieu, up to the former, a distance of two leagues, from whence there is a ferry to La Valtrie on the opposite side; the fare is two shillings for each person, and seven shillings and sixpence for a horsé and carriage. In the second range of concessions is the Brulé St. Antoine, and in the fourth Le Grand Brulé: these places derive their appellations from the method sometimes adopted of clearing the lands by burning the wood upon the ground where it is felled, after such parts of it as are wanted for immediate use are removed; or else by setting fire to the trees and underwood while standing: when once fairly on fire, they will often continue to burn for weeks before the flames are again subdued. How far the conflagration has spread is shewn by the blackened and scorched appearance of the contiguous woods, and many of the half consumed trunks and roots, that remain for years in the ground; being extirpated only as the farmer's leisure offers convenient opportunities. Accidental fires sometimes occur in the forests, which, being spread by the wind, and no means taken to extinguish them, occasion brulés to a great extent. There are two neat churches and parsonage-houses in the seigniory, but no village; the houses however are numerous, distributed along the different roads in the concessions, and towards the banks of the Saint Laurence. The group of small islands in front, called Les Islets de Contrecoeur, is an appendage to the property.

St. Ours (the seigniory of) and its augmenta-

tion, lies on the south side of the St. Laurence;
a small part in the county of Surrey, and the
rest in Richelieu; bounded on the south-west
by the seigniories of Contrecoeur, St. Denis and
St. Hyacinthe, on the north-east by those of
Sorel and Bourchemin, and in the rear by the
river Yamaska; is two leagues in breadth by
rather more than seven in depth; was granted
29th October, 1672, to Sieur de St. Ours, and
is now in possession of Charles de St. Ours,
Esq. The land in this extensive grant is every
where of a good quality, with varieties adapted
to almost every species of agriculture; full nine-
tenths of the whole of it is in a state of cultivation.   There are ten ranges, containing altogether 800 concessions; those situated along the
Saint Laurence and on both banks of the Richelieu are perhaps the richest parts of the soil,
and greatly superior, as to cultivation, to those
in the rear of the seigniory.   Some timber of
the best kind and largest dimensions still remains, and also some of the inferior sorts.   The
river Richelieu, that traverses the upper part
diagonally, is navigable from the St. Laurence
for craft of 150 tons burthen; the Yamaska, at
the lower extremity of it, is also navigable, by
both of which it possesses the advantages of
expeditious water conveyance in an eminent
degree: in addition to these, it is watered by

three other rivers (not navigable) called La
Prade, La Plante, and Salvayle.   On the right
bank of the Richelieu is the village of St. Ours,
of about sixty houses, many of them substantially and well constructed of stone ; in the
centre of it is a handsome church and parsonage-house, and at a little distance the manor-
house : besides traders and artizans, many persons of considerable property reside here, who
are corn-dealers, and make large purchases of
grain of all kinds, that is produced in abundance
throughout this and the adjoining seigniories,
which is put on board large river craft in the
Richelieu and Yamaska, and sent to Quebec
for exportation.   Nearly in every direction there
are many public roads, kept in good repair,
particularly on both sides of the two large
rivers, and those leading from the Saint Laurence to the Yamaska.   From the village there
is a ferry across the Richelieu, on the left bank
of which are two excellent grist-mills.   The
Island Deschaillons, a short distance from the
village, is full a mile-long and half a mile wide.
In front of the seigniory there is a group of
islands belonging to it; the largest of them is
called Isle Commune, and has some good pasture on it.   Under the various considerations
of extent, situation, local advantages, the quantity of land in cultivation, the state of husbandry,

and the population, which amounts to 3000 souls, there are certainly but few possessions in the province superior in value to this one.

BELOEIL (the seigniory of), on the north-west side of the Richelieu, in the county of Surrey, is bounded to the westward by the seigniory of Chambly, to the eastward by that of Cournoyer, to the southward by the river, and to the northward by lands stretching to the rear of the seigniory of Cap St. Michel and the adjoining small fiefs, and which form an augmentation to Beloeil; its dimensions are two leagues in front by one and a half deep; the augmentation is nearly of the same superficies. The principal grant was made, January 18, 1694, to Sieur Joseph Hertel, and the accessory one, March 24, 1731, to Sieur de Longeuil. The Baroness de Longeuil is now proprietor of both. The land of this tract is good, resembling in its varieties that of Chambly, having some patches of as rich a soil as any in the district of Montreal. On the border of the river and the eastern side the settlements are numerous; about three-fourths of the whole being in cultivation. The uncleared parts afford some beech, maple, and birch timber, but more of spruce fir, cedar, and inferior sorts. The north-eastern part is well watered by the little river Beloeil, that flows into the Richelieu,

and along whose banks is a range of excellent
concessions ; in its course it works a grist-mill
and a saw-mill : some smaller streams traverse
the lower part, and likewise fall into the Richelieu.　Various good roads lead through the
seigniory ; but the one that follows the course
of the river is the main public one.　The houses
of the settlers, many of which are extremely
well built, are dispersed through the different
concessions ; here and there a few together, but
no village.　The church and parsonage-house
are near the Richelieu.

ROUVILLE (the seigniory of), on the river
Richelieu, opposite to Beloeil, is in the county
of Bedford ; bounded on the west by Chambly,
on the east by St. Charles, on the south by the
seigniory of St. Hyacinthe, and in front by the
river ; two leagues in front by one and a half in
depth ; was granted January 18th, 1694, to
Jean Baptiste Hertel, Sieur de Rouville, and
now the property of J. B. M. H. de Rouville,
Esq.　This tract contains land of so good a
quality that nearly the whole of it is in a very
advanced state of improvement, principally
under grain : the concessions are divided into
eight ranges, all running nearly parallel to the
river ; they are watered by several small streams
besides the Riviere des Hurons, which is one of
considerable magnitude, that winds through the

lower part, and, continuing the same serpentine course, falls into the Basin of Chambly; it rises in the seigniory of St. Charles, and runs about twenty miles, not only contributing to the fertility of the soil, but by its sinuous meanders forming a strong feature of embellishment. Towards the middle of the seigniory, between the second and third ranges, is the Mountain, frequently called Chambly and Beloeil; but most correctly Mount Rouville: at its base it spreads over about 600 acres, extending principally from south-west to north-east, and rising to an elevation little inferior to the mountain of Montreal; on the south side the acclivity is gentle, but in the opposite direction it is very steep and abrupt. On the summit of this mountain there is a beautiful little lake of fine clear water, from whence a rivulet flows, in a pretty winding stream, into the Riviere des Hurons, turning in the upper part of its course a grist-mill. The slopes of the mount are in many places broken by woods that greatly increase its picturesque beauty. The church of St. Jean Baptiste is situated to the southward, and a little in the rear of the height; in its front, near the Richelieu, is the church and parish of St. Hilaire, facing that of Beloeil in the opposite seigniory. The roads leading along the bank of the Richelieu and on both sides of the Riviere des Hurons are good; there are also two that take a southerly direction, and open a direct communication with the river Yamaska.

St. Charles (the seigniory of), on the south side of the river Richelieu, in the county of Richelieu, is bounded on the south-west by the seigniory of Rouville, on the north-east by the seigniory of St. Denis, on the south by the seigniory of St. Hyacinthe, and on the front by the river; containing a space two leagues square: it was granted, March 1st, 1695, to Sieur Hertel de la Fresniere, and at present belongs to the Honourable P. D. Debartzch. The generality of the land in this grant is not surpassed by that of any one that surrounds it: the soil most prevalent is a fine strong loam; in some places there is a rich vegetable mould upon a stratum of clay, and in others a mixture of clay and sand: an inconsiderable proportion of it remains uncultivated. The mode of husbandry is very fair, and is most years rewarded with abundant harvests. The population of the settled parts is somewhat above the numerical ratio in proportion to their extent. The lower part of the seigniory is watered by the Riviere des Hurons, and the north-east or upper angle of it is crossed by the little river Miot. The houses of the tenantry are scattered about the concessions, but there is no village: the church,

P

dedicated to St. Charles, and the parsonage-house, stand on the bank of the Richelieu, about midway between the lateral boundaries; and near the same spot is a handsome manor-house, where the proprietor resides. At the western extremity of its front the Richelieu, by a sudden turn, spreads to a breadth of more than half a mile, in which expansion there are two small islands, called Les Isle aux Cerfs, that form part of the seignorial property.

Cournoyer (the seigniory of), on the river Richelieu, in the county of Surrey, is bounded on the north-west by Vercheres and Bellevue, on the south-west by Beloeil, on the north-east by Contrecoeur, and in the rear by the river; two leagues in front by an equal depth; was granted, March 1st, 1695, to Sieur de Cournoyer, and now possessed by A. Bellefeuille, Esq. The land in this seigniory is nearly similar to that of Vercheres and Contrecoeur, and for the most part of a good quality, producing, like many of the adjacent properties, wheat and other grain in abundance: the best cultivated part is on the bank of the river and towards Contrecoeur: the quantity under management is about two thirds of the whole. The uncleared lands are chiefly at the north-west angle, and afford wood of the inferior species only. It is watered by the Richelieu, but has no stream in

its interior. An excellent road leads from the
village of Vercheres, close to the St. Laurence,
down the Richelieu, where it joins the main
public road to Chambly, &c. The church of
St. Mark is on the bank of the river, but there
is no village.

St. Denis (the seigniory of), in the county
of Richelieu, is bounded in front by the seigniory of Contrecoeur, on the north-east by that
of St. Ours, on the south-west by Vercheres,
and in the rear by St. Hyacinthe; it is two
leagues in breadth by as many in depth; and
was granted, September 20th, 1694, to Louis
de Ganne, Sieur de Falaise. The property now
belongs to the heirs of ———— Montarville, Esq.
Nearly all the land within these limits is of a
good sort and very fertile, being chiefly a light
earth covering a yellow loam : wheat and other
grain is found to thrive extremely well upon it,
and yield ample returns. Rather more than
two-thirds of it are cleared and under tillage,
there being five ranges of concessions, making
together 300 lots, very few of which are unoc-
cupied. The river Richelieu runs across the
front, and the rear is watered by the little river,
or rather rivulet, called Le Miot. On the south
bank of the Richelieu is the village of St. Denis,
that numbers about eighty houses, and a very

fine church, the whole tolerably well built, in
an agreeable and pleasant situation, which when
seen from the opposite side of the river, where
some of the best houses, and the church, with
its three handsome spires, present a front view,
exhibit a favourable specimen of picturesque
beauty: between the main street and the river
are some capacious store-houses, chiefly used
as granaries, and wherein large quantities of
corn are collected from the adjacent seigniories
for exportation; as the lands for many leagues
about this part are considered the most productive in grain of the whole district of Montreal.
In the river, nearly fronting the village, is the
Isle de Madere, and a smaller one : from this
place there is a ferry to the opposite seigniory
of Contrecoeur. It is remarkable that there are
neither saw nor grist-mills on either of the streams;
wind-mills supply the place of the latter. There
is a school for females, conducted by two sisters
of the congregation of Notre-Dame, missionaries
from Montreal. In proportion to the superficies of this seigniory it is very well inhabited;
the number of houses dispersed over it (including the village) exceeding 400. There is a fief
of twelve acres in front, called Cascarinette,
but it is now the property of the seignior. The
public roads in all directions are numerous; the

principal ones are those by which the communication between the rivers St. Laurence
and Yamaska is kept up.

: St. Hyacinthe (the seigniory of), in the
county of Richelieu, is bounded on the south-
west by the seigniory of Monnoir and the township of Farnham, on the north-east by the seigniories of St. Ours and de Ramzay, on the
north-west by those of Rouville, St. Charles, and
St. Denis, on the south-east by the townships
of Milton and Granby; six leagues in front by
six in depth, being three leagues on each side
of the river Yamaska; was granted, November
23, 1748, to Sieur François de Rigaud, Seigneur
de Vaudreuil, and is now the property of Monsieur Desolles and the Honourable P. D. Debartzch, heirs of the late H. M. Delorme, Esq.
This capacious grant is in a situation that,
combined with its many other advantages, renders it a most valuable and highly improvable
possession. So great an extent naturally embraces many varieties of soil; but the best
species here predominate, and the proportion
anywise below mediocrity is very trifling; the
least improvable is towards the north and north-
east side, where it is low, and in some places
rather swampy; approaching the township of
Granby it rises higher, presenting a valuable
tract for every species of culture requiring a

rich dry soil. In many parts there are lands admirably well adapted to the production of hemp and flax in large quantities; to the growth of all the grains peculiar to the country no part of the district is more congenial. The banks of the Yamaska and the other streams afford plenty of good meadow land; in fact, the different classes of arable, meadow, and pasture may be nearly all denominated of first rate superiority. There is much fine beach, maple, and bass-wood timber; cedar and spruce-fir are abundant on the low wet lands; oak and pine are found in tolerable quantities, and of large scantling towards the townships of Granby and Farnham. The part of the seigniory lying on the north-west side of the Yamaska is nearly all employed in agriculture; the opposite bank, and the parts towards the south-eastern extremity, also present many wide ranges of cultivated grounds. The Yamaska flowing along the middle of this spacious property, and being navigable for large boats and rafts, affords ample means of speedy conveyance for the fruits of the field, and the produce of the forests. A branch of the same river diverging to the eastward into the new townships, and which receives several minor streams, plentifully waters that division; while the river Salvayle, that has its rise near the boundary of St. Charles, with some of less note, completely answer the purpose of irrigation for the western part. The roads are well kept, and pass in almost every direction; those on each side of the river are the main public ones, by which the communication between Three Rivers, Quebec, and the state of Vermont, is directly maintained; and, in consequence of the importance of this route, every attention is paid by the proper officers of the different districts to preserve it in the best possible state of public accommodation. From these roads others of no less general utility strike off, into the new townships, and thence in several ramifications to the state of New Hampshire, &c.; together forming the means of intercourse invaluable to this part of the province. There are several parishes within the seigniory, and although they are tolerably well inhabited, there is only the single village of St. Hyacinthe, which is most conveniently situated on an angle, formed in the north-east part by a large bend of the Yamaska, containing from eighty to ninety houses, for the most part built in a superior style, and very respectably tenanted, a large handsome church and good parsonage-house, and a college, or rather public school. Being in the main road, there is a continual influx of strangers travelling to and from the frontiers, for whose reception there are one or two inns, wherein the accommodation is every way respectable; the environs are most agreeably diversified by gardens and orchards in a flourishing state, meadows, pastures, and other farm inclosures. At a short distance from the village are a grist and a saw-mill. Near the boundary of the seigniory of Rouville there is a single mountain, similar to that of Beloeil, but inferior in elevation and extent, adorned nearly to the summit with woods, beautiful in their appearance on the slopes, and containing some fine timber. On the south-west side of the river is another, called the Yamaska Mountain, almost of the same form and magnitude, but having, among the woods that spread over it, some excellent fine timber.

BOURCHEMIN (the seigniory of), on the river Yamaska, in the county of Richelieu, is bounded by the seigniories of St. Hyacinthe and St. Ours on the south-west, St. Charles, Yamaska, and de Ramzay on the north-east, and by Sorel on the north-west; a league and a half in breadth, by each side of the river, and three leagues in depth; was granted, 22d June, 1695, to Sieur Jacques François Bourchemin, and is now the property of Mrs. Barrow.

BOURGMARIE WEST (the seigniory of), extending from the rear of the seigniory of Sorel to the river Yamaska, joins Bourchemin on the

south-west; it is sixty arpens in front by a
league and a half in depth, and was granted,
August 1, 1708, to Marie Fézéret, and now the
property of Mrs. Barrow.

LOUISE DE RAMZAY is a small piece of land,
about a league and a half superficial, of a triangular form, lying in the rear of the seigniory of
Sorel, between those of St. Ours, Bourchemin,
and Bonsecours; granted, June 18, 1739, to
the Demoiselles Angelique, Louise, and Elizabeth de Ramzay.

BONSECOURS (the seigniory of), lies between
the seigniory of Sorel and the river Yamaska,
having the seigniory of Yamaska for its north-
eastern boundary; it is seventy-four French
arpens broad by two leagues deep; granted,
April 16, 1678, to Sieur Villeneuve, and now
possessed by Mrs. Barrow. The same kind of
land prevails generally throughout these four
several concessions, of which but a small part
can be deemed of superior quality. Bourchemin, where the Yamaska runs through it, is the
best settled, but even there cultivation has not
made a very favourable progress; in fact, much
the largest proportion of each grant still remains covered with its natural wood: among
it a little good timber may be found; but the
inferior species are abundant enough.

DE RAMZAY (the seigniory of), in the county of Richelieu, is bounded on the south-west by St. Hyacinthe, on the east and north-east by the township of Upton, and on the north-west by St. Charles Yamaska and Bourchemin; three leagues in front by as many in depth; was granted, 17th October, 1710, to Sieur de Ramzay, and is now the property of the heirs of P. Langan, Esq. Of this seigniory very little is cultivated, or even cleared. Judging of the quality of the land from the timber growing thereon, gives every reason to suppose that it might be brought into use with very good prospects. Towards the north-east there are some swamps, thickly covered with cedar and spruce fir, the certain indication of such a soil; but the woods on the higher parts are of much better kinds, and in some places shew the ground to be of a strong and good quality. It is watered by the river Chibouet, that has its source in the recesses of the forests, and after an irregular course falls into the Yamaska.

ST. CHARLES YAMASKA (the seigniory of), on the eastern bank of the Yamaska, in the county of Richelieu, is bounded on the north by the seigniory of Bourgmarie East, on the south by Bourchemin, on the east by de Ramzay, and on the west by the river; it contains a league and a half in superficies; granted, August 14, 1701, to Sieur Réné Fézéret, and is now the property of Mrs. Barrow. The best and only cultivated part of the land lies along the bank of the river, but extends only a short distance from it, producing grain in moderately good crops. With the exceptions of this tract the seigniory is nearly all wood-land, in some places bearing the appearance of a soil that would reimburse the expense and trouble of bringing it into use, if persevered in with industry and managed with a little skill.

SOREL (the seigniory of), on the south side of the Saint Laurence, in the county of Richelieu and Surrey, is bounded on the south-west by the seigniory of St. Ours, on the north-east by the seigniory of Yamaska, and in the rear by the little grants of Bourgmarie West and Louise de Ramzay; two leagues and a half in breadth by two in depth (one on each side of the river Richelieu); was granted, 29th October, 1672, to Sorel, Sieur de Saurel; it was purchased, in 1781, from its then possessor, for the use of government, by Sir Frederick Haldimand, governor and commander in chief. Part of this seigniory is of a lightish, good soil, in some places inclining to a mixture of sand and clay; on the north-east it is low, where the Bay of La Valliere or Yamaska cuts into it, occasion-

ing swamps and marshes of considerable extent. Of the whole grant about two-thirds are
cultivated, and afford a tolerable proof that
where a proper mode of husbandry is introduced
the land is rendered very productive. The low,
wet parts, particularly that called the Great
Swamp, lying between the Riviere Pot au
Beurre and the town of William Henry, now
covered with spruce fir and cedar-trees, might
by ditching and draining be converted into
good meadow and pasture, and some spots
made fit for the growth of hemp. The rising
grounds afford timber of the best sorts, in small
quantities, and also some situations where the
culture of flax could be introduced with good
prospects of success. The Riviere Pot au Beurre,
branching into three distinct streams that flow
into the Bay of La Valliere, waters the rear of
the seigniory; the Richelieu traverses the upper
part, and here discharges itself into the St.
Laurence; on the banks of these streams there
are some of the concessions and farms in a
state of improvement much superior to the
other ranges. From the town of Sorel there
are roads in many directions, of which the two
main ones leading to Yamaska and along the
course of the Richelieu are the best, and of
most importance. The town of Sorel, or William Henry, is very well and pleasantly situated

at the confluence of the Richelieu, Sorel or Chambly River (known by each appellation), with the Saint Laurence, on the scite of a fort built in the year 1665, by order of Mons. de Tracy, similar to those erected in the neighbourhood of Montreal, &c. as a defence against the incursions of the Indians, and which received its name from Sorel, a captain of engineers, who superintended its construction. The plan of it covers about 120 acres of ground, although at present the number of houses does not much exceed 150, exclusive of stores, barracks, and government buildings. It is laid out with regularity, the streets intersecting each other at right angles, and having in the centre a square 170 yards on each side; the dwelling-houses are of wood, substantially and well constructed, but the Protestant and the Catholic churches are both stone buildings; there are eight principal streets, that, like the town itself, are named after different branches of the royal family; the whole population is about one thousand five hundred. Before the town the bank of the Richelieu is from ten to twelve feet high, having near the point two small wharfs or landing-places; the river is here two hundred and fifty yards broad, with from two and a half to five and a half fathoms of water. On the opposite shore there are convenient places for building vessels, and where some of large tonnage have been constructed; but latterly this branch of trade has not been so much attended to here as it used to be, notwithstanding the accommodations for carrying it on would induce a belief that great encouragement would be given to it. A small distance from a little rivulet to the southward of the place is a blockhouse and an hospital, and a little further on a good wooden building, with out-houses, gardens, &c. called the Government-house, serving as a residence for the commanding officer of the troops stationed here, usually one or two companies of infantry. On the south-east side of the town there is a rising ground, whereon it was once in contemplation to erect some substantial military works, but hitherto slight field works have been the only defences thrown up. Such a measure ought not to be entirely neglected, for the position being one of importance to the safety of the province, supposing it necessary to contend against a well directed invasion, and not naturally a strong one, should receive such assistance from art as would render it tenable for a long time to oppose a considerable force, as it is a point against which an enterprising enemy would endeavour, for several reasons, to direct a main attack. The present town of Sorel was begun

about the year 1785, when some loyalists and
disbanded soldiers settled at it, and it still conti-
-nues to be the residence of many old military
servants of the crown, who exist upon pensions
allowed them by government. Some trade is
carried on here, but not so much as might be
supposed its situation at the junction of two
navigable rivers would command : the timber
trade, the export of grain from this part of the
country, and the interchange between the American states, might be extended to a considerable
amount, and apparently with many advantages.
Within a short time there has been established
a regular post road from William Henry to St.
John's, whereon travellers from Quebec to the
new townships and into the United States
proceed with expedition, and find every requisite accommodation of horses and carriages, at
rates fixed by the government of the province.
The Richelieu, affording a quick and easy water
communication from the American territory
into the very centre of the province, is entitled
to consideration in more than one point of view.
As a medium of commerce between the fertile
districts of each country, it merits attention;
and it has a forcible claim to consideration from
being a main inlet into the British territory,
through which hostile operations might be directed with an alarming rapidity, and perhaps

for some time with serious consequences, before they could be checked and repelled. The first may be encouraged, and in all probability advantageously extended, as easily as the latter can be guarded against when the possibility of the attempt and its contingencies are understood. This river flows from Lake Champlain in a northerly course, to its confluence with the St. Laurence, through the well cultivated seigniories that have been already described. Its banks are generally between eight and twelve feet high, diversified on each side by many farms and extensive settlements, in a very high state of improvement; some neat, populous, and flourishing villages, handsome churches, numerous mills of various kinds, good roads in all directions, with every other characteristic of a country inhabited by an industrious population. The navigation is carried on by boats, canoes, and other craft of large dimension and burthen, and by rafts. From its junction with the St. Laurence, decked vessels of one hundred and fifty tons may ascend from twelve to fourteen miles. This river is noticeable for the unusual circumstance of being much narrower at its discharge than at the place from whence it flows; and for the gradual diminution of the breadth of its bed. At its mouth it is about two hundred and fifty yards wide, which it preserves,

with the exception of one or two expansions
occasioned by some small islands, which greatly
increase the beauty of its scenery, up to the
bason of Chambly, that has been already mentioned; from hence to the Isle du Portage the
breadth is five hundred yards; beyond this it
spreads to double that distance, and continues
to widen still more up to St. Johns, from whence
there is a ship navigation to the towns on Lake
Champlain. From the bason down to the St.
Lawrence the current is regular and gentle, and
although there are some shoals and flats, they do
not disturb the smoothness of its course; but
from Lake Champlain the stream is hurried, in
some places rather violent, and in others broken
by rapids. The passage downwards for loaded
boats, &c. is in general quick and unattended
with the smallest difficulty, except what is occasioned by the rapids. Upwards to Chambly
nothing more than ordinary care is required to
avoid the shallows, but from thence to St.
Johns the ascent is attended with more labour,
from the causes just spoken of. The number
of river craft, canoes, &c. with their various
ladings, with the immense quantities of timber
composing the numerous rafts that are continually descending, and upon which many hundred tons of pot and pearl ashes, and large cargoes of flour are brought down every summer,

Q

exclusive of what is conveyed by the boats, unequivocally point out the value and import- ance of this communication. The Isle St. Therese, between Chambly and St. Johns, is two miles long, and about half a mile broad, and with the smaller island adjacent, was granted Nov. 3, 1672, to Sieur Dugué; it is flat and low, partly covered with small timber and brush-wood, but where it is clear there are some good meadows and fine pasturage for cattle. The Isle du Portage, a little below it, is of no value. Near Isle Therese is a ferry, where the charge for taking across a horse and carriage is one shilling and three-pence; a single horse, seven-pence halfpenny; and two-pence half- penny each person: in several other places there are ferries, in the vicinity of the main roads from Montreal to the new townships.

LA CHENAIE (the seigniory of) lies on the north side of the river St. Jean, or Jesus, in the county of Leinster; bounded on the north-east by the seigniory of St. Sulpice, on the south- west by that of Terrebonne, and by the town- ships of Kilkenny and Rawdon in the rear; it contains four leagues in front by six in depth, and was granted 16th April, 1647, to Pierre Legardeur. This tract was afterwards divided, and at present forms the two distinct seig- niories of La Chenaie and L'Assomption; the

former is the property of Peter Pangman, Esq.
and the latter belongs to the heirs of the late
P. R. de St. Ours, Esq. except a small portion,
which is the property of General Christie Burton. La Chenaie adjoins Terrebonne, and has
a front of two leagues. The quality of the land
is various, but throughout proves tolerably good,
as very few parts indeed fall below mediocrity.
The usual sorts of grain, and other produce of
the country, are cultivated here, and return excellent crops: there are also many patches well
suited to the growth of flax, that might be carried on with success to a considerable extent.
The rivers Achigan and Mascouche, with several smaller streams and rivulets branching from
them, water it very favourably; neither river is
navigable for boats, but timber is brought down
them to the St. Lawrence. In the spring and
autumn their waters greatly increase, and in
these seasons some rapids in them are very violent; but even in the usual periods of drought
there is seldom any want of a sufficient supply
to keep the mills at work. On the borders of
the St. Jean, Achigan, Mascouche, Ruisseau
des Anges, St. Pierre, and the other streams,
there are nine ranges of concessions, containing
together 456 lots, nearly equal to one half of
the seigniory; of this number rather more than
400 are cleared, well settled, and much im-

.proved. Although so well inhabited, there is not a village worth notice; of two churches, one is dedicated to St. Henri, and the other named La Chenaie. On the Achigan there is a grist-mill, and upon the Mascouche a grist and a saw-mill. About a mile from the river Jesus is a fief, of 18 acres in front, that runs into the adjoining seigniory of L'Assomption as far as the limits of St. Sulpice, and of which Mrs. Deviene is the proprietor. Over the different rivers there are good bridges, and from La Chenaie two ferries, one to the Riviere des Prairies, where one shilling and eight-pence is charged; the other to isle Jesus, where only ten-pence is demanded for each person.

L'Assomption (the seigniory of) possesses many local advantages, and a variety of soil favourable to the encouragement of cultivation in almost every branch. Towards the township of Rawdon the land is higher than it is in the front; consisting chiefly of a yellow loam, mixed in some places with sand, which, when tilled, is very fertile, but still perhaps something inferior to the lower parts, where there are many exceeding fine tracts fit for the culture of every species of grain. On the uplands, birch, beech, and maple timber is found in great perfection, with some pine of a good growth; but in the valleys the wood is inferior

in quality; the best sorts very partially intermixed. The River Assomption falls into the
Riviere St. Jean and waters the lower part;
the Achigan crosses the seigniory of La Chenaie, enters L'Assomption towards the middle
of its depth, forms a considerable bend in it,
and afterwards recrosses the division line: the
upper part is intersected by some smaller
streams that contribute greatly to its fertility,
and are no less ornamental to it. The Assomption and Achigan may both be called large
rivers, but neither of them are navigable, although both of them are made use of to bring
down the timber felled in the upper parts of
the adjacent seigniories and townships. Very
few grants exceed this property in the proportion of cultivated land, four-fifths of it being
cleared and well settled; there are ten ranges of
concessions, containing 1000 lots; upon them
are nearly 700 houses of all classes. The most
improved settlements are those situated on the
banks of the two large rivers. In the bend of
the Achigan, upon a beautiful and well chosen
spot, is the handsome church of St. Roc, and
around it a few well-built houses, the commencement of a village; and although as yet
not very considerable, there is a good public
school in it. Beside the church of St. Roc,
there is another towards the rear of the seig-

niory. The Achigan turns two corn-mills and one saw-mill.

St. Sulpice (the seigniory of) on the north side of the Saint Lawrence, in the county of Leinster, is bounded in front by the river, in the rear by the township of Rawdon, on the north-east by the seigniory of La Valtrie, and on the south-west by that of L'Assomption; two leagues in front by six in depth; was grant-éd, 17th December, 1640, to Messrs. Cherrier and Le Royer, and is now the property of the seminary of St. Sulpice at Montreal. More than three-fourths of this seigniory is well cul-tivated, and for the goodness of its soil, the quality of the timber, and state of improve-ment, is not surpassed by any that surround it. It is particularly well watered by the River L'Assomption, the Achigan, St. Esprit, Ruis-seau St. George, Ruisseau Vacher, Riviere Rouge, Ruisseau Point de Jour, and Lake Ouareau, most of them flowing into the Assomption after a mazy course, that in some parts, where the ground is high and clothed with wood, present points of view truly picturesque and beautiful. The different ranges of concessions contain up-wards of 300 lots of various dimensions, nearly all of which are settled upon, and generally speaking under a respectable system of hus-bandry; but those in the greatest state of improvement lie on the banks of the St. Lawrence; and on both sides of the Assomption. The seigniory contains two churches and parsonage-houses, and one village; many grist and saw-mills are worked by the different streams and rivers. The village is situated on the south-west side of the Assomption, and covers about half a mile square, having from eighty to ninety houses, besides many storehouses, some for general merchandise and the others for grain, as large quantities are collected here for exportation; and from hence also are dispersed over the other seigniories, and the townships towards the Ottawa, a good deal of merchandise, and many articles of general consumption, so that it is a place of some little trade: the houses of the most wealthy inhabitants are exceedingly well built of stone. From hence there are many good roads leading to the interior of this and into the adjacent seigniories; and over the large rivers, bridges at convenient intervals.

La Valtrie (the seigniory of) and its augmentation, in the county of Warwick, has the River St. Lawrence on its front, the seigniory of St. Sulpice on its south-west, that of La Noraye on the north-east, and the township of Kildare in the rear; a league and a half in breadth by the same depth; was granted 29th October, 1672, to Sieur de la Valtrie. The

augmentation, similar in breadth to the seigniory, but having a depth of two leagues and
a half, was granted 21st April, 1734, to Sieur
Marganne de la Valtrie; they both remain in
possession of the heirs of the original grantee.
This is a very valuable property; the land, generally speaking, is level from the rear to the
St. Lawrence, whose banks hereabouts are rather
low.   The quality of the soil varies a little, but
the major part of it is good and productive,
either of a light greyish earth, a yellowish loam,
or clay mixed with sand; nearly the whole of
it under culture, and yielding ample crops to a
system of husbandry that in several respects is
creditable to the farmers.   The Riviere L'Assomption winds its broad but shallow stream
through the upper part of the seigniory, and
the lower portion of it is watered by La petite
Riviere de la Valtrie, that falls into the St. Lawrence.   Wheat and other grain forms the chief
part of the disposable produce of this tract;
good hay in great abundance is made from
some very extensive and excellent ranges of
meadow land.   Although well inhabited, yet
there is not a village in La Valtrie; the houses
are spread about among the concessions, and
thickly placed by the sides of the roads that
lead along the St. Lawrence; the church, with
the parsonage, a chapel, the manor-house, with

a few others, are situated a little to the eastward of the Riviere La Valtrie; and from thence
at no great distance is the wood of La Valtrie;
that, even in Canada, is worthy of notice, for
the fine, lofty, and well grown timber trees of
various kinds that compose it. The main road
from Quebec to Montreal passes through this
wood and along the bank of the river, offering
to the traveller in the summer season for several miles a succession of beautiful and romantic
scenery. Besides the main road, there are several that lead into the populous seigniories on
each side, which are intersected by others running at right angles into Kildare, and opening
a most convenient and easy intercourse with the
neighbouring townships. On the River La Valtrie there is a grist and a saw-mill. The rear
boundary line of this seigniory had not until
very recently been accurately measured, when
it was discovered, that in addition to its proper
depth of four leagues, there was still a space of
about a mile in breadth between it and Kildare,
which had always been supposed to form part
of the grant, and many persons had settled
thereon with titles from the seignior of La Valtrie; this extra space is very well cultivated, and
has a church, with a great many houses, built
within it, from the erroneous confidence of all
parties that they were within the just limits of

the grant. Under these circumstances of encroachment, occasioned by ineffectual measurement at first, a compromise has been made, and an order passed the governor and council to grant the cultivated part to the present proprietor of La Valtrie, and to reserve the remainder for the use of the Protestant clergy and future disposition of government. In front of the seigniory are the two Isles de la Valtrie, appendages to it.

La Noraye and Dautre'(the seigniories of) with their augmentation, lie on the north side of the River St. Lawrence, in the county of Warwick; are bounded on the south-west by La Valtrie, on the north-east by the seigniory of Berthier, in front by the river, and in the rear by the seigniories of D'Aillebout D'Argenteuil and De Ramzay. La Noraye, two leagues broad and two deep, was granted April 7th, 1688, to Sieur de la Noraye. Dautré was granted in two portions; the westerly one, half a league broad by two leagues deep, to Sieur Jean Bourdon on the 1st December, 1637; the easterly one, of precisely the same dimensions, on the 16th April, 1647, to Sieur Jean Bourdon also. The augmentation, under the title of Derriere Dautré, and La Noraye, being the breadth of the two former (three leagues) and extending to the Riviere L'Assomption, about

four leagues, was granted 4th July, 1739, to
Sieur Jean Baptiste Neveu. The whole is now
the property of the Hon. Ross Cuthbert. The
extensive tract included in these several grants
contains a vast quantity of excellent arable
land, that lies in general pretty level. The soil
is various; in the front a light reddish earth
with some clay, but growing stronger by the
mixture of different loams towards the rear,
where it is a strong, rich, black earth. The timber embraces almost every variety, with much
of a superior quality in the different classes,
and some very good oak and pine. It is conveniently watered on the south-west side by the
rivers St. Joseph, St. John, and the little Lake
Romer; a little westward of the St. John is another small lake connected with that river by a
short canal that always ensures to it a permanent stream. The rivers La Chaloupe and Bayonne cross its north-east side into Berthier;
on them there are several good corn and saw-
mills. In the rear of the seigniory, towards the
River L'Assomption, is an eminence called
Castle Hill, commanding a diversified and beautiful prospect over the surrounding country, on
which the present proprietor is about erecting
a handsome house for his future residence. In
this property cultivation is in a very advanced
state, about two-thirds of it being thickly settled,

of which the parishes of St. Elizabeth in the rear, the banks of the St. Lawrence, the Coteaus St. Martin and St. Emily, are perhaps the most flourishing. There is no village; but good houses, with substantial and extensive farm buildings, are dispersed over it in all parts.

D'Aillebout D'Argenteuil (the seigniory of), in the county of Warwick, is bounded in front by the Riviere L'Assomption, on the south-west by the township of Kildare, on the north-east by the seigniory of De Ramzay, and in the rear by waste crown lands; a league and a half in front by four leagues in depth: was granted October 6th, 1736, to Sieur Jean D'Aillebout d'Argenteuil.

De Ramzay (the seigniory of) joins d'Aillebout, and is bounded on the north-east by the township of Brandon; of precisely the same dimensions as the preceding one; was granted 7th October, 1736, to Dame Genevieve de Ramzay, widow of Sieur de Boishebert. Both seigniories are now the property of the heirs of the late Hon. P. L. Panet. These grants consist of good rich land in the lower part, but in the rear, approaching the mountains, the soil is either a hard unfruitful clay, upon which the farmer's labour would be thrown away, or irregular and broken strata of rock. It is however tolerably well timbered, beside the common sorts for fuel, with beech, birch, and maple, some oak, and a little pine. A small range on the west bank of L'Assomption is all that in either seigniory is under culture.

BERTHIER (the seigniory of), on the north bank of the St. Lawrence, in the county of Warwick, with its fiefs and augmentations, is bounded on the south-west by the seigniory of Dautré and augmentation, as recently described; on the north-east by those of Dusablé or New York, and Maskinongé; in the rear by the township of Brandon, and in front by the St. Lawrence; was granted 27th April, 1674, to M. Berthier; the augmentation was granted 31st December, 1732, to Sieur Pierre L'Etage: the property, as it is at present possessed by the Hon. James Cuthbert, is two leagues and three quarters in front, by four and a half in depth. Of ten ranges of concessions, containing 600 lots or thereabouts, nearly all are in the hands of tenants, but many of them retained as woodlands, and not settled upon. The soil in general is good, except towards the rear, where it is rocky and sterile; in the concession called St. Cuthbert it is a fine vegetable earth several inches deep, on a subsoil of strong clay; in that of St. Esprit a strong deep loam; in St. Pierre a rich light earth; in St. Catherine a small part is a good loam, and the rest of some-

what inferior quality; in St. Jean there is a
mixture of several species, which taken together is fully equal in fertility to either of the
others.   In front the land is low, especially. towards the north-east boundary, but the arable
is very productive, and the remainder a succession of very fine meadows.   The other parts of
the seigniory are but indifferent in quality, and
some of it about the back boundary even .bar-
ren and unfit for tillage.   Most of these concessions are farmed in a very good style; but those
whereon the greatest improvement is visible are
St. Cuthbert, St. Esprit, and St. Pierre, where
industry and careful arrangement has given an
appearance to much the greatest number of the
farms that conveys an idea of the ease and even
affluence enjoyed by their occupiers.   Wheat
is the chief production of these lands, but they
are fit, generally speaking, for every species of
culture; and the important articles of hemp
and flax might be raised in almost any quantities, would the farmers attend to it properly,
and adopt a different method in its cultivation to that hitherto used in the province. The
Rivers Chicot, La Chaloupe, Bayonne, and the
Bonaventure Creek, a branch of the latter that
runs almost to the rear boundary, afford a convenient and equal irrigation: the first is navigable for boats up to the seignorial mill, about

two leagues, but the two others only a mile or
two from their mouths. Near the Bayonne
there is a spring highly impregnated with salt,
from the waters of which that article may and
sometimes is made of a very good quality. On
the best cultivated ranges the wood is nearly all
cleared away; but on the others, and in the back
districts, there still remains abundance of *bois
de chauffage,* or fuel, with some little maple,
beech, and cedar. The village of Berthier is
pleasantly situated on the north side of the
Chenail du Nord, and forms one principal street,
consisting of at least eighty houses; or rather,
they are placed sometimes at long intervals on
the side of the main road to Quebec: many of
them are extremely well-built and handsome.
There are, exclusive of dwellings, a great many
granaries and store-houses for general merchandise, it being a place of some trade, from whence
British manufactured goods are dispersed over
the neighbouring populous seigniories, and from
whence also large quantities of grain are annually exported. The church, that claims notice not only as being a handsome structure,
but for the elegance of its interior decoration,
is situated at a small distance behind the main
street. This village being about mid-way between Montreal and Three Rivers, in the direct
route of the public stage coaches that have been

established upon the plan of those in England between the former place and Quebec, and also the principal intermediate post-office station, makes it a place of great resort and considerable traffic: several inns are kept, where travellers will always find good and comfortable accommodation. On passing through the Chenail du Nord, the village with its gardens, orchards, meadows, and surrounding cultivated fields, form together an agreeable and pleasing assemblage of objects, although from the flatness of the country it is not marked by any of those traits of grandeur so frequently observable on the north side of the St. Lawrence, descending towards Quebec. Indeed, it is so little above the level of the river, that in the spring, when the melted snow and ice occasion a rise of the waters, it is sometimes overflowed to a considerable distance inland, causing much damage to the lower parts of the houses in the village, and goods deposited in the stores; so great has been the rise as to make it necessary to remove large quantities of wheat from the upper stories of the granaries to save it from injury. A similar inconvenience happens at Vercheres and its vicinity, on the south side of the river. Besides the village of Berthier, there is another in the upper part of the seigniory called Pierreville, of about twenty houses, all of wood. On the west side of the River Chicot, and about two leagues in the interior,. is the church called St. Cuthbert's, belonging to a parish of the same name, that spreads over a large portion of this and the adjoining seigniory to the north-east. There are also four schools; two of them supported by the Roman Catholic clergy. Including the villages, the dwelling-houses dispersed in the various concessions amount to about 500, and the total population of the seigniory is estimated to exceed 5000, which certainly will not be supposed an exaggerated computation, when it is known that it furnishes 1000 able-bodied men for the militia. In Berthier and its dependencies there are two grist-mills, two saw-mills, and one pot-ash manufactory. The main road by the St. Lawrence, and the different roads through the concessions, are maintained in excellent repair. Across the rivers there are bridges, all free of tolls. The domain of Berthier is on the south-west side of the River Bayonne, and contains 335 arpens, approaching in goodness to the best of the district. In front of the seigniory several fine islands form the south boundary of the Chenail du Nord; they are named Isles Randin, Du Pas, Castor, &c. On Dupas, which is the largest, and was granted November 3d, 1672, to Sieur Dupas, there is a church and several

flourishing settlements; the others consist principally of meadow and grazing land. A little
to the southward of this group are Isles St.
Ignace, Isle Madame, Isle aux Oies, Isle Ronde,
and Isle de Grace, belonging to government;
these, and some others to the eastward, at the
entrance into Lake St. Peter, are very low, but
clothed with good timber; they abound with
all sorts of wild fowl, as do the intervals between them with excellent fish of various kinds.

LA PETITE NATION (the seigniory of), is
situated on the north side of the Grand or Ottawa River, in the county of York, occupying
the ground of two projected townships, between
those of Grenville and Lochaber, five leagues in
front by five in depth; was granted May 16th,
1674, to Messire Francois de Laval, Bishop of
Pétrée, the first Bishop of Quebec. It is now
the property of I. Papineau, Esq. The whole
of this grant, with the exception of a small spot,
remains in a state of wood-land; recently, however, the present proprietor, a gentleman of
Montreal, and for many years a member of the
provincial parliament, has retired to it with an
intention to commence a plan of improvement,
that, if persevered in, will be likely to realise
many of the advantages that its situation and
other favourable contingencies hold forth the
promise of. The Ottawa indents the front by

several bays and large ponds, towards which
the land is low, but of excellent quality, where
there are ranges of soil stretching a great distance
to the interior, fit for the cultivation of every
species of grain, hemp, flax, and grasses of all
descriptions. On the margin of the rivers,
large tracts of fine natural meadows and pastures at present enrich only the earth with their
exuberant plenty. The inlets and ponds abound
with fish in great variety, and the neighbouring
grounds with game, duck, teal, and other wild
fowl, in great quantities. Penetrating deeper
into the seigniory, the land has a gradual
ascent, and is clothed with timber of the best
kinds; the oak is of superior quality, particularly some of the largest dimensions, fit for ship-
building. The main ridge of mountains, that
runs a westerly course from Quebec until it
falls upon the Ottawa, crosses La Petite Nation
about the middle; beyond this intersection the
remainder of the grant has been only partially
explored, but the quality of the part that has
been observed is much inferior to that of the
south; although the various sorts of timber appear to retain their superiority, or at any rate it
is but very little diminished. From the range
of heights and the upper lands several small
streams have their sources, from whence in
various directions they water the valleys in their

way to the grand river, but they are too inconsiderable for other purposes than irrigation and
working of mills.

LES ISLES BOUCHARD, lying in front of the
seigniories of Vercheres and Contrecœur, in the
St. Lawrence, were granted Oct. 29th, 1672,
to Sieur Fortel. They are together about five
miles in length by half a mile broad. Some
good meadow and pasture land is found upon
them, the rest is covered with wood, and among
it some very fine timber. On all of them the
soil is excellent.

Having now finished a compressed description
of all the feudal tenures in the district of Montreal, I will next notice such grants as have
been made by the English government in free
and common soccage under the title of

TOWNSHIPS.

KILPARE is situated in the county of Warwick, and in the rear of the seigniory of La
Valtrie; it was erected into a township by
letters patent, dated June 24, 1803 *, and lands

* As a list of the several grants in free and common soccage, made since the year 1796, under the great seal, in such
tracts as are actually erected into townships within the province
of Lower Canada, specifying by whom each was made, the
time when, to whom, what quantity, and the proportion of

therein, equal to one-fourth of a township, granted to P. P. M. de la Valtrie and his associates; which grant is now the property of the heirs of the said M. de la Valtrie, and the widow of William Vondenvelden, Esq. This township has twelve ranges of concessions, but is only thirteen lots wide *. No part of it has

crown and clergy reservations, is given in the appendix, a recital of the same individually is thereby rendered unnecessary. The reader will please to refer to it for whatever concerns any original township grant. In the description, where individuals may be named, they are the actual proprietors of large tracts, either by purchase or otherwise.

* To avoid repeating the dimensions of townships and their subdivisions, the same is here given precisely. The most exact content of ten miles square, the usual dimensions of an *inland township*, as prescribed by the warrants of survey, is sixty-one thousand acres, exclusive of the usual allowance of five acres on every hundred for highways. This quantity is contained in a tract of ten miles and five chains in length; by ten miles, three chains, and fifty links, in perpendicular breadth; or such other length and breadth as may be equivalent thereto. A rectangular township of this admeasurement contains eleven concessions or ranges of lots, each lot being seventy-three chains and five links long, and twenty-eight chains seventy-five links broad. Each range is divided into twenty-eight lots, so that each township contains three hundred and eight lots of two hundred acres, with the allowance for highways. Of these lots two hundred and twenty are granted to settlers, and the remaining eighty-eight reserved for the crown and protestant clergy. In like manner it may be observed, that the quantity nearest to the content of nine miles broad by twelve miles deep, the usual dimensions of a river township, is sixty-seven thousand two hundred acres, exclusive of the allowance for highways. These are contained in a tract of seven hundred and twenty-eight chains broad, by nine hundred and sixty-nine chains and sixty

yet been cultivated, although the soil appears
to be of a superior quality, and some of it fit
for hemp and flax, as well as all sorts of grain.
Most of the timber is good. It is watered by
part of Rivière L'Assómption and some inferior streams.

RAWDON, in the county of Leinster, joins
Kildare on the south-west. This is a full
township, of which very little has yet been
granted or even surveyed. The surface of it is
uneven, in many places rocky, but in others
having extents of good land upon which grain
might be raised with profit, and on some few
hemp and flax. On the uplands the greater
part of the timber is maple, beech, and birch;
cedar and spruce fir abound on the lower ones.
It is watered by several small streams.

KILKENNY and ABERCROMBIE are on the
south-west of Rawdon; they have both been surveyed, but from the badness of the soil, which
in fact is scarcely improvable by any means,
at least such as settlers could have recourse to,

links long, or other equivalent length and breadth. A rectangular township of these dimensions contains twelve concessions
or ranges of lots, each lot being eighty chains and eighty links
long, and twenty-six chains broad, and in each range twenty-
eight lots, making in all three hundred and thirty-six lots of two
hundred acres, with the highways. Of this number two hundred and forty are grantable to settlers, and the remaining
ninety-six are reserved as before mentioned.

some persons who had obtained grants therein were on these considerations-permitted to locate their lands in the township of Acton.

CHATHAM is situated on the north side of the Ottawa River, in the county of York, bounded on the east by the seigniory of Argenteuil, on the west by Grenville, and in the rear by Wentworth. It has been surveyed, divided into farm lots, and all granted. Colonel Robertson, who obtained the largest proportion of any person therein, has been the active promoter of an extensive settlement along the river, where the soil is well varied and good, fit for grain, hemp, flax, or indeed most other productions, and which is also the case with the greatest portion of the township. There are also many fine tracts of natural meadow, and some rich pastures. In the rear the surface is broken and uneven, the land inferior in quality, and choked with rocks and other impediments to cultivation. The timber in general is of the best sorts, with much valuable pine and oak, fit for naval purposes. By the side of the Ottawa there is a good road, that is the main route from Montreal to the upper townships on the bank of that river. The Rivière du Nord and several smaller streams water it; by the first mentioned, the timber felled in this and some of the adjoining townships is floated down to the Ottawa. In front of the township are some small islands, that in the intervals between them form several rapids.

WENTWORTH is situated in the rear of Chatham, and has the full dimensions of an inland township, about one quarter of which is subdivided and granted. The greater part of this tract is mountainous and rocky, very inapplicable to arable purposes; but on the three first ranges, all that has hitherto been surveyed, the land is found to be of a tolerable good quality, but not any part of it is yet settled upon. Although there are no very strong inducements to attempt cultivation, this township produces most excellent timber for naval purposes, in great abundance, with the advantage of easy conveyance by the Rivière du Nord, by which it is watered, besides several other streams and small lakes.

GRENVILLE, including an additional parcel of land added thereto since the original grant, is the second township to the westward on the Ottawa River, situated between the seigniory of La Petite Nation and Chatham, and bounded in the rear by unsurveyed lands of the township of Harrington. In the nature of the soil, the species and quality of the timber, it greatly resembles Chatham. A grant of large extent has been made to Archibald M'Millan and others, emigrants from Scotland, but very little of it is at present under culture.

LOCHABER, on the north side of the Ottawa River, between the seigniory of La Petite Nation and the township of Buckingham, in the county of York, has been partly surveyed; thirteen thousand two hundred and sixty-one acres were granted in the year 1807, to Archibald M'Millan and others, emigrants from Scotland; of this portion very little has been yet cultivated. Along the front, the river forms several deep bays, in which direction the land is so low, that it is frequently overflowed; but if the settlements should become more numerous, embankments might be raised to repress the incursion of the waters; this part would then become good meadow, and a short distance towards the interior, much of it would be good arable. Proceeding to the rear, the land is broken and rugged up to the ridge of mountains, beyond which there is nothing at all improvable, at least in their vicinity. Much of the timber within this tract, both oak and pine, is fit for naval purposes. Several rivers and streams wind through the township; neither of the former are navigable for boats, though timber may be floated down them to the Ottawa, which here expands greatly in breadth, and has several islands in it that are all well covered with wood;

the largest of them is a mile long, and about a quarter of a mile broad.

BUCKINGHAM, on the north bank of the Ottawa, in the county of York, joins Lochaber; four ranges of it have been surveyed, and little more than one quarter granted. Bordering the river the land is low, and from several large bays and ponds that run a great way into it, is frequently overflowed; but when that is not the case, there is some excellent meadow land, and also some that is tolerably good for other purposes. In the rear the soil is but indifferent; in places, so uneven and stony as to be fit for no sort of tillage. It is watered by several small streams, descending from the rear into the Ottawa. A few families have settled on convenient spots in front of the township, and pursue their agricultural labours with success, and favourable prospects of improvement.

TEMPLETON is the next township to Buckingham; about one half thereof has been granted to Archibald M'Millan and others, his associates, but as yet very few persons have settled upon it. The land approaching the Ottawa is rather low, but the soil tolerably good for the production of most species of grain and many of the most useful succulents; the back parts are not much inferior to the front. The timber is mostly beech, maple, basswood, pine, and some oak, with cedar and hemlock on the lower grounds. It is well watered by the River Gatineau, the Riviere Blanche, and some smaller streams.

Hull joins Templeton on the west. In 1806 one quarter of this township was surveyed and granted to Philemon Wright and his associates. This portion is situated on a large bend or turn of the Ottawa, and as the mountains here abut upon the river, and the land behind them not being arable, the whole of it was laid out along the front. The soil is of a fair medium quality, fit for all the farmer's general purposes; what part of it is cultivated produces very good crops of all kinds of grain, &c. About thirty families are settled here, and have their farms in a very respectable state of cultivation and progressive improvement. The timber is for the most part of the best sort, the oak fit for naval purposes, and much of the pine for masts of large dimensions. Mr. Wright, as the head of the township, has been indefatigable in promoting the increase and prosperity of this infant settlement. In viewing the progress already made, the greatest encomiums will be called forth for the manner in which, by his own example and encouragement, he has so essentially promoted it, and for settling upon the lands himself. He carries on the timber trade

to a great extent, and a large manufactory
of pot and pearl ashes; he has established a
school, erected a meeting-house, and adopted
various means to excite the industry, and secure
comfort and happiness to all classes of his little
society. His own habitation is pleasantly situated at the east end of the township, on the
bank of the Ottawa; close by it there is a short
portage, and nearly fronting it are some small
islands that greatly obstruct and break the current of the river; on the opposite side a fall,
twenty-six feet high, forms an agreeable object in
the prospect; a little above this place is a reef
of rocks, stretching nearly across the river, and
the falls of La Petite Chaudiere. The townships on the Ottawa abounding with timber of
the best growth, either for ship-building, mast-
ing, planking, or staves, it may be worth while
to remark that a very great proportion of that
trade has been furnished from them to Montreal
and Quebec; not from those on the north side
only, but vast quantities have been supplied
from those on the south, in the Upper Province,
and the rafts of it brought down the rivers
Rideau and Petite Nation, into the Ottawa.
From the former, a road leading to the settlements in the neighbourhood of Kingston will in
a short period, from the increasing population
and consequence of that district, become of

great necessity. It is an object therefore worthy the attention of the government of that province to give every encouragement to facilitate its immediate formation: when completed, a communication from the back townships to Montreal will be opened, more direct and much shorter than the present one, for the conveyance of their produce to a certain market.

EARDLEY and ONSLOW are the two last townships on the Ottawa that have been surveyed, and partial grants made therein, although several others are projected, and names given to them. The front of both of them extends along Lake Chaudiere, or Kettle Lake. The lands that have been examined in the former are found to be of a favourable description; many parts suitable both for hemp and flax, as well as grain, but no settlements have been yet established upon them. The main westerly ranges of mountains terminate upon the river hereabouts. In the latter township, the first range and part of the second are an almost continued ledge of flat rocks, with scarce any soil upon them, except only a very few lots that have been granted; the third and fourth ranges appear to be very good land, that would soon become profitable with careful culture; but the fifth and sixth are poor and swampy, not worth the trouble of draining, and covered with hemlock and other woods of small value. At the west end of this township is one of the many rapids of the Ottawa, called the Rapide des Chats.

NEWTON, in the county of York, lying between the seigniories of Rigaud, Soulange, and New Longeuil, is of an irregular figure, and very advantageously situated, contiguous to the settlements in the Upper Province. On the western side the land is of a very superior quality, and will produce all sorts of grain; many parts also might be employed to great advantage in growing hemp and flax. The eastern side is much lower, inclining here and there for short distances to be marshy : there is, however, no actual swamp; and if the low grounds, that are rather wet, were carefully ditched and drained, they would prove most excellent land, and furnish luxuriant meadow and pasture, as well as good arable. On the most elevated parts, the principal timber is maple, beech, and birch; on the others, cedar, red spruce, alder, and hemlock. As the grants in this township are all recent, only a few of the lots are yet cultivated, but the goodness of situation and several other local advantages are likely soon to induce settlers in much greater numbers. The greatest landholders are the Honourable A. C. de Lotbiniere, Saveuse de Beaujeu, Esq. and Mr. John Mᶜ Nider.

GODMANCHESTER is situated on the south side of Lake St. Francis, in the county of Huntingdon, bounded in the rear by the River Chateauguay, that separates it from Hinchinbrook, and by a small part of the Province Line, or the forty-fifth parallel of north latitude, which is the boundary between the British and American dominions. This township was laid out in the year 1785, and lands assigned therein to officers and soldiers of disbanded Canadian corps. It is divided into five ranges, and these into lots differing a little from the usual dimensions, being nineteen chains wide, and one hundred and five in depth. The whole of it is granted, though only a very small proportion is yet settled upon, and which is about the margin of the lake, where a few houses now and then present themselves, at considerable distances from each other; on the bank of the Chateauguay, also, there are a few settlements. About the front of the township the land is low and flat, but the soil generally good, although in some places wet; further towards the interior, and stretching onward to the Chateauguay, it is greatly superior, being in every respect suitable for the cultivation of any sort of grain, hemp, flax, or other productions of the country. The timber, of which much still remains, although immense quantities have been felled and carried to market, is of the first rate quality. On the north bank of the Chateauguay there is a good road, leading into the state of New York. Among the holders of large tracts of land in this township are the heirs of the late Alexander Ellice, Esq. who now retain twenty-five thousand nine hundred acres, which that gentleman acquired by purchase, and afterwards had secured to him by patent. Adjoining Godmanchester, on the west, is a space reserved for the use of the domiciliated Indians of St. Regis, and commonly known by the name of the Indian Lands: it forms a triangle bounded by Lake St. Francis, Godmanchester, and the line of 45°; its side on the lake is about ten miles, and that on the line twelve miles and a half. The land is of a very superior class, and well furnished with fine timber, but much neglected by the proprietors, as there are no other settlements upon it than a few of their own around the village, which is very well situated, at the western extremity of the tract, close to the St. Lawrence. The boundary line runs through the middle of it, and from hence divides the river upwards, in mid-channel. That the village of St. Regis should be thus circumstanced is a subject of regret, on account of the animosity it frequently occasions among people of the same tribe, from the residents of the huts on one side of it being inhabitants of a different country, as it may be termed, from those on the other. During the late war with America, part of them espoused the cause of each belligerent, but a more prudent few remained neutral; quarrels and bloodshed ensued; indeed no precautions could have prevented such events among so many turbulent and untamed spirits living together, and supposing themselves of political consequence to the contending powers. About fifty houses, or more properly speaking, hovels, a church, a chapel, and a house for the Catholic minister resident with them as missionary, compose their village. The habitations are poor, ill-built, and more than commonly dirty; attached to them are small gardens, or rather enclosures, wherein Indian corn and potatoes are planted, and which, with what they raise on the Petite Isle St. Regis, and some others in the St. Lawrence, near the village, that are their own property, increased by the produce of their fishing, and sometimes hunting parties, constitute nearly their whole means of subsistence; as indolence, mistaken for the spirit of independence, destroys every idea of improving their condition by the profits of agriculture. A similar reservation of

s

land has also been made for them by the American government on that side of the line.

- HINCHINBROOK is in the county of Huntingdon, on the boundary line; joining the seigniory of Beauharnois on the north-east, and separated from Godmanchester by the River Chateauguay. Nearly the whole of this township is granted. From the province line northward there are three full ranges, but the remainder of it is more irregularly divided and appropriated to crown and clergy reservations, in large portions, or blocks, as they are technically termed. The land is somewhat uneven, but the soil is excellent, excepting only a very few swampy tracts, that are covered with cedar, spruce fir, and hemlock trees. The large knolls, or rising grounds, are thickly clothed with good timber, as beech, maple, birch, pine, oak, butternut, and basswood. Towards the Chateauguay, in some places, it subsides into valleys and gentle slopes, where there are large breadths of fine meadows, well watered by several branches of that river. At present the township contains but few inhabitants, some of them settled on thriving farms by the river side, and others in very eligible situations along the frontier, in which direction there are several roads passing into the state of New York. An immense stock of fine timber still remains in this township, although for years past vast quantities have been cut and rafted down the Chateauguay, to Montreal and Quebec.

HEMMINGFORD, in the county of Huntingdon, is also situated on the boundary line, having on its north-west side the seigniory of Beauharnois, and that of La Colle on the north-east. This township has been laid out for close settlements, that is, to be granted by single lots to persons, upon condition of immediately taking possession and beginning to improve them; indeed its situation, as well as that of Hinchinbrook, and generally those along this line of frontier, require every attention and encouragement in this respect; the political results of any measures that increase the settlements and population of this part of the district will appear obvious when it is recollected that every male, from the age of sixteen to sixty, must become a militia-man. There are five complete ranges of two hundred acre lots, and the remainder of the township is divided in a similar manner to Hinchinbrook; but a proportion of these reservations has been let under lease. Although the surface is very uneven, and several high ridges rise in various directions, with many places where there are large seams of flat rock a little below the surface, there are nevertheless many tracts whereon the soil is of a rich and very su-

perior quality, fit for the growth of grain, hemp,
flax, and indeed for every other agricultural
purpose. On the north-west and north-east
sides are found some swamps, abundantly covered with cedar, spruce fir, tammarack, and
trees of similar nature. On the high lands the
timber is of the best sorts, and consists of beech,
maple, elm, birch, &c.; along the second range
some oak and pine, of large dimensions and
good quality, is found. It is very well watered
by the little river Montreal, that falls into the
Richelieu, and many small streams that descend
from the heights to the Chateauguay. In this
township very considerable settlements have
been made, and some of the farms are in a very
thriving state. On the different streams there
are several mills of both kinds. Of the many
roads that traverse the township, the greater
number are but very indifferent ones, and practicable only in the winter time, when rendered
firm and solid by the frost.

SHERRINGTON is an irregular township lying
between the seigniories of La Salle and De
Lery, in the county of Huntingdon, bounded
on the south-west by Beauharnois and Hemmingford, and on the north-east by the seigniory
of La Prairie de la Magdelaine. This tract is
greatly diversified both with respect to quality
of soil and species of timber. On the south-

west the lands rise gently in many places to considerable eminences; in this part there are several sorts of soil, but almost the whole unexceptionable and plentifully covered with beech, elm, maple, basswood and white ash. To the north-east there are many swamps, some of them overgrown with black ash, and others with cedar, &c.; those covered with ash might soon be rendered fit for culture, and would, by ditching, become very good meadow land. The river La Tortue winds through the township, and with many smaller streams conveniently waters it; it is not navigable for boats, but rafts are brought down to La Tortue mills. The eleventh, twelfth, thirteenth, and fourteenth ranges are settled by Canadians, who had their titles originally from Mr. Sanguinet, proprietor of the seigniory of La Salle, under an erroneous belief of the same being within his boundary. About the eighth and ninth range is a small settlement of twelve English families, who have made great progress, and got their farms into a very thriving state, considering how recently they have taken possession of them. The road from La Tortue into Hemmingford passes through Sherrington, and there is also another leading by the Douglass settlement. Surrounded as this township is by settlements in a good state of cultivation, and possessing within itself great inducements for settlers, it is likely to become in a few years a very fertile and valuable tract. The principal landowners are the Lord Bishop of Quebec, the Honourable F. Baby, and Mr. M'Callum of Quebec, who has acquired his proportion from the Honourable John Young.

SUTTON is situated on the province line, in the county of Bedford, having the seigniory of St. Armand on the west, the township of Potton on the east, and that of Brome on the north. It consists of very good land, generally speaking, on which cultivation in every branch might be carried on to advantage, except on some few marshy parts, but which could easily be drained, and would then become very good meadow land. The timber is chiefly ash, elm, maple, and beech; and on the low parts, the species usually found on wet soils, as cedar, spruce fir, hemlock, &c. It is watered by the River Mississqui, that crosses the south-east corner of it, and by many small rivers; several roads have opened in different directions towards Mississqui bay, the other townships, and the state of Vermont. In this township settlements to a large extent have been made, and agriculture appears to be carried on with a spirit that promises both an increase in tillage and improvement in method; on the streams that intersect the cultivated parts there are two grist and three saw-mills. The whole population at present exceeds 1200 souls.

POTTON joins the eastern boundary of Sutton, and extends along the province line as far as Lake Memphremagog; the western part of it is in the county of Bedford, and the eastern in that of Richelieu. Though having a surface for the most part hilly and uneven, the land is of a good quality; the different species of soil offering good situations for raising all sorts of grain, as well as most other productions. It is watered by the River Mississqui, and a great number of tributary streams flowing from the hills into it in almost every direction, and many others that fall into the lake. The timber consists of elm, beech, and maple, with all the common sorts. There are some thriving settlements on the banks of the Mississqui River, and the margin of the lake, where the land is particularly good; the population thereon amounts to upwards of 800 souls. A few roads leading into the neighbouring townships are the only ones that have yet been made, and these are not very good.

STANSTEAD, on the eastern side of Lake Memphremagog, in the county of Richelieu, stretches along the province line until it is bounded by Barnston on the east, and Hatley on the north. This certainly obtains a superiority over all the new townships on this frontier, both in the advantages of its locality, the excellence of its soil, and the quality of its timber. There are many large swells of land, some of them of considerable elevation, that are clothed with oak, pine, and nearly all of the best sorts of hard woods; in the low parts there is great abundance of common timber. Besides Lake Memphremagog and Lake Scaswinepus, it is watered by numerous streams that flow into them, and turn several mills of both sorts. The southerly half of this township, that was granted in the year 1800 to Isaac Ogden, Esq. is well settled and in a very thriving state of cultivation, producing every species of grain peculiar to the province; the wheat superior in quality to most other parts of it; many excellent situations and congenial soil offer opportunities to promote the growth of hemp and flax to almost any extent. The northerly half is not so well settled as the opposite one, but for no other reason than having been granted only in the year 1810, as the land is good, and fit for every species of agriculture. It is the property of Sir R. S. Milnes, Bart. being a portion of 48,000 acres granted to him by the crown, as a special mark of his Majesty's approbation and royal favour for the many important services rendered by him to the province,

during the period of his being its lieutenant-
governor; at present it is greatly inferior to the
other half in the number of its population, yet
as it holds forth almost every strong inducement for such persons as may be desirous of
settling upon new lands, its improvement is
likely to be rapid. The remainder of Sir R.
Milne's grant is located in Compton and Barnston. In the south-east part of the township is
the village of Stanstead, which though small
has some good houses in it; the main stage
road from Quebec into the states of Vermont, New Hampshire, &c. passes through it,
from which, as bringing a continual influx of
strangers, some little consequence is derived.
From hence the same road leads to Derby in
Vermont; at that place the communication to
almost every part of the United States is easy.
The settlements along the border of the beautiful Lake Memphremagog are most delightfully
situated, and in a very forward and promising
state of improvement. The houses dispersed
over them are well built, and surrounded by
neat well-stocked gardens, fine young orchards,
and every requisite comfort of rustic life; their
appearance conveys to the traveller a very favourable opinion of the content and happiness
of their owners. In the township there are several manufactories of pot and pearl ashes.
The aggregate population exceeds 2500 souls.

BARNSTON, in the county of Richelieu, is on the province line, and next to Stanstead. In this township, where the surface is a continual succession of hill and dale alternately, the chief part of the land is good, answering very well for the growth of grain and other usual productions; some swamps are met with in the low parts. The timber upon it embraces almost every sort, but the best are beech, maple, elm, ash, fir, and some oak. The soil is watered by several small lakes, rivers, and streams, on which there are mills of both sorts. The westerly half of the township was granted in 1801 to Messrs. Lester and Morrogh, and contains at present a population of 500 souls. The largest part of the easterly half belongs to Sir R. S. Milnes, Bart. none of which is settled.

BARFORD is situated between Hereford and Barnston, in the counties of Richelieu and Buckingham. It is not a full township, having only seventeen lots in each range. Isaac W. Clarke, Esq. obtained a grant of the greatest part of it in 1802. None of it is yet settled, although it is a tract that promises to become valuable, as the land is every where excellent and the timber good. It is watered by many rivulets and streams.

HATLEY is in the second row of townships northward from the province line, in the counties of Richelieu and Buckingham; bounded by Stanstead on the south, Ascot on the north, Compton on the east, and by Lake Memphremagog, a branch of the River St. Francis, and Lake Scaswinepus on the west. The surface is irregular, in some places hilly, and the quality of the land very variable. On the east and north-east the soil is good, whereon most species of grain might be grown; to the west it is rather superior, but about the middle it is very indifferent, rugged, and swampy. On the best lands beech, elm, maple, and ash timber grows in abundance; in the swamps spruce fir, cedar, and alder. Towards Ascot and Compton some extensive settlements present themselves, where the houses and out-buildings are substantially constructed, the farms cultivated with industry and much ability, and well stocked with cattle. On the border of Lake Memphremagog is another range of improving settlements. The township is watered by several lakes, some small rivers and streams, which as they wind their courses through the cultivated lands turn mills of both sorts. Lake Tomefobi extends diagonally from the fourth range to the ninth, a distance of about eight miles; its breadth is one mile. The banks are beautiful and picturesque, with landscape and woodland scenery as romantic as the most fertile genius of an artist could well imagine; it abounds with excellent fish of many sorts, and is the resort of innumerable wild fowl of various descriptions, as indeed are all the smaller ones. Many roads lead to the adjacent townships, and also communicate with the main ones, leading into the states of Vermont and New Hampshire. One of the most extensive landholders is Henry Cull, Esq. Lieutenant-Colonel of the Militia; a gentleman highly esteemed in this part of the country for his public spirit, for the industry and good will with which at all times he is ready to set an example, or to second and encourage every species of improvement having the welfare of this newly settled district for its object, as well as for supporting every measure of government introduced with the same laudable intention. The population of this township at present is but little more than 1000 souls.

BOLTON, on the west side of Lake Memphremagog, in the county of Richelieu, is bounded by Stukeley and Oxford on the north, Potton on the south, and Brome on the west. This is one of the first townships that was laid out. The surface of it is uneven and rather mountainous, being crossed diagonally by an irregular chain of heights, wherein several rivers have their sources, and which divides the waters that fall into the Yamaska, and other large rivers to the northward, from those flowing into Lake Memphremagog and the Mississqui in the opposite direction. The lands on the low parts are tolerably good, but those to the eastward are the best, whereon there are some fine settlements, well cultivated and producing every sort of grain. On the streams that intersect this part are several corn and grist-mills. Some tolerably good roads have also been opened into the other townships. The population is not very great, being about 800 souls.

BROME, in the county of Richelieu, is next to Bolton, and joins Dunham and Farnham on the west, Sutton on the south, and Shefford on the north. Some part of the land in this township is good, but the other is so mountainous and rocky as to be unfit for culture. The best kind will produce grain of most sorts; hemp and flax might also be grown in several places. On the north-west side, where it is rugged and high, some good timber is to be found, and also great quantities of a very good species of iron-ore. Near Lake Brome, about nine miles in circumference, a few settlements have been made, that afford a favourable specimen of what may be done, upon the lands that are at all susceptible of tillage. Several small rivers fall into the lake, upon which some grist and saw-mills have been erected. The population is 600 souls or thereabouts.

DUNHAM, between the seigniory of St. Armand's and Farnham, in the county of Bedford, touches upon Sutton and Brome to the eastward, and Stanbridge to the westward. The situation and quality of the land throughout renders it a valuable tract; it has plenty of timber, such as maple, beech, birch, elm, butternut, iron-wood, white and black ash; also good oak and pine. The upper lands are rather hilly, having many horizontal seams of rock lying a little below the surface; but on the more level parts the soil is found to be generally a rich black mould, with here and there a mixture of sand. It yields all sorts of grain in abundance; in many places it is peculiarly fit for the growth of flax, and in some others for hemp. Swamps, but not very extensive ones or numerous, are met with, covered generally with cedar and tammarack, but they might be drained without much trouble, and cleared to great advantage. The township is watered by several branches of the Yamaska and the Pike River, and by two beautiful little lakes, the largest spreading over about 600 acres in the sixth range. There are a greater number of roads, and mostly kept in good repair, within this township, than perhaps will be found in any other, connecting it with the surrounding ones, leading through Farnham to the Yamaska, and also to the state of Vermont. The Pike River, and some of the smaller streams, work three or four mills of both sorts. This was the first of the townships erected, in Lower Canada, by letters patent, bearing date in the year 1796; it was granted to the Honourable Thomas Dunn, who is at present the greatest landholder therein. Nearly the whole of it is settled, and many extensive farms are worthy of notice for their flourishing and improved state, producing great quantities of wheat, barley, and oats, besides most other articles peculiar to the country; and in fact the same may be said of the major part of the settlements within it. Perhaps no tract of land of similar extent through the whole of the lower province is better calculated than this for a judicious experimental farmer to demonstrate how much the present stock of agricultural knowledge among the Canadian husbandmen may be increased. Several pot and pearlash manufactories are carried on here. The population is 1600 souls.

STANBRIDGE, in the county of Bedford, is situated between Dunham and the seigniories of Sabrevois and Noyan, having St. Armand's on the south, and Farnham on the north. This

township presents a great variety both of land
and timber; the westerly part is low and rather.
marshy, with a good deal of cedar, hemlock,
tammarack, and some white oak. - Near Mississqui Bay and Pike River the soil is chiefly of
clay mixed with sand; to the eastward it is
higher and better, composed of rich black
and yellow loam, with a little sand. The timber is beech, elm, and maple, with some fine
oak; but bearing only a small proportion to
the other sorts. The Pike River and its numerous branches water it very conveniently, and
work several saw and corn-mills. It is intersected by many roads; the two principal ones
are those that lead southward, through St. Armand's into the state of Vermont, and northward. through Farnham to St. John's on the
Richelieu, and Montreal; whither the inhabitants of these parts convey the greatest portion
of their disposable produce. A large tract of
this township is settled, especially on the north-
eastern side, where, on the elevated ridges, are
many farms, exceedingly well situated, and in a
state of cultivation that bespeaks much practical knowledge of agriculture; the houses. well
built, the gardens and orchards well laid out,
and the general arrangements not unworthy of
being imitated in many of the townships more
recently settled.

FARNHAM, in the counties of Bedford and Richelieu, extends along Stanbridge and Dun-. ham to the south, bounded by the seigniory of St. Hyacinthe and Granby on the north, Monnoir on the west, and Brome on the east. The land is here of a good quality, generally similar to that of Stanbridge, though perhaps with a greater proportion of indifferent tracts: the north-west has swamps that spread widely. The best is timbered principally with beech, elm, and maple; on the marshy parts there are the usual inferior species. It is watered by large branches of the river Yamaska, on which there are many corn and saw-mills. Several roads cross it in every direction, besides the two principal ones mentioned in the preceding article. Along the banks of the streams some good patches of settlements shew themselves. Nearly all this township has been granted. In 1798, Samuel Gale and others obtained a large portion of it, and still continue the greatest landholders: in 1805, a grant was made to the family of the late Colonel Cuyler; and in 1809 the westerly part, being the " rest and residue of Farnham," was laid out, and 10,176 acres thereof granted to John Allsop, Esq. and others his associates, who still retain the property.

GRANBY and MILTON: the first in the counties of Bedford and Richelieu, and the

other wholly in Richelieu, reaching along St.
Hyacinthe on the west; bounded by Roxton,
Shefford, and part of Farnham on the south,
and by Upton on the north. In the former
the land is for the most part of a serviceable
description, composed principally of a blackish
loam, over which, in some places, there is a
layer of fine vegetable mould : good crops of
wheat and other grain might reasonably be expected from it; many parts are particularly
eligible for hemp, and some also for flax. The
timber consists of beech, elm, butternut, maple,
pine, and a little oak. The lands of Milton are
not so good, as they lie much lower, and in
many places run into swamps that would require much perseverance in a good system of
draining to be rendered of any utility; but
while there remain so many thousands of acres
to be granted, not needing this operation, it is
not probable that it will be undertaken here.
There is however abundance of very fine grass-
land : the timber is a mixture of beech, pine,
cedar, and tammarack. The parts of these
townships that have been laid out were granted,
in 1785, to officers and privates of the British
militia, who served during the blockade of
Quebec by the Americans in 1775-6.

SHEFFORD, in the county of Richelieu, between Granby and Stukely, joins Brome on the

south, and Roxton on the north. The face of
the country in this township is uneven, and towards the west mountainous; the soil in most
places is exceedingly rich, but the uplands and
high ridges are too stony to be of much value:
the timber almost universally of the best species.
It is watered by several branches of the Yamaska and other streams, and intersected by
many roads communicating with the other
townships. The south-east part is the best and
most populous, where some fine settlements
present themselves, that are, to the extent of
their cultivation, in a very flourishing state.
The banks of the rivers display many good
breadths of meadow and grazing land. In the
inhabited parts some corn and saw-mills have
been erected. The population of the whole
township is but small, scarcely exceeding 500
souls.

STUKELY, in the county of Richelieu, between Shefford and Orford, has Ely on the
north, and Bolton on the south. Although the
surface of this tract is generally uneven and
broken, the land in some parts of it is rather
above the medium quality. Beech, maple, and
bass-wood, with hemlock and cedar in the hollows and moist lands, are the prevailing sorts of
timber. It is watered by streams falling into
the Yamaska, that have their sources among

T 2

the hills stretching across it, and also by some small lakes. But little progress has been made by settlers, as the entire population is but 250 souls, occupying a few small farms in the southern part of the township.

ORFORD, partly in the two counties of Richelieu and Buckingham, has its front to the river St. Francis and Lake Scaswinepus, joins Stukely in the rear, Brompton on the north, and Bolton on the south. But little can be said of this township, and that little not very favourable. It is mountainous, rough, and almost unfit for tillage. Some good timber, however, is to be had in it. In the interior there are some large lakes, one of which, about four miles long and three-quarters of a mile broad, stretches into Brompton. As may naturally be inferred, but few lots of it are occupied; its population numbering only about 100 souls.

ELY and ROXTON : the first in the counties of Richelieu and Buckingham, and the other in Richelieu; they are between Shefford and Stukely on the south; Acton, Dunham, and Melbourne on the north. Ely has been all surveyed, and the south-easterly quarter of it granted; of Roxton, the southerly half has been surveyed and granted. The land of both townships is good, and if cultivated would prove fertile. The low land is rather wet, but not unfit for tillage. It produces some of the best species of hard, black woods. Branches of the Yamaska and several other streams water these townships. Only a very few persons are settled in either.

ACTON is partly in the counties of Richelieu and Buckingham, stretching along Roxton and Ely on the south, bounded by Upton on the west, and by Grantham, Wickham, and Durham on the north and north-east. About one-half of it has been surveyed and granted, but no part thereof is settled upon. The land is level, and lying rather low, is overspread with several swamps, that are covered with spruce fir, white pine, cedar, &c.; the drier tracts are timbered with ash, beech, maple, and birch. It is watered by two large branches of the Yamaska.

UPTON, in the counties of Richelieu and Buckingham, is of an irregular figure, extending along the boundaries of the seigniories of De Ramzay and De Guir, to the river St. Francis; it is bounded on the south-east by Acton and Grantham, and abuts upon Milton on the south. The land is here flat and low, with many extensive swamps spreading over it, covered with tammarack, alder, and cedar. By the side of the St. Francis, and other streams that intersect it, there are some few spots of land, that, if under cultivation, might produce good crops of grain ; but the general soil does not admit of a description much in its favour. Neither roads nor settlements have yet been made, if a few scattered houses, with small patches of ground attached to them along the line of De Guir, be excepted. It is watered by some branches of the river David.

Having given a detailed account of the seigniories and townships in the district of Montreal, a convenient opportunity now offers to make an observation or two upon this part of the frontier of Lower Canada, and of the line of demarcation between it and the states of New Hampshire, Vermont, and New York, which extends from a stone monument erected on the west bank of the Connecticut River, for the purpose of marking its commencement, to the village of St. Regis, on the river St. Lawrence, a distance of $146\frac{1}{4}$ miles. In the years 1771, 2, 3, and 4, this line was established by actual measurement, in pursuance to orders from the respective governments of the provinces of Quebec and New York, at that period both under the British dominion ; and, more particularly, according to specific instructions issued by the late Lieutenant-Governor, Cramahé, to the Honourable John Collins, Deputy

Surveyor-General of the former province. By
more recent surveys that have been made in
laying out the several townships now established
along this line, its course is accurately ascertained, and clearly demonstrated to be irregular
in the field, at some places inclining towards
the north, and at others diverging to the south.
These points of aberration will be readily discovered by inspecting the delineations upon
my Topographical Map. The correctness of its
position at St. Regis is unimpeachable; but it
deviates widely from its true latitude at the
monument on the Connecticut, which spot is
nearly on the meridian of Quebec. The exact
latitude and longitude of that city has been so
repeatedly corroborated by eminent astrono-
mers, that it may be assumed with safety as a
correct point of departure. Proceeding upon
that datum, which will hardly be controverted,
the boundary line, fixed as it now is, proves to
be at the Connecticut, an encroachment upon
the province of Lower Canada exceeding three
geographical miles. An assertion, however, has
been made to the contrary; for in a report made
in the year 1806 to the government of the state
of Vermont by Dr. Williams, it is stated to be
no less than fourteen miles too far south at the
monument, and seven miles too far south where
it intersects Lake Memphremagog; and the

same is maintained to be an infringement to that extent upon the state: but assertion does not establish a fact. I do not permit myself to question that gentleman's scientific abilities, and can therefore attribute the result of his operations, differing so widely as it does from that of others, which have been carefully performed, only to the use of very imperfect astronomical instruments, which have betrayed him into so serious an error with respect to the true position of that line. But, for argument's sake, admitting the doctor to have been correct, no advantage could accrue to the United States from the supposed discovery; for it is palpably evident, that a line drawn through these two fixed points of latitude, and extending westerly to the St. Lawrence, would take a much greater superficies from the state of New York than what it cuts off from Lower Canada. This, however, is a subject that will no doubt be critically investigated, and satisfactorily adjusted, by carrying into effect the provisions of the fourth and fifth articles of the treaty of peace of 1815, between his Britannic Majesty and the United States of America. It has indeed become a case of necessity, and a matter of great importance to each government respectively, as there are numerous settlements on each side of the boundary already in a flourishing state of cultivation, and rapidly increasing both in population and improvement. From the Connecticut River the height of land on which the boundary is supposed to pass runs to the north-east, and divides the waters that fall into the Saint Lawrence from those flowing into the Atlantic; and which height, after running some distance upon that course, sends off a branch to the eastward, that separates the heads of the streams falling into Lake Timiscouata and River St. John, and by that channel into the Bay of Fundy, from those that descend in a more direct course to the Atlantic. The main ridge, continuing its north-easterly direction, is intersected by an imaginary line, prolonged in a course astronomically due north, from the head of the river St. Croix, and which ridge is supposed to be the boundary between Lower Canada and the United States; at least such appears to be the way in which the treaty of 1783 is construed by the American government; but which ought, more fairly, to be understood as follows, viz. That the astronomical line running north from the St. Croix should extend only to the first or easterly ridge, and thence run westerly, along the crest of the said ridge, to the Connecticut; thereby equitably dividing the waters flowing into the St. Lawrence from those that empty into the Atlantic *within the limits of the United States;*

and those that have their estuaries within the
British province of New Brunswick. It is important, and must always have been had in contemplation, that an uninterrupted communication and connexion should exist between all his
Majesty's North American possessions; but by
the manner in which the treaty is insisted upon
by the opposite party, a space of more than
eighty-five miles would be placed within the
American limits, and by which the British provinces would be completely severed; it would
also produce the inconvenience of having the
mail from England to Quebec carried over that
distance of American territory; and which may
either be deemed a matter of indulgence, or
complained of as an encroachment, according
to the temper of the times. Within this tract
also is the Madawaska settlement, consisting of
nearly 200 families, all holding their grants from
the British government. England, at all times
high minded and generous, never shrinks from
the strict fulfilment of her engagements; even
though from oversight, or want of political
acuteness in the persons employed, they may
have been framed in a way prejudicial to
her true interests. But at the same time she
has a right to require that the interpretation of
them should not be overstrained or twisted
from their obvious meaning and intent by a

grasping-cupidity after a few miles of territory; which if acquired, could be but of little available advantage to the other party. To her, however, this tract is of more value, as securing a free access to all the British provinces, without being obliged to the forbearance of any neighbouring state for that enjoyment. If in the final fulfilment of the fourth and fifth articles of the treaty of 1815 it should be awarded that the claim of the American government to have the boundary pass along the north-easterly ridge of land is just, and ought to be acceded to, it is very desirable, and even important to his Majesty's colonies, that one of the instructions to the British negociator should be, to obtain the cession of this tract of country, either by exchange or other equivalent means, in order that the communication from Nova Scotia and New Brunswick with Lower Canada may be henceforth secured from the chance of interruption.

In addition to these exterior boundaries between us and a *foreign* territory, the settlement of which is in the hands of the imperial government, there are also some relating to interior division that ought to occupy the attention of the provincial legislature. Of these the most prominent are the district boundaries, that, as they are now fixed, produce embarrassment

and inconvenience. On the north side of the
St. Lawrence they are, it is true, identified with
the seignorial divisions ; but on the south side
they are only ideal lines, prolonged to the
boundary of the province, not only cutting several townships, but even farm lots in them, by
which they are placed in two districts. The
evil consequence of this has been frequently
apparent in judicial proceedings, when persons
summoned to attend the courts of law have
gone from a great distance, and at much expense,—to Montreal, for instance,—before they
discovered that their attendance was required
in the district court of Three Rivers, and so
with respect to the others. Men living far in
the interior cannot be supposed to have a critical knowledge of the direction that an imaginary line should take, even though it be liable
to interfere with their rights and privileges ; it
ought, therefore, to be made plain to them, and
which certainly could be accomplished without
difficulty. It might be done by having the
boundaries surveyed and marked in the field
along their whole line, if it be deemed prefer-
able for them to preserve a straight direction; or
otherwise, they might be made to run along the
limits of the townships that they now intersect,
and which, although irregular, would thereby
be as exactly defined as by any other method,

and indeed with less trouble, as nothing more
would be required than to establish the same
by *proces verbal*. At all events some regulation
in this respect is necessary, in order that the
southern townships, now containing a population of nearly 20,000, and that is every year
acquiring fresh accessions, may no longer be
involved in similar inconvenience. The county
boundaries from the same cause call for a revision.

THE DISTRICT OF THREE RIVERS

Lies between those of Montreal and Quebec,
is bounded on the south by part of the line of
45 degrees of north latitude, and the ridge of
mountains stretching to the north-east; northward its limit is indefinite, or it may be presumed to have only the province boundary for
its limit in that direction. Its breadth, on the
north side of the St. Lawrence, from the seigniory of Berthier to that of St. Anne, is fifty-
two miles and a half; but on the south side,
from Sorel to Deschaillors, no more than fifty
miles and a half. It contains the county of St.
Maurice, and the greater part of Buckingham,
forty seigniories and fiefs, thirty-two whole
townships, part of eleven others that are divided by the district lines, thirty-two that are pro-

jected only, and twenty-two parishes. The lands granted " *en fief. et seigneurie*" are 1,039,549 superficial acres, or 1,220,308 superficial French arpents. In the townships 824,679 acres have been granted in free and common soccage. The cultivated part of the seigniories may be taken at a little more than one third ; but the townships fall very short of the same proportion, and the recent date of their grants sufficiently assign the reason of it.

MASKINONGE' (the seigniory of), situated on the north side of Lake St. Peter's, in the county of St. Maurice, is bounded on the south-west by Berthier, on the north-east by the seigniory of Riviere du Loup, and in the rear by Dusablé or Nouvelle York and Carufel : it contains two separate grants ; that of the north-east part, a league and a half in front by the same depth, was made November 3, 1672, to Sieur Baptiste Le Gardeur de St. Michel ; and the south-west part, a league in front by a league in depth, on the same date, and to the same person. The soil is rich, fertile in the production of all sorts of grain, and in some places would be excellent for hemp and flax. The land in general is rather flat; and towards the front is so low as to be sometimes overflowed in the spring ; but this only serves to enrich the fine meadows and good pasture grounds that border the river.

The timber has been very much thinned in this seigniory, but it is very well watered by the large river Maskinongé that winds through the centre of it, and is navigable for boats and canoes for several miles up, and by some small streams. About two-thirds of it is in cultivation. The best settlements are on the borders of Chenail du Nord, on both sides of the road leading to Quebec, and on the east bank of the Maskinongé, over which there is a bridge. There is no village in the seigniory, but it has a church and parsonage-house, one grist-mill and one saw-mill. At the entrance of the Masquinongé there are two or three large islands, forming different channels into it; they are all flat and low, but covered with various sorts of inferior wood. Timber from Carufel, &c. and the townships in its rear, are brought down it into the St. Lawrence.

DUSABLE' or NOUVELLE YORK (the seigniory of), in the county of St. Maurice, is situated in the rear of Maskinongé, between Berthier and Carufel, one league in front by three in depth; was granted, August 15, 1739, to Adrien Dandonneau Dusablé, and is now the property of the Honourable Ross Cuthbert. A small ridge of rising ground crosses this grant a little to the northward of the road to Quebec, which seems to separate the fertile from the barren parts, for to the southward of it the soil is rich, productive, well settled, and under good cultivation; but on the opposite side of the height it is very indifferent, and thinly settled by a few farmers, who have occasion to exert their utmost industry to procure a living. The whole tract is almost free from wood; the little remaining is only fit for fuel. A small stream, called Riviere Cachée, runs through the lower part, and works one corn and one saw-mill.

CARUFEL (the seigniory of), in the county of St. Maurice, lies in the rear of the seigniory of Maskinongé, between Dusablé and fief St. John, about two leagues in front by two in depth; was granted, in March 1705, to Jean Sicard, Sieur de Carufel, and is now possessed by the heirs of the late Honourable Charles de Lanaudiere. In this grant the land is of a pretty good quality, mixed here and there with a reddish clay and sand. Almost every kind of good timber is found upon it, and some of the pine rising to large dimensions. The river Maskinongé traverses it from the north-west, by which the timber felled here is sent down to the St. Lawrence. A small part of it lying on the front is all that is yet cultivated, where, however, there are some very respectable farms and good houses by the side of the main road.

LAKE MASKINONGE' or LANAUDIERE (the

seigniory of), in the counties of St. Maurice
and Warwick, lies in the rear of Berthier, Dusablé and Carufel; it is two leagues in front, and
extends in depth so far as to comprehend Lake
Maskinongé; it was granted, March 1, 1750, to
Charles François Tarieu de Lanaudiere, and is
now the property of T. Pothier, Esq. Some difficulties have occurred with respect to the depth
and other limits of this seigniory, because the
Lake Maskinongé has been found to lie much
further to the westward than it was supposed to
do at the time it was granted; however, it was
at that period sufficiently known not to be mistaken for any of the inferior lakes. The claims
to this property set up by the heirs of the late
M. de Lanaudiere are marked on the topogra-
phical map by the letters *a*, *b*, *c*, *d*, *e*, *f*, *g*, *h*,
i, *k*, *l*. It is a fine tract of land, of a strong
rich soil, and very well timbered with beech,
maple, birch, pine, and some oak. It is watered
by several small lakes, but principally by the river
Maskinongé, whose stream flows from the lake
of that name, which is about nine miles in circumference, and well stocked with various sorts
of excellent fish. The scenery around it possesses many natural beauties of the wild and
sublime description, presenting an amphitheatre
of rising grounds and lofty hills, backed by the
magnificent ridge of mountains running westerly

from Quebec, and many other bold features of a romantic country. Very few settlements have yet been made here, but it certainly may be improved in a very short time into a valuable estate.

St. Jean (fief), in the county of St. Maurice, is placed between the seigniories of Riviere du Loup, Maskinongé and Carufel; three-quarters of a league in front by two leagues in depth; granted, October 13, 1701, to Les Dames religieuses Ursulines des Trois Rivieres. A confirmation of this grant, with its augmentation, bearing date December 10, 1737, gives it one league more in depth. The Ursulines still retain the property. The land is good and productive; of the fief nearly the whole is cultivated, but very little of the augmentation. It has some fine timber upon it.

Riviere du Loup (the seigniory of), in the county of St. Maurice, is situated on the north side of Lake St. Peter, between the fief St. Jean and Grand Pré: one league in front, that is, half a league on each side of the river, by four leagues in depth; it was granted, with an augmentation, April 5th, 1689, to Sieur Villeraie for Sieur D'Artigny. This seigniory surpasses in value, perhaps, every property of similar extent in the province; its soil is commonly a light reddish earth, a little sandy, sometimes

mixed with clay; in many places it is a fine
yellow loam, altogether very fertile, producing
abundant crops of grain, and every article of
general growth in the country; some parts are
particularly eligible for raising hemp and flax.
It is generally level, but towards the margin of
the lake it is flat and low, consisting chiefly
of meadow and grazing land, both excellent.
About the front there is no timber of superior
growth remaining, and indeed not much of any
other; but towards the rear there are many
spots where some of the largest size both of
pine and oak is to be found. The Grande and
Petite Rivières du Loup, and some inferior
streams, water the seigniory extremely well; the
former crosses it diagonally, and by its serpentine course greatly heightens the other natural
attractions of the place. A variety of good
roads lead in every direction. The Quebec
road is embellished on each side by many good
houses, and farms in a very improved state.
Numerous settlements and roads extend on
each side of the two Rivières du Loup, whose
banks for several miles upwards are lofty, and
agreeably varied with woodland and landscape
scenery, which, combining with the luxuriance
of the well cultivated fields, leaves very little to
be desired with respect to prospect. On the
westerly side of the great River is the village du

Loup, containing about 30 or 40 houses only;
but the settlements on each side of the road are
so thickly inhabited, that they may be almost
considered as an extension of it to a great distance. In the village fronting the road is a
new church, remarkable for its size, the elegance
of its structure, and the good taste of its interior
decoration; of three steeples that surmount it,
the two in front are covered with tin, which
renders them conspicuous objects at a considerable distance. Near the village the Grand
Rivière du Loup is crossed by a very fine
bridge, both handsomely and solidly constructed of timber. The population and wealth of
this place are considerable; many trades are carried on, and many shops kept open for the sale
of all kinds of manufactured goods and produce;
large quantities of grain are collected here for
exportation, and deposited in store-houses kept
for that purpose. The whole of the seigniory
and part of the augmentation are cultivated.
On the rivers there are some grist and saw mills.

GRAND PRE' (the seigniory of), in the county
of St. Maurice, is situated on the north side of
Lake St. Peter, between the augmentation to
Rivière du Loup, Grosbois, and Dumontier, a
league in front by three in depth; was granted
3d July, 1695, to Pierre Boucher, Sieur de
Grand Pré. This seigniory is singularly over-

laid by that of Rivière du Loup, which from being a prior concession to this one, and the term of the grant expressing half a league on each side of the river, leaves but a small irregular frontage on the lake for Grand Pré. This tract, in the quality of the land and species of the timber, strongly resembles that of Rivière du Loup, but is not near so well settled as that property, although there is every probability of its becoming, in a few years, an estate of considerable value.

Gros Bois or Yamachiche (the seigniory of), in the county of St. Maurice, on the north side of Lake St. Peter, between Grand Pré and Gatineau, is bounded in the rear by Fief Dumontier; it is a league and a half in front by two leagues in depth; was granted Nov. 3, 1672, to Sieur Boucher, and is now the property of Louis Gugy, Esq. It is rather low towards the front, but retiring from the lake there are some few rising grounds. The soils and different kinds of timber upon it are very similar to the two last mentioned grants. The Rivière du Loup and the Grande and Petite Rivières Machiche water it, over which, where they are intersected by the main roads, bridges, substantially built of timber, that have a light and pleasing appearance, have been erected. About three-fourths of the grant are conceded;

the settlements in front and on the banks of the river are in good order, and very flourishing; the houses and farm buildings, well constructed, bespeak their proprietors to be very industrious and in easy circumstances. On the east side of the main or Quebec road, that here resumes its course close to the River St. Lawrence, are the church and parsonage-house of Machiche, with a cluster of houses, forming a small neat village around them. The interior is traversed by many roads leading to the seigniories in the rear, as well as those on each side. On the different streams there are some good mills of both descriptions.

GATINEAU (fief and augmentation), in the county of St. Maurice, joins Yamachiche; it is three quarters of a league in front by a league and a half in depth; was granted Nov. 3, 1672, to Sieur Boucher, fils; the augmentation, of the same breadth as the fief, and four leagues deep, was granted Oct. 3, 1750, to Demoiselle Marie Josephe Gatineau Duplessis. The land in this fief is of rather a lighter soil than the adjoining grants, equally fertile, and subject to nearly the same mode of culture. It is watered by the two rivers Machiche, whose banks for a considerable distance upwards display some good and thriving settlements, connected by many good roads, beside the public one that crosses them.

Pointe du Lac or Tonnancour (the seigniory of), in the county of St. Maurice, has part of Lake St. Peter and the St. Lawrence in front, St. Marguerite and St. Maurice on the north-east, and Gatineau on the south-west; it is a league and a quarter in front by two leagues in depth, comprising therein the fiefs Normanville and Sauvaget; was granted Nov. 3, 1734, to Sieur Réné Godefroi de Tonnancour, and is now possessed by the heirs of the late Nicholas Montour, Esq. A reddish light soil, upon clay or a good marl, spreads over the greatest part of this seigniory; the front of it is flat and low, towards the interior it gradually gets higher, and rises more abruptly to the rear. Beech, ash, birch, and some pine, are the prevailing species of timber. It is watered by La Rivière de la Pointe du Lac, that passes through it in a northerly direction, by part of the River Machiche, and some smaller streams; on their banks there are some good settlements, which with those along its front embrace about one half of the grant. Several roads pass through the interior; the main one crossing the front on the bank of the river. The Pointe du Lac is a large projection from the front of the seigniory, forming the north-east extremity of Lake St. Peter: on this promontory are some remains of barracks that were erected for the accommodation of troops during the first American war, when it was necessary to have a force stationed at different places above Quebec, to defend the passage of the St. Lawrence. On the east side of La Rivière de la Pointe du Lac stands a good-looking church, parsonage-house, and a chapel; not far removed from this spot are Montour's Mills, large, commodious, and well-built; near to them are some extensive store-houses and dwellings; on the opposite side of the road, a little above the mills, stands the proprietor's manor-house, a very handsome building, finely situated, and commanding a fine prospect over a tract of country abounding in picturesque beauties.

St. MARGUERITE (the seigniory of), in the county of St. Maurice, is situated in the rear of several small grants made to the late order of Jesuits, Sieur de St. Paul, and others; it is bounded on the north-east by the River St. Maurice, on the south-west by Tonnancour or Pointe du Lac, and on the north-west by the seigniory of St. Maurice; it is about three quarters of a league in front by a league in depth, and was granted 27th July, 1691, to Sieur Jacques Dubois de Boguinet. The little fief of Vieux Pont, about a quarter of a mile in front, is within the seigniory of St. Marguerite, and extends from the Saint Lawrence

.to the rear boundary; was granted August 23, 1674, to Joseph Godefroi, Sieur de Vieux Pont. This seigniory is of a light sandy soil, mixed in some places with clay, in others .with loam; it has some good timber upon it, is watered by several small streams, and the greatest part of it is well cultivated. The small tracts marked *a, b, c, d,* on the topographical map, were granted at different periods to the Jesuits and others. The soil of these pieces is the same as the rest of the seigniory, but they are entirely cleared of timber, and all in a good state of cultivation. All these grants are intersected by the roads from Three Rivers to Montreal and the different seigniories, and on the north-east by those to the forges of St. Maurice.

The town of Three Rivers is situated on the north-west side of the River St. Maurice, at its confluence with the St. Lawrence: it derives its name from the entrance into the former river being separated, by two islands lying at the mouth, into three channels. The town plot covers nearly 400 acres, forming a front of rather more than 1300 yards on the bank of the St. Lawrence. It stands on an exceeding light and sandy soil, which extends also over the environs; to the bank of the St. Maurice the ground rises very considerably; but in the op-

posite direction it sinks almost to a level with.
the river. Three Rivers ranks as the third town
in the province, but compared with either of the
others it is small indeed, containing only about
320 houses, with a population not much exceeding 2500 souls. It sends two members to the
provincial parliament. In the year 1618 some
French colonists began building this place, with
a view of making it a depot from whence the
fur trade might be carried on with the Indians
to the northward; their plan experienced at
first many flattering indications of success, but
after Montreal was founded, and had so increased as to be able to defend itself against
the attacks of the natives of the country, it was
supposed to be a situation better suited to this
improving traffic, and was consequently preferred; from that period Three Rivers, being
greatly neglected, did not much enlarge either
its extent or population. About the beginning
of last century, however, it began again to entertain hopes of rising into some consequence
by opening the iron mines at Saint Maurice;
but they proved nearly as delusive as the former, and up to the present time its improvement has been upon a very moderate scale.
The trade carried on here is chiefly in British
manufactured goods, that from hence are plentifully distributed through the middle district

of the province; the exports consist of wheat,
timber, though now not so much as formerly,
and the produce of its iron foundery, added to
that of the mines of St. Maurice: peltry in
small quantities still continues to be brought
hither by the Indians from the northward, and
which is received by the agents of the North
West Company. Several pot and pearl ash
manufactories, two or three breweries, and an
extensive brick manufactory, considerably increase the general trade of the place: many of
the bark canoes used in the north-west voyages
are built here, and of the same material a variety of ingenious and ornamental works and
toys are made. As a shipping port it is conveniently situated, there being a sufficient depth
of water for ships of large tonnage to lie close
to the wharfs and receive or discharge their
cargoes by a temporary stage from their gang-
ways. The town itself possesses but little to
attract a stranger's notice; the streets are narrow and unpaved; the principal one is Rue
Notre Dame, running the whole length of it,
almost parallel with the river; next to this are
the Rues des Forges, du Fleuve, du Rempart,
St. Maurice, du Platon, des Casernes, St. Louis,
St. Jean, and St. Pierre, which may be said to
constitute nearly all the inhabited part of the
place. The shops and storehouses are numer-

ous, wherein may be had British goods of all denominations; several inns afford to travellers very respectable accommodations. On the south-west side of the town are the remains of some military works thrown up for its defence by the English army, during the war of the rebellion, which are now honoured by the inhabitants with the high-sounding title of " *Anciennes Fortifications.*" On the outside of these works is an extensive tract of common land. The principal public buildings in the town are the Ursuline convent, the protestant and catholic churches, the court-house, gaol, and barracks. The major part of the private dwelling-houses, &c. are built of wood, the oldest of them only one story high, having small gardens about them; but those of more recent date are in a much better style, many of them higher than the old ones, and rather of handsome appearance. The Ursuline convent was founded in 1677, by Mons. de St. Vallier, Bishop of Quebec, for the education of youth, chiefly females, and as an asylum for the sick and infirm poor. The establishment is for a superior and twenty-four nuns. In 1806, the old building was destroyed by fire, when its inhabitants, dispersed by that calamity, were received into the different religious houses of Quebec and Montreal, until the present edifice was erected. It is a regular stone building, two stories high, of considerable extent, surrounded by fine gardens; it includes a parochial church and hospital, with all the apartments and offices requisite both for the dwellings and carrying on the different functions of the establishment. As the Ursulines were held in great estimation for the general utility and the charitable nature of their institution, public subscriptions were opened immediately after the accident that deprived them of their residence, from the proceeds of which, with a little pecuniary aid from the legislature, they were able to rebuild their convent in its present improved and substantial manner, and which, though not quite finished, they took possession of in 1808. The old monastery of the Recollets, a stone building, is now delapidated; near it is a powder magazine. The protestant and catholic churches are good plain buildings, but neither of them sufficiently remarkable to attract particular attention. The court-house and gaol are handsome modern stone edifices, both in good situations, and well designed for their respective purposes. The building now occupied as barracks is solidly constructed of stone, situated on the north side of Notre Dame Street, and on the highest ground about the town. It was originally erected as a residence for the French governor.

From Rue des Forges there is a road leading
to the foundery of St. Maurice. On the eastern
side of the town are several small fiefs and separate lots of ground belonging to different
proprietors, most of them in a good state of
cultivation.

St. Maurice (the seigniory of), in the
county of Saint Maurice, lies on the west side
of River St. Maurice, a league in breadth by a
league and a half in depth: the original grant
was two leagues in depth, but owing to the
seigniory of Pointe du Lac, by which it is
bounded on the south-west, being of a prior
date, so great an extent could not be taken.
St. Maurice was reunited to the king's domain
on the 6th April, 1740, and on the 13th of the
same month granted to the company of the
forges, with an additional piece of land three
leagues in depth by two in breadth, called fief
St. Etienne; on the north-west of St. Etienne
is another tract of the same dimensions, that
has lately been annexed to the above grants, as
part of the lands belonging to the forges. The
whole is the property of the crown, but let on
lease for twenty-one years, together with the
forges, &c. to Messrs. Munro and Bell, for the
sum of 500l. per annum only. The soil in St.
Maurice (seigniory) is light and sandy, generally
upon a bottom of clay or good marl; the sur-

face is a continual alternation of gradual rise and fall; in the low parts there are a few swamps, with a good deal of hemlock and cedar upon them; the acclivities are mostly clothed with a general mixture of timber trees, but the chief sort is pine of a middling growth: a very small part only of this grant is cultivated. A fine road from Three Rivers crosses it, leading mostly through the woods to the foundery. The fief St. Etienne is but little cultivated, though of a better soil, having a superior mixture of marl, and in many places a rich black vegetable earth; the ground is irregular, as in St. Maurice, but rising into stronger ridges on the north-west. The fief has several divisions called *Cotes* Rouge, de Grand Pont, Croche, Turcotte, de 14 Arpens, and St. Jean. The upper lands are well covered with maple, birch, beech, and ash, but on the low grounds, that are wet in some places, there are only the usual inferior species, but these in great abundance. In this grant there are several pineries, which produce trees of a superior growth, particularly the one a little below and on Pigeon Island. Iron ore, that at one time was found plentifully in several parts of this fief, is now only met with in the rear. Quarries of lime-stone, a good grey stone, and some other hard species fit for building, are opened on the banks of the St. Maurice, near the falls of Gros, and those of Gabelle a little below. Wood for the purposes of the forges is produced in abundance; great quantities of it are felled and carried by sleighs every winter to the furnaces, where it is made into charcoal for the use of the melting-houses; it was in consequence of the great demand, from the continual consumption of this article, that the additional tract of crown land was super-added to the others on the renewal of the lease. The foundery of St. Maurice is situated in this fief, in a beautiful valley, at the con-fluence of a small stream with the St. Maurice, about eight miles above the town of Three Ri-vers; the high banks of the river, embellished with every variety of fine trees in groups on each side, the dark hue of the large pineries and immense surrounding forests, and the more distant and softened shades of the lofty moun-tains that bound the view, form together a bold and magnificent prospect, when viewed from the place where the road ascends the brow of the ridge that overlooks the valley. The foun-dery itself is replete with convenience for carry-ing on an extensive concern; furnaces, forges, casting-houses, workshops, &c. with the dwell-ing-houses and other buildings, have altogether the appearance of a tolerably large village. The articles manufactured here consist of stoves of all descriptions, that are used throughout the provinces, large cauldrons or kettles for making pot-ashes, machinery for mills, with cast and wrought iron work of all denominations; there are likewise large quantities of pig and bar iron exported: the number of men employed is from 250 to 300; the principal foremen and persons engaged in making models, &c. are either English or Scotch men; the workmen are generally Canadians. In the early establishment of this foundery, about 1737, the ore was found in great abundance near the surface, of a quality not inferior to many of the best mines of Europe for the pliability of the metal. At first the mode of working the different veins was managed with very little skill, but in 1739 an artizan was brought from France, who combined a knowledge of the different branches of manufacturing wrought and cast iron with a competent skill in working the mines; from this acquisition great improvements took place, which have progressively increased, and the establishment is now carried on with almost as much ability, and on the same principle, as similar concerns in England and Scotland. It will appear somewhat singular that neither of the provinces should produce sand proper for the purposes of casting iron, but such is the fact, and the proprietors of these works, in conse-

x

quence, import from England all they use in that operation. Since the year 1806, Messrs. Munro and Bell have occupied these valuable premises on the terms before named; previous to that period their annual rent was 800*l.* per annum; on the termination of their former lease they were, very reasonably, entitled to the consideration of the government in reletting them, as indeed is every tenant on the expiration of a given term, after his ability and exertions have materially enhanced the value of the property; but it very rarely occurs that similar circumstances of improvement have operated as a cause for a reduction of the rent almost fifty per cent; at any rate these gentlemen, whose industry and skill prove undoubtedly useful to the province, have many good reasons to be satisfied with their bargain.

CAP DE LA MAGDELAINE (the scigniory of), in the county of St. Maurice, is bounded by the river St. Maurice on the south-west, the seigniory of Champlain and its augmentation on the north-east, and by the river St. Lawrence on the front; its breadth is two leagues, its depth extends twenty leagues into the interior northwards; it was granted March 20, 1651, to the Order of Jesuits, and has now devolved to the crown. The soil of this extensive seigniory, in such parts of it as have yet come

under observation, nearly resembles that of the
lands belonging to the foundery of St. Maurice;
but where it differs therefrom there is rather less
of a sandy earth, with a bluish and a yellow
loam prevailing in a greater proportion. The
timber is almost of the same species, and towards the interior much of it has attained a
very fine growth. Compared with the great
extent of the grant, a small portion only is
under cultivation, which lies principally on
the St. Lawrence, and on the bank of the St.
Maurice, almost up to the Falls of Gabelle:
the settlements, however, are not noticeable for
any thing in their system of management above
mediocrity; in consequence their wheat and
other crops are but indifferent, on land that
might be made to yield abundantly. The
situation of the farms on the banks of the rivers,
and the quality of the soil, are both favourable
to agricultural improvement; circumstances,
that if judiciously attended to could not fail of
rendering this part of the seigniory extremely
valuable. The Quebec road passes almost close
to the St. Lawrence, by the ferry over the St.
Maurice to the town of Three Rivers; this ferry,
by which the established post-road is continued,
is nearly two miles across; the price demanded
from each person is two shillings and sixpence,
and in like proportion for horses and carriages;

but about a mile and a half higher up the river there is another, where the charge is only three-pence each person, and fifteen-pence for a horse and carriage. By the side of this road stands the church of the seigniory, with its parsonage-house. At the mouth of the Saint Maurice are the islands Bellerive, au Cochon, St. Christophe, La Croix, and L'Abri; they are low, and almost covered with wood of the inferior sorts, but afford some very good grazing land. It was in contemplation some time since to throw a bridge across this river opposite to the Isle St. Christophe. Such a measure would prove of so great public utility as to ex-cite hopes that the design is not abandoned. On a route so much frequented as this is, the undertakers of the plan could hardly fail of deriving a handsome profit by their speculation; the impediments to carrying it into effect, from the experience derived already in the execution of similar projects, are not very difficult to be overcome. Between Isle Bellerive and the main there is a very good situation for laying up river craft during the winter season, where they remain secure, in about eight feet water, and escape all injury from the breaking up of the ice in the spring. The St. Maurice is one of the large rivers that pour their streams into the St. Lawrence: the depth of it is inconsider-

able, being navigable for small boats and canoes
to a short distance only upwards from its mouth.
It takes its rise in the interior, about the skirts
of the north-west ridge of mountains, and flows
through Lake St. Thomas, from whence the
magnitude of its stream is greatly increased;
the banks on each side are high, and covered
with large groups of fine majestic trees; some
of the small islands in it are thickly clothed
with large pine-trees. In the interior the stream
is passable for some of the Indian canoes, but
not without many difficulties and much labour,
caused by the numerous falls and rapids, that
occasion very long portages; however, a party
or two of the Indian hunters persevere through
this toilsome route, and descend every season to
Three Rivers with a few furs.

CHAMPLAIN (the seigniory of and its augmentation), in the county of St. Maurice, on the
north side of the River St. Lawrence, lies between
Cap de la Magdelaine (seigniory) and Batiscan,
a league and a half in front by a league in depth;
was granted Sept. 22, 1664, to Etienne Pezard,
Sieur de la Touche; the augmentation, of the
same breadth as the seigniory, and three leagues
deep, is bounded in the rear by the township of
Radnor, and waste crown lands; it was granted
April 28th, 1697, to Madame de la Touche. In
this seigniory the soil is favourable to the growth

of all sorts of grain, and in many places so excellent for the cultivation of flax, that it is a
subject of regret so profitable and important an
article is not attended to. The timber is various, and though not of first rate quality, yet is
not overstocked with the more useless sorts.
It is watered by the little River Champlain,
and by many small streams, whose sources are
at a short distance in the interior, which winding down the gradual descent to the St. Lawrence in little rivulets, cross the main road,
and agreeably diversify the meadows and cultivated grounds along the front. The little Champlain works a grist and a saw-mill. About one
third of this seigniory is cultivated in a neat
style, and by the side of the Quebec road displays many good houses with thriving farms,
almost wholly cleared of the wood: it has one
church, and a parsonage-house near the road.
Only a very small proportion of the augmentation is yet brought into use; the remainder
continues in a state of woodland, which produces some capital timber.

BATISCAN (the seigniory of), in the county
of St. Maurice, has the St. Lawrence in front,
Champlain and its augmentation on the south-
west, and Ste. Marie with the augmentation
to Ste. Anne on the north-east; its breadth is
about two leagues, and its depth twenty;

granted March 3d, 1639, to the Order of Jesuits, and now reverted to the crown. Bordering the St. Lawrence the land is low, but it soon obtains a gradual rise for the distance of nearly four leagues and a half to the interior; it then becomes mountainous, as it gains upon the north-western ridge. The soil in the lower parts, like the adjacent seigniories, is a light earth, rather sandy, laid over a stratum of good clay; but proceeding northward, it gets stronger, and is enriched for a considerable space with fine black mould, affording many capital tracts for the growth of all kinds of grain. On the front the wood is nearly all cleared away and the land cultivated for two or three miles inward, and rather more than five miles upwards, on both sides of the River Batiscan, upon which there are many good settlements, where the different farms appear very neat and well managed. The whole of its depth has not been explored, but as far as it has been visited is found to produce timber of the best species, and excellent of the different kinds. La Petite Riviere Champlain, with some smaller streams, water the front, besides the large River Batiscan, that rolls a much broader current, but is so shallow as not to be accessible for boats higher than six or seven miles from its mouth. Over this and the Champlain there are ferries, where canoes and scows are always in readiness on either side for travellers, carriages, &c. In addition to the main road that crosses the seigniory, others ascend for several miles on each side of the Batiscan, and communicate with the adjacent grants. About six miles up on the east side of this river is the foundery of the same name; it consists of a furnace or smelting-house, a casting-house, two forges, dwelling-houses, and various other buildings. The manufactures carried on here are similar to those of St. Maurice; some pig and bar iron are also exported, but neither upon so extensive a scale as from the other foundery. The establishment is the property of several individuals; the chief owners were formerly the Hon. T. Dunn, John Craigie, Esq., Mr. Frobisher, and Mr. Coffin; the first named gentleman has for some time past withdrawn himself from the concern, and one or two of the latter are deceased: it is now continued by their heirs and successors. From the expensive nature of these works, that require the continual application of large sums of money to keep them going, the revenue in proportion to the trade is by no means equal to that of St. Maurice. In opening a field for ingenuity and industry, as well as causing a competition in supplying articles of internal consumption, they are undoubtedly of service to the provinces, yet they are said not to be a very profitable speculation to the owners of the property.

STE. MARIE (the seigniory of), in the county of St. Maurice, joins Batiscan ; it is three quarters of a league in breadth, by half a league in depth ; was granted Nov. 3d, 1672, to Sieur le Moine, and is now the property of M. Boisvert. STE. ANNE, next to Ste. Marie, nearly of the same breadth, and a league in depth, was granted Oct. 29th, 1672, to Messieurs Sueur and La-. naudiere. This grant has three augmentations : the first, extending in breadth from the seigniory. of Grondines to Batiscan, and three leagues in depth, was granted March 4th, 1697, to Madame Denis, veuve de Sieur Lanaudiere : the second, one league and a half deep, and the breadth of the former, granted Oct. 30th, 1700, to Sieur Thomas Tarieu de la Perade : and the third, three leagues deep by a similar breadth, granted April 20th, 1735, to Thomas Tarieu de la Perade : they are now the property of the heirs of C. Lanaudiere, Esq. The front of these two seigniories is so low as to be inundated in the spring of the year by the rising of the St. Lawrence, but this temporary inconvenience contributes greatly to the luxuriance of the fine meadows that border the river. The soil is sufficiently fertile, and consists of a light

sandy earth lying upon a reddish clay about
the front, but further to the rear is found a
mixture of yellow loam and black mould;
altogether it is very productive in grain of all
kinds, and most other articles of general growth.
In Ste. Marie the quantity of land under cultivation is nearly two-thirds of the grant, and in
Ste. Anne it amounts to nearly 300 lots or farms,
somewhat irregularly dispersed along each branch
of the River St. Anne, and at the descent of a
small ridge that stretches across the seigniory
a short distance from its front. Of the augmentations to Ste. Anne but very little is cultivated; it is almost wholly woodland, producing
timber of all species, and some of excellent
growth and great value: the quality of the
land, as indicated by the various kinds of wood
growing upon it, is very good. Both grants
are watered by the Rivers Batiscan and St.
Anne, with a few other streams, not of much
consequence; the two rivers are large, but
scarcely at all navigable; the former is about
350 and the latter 400 yards wide; they run
nearly parallel to each other, about seven miles
apart, and in a direction almost opposite to the
other large streams, as they take a north-easterly course for about 70 miles, until they come
to the rear of the city of Quebec, at about 30
miles distant in the township of Stoneham,

when they strike off to the northward, in which direction they are supposed to have their sources in some of the lakes of that part of the country which at present is but very little known. Their streams are interrupted by many falls and rapids, that would render them unnavigable, even if the shallowness of the water did not do so: near where they discharge into the St. Lawrence, their banks are low, but more to the interior they are much higher, in some places rocky, but generally covered with fine timber. On the east side of River St. Anne, and near the St. Lawrence, is the village of St. Anne, containing about 30 houses, a handsome church, a parsonage-house, and a chapel; here are also a few shopkeepers, and an inn with good accommodations, where the stage-coaches put up, and also a post-house. At the village is a ferry, where canoes and scows are always to be had for transporting travellers, carriages, &c. The river is here so shallow that the large boats are set across by poles: the charge for each person is three-pence, and one shilling for a horse and carriage. The property of this ferry was granted in perpetuity by letters patent to the late Honourable C. de Lanaudiere, his heirs, &c. Owing to the inundation during the spring, the main road from Quebec is further retired from the bank of the St. Lawrence at

this place than at most others ; it passes along
the ridge or eminence before mentioned, until
it arrives near to the village, where it resumes
its usual direction :- on both sides of the river
St. Anne there are roads that follow its course
through several seigniories to the north-east.
There is a grist-mill in Ste. Anne, and a grist
and a saw-mill in Ste. Marie. The manor-houses
in each seigniory are agreeably situated near
the two points formed by the rivers St. Anne
and St. Lawrence. That belonging to the
family of Lanaudiere is surrounded by excellent gardens, and many fine groups of beautiful
trees. On the eastern side of the seigniory of
Ste. Anne is fief Dorvilliers, containing one
league superficial measure. At the confluence
of the two rivers lie the Isles St. Ignace, Ste.
Marguerite, Dularge and Dusable, all belonging to the seigniory ; they are low, but yield
fine pasture and some good meadow land ; being well clothed with wood, they afford several
very pleasing prospects from both the houses.

YAMASKA (the seigniory of), on the south
side of the river St. Lawrence, in the county of
Buckingham, is bounded on the south-west by the
seigniory of Sorel and Bonsecours, on the north-
east by St. François, and in the rear by Bourgmarie East ; a league and a half in front by
three leagues deep ; it was granted September

24th, 1683, to Sieur de la Valliere, and is now the property of J. M. Tonnancour, Esq. Cultivation of a favourable description extends over nearly one half of the seigniory; the different concessions, large and small, amount to upwards of 160, lying on each side of the River Yamaska, by the Petit Chenail, and in the Cotes St. Louis, and Ste. Catherine. The Bay of La Vallier, or Yamaska, extends across the upper part of it into Sorel, and that of St. François makes rather a deep incision on its eastern side; immediately surrounding these bays the land is low and marshy, but a short distance from them are many large tracts of most excellent meadow; further to the rear the soil is rich, and very productive, consisting of good yellow loam, and a fine clay intermixed with light earth, affording much good arable for grain of all sorts, and some spots well adapted to the culture of flax and hemp. The front part of the seigniory is moderately well furnished with timber of a middling and inferior quality, as white fir, spruce fir, hemlock, &c.; but in the rear upon the drier grounds, some of a superior description is produced, as plane, beech, hickory, and oak. The land is tolerably well watered by several small streams, in addition to the little river David that has its source in the adjoining savannes, or large swamps. The

convenience of good roads is afforded in every direction. The main one, from the eastward, leading to the town of William Henry, crosses the
Yamaska at a ferry, just above la Petite Isle Tonnancour: the price of passage is three-pence
each person, six-pence for a horse, and one shilling for a carriage. A grist-mill and a wind-mill
are near the ferry. In front of the seigniory are
the Isles du Moine, aux Raisins, and some others;
in the mouth of the river is the large island St.
Jean, entirely covered with wood, some of it
of good quality. The bays beforementioned
yield a great variety of fine fish, and along their
shores game of several sorts is found in abundance. The river Yamaska admits of inland
navigation of some importance for batteaux and
rafts: its medium breadth is about 400 yards.
Its sources are in the high lands about the
townships of Bolton and Brome; the current is also
supplied by some of the large lakes in the same
neighbourhood: one large branch of it crosses
the township of Farnham, and another, at about
22 miles further on, diverges into the adjoining
townships: from thence it pursues a north or
north-westerly direction to Lake St. Peter; the
whole of its course is about 90 miles. As the
new townships in this part of the province
become more populous, and the increase of
agriculture furnishes produce beyond their own

consumption, this route of communication will prove not much inferior in consequence to that by the River Richelieu.

ST. FRANÇOIS (the seigniory of), on the south side of the St. Lawrence, in the county of Buckingham, has Yamaska on the south-west, Lussaudiere on the north-east, and De Guir and Pierrcville in the rear: it is one league in front by nearly two in depth; granted October 8th, 1678, to Sieur de Crevier, and is now the property of Mons. Le Gendre, and some families of the Abenaqui Indians. This seigniory, like the preceding one, is low towards the Lake St. Peter. The Bay of St. François, and some others, indent it rather deeply, and occasion large tracts of marsh land along their shores; a little removed from them are some very fine meadows, and further to the interior the soil is good, in most parts rather light and sandy. The timber is but of indifferent quality, and consists more of spruce fir, hemlock, and cedar, than any other; on the driest land there is a little maple and beech. The River St. Francis, with a few smaller streams, water it very well. About one half of this grant is in a state of cultivation; the best settled and most improved parts lie on each side of the St. Francis. At the descent of this river into the St. Lawrence are several islands that are attached to the grant; the largest of them is nearly four miles long, partly cultivated, and very well settled; the church and parsonage-house belonging to the seigniory stand on this island, from whence, although not an established ferry, there are always in readiness canoes to convey travellers to William Henry, at the rate of five shillings each person; a route generally preferred in summer-time to that by the post roads. The other islands are low, some of them affording a little meadow land, but they are principally covered with wood. On the east side of the river is situated the Indian village of St. François, of about 25 or 30 very indifferently built wooden houses, inhabited by some families of the converted Indians of the Abenaqui tribe, who subsist themselves upon the lands that are their own property within this seigniory, by raising, in their peculiarly careless manner, some Indian corn, growing potatoes, and rearing poultry and pigs; they sometimes increase these means by fishing, and during the winter months by hunting parties; the latter is but a precarious resource, as they are compelled to go an immense distance before they can meet with game to repay their labour; for as the habitations of civilized man have spread over the province, the animals that were the prior occupants have fled for pro-

tection to the recesses of more distant forests.
In this village, there is a church and a parsonage-house, at which the missionary, who super-
intends the religious concerns of the tribe, always resides. An interpreter also has a permanent residence among them. There are several roads leading through this property; the
main one, from the eastward to William Henry,
crosses the river at a ferry by the Abenaqui
village, where three-pence is paid for each person, and one shilling for a horse and carriage.
The river St. Francis is another of the communications by which a considerable and increasing traffic is carried on with the southern townships, and also with the United States. The
navigation of it is difficult and exceedingly laborious, owing to the great number of violent
rapids and falls that occur in its course; but
as it presents a direct route for sending the produce of these districts to a certain market, these
obstacles are resolutely overcome by the industrious settlers on each side of the boundaries,
and large quantities of pot and pearl-ashes,
and various other commodities, are every summer brought down by it into the St. Lawrence
for Quebec. Great quantities of British manufactured goods are also sent upwards to the
States. The source of the St. Francis is a large
lake of the same name, lying in the townships

Y

of Garthby and Colerain, from whence it flows
in a south-westerly direction for about thirty
miles; part of this distance is but imperfectly
known, never having been correctly surveyed:
it then assumes a course nearly north-westerly,
runs about eighty miles, and discharges itself
into Lake St. Peter. In the township of Ascott
a branch of it connects with Lake Memphremagog, from the extremity of which several streams
descend into the state of Vermont; by this
means the transport of goods is continued in
that direction. As the navigation from Lake
Memphremagog to the St. Lawrence is op-
posed by many and powerful natural obstructions, a particular account of it will help to.
shew what patient and persevering industry is
required to surmount them. From the outlet of
the lake to the place where the stream joins the
St. Francis is about 19 miles, in which distance
there is a singular alternation of violent rapids
and still water where the current is most tedi-
ously slow; about three quarters of a mile
before, it enters the river there is what is
termed a *fall*, not indeed from a perpendicular
height, but the bed of the river being very
much contracted, and the current broken by
high ledges of rock, it is impossible for boats
to pass it; even single sticks of timber are seldom sent down it, as experience has proved

that they never escape without being much bruised, if not absolutely shivered to pieces : in this distance of three quarters of a mile the whole descent is from 170 to 180 feet. At this place the scows and boats are unloaded, their contents carried to the end of the fall, and there re-embarked in other craft ready to receive them; from hence they are borne down by a gentle current about six miles, to the Great Brompton Falls, that are about two miles in length : as empty boats can run down them on the west side only, the cargoes are again taken out and conveyed to the foot of the falls, where the boats are re-laden, and proceed about seven miles further to the Little Brompton Falls; a repetition of the former labours must again take place, as they can be passed by nothing but light craft : at this point the portage is no more than 250 yards. A mile or two further on is Dutchman's Shoot, where the river is narrowed by a ledge of rocks, and two small islands forming a rapid, that with much care and some difficulty loaded boats may pass through. After this a current, rapid and slow in succession, continues without impediment for fifteen miles to Kingsey portage; this is a confined part of the river, with a large rock in the middle of it, that is covered when the water is very high, and at which time only the loaded boats are able to pass it; the current rushes through the channel with great impetuosity, and retains its violence for more than a mile beyond it. From hence no material obstacles present themselves until arriving at Menue Falls, a distance of about twenty miles; these are three-quarters of a mile long, and only practicable for the empty boats: Lord's Falls, two miles further down, and about the same length as those of Menue, are subject to the same inconvenience, or even greater, for unless the water be very high they cannot be passed by the light boats. At six miles below this fall is the commencement of a very rapid current, that continues for fifteen miles, and when passed all difficulties are overcome, and the river is free into Lake St. Peter. From the upper to the lower part of the river it varies in breadth from 100 yards to nearly a mile. Notwithstanding this troublesome medley of land and water carriage, the trade carried on by it is now very considerable, as more than 1500 barrels of ashes only have been brought down it in one summer very lately.

LUSSAUDIERE (the seigniory of), in the county of Buckingham, is situated next to St. François, one league square; was granted 26th July, 1683, to Sieur de la Motte de Luciere. In this grant the land is generally of a better quality than that in the preceding one, with less of a sandy description: the front is so low as to be overflowed in the spring by Lake St. Peter, and consists of very fine meadow and good pasturage: proceeding to the rear the ground rises gradually; in this direction there are some patches of fair arable land. The timber is not of the best kinds, particularly in front, although it improves further back. About one third of the scigniory is cultivated; the most improved settlements are contiguous to the main road on each side of it, where some of the lots and farms bespeak an attention to husbandry that shews them in a very favourable light.

PIERREVILLE (the seigniory of), in the county of Buckingham, is situated in the rear of St. François, bounded on its south and south-west sides by the seigniory of De Guir, and on the north and north-east by waste lands of the crown, a league and a half in front by a league in depth; it was granted August 3, 1683, to Sieur Laurent Phillippe, and is now the property of the Baroness de Longeuil. A middling good soil is the general characteristic of the whole of this grant; in some parts it lies low, but not so as to occasion swamps. The best land is found close on each side of the St. Francis, where are the principal settlements and the best cultivation; the quantity under hand amounts to one third of the whole, or a little more. The River St. Francis runs through the seigniory, dividing it nearly in half, and affords the advantages of easy and expeditious conveyance; as its current hereabouts, and towards the St. Lawrence, is very rapid. An inferior description of timber prevails; enough however of the better sorts is found to supply the wants of the inhabitants. The river turns a grist and a saw-mill; in it there are two or three small islands covered with trees of no real value, although exceedingly decorative.

DE GUIR (the seigniory of), in the county of Buckingham, bounded on the north and north-west by Pierreville and St. François, on the south-east by the township of Upton, on the south-west by Bourgmarie East, and on the north-east by Courval; its figure is irregular, the greatest length being two leagues and a half; as it is now possessed, it does not agree at all with the original grant, which specifies two leagues of front by two leagues deep: it was granted September 23, 1751, to Sieur Josephe De Guir, dit des Rosiers; the property now belongs to Josias Wurtel, Esq. Nearly all this tract remains in a state of woodland; in many places it is low, but of a soil that if cleared would be fit for the productions of every sort common to the country. The timber is generally of a superior class. Several branches of the River David water it, and along them are dispersed a few settlers who have their farms in a forward state of cultivation: were a critical revision of the boundaries to take place, some of these tenants now holding from the seignior of De Guir would prove to be located within the township of Upton.

BOURGMARIE EAST (the seigniory of) is an instance in support of the observations made some pages back relating to the inconvenience of the present district and county boundaries, as it lies within the districts of Montreal and Three Rivers, and in the counties of Richelieu and Buckingham; it is situated in the rear of the seigniory of Yamaska, bounded on the west by the river Yamaska, on the south by St. Charles, and on the east by De Guir; fifty arpents in front by nearly two leagues in depth; it was granted on the 1st of August, 1708, to Marie Fézéret, and is now the property of Mrs. Barrow. This tract is what the Canadian farmers term very good land; in fact it is of rather a superior quality, and such as if moderately well managed would yield abundant crops of grain; at present about a third part of it is under cultivation. A little good timber is found upon it, with abundance of the inferior sorts, such as basswood, spruce fir, hemlock and cedar. Besides having the navigable river for one of the boundaries, it is watered by the River David, that winds a very mazy course through it, and turns one grist-mill. On each side of this river there is a road, and one that coasts the Yamaska. The church of this seigniory has no resident *Curé*, but the duties of it are performed by the minister of St. Michael de Yamaska.

BAIE ST. ANTOINE or LEFEBVRE (the seigniory of) is on the south side of the St. Lawrence, in the county of Buckingham; bounded on the south-west by Lussaudiere, on the north-east by Nicolet, and in the rear by Courval; two leagues in front and the same in depth; granted September 4th, 1683, to Sieur Lefebvre, and is now the property of Louis Guoin, Esq. This is in all respects a very productive tract of ground: in the front the Longue Pointe, Pointe aux Pois, and Pointe à la Garenne, all stretching boldly into the St. Lawrence, form the extremities of two large bays; to the east of Pointe à la Garenne is the Baie de Febvre, also trenching deeply upon the seigniory; for some distance on the margin of these bays is a marsh that in the summer affords excellent pasture, singularly intersected in all directions by numerous small and clear rivulets;

rising from hence to the main road crossing the seigniory from east to west, are some very rich and luxuriant meadows. From this road, the land continues a gradual elevation to the rear; the soil is mostly a fat clay or good black mould highly fertile. Except in the marshes and meadows, that have plenty of common wood, the timber is of the best kinds. The River Nicolet, crossing a small part of the south-east corner, is the only stream towards the back of the seigniory: full one half of this property is under culture, and can boast of some farms in a very flourishing state, particularly by the road side. The want of water corn-mills is supplied by several wind-mills. The church is placed about the middle of the grant, on a rising ground; below it are many good houses, almost sufficient in number to form a respectable village; among them are two or three shops, and a *tavern*, for which the situation is not ill chosen, as the place is a great thoroughfare; from whence a main road strikes off towards the southern townships.

COURVAL (the seigniory of), in the county of Buckingham, is situated in the rear of Baie St. Antoine or Lefebvre, two leagues in breadth by three in depth, and stretching in that direction to the township of Wendover; it was granted September 25th, 1754, to Sieur Cressé, and is now possessed by Louis Guoin, Esq. But little of this grant is cleared; the land however is much above mediocrity: a few swampy places present the usual kinds of timber upon a wet soil, but the uplands produce beech, maple, birch, and pine. The south-west branch of the Nicolet and the St. Francis water it; on the latter is a grist-mill belonging to the seignior. The few settlers who have began to cultivate are established upon the banks of the two rivers, and have managed to improve their farms very fast. The only road is the one from St. Antoine to the new townships.

NICOLET (the seigniory of, and its augmentation), on the south side of the St. Lawrence, or rather Lake St. Peter, in the county of Buckingham, is bounded by Baie St. Antoine (seigniory) and Courval on the south-west, Roquetaillade and the township of Aston on the north-east, and the township of Wendover in the rear; two leagues in front by two in depth; was granted October 29th, 1672, to Sieur de Laubia: the augmentation, two leagues in breadth by three in depth, was granted November 4th, 1680, to Sieur de Cressé; they are at present possessed by Mons. Cressé, a lineal descendant of the original proprietor. The soil of this grant is not remarkably good, but industry has

Village of Nauvoo.

in some degree made up for its natural deficiencies, as there are 250 concessions in a very
fair state of cultivation, producing good crops
of grain of most kinds. Towards the St. Lawrence the land is poor, of a light sandy nature,
but more in the interior it grows stronger and
obtains a better heart: it lies rather low, and
is generally level, timbered with the ordinary
sorts of wood, and but little of a superior quality or growth. The River Nicolet waters it advantageously. A village containing 50 houses,
with the church in the midst of them, is noticeable for its beautiful situation on the side of a
gentle acclivity, covered with some majestic
oaks (the best timber of the seigniory), and
crested with a tuft of lofty pines: below the
village, and on the opposite side of the river,
are the remains of the old church and parsonage of Nicolet. Both sides of the river, for
about three leagues upwards, are embellished
by settlements, and the appearance greatly enlivened by a number of neat houses, which in
various parts of the seigniory, including the
village, exceed 300; many of them well built
of stone. At the entrance of the river is Isle
Moran, the property of Mons. Paul Beaubien,
of which a grant was made October 29th,
1672, to Sieur de Moran. The main road to
William Henry passes through the village, and

crosses the river at a ferry, where the toll is three-pence each person, nine-pence for a horse, and fifteen-pence for a horse and carriage; besides this road, several others intersect the seigniory in different directions, and pass along each side of the river, upon which there are three grist-mills and as many saw-mills. The Nicolet takes its source from a lake of the same name, in the township of Weedon, and runs north-westerly through the townships of Ham, Arthabaska, Bulstrode, &c. for about 47 miles, when it is met by a large branch from the townships of Simpson, Kingsey, and Shipton, navigable for boats and scows, and which sends off numerous streams on each side; this point of junction is called the second forks: from hence its course through the augmentation and seigniory, until it falls into Lake St. Peter, is about twenty-one miles. The banks, in the interior townships, are high, and generally covered with woods down to the water; but in the lower part of its course they diminish their height very much, and are less woody: from the village downward there are several small islands covered with trees, that form very pleasing groups from the acclivity before mentioned. In the upper part of the river there are some rapids, but of no great impediment, as the Indians frequently ascend and descend them in canoes. In the spring, when the stream is increased by the freshes, small decked vessels can sometimes get up from the St. Lawrence as high as the village, but this cannot be depended upon, as the entrance is obstructed by a sandy bar, upon which craft drawing two feet water frequently strike in the summer or dry season: it is called the Batture aux Sables. The scenery on both banks is varied and beautiful in many places, but especially on the north-east side it is particularly interesting: in passing down the St. Lawrence, the front of the seigniory presents a prospect peculiarly pleasing, as bordering on that river the wood is pretty thick, with several clear intervals, through which the settlements and the village are seen in different points of view to the greatest advantage. A little above the village is the college of Nicolet, founded about ten years ago, and maintained in its infancy by the liberality of the Catholic Bishop of Quebec. It stands on a spot well calculated by the natural beauties of its situation to assist the views of so excellent an establishment. The building is on a simple, unostentatious, but convenient plan, possessing all requisite accommodation for the director, masters, and seventy pensioners. This institution is entirely for instruction, and since its foundation has been so much encouraged as to exhibit many pleasing proofs of having completely answered the expectations of its benevolent patron. There are six professors in the different branches of philosophy, classics, belles lettres, &c. and one for the English language; the whole system and progress of the studies are carried on under the immediate inspection of a director, who always resides at the college. In addition to the advantages of a liberal and polished education, the pupils here enjoy a salubrious air, with every means of acquiring vigour of body, as well as cultivating the mind.

ROQUETAILLADE (fief), on the south side of the St. Lawrence, in the county of Buckingham, joins Nicolet on the south-west, and is bounded by the township of Aston in the rear, half a league in front by three leagues in depth; was granted April 22, 1675, to Sieur Pierre Godefroi de Roquetaillade.

GODEFROI (fief), adjoining Roquetaillade, is three quarters of a league in front by three leagues in depth; was granted August 31, 1638, to Sieur Godefroi, and is now the property of Etienne Le Blanc, Esq. and Mons. Loiseau. Estimated generally, the land of these two fiefs is valuable; in the front, indeed, it is rather light and sandy, but it soon loses that character, and towards the interior improves into a fine black mould; in the rear it lies low, and has one or two small swamps, and perhaps as many *brulés:* a little draining would, in a short time, convert the first into fine meadows, and the latter might be as easily improved into good arable land. Wood is plentiful, although but little of first rate quality among it. The Rivers Ste. Marguerite and Godefroi, with many small rivulets, wind through both fiefs so as to water them completely; two mills are turned by them. About two-thirds of each property is settled, and some of it in a state of superior cultivation, particularly on the road, or *Chemin du Village* as it is called, that goes from Becancour to Nicolet, the Coteaux Vuide Poche, Beausejour, St. Charles and Cote du Brulé; between the different ranges there are roads leading to the Route de St. Gregoire, which communicates with the main road near the ferry across the St. Lawrence. The church of St. Gregoire, surrounded by a few well built houses, is situated on the east side of the route near the Chemin du Village. The easterly boundary of Godefroi is supposed to pass down the middle of the River Godefroi from Lake St. Paul.

BECANCOUR (the seigniory of), on the south side of the St. Lawrence, in the county of Buckingham, is bounded by Godefroi on the south-west, by fief Dutord on the north-east, and by the townships of Aston and Maddington in the rear; two leagues and a quarter in front by two in depth; was granted April 16, 1647, to Sieur de Becancour, and is now the property of the heirs of the late Lieut. Colonel Bruere, Etienne Le Blanc, Esq. and Mr. Ezekiel Hart. This grant, which towards the river is flat, possesses an excellent and exuberant soil, not materially differing in its peculiarities from that of the two preceding descriptions; the wheat, oats, and barley produced upon it, but particularly the former, are considered as fine, if not better than any other in the province. Hemp and flax are both grown here, and both excellent in quality. The timber is not much entitled to notice, the lowlands affording none but of the most inferior sorts, and the higher situations only beech, maple, birch, and a little pine. More than one half of the seigniory is in cultivation, and several of the farms exhibit a high state of improvement; the best of which are situated on the St. Lawrence, and on each side of the Becancour and Blanche. It is watered by the Rivers Becancour, Godefroi, and Blanche, Lake St. Paul, and Lac aux Outardes: the first is a large river, winding in a beautiful manner through the middle of the seigniory; its source is in the townships of

Broughton and Leeds, from whence it branches
into those of Inverness, Halifax, and Ireland,
where many minor streams flowing from numerous small lakes fall into it. After traversing
the townships of Nelson and Somerset, and the
front of Stanfold and Bulstrode, in an easterly
direction, for about 46 miles, it alters its course
to north-west, flowing about 21 miles more between Aston and Maddington, and through
the seigniory, it discharges itself into the St.
Lawrence. The banks towards its source arc
high, steep, and frequently rocky, but they decrease their elevation very much as they descend towards its mouth. The current being
greatly embarrassed by falls, rapids, and shoals,
is not navigable. In the broader parts there are
some small islands covered with fine trees,
that viewed from the banks display the varied
hues of their foliage with pleasing effect. Within
the limits of Becancour there are two mills
upon the river. Lake St. Paul is an expanse
about four miles and a half long and half a
mile broad, not very deep, but abounding in
fish of many sorts: its waters pass by the
channel of the river Godefroi into the St. Lawrence. The margin of it is a perfect landscape,
set off by almost every description of charming
scenery: well cultivated farms, with neat and
good houses belonging to them, are seen in all

directions round it, and in many places groups
of fine trees, as decorative as they can be conceived to be in a well preserved park, give to
the whole view an appearance most beautifully
picturesque. Lac aux Outardes connects with
St. Paul, and participates in the general amenity
of the situation; it derives its name from the
immense quantities of birds of that species
(bustards) that formerly frequented its borders,
although now even one of them is but rarely seen,
as the increase of settlements has long since
driven them to more solitary situations. The
Isle Dorval, a small low island, covered with
underwood, divides the entrance of the Becancour into two channels. Just above this island,
and on the west side of the river, are the hemp-
mills, &c. established by government, and
placed under the direction of Mr. Campbell:
the spot was selected by him, and with respect
to situation and soil is admirably well calculated for the production of that article; but
whatever pains have been taken to give full
effect to the plan, the success has been only
partial: perhaps something like the real cause
of failure may have been mentioned in a former
page of this work, as well as some of the means
that might be adopted, and would ensure more
favourable results in the cultivation of that valuable plant. The church of Becancour, with

the parsonage-house and a few others surrounding it, is situated on the east side of the
river: a short distance above it is a village of
Abenaqui Indians, consisting of a few ill-built
wooden houses, or, more correctly speaking,
hovels; the manners and occupations of these
people are precisely similar to those of the
village in St. François. The main road to the
westward crosses the river just above Isle
Dorval, two others ascend it for some distance
on each side, and one or two range in different
directions among the settlements. From the
front of the seigniory, there is a ferry over the
St. Lawrence to Three Rivers.

DUTORD (fief), adjoining Becancour on the
south-west, is bounded in the rear by the township of Maddington. The original title of this
concession has not been found among the
other records, therefore its date and dimensions,
as granted, are both uncertain; it is however
at present a quarter of a league in front by
nearly three leagues in depth.

COURNOYER (fief) lies contiguous to Dutord,
and is bounded on the north-east by Gentilly.
The extent of this fief is half a league in front
by three leagues in depth, but, as with the
preceding grant, neither the original title nor
other record relative to it have been discovered.
The former is the property of Mons. Bellefeuille;

and the latter belongs to Etienne Le Blanc, Esq:
Towards the rear of these two fiefs the land is
higher, but in all other respects precisely similar
to Becancour, and the timber nearly of the
same species that prevails there. Two thirds
of the land is well settled, and in a superior
state of cultivation.

' GENTILLY (the seigniory of), in the county
of Buckingham, is bounded on the north-east
by Livrard, on the south-west by fief Cournoyer, and in the rear by the townships
of Maddington and Blandford; two leagues
and a half in front by two in depth; was
granted August 14th, 1676, to Michel Pelletier, Sieur de la Perade: it is now the property of Messrs. de Lery. For a great distance
the southern bank of the St. Lawrence has
been described as low, in many places but
little above the water's level; it here assumes a
different character, rising high and steep, from
whence there is a gradual descent towards the
rear. The soil in front is a sandy loam and
good clay, but further back it changes to a
strong black mould, that is very favourable to
most species of agriculture. The first and
second ranges of concessions near the St. Lawrence, and on the river Gentilly, shew a very
good specimen of judicious management: the
whole of the land in culture will amount to

about one third of the seigniory. The timber upon the banks of the latter river is of the best kind and capital quality, but that in other parts is only fit for fire-wood; and as such, large quantities are cut and rafted down to Quebec. This property is watered by the river Gentilly and two or three smaller streams, which work one grist and one saw-mill.

LIVRARD or ST. PIERRE LES BECQUETS (the seigniory of), in the county of Buckingham, is bounded in front by the St. Lawrence, by the district line between Quebec and Three Rivers on the north-east, the seigniory of Gentilly on the south-west, and by the township of Blandford in the rear; two leagues in front and four deep; granted April 27, 1683, to Sieur Livrard, together with Isle Madame below the Island of Orleans. It is now the property of A. Lanaudiere, Esq. and the Honorable F. Baby. This seigniory is but very little settled, although the soil is fertile, and yields good crops of grain in all its varieties; it is composed generally of fine clay and a rich black mould. It is plentifully stocked with timber, some of which is of the best description, but much the greater proportion is *bois de chauffage*, that is supplied in large quantities for the consumption of the capital. It is watered by part of the Rivière du Chêne, and some small streams. In the first and second ranges of concessions, there are a few farms in a very improved state. The church of St. Pierre, the parsonage, and a chapel, are situated on the bank of the St. Lawrence, along which the main road passes.

TOWNSHIPS.

GRANTHAM, on the west side of the St. Francis, in the county of Buckingham, is bounded by Upton on the west and northwest, and Wickham on the south. On the bank of the river the ground is high, but broken by several deep ravines; in other directions it is considerably lower, and very level. The soil almost every where is good, being, on the uplands, either a yellow or a blackish loam with sand below it; in other situations it is more incorporated with sand. The timb eron the land contiguous to the river is birch, pine, maple, elm, beech, basswood, and iron wood; cedar, fir, and tammarack, are abundant in the inferior parts. The Black River, with a few other streams, water it, and present many excellent situations for the erection of mills.

A very small number of settlers have established themselves on the margin of the rivers, upon well chosen spots, where the land is propitious to almost every species of culture; and so it is upon a great many others that might be selected. In several parts of this township are large extents, producing a fine luxuriant natural grass, that after coming to maturity dries upon the ground, and in that state is but little inferior to good meadow hay. The principal proprietors are the heirs of the original grantee, the late William Grant, Esq.

WENDOVER, in the county of Buckingham, has its front on the east bank of the St. Francis, opposite to Grantham; bounded on the north-west by Courval and the augmentation to Nicolet, on the south-east by Simpson, and in the rear by waste crown lands. The quality of this tract cannot be highly praised: the land near the river is the best, and will admit of cultivation; but a short distance from thence it sinks into low deep swamps, where the soil is chiefly yellow sand and gravel; these extend nearly as far back as the rear boundary, and are overflowed in the spring. On the driest situations the timber is maple, birch, beech, and pine; in the swamps, hemlock, &c. Two branches of the Nicolet and some other streams

water it. Only a quarter of this township has
been yet surveyed, and with the trifling exception of two single lots, none of it settled; but
possibly, as the main road from the St. Lawrence into the United States passes through it,
and is likely to become a route of much importance, some adventurous cultivators may
hereafter be induced to establish themselves
in its vicinity.

SIMPSON, in the county of Buckingham,
lies between Wendover and Kingsey, on the
east side of the River St. Francis; is bounded
in the rear by Warwick, and waste lands of the
crown. The whole of this tract has been surveyed, and granted to officers and privates of
the Canadian Militia, who served during the
blockade of Quebec, in 1775 and 6. The
land is low and level, with very few swamps:
it is of a good quality, and if brought under
cultivation would produce grain of all sorts;
hemp and flax in many places would find a
soil highly favourable to their growth. Good
timber, principally beech and maple, is found
partially, but the kinds of little value are in
abundance. It is watered by several branches
of the Nicolet, and some small streams that fall
into the St. Francis; the former presenting
many excellent situations for the erection of

mills. A few lots, situated by the road side, contiguous to the river, are settled upon, and agriculture has already made some progress thereon.

WICKHAM, in the county of Buckingham, on the west side of the River St. Francis, opposite to Simpson. The interior and rear of this tract are so swampy and thickly covered with cedar, spruce fir, and hemlock, as to be little capable of being converted to any agricultural purpose. Near the river, and also drawing towards the townships of Grantham and Dunham, the land is more elevated, considerably better in quality; and might soon be made fit for production of most species of grain, and useful for most other purposes of the farm. In these districts the timber consists of oak, pine, maple, and beech, each of good dimensions. In the interior there are but a few rivulets, and these very diminutive; but it has the advantage of being traversed in front by a very beautiful and serpentine course of the St. Francis, that affords complete irrigation to the best lands. In this township, 23,786 acres have been granted to William Lindsay and others; but settlement or clearing any parts of it has scarcely yet commenced.

DURHAM, in the county of Buckingham, on the west side of the St. Francis, joins Wickham on the north-west, Melbourne on the south-east, and Acton and Ely on the south-west. The land here is generally good, presenting several extensive and improvable tracts that might be turned to advantage under most sorts of cultivation. On the bank of the river a small settlement is forming, and if in good hands, from the nature of the soil fixed upon, it will undoubtedly be attended with success. Beech, maple, birch, butternut, pine, ash, and cedar, are to be found in great plenty; there is some oak, but it is less abundant than the others. It is watered by numerous small rivulets. The principal proprietors of lands are the heirs of the late Thomas Scott, Esq. The Abenaqui Indians of the village in the seigniory of St. Francois hold 8150 acres by letters patent.

KINGSEY, in the county of Buckingham, is on the east side of the river St. Francis; bounded by Simpson on the north-west, Shipton on the south-east, and Warwick on the rear. A line drawn through this township from west to east would nearly separate the two qualities of land that compose it. The front, and the side next to Shipton, are of the very best quality, and equal to every species of cultivation: they produce beech, birch, maple, butternut, basswood, and oak timber. The part adjoining

Warwick and Simpson is low and swampy, covered with cedar, spruce-fir, and similar woods. Several branches of the Nicolet water it advantageously enough; on the banks of these streams a few settlers have established themselves, but the greatest shew of cultivation is in front, upon the St. Francis, where some industrious farmers have made great progress, considering how recently they have begun to clear the land ; their successful example will be likely to attract other settlers of similar habits, and in a few years, from the natural fertility of the soil, aided by their exertions, this, in all probability, will become a populous and thriving township. The principal proprietors are the heirs of the late Major Samuel Holland, Surveyor-General of the northern district' in America, previous to the rebellion ; also the heirs of the late Doctor George Longmore : a small proportion is held by the family of Donald Maclean.

SHIPTON, in the county of Buckingham, lies between Kingscy and Windsor, having Tingwick in the rear. This tract, equally good in nearly all its parts, is of a very superior quality, and decidedly the best of all the townships within this district: cultivation of every description may be carried on with the greatest success, but hemp, flax, and wheat, would be found particularly beneficial; the latter, indeed, is scarcely surpassed in goodness upon any tract of the province. Numerous gradual rises in several parts of the township are peculiarly fit for such productions as require a rich dry soil. The timber is beech, oak, maple, birch, and pine, intermixed with great abundance of inferior kinds. It is exceedingly well watered by a large branch of the Nicolet, and by several small rivulets that rise in the uplands, and after winding very sinuous courses, descend into the St. Francis. Agriculture is pursued here with great attention, and over a large extent of land : the farms are dispersed on the banks of the St. Francis, the Nicolet, and the rivulets, many of them displaying an advanced state of improvement. The Nicolet is navigable for boats and scows from hence to the St. Lawrence, and, with the St. Francis, furnishes water conveyance from nearly every part of the township; by which routes large quantities of pot and pearl ash, made here, are transported to Quebec. Besides these means of sending its surplus produce to market, there is also the advantage of Craigs' Road passing nearly through the middle of it ; that certainly, and at no very distant period, is destined to be the direct communication between the capital of Canada and the United States: the main road on the east side of the St. Francis to the St. Lawrence, as before noticed, and some others leading into the neighbouring townships, are considerations that, ere long, will have great influence in rendering this a rich, populous, and flourishing part of the district of Three Rivers. Industrious men are not always speculative, but there are inducements here sufficiently strong to excite the most parsimonious to extend their views; while to new settlers a rich and luxuriant soil is presented, that with care and industry, under the guidance of a moderate degree of agricultural skill, will hardly fail to realize the most flattering expectations: some good corn and saw-mills have been erected already: the present population is about 1000 souls. Elmer Cushing and William Bernard are the principal proprietors of land in this township.

MELBOURNE, in the county of Buckingham, on the west side of the St. Francis, joins Durham on the north-west. The land here is, in general, but little inferior to that in the township of Shipton, and well clothed with good maple, beech, elm, pine, and oak timber; several rivers and streams spread over it in every direction; and after completely answering all the purposes of irrigation, fall into the St. Francis. Large settlements have been made in this township, and considering them as lands but newly redeemed from the state of nature, great advances in cultivation are perceptible, and which have been guided by a competent knowledge in a judicious system of husbandry. The soil is excellent, and requires but little aid to render it uncommonly fertile; it will produce grain of all sorts in great perfection, and most species of succulents. In several parts flax and hemp could be raised in great quantities. Pot and pearl ash are made here, and with the wheat form a principal part of the traffic that is carried on; there are, however, several saw-mills in almost constant work. A communication by roads in various directions has been opened with the adjacent townships. In the River St. Francis there are several small islands along the front of this tract, and although they are rather obstructive to the navigation, yet from their beauty, and the picturesque variety exhibited by the foliage of the different species of trees they are covered with to the water's edge, they can hardly be wished away. A large extent of this valuable land is the property of the Honourable John Caldwell. The population is about 350 persons.

BROMPTON, in the county of Buckingham, is irregular in figure, bounded on the north-east and north-west by Melbourne, on the south by Orford, on the east by the St. Francis, and on the west by Ely. In the northerly part and by

the river the land is of a very fair quality, fit
for cultivation, and likely to produce good
crops of wheat or other grain ; the superior sorts
of the timber consist of elm, maple, beech,
basswood, and birch. The southerly part is
uneven, rough, and rocky, and generally speaking, useless untractable land. It is watered by
several brooks and streams; there is also a lake
covering several lots in the tenth and eleventh
range, and spreading thence into Orford. On
the River St. Francis, and contiguous to Melbourne, some settlements have been formed,
where a few well cultivated farms display
themselves The portages, occasioned by the
great and little Brompton falls, are on the west
side of the river within this township. The
population at present amounts to about 200
souls : the principal landholders are William
Bernard and his associates, who were the original patentees.

WINDSOR, in the county of Buckingham,
on the east side of the River St. Francis, lies
between Shipton and Stoke, bounded in the
rear by Wotton. This is a very fine tract of
land, of an excellent rich soil, with varieties
suitable to almost every species of culture, and
particularly hemp and flax. The surface is
undulated by moderate elevations that are well

clothed with maple, beech, birch, and fir-trees
of good size ; on the flat lands ash and cedar
prevail. A few swamps occur here and there,
but they are of so trifling a depth as to be
drained with very little trouble, and might
then be converted into excellent meadows.
It is watered by two large streams and several
small ones flowing into the St. Francis. Notwithstanding the superior excellence of the
land, this township is badly settled ; but the
whole of it has been granted to the officers and
privates of the Canadian Militia, who served in
1775 and 6; it was intended as some compensation for their past services, but scarcely any
of them were inclined to make the most advantage of the reward, by turning their swords into
ploughshares; and themselves into industrious
cultivators ; instead of which, they preferred
disposing of their lots for whatever present
profit they could turn them to: indeed, the
lands granted in this manner have been almost
generally neglected. The population of this
township scarcely exceeds 50 souls, a circumstance difficult to be accounted for, when the
advantages of its locality and goodness of soil
are taken into consideration.

STOKE, in the county of Buckingham, on
the east side of the St. Francis, joins Windsor

on the north-west, Ascott, Eaton, and Westbury on the south-east, and Dudswell on the
north-east. This tract is likewise in the same
neglected state as Windsor, most probably
from being granted in the same manner. The
land is of first rate quality, and fit for all the
purposes of agriculture: in general, beech, basswood, ironwood, and maple, are the most prevalent kinds of timber. A few swamps occur,
but neither extensive nor deep; in fact, they
are scarcely more than common wet-lands, and
require only careful ditching to become very
good meadows, of which there are already, in
different parts, many large extents of the most
luxuriant kind. It is uncommonly well watered
by several rivers and streams, that, after winding in all directions, fall into the St. Francis;
in the fourteenth range there is a small lake.
On the banks of some of the minor rivulets
many good patches for the growth of hemp can
be found, and on the parts that lie a little
higher is a fine soil for the culture of flax.
The population hardly merits an estimate.

ASCOTT, in the county of Buckingham, is
advantageously situated at the forks of the
River St. Francis, bounded on the north by
Stoke, on the south by Hatley and Compton,
on the east by Eaton, and on the west by part
of the branch of the St. Francis that connects

A A

with Lake Memphremagog. In every point
of view, this is a desirable tract : the land is of
an exceeding good quality, and so well varied
in the nature of its soil as to answer all the
purposes of the farmer; the timber is beech,
maple, pine, basswood, and oak. It is watered
by some rivers of considerable magnitude
branching off into the adjacent townships of
Compton, Clifton, and Eaton, that in their
course through this one turn several grist and
saw-mills. Settlements on a very large scale
have been made here, and several farms by the
sides of the rivers have attained a degree of
flourishing superiority, that shows their improvement to have been very rapid, as no part of
the land was granted prior to the year 1803.
The majority of the settlers here, as well as in
most of the neighbouring townships, are Americans, who, since their domiciliation, have taken
the oaths of allegiance to the British Government : these people are in general very industrious and persevering, unquestionably much
better managers upon their farms than the Canadians are, particularly when they take the
land in a state of nature ; by the system they
pursue, a tract of ground from its first clearing
becomes fruitful, and turns to account in a
much shorter period than it would under the
hands of provincial farmers ; the latter would

proceed by the methods of his forefathers, but the other is an experimentalist, and varies his operations in whatever way he thinks the nature and quality of the materials he has to work upon may be most speedily made to produce his only object, gain. The population of this township is at present 1000 souls. Several pot-ash manufactories, and mills of both descriptions, have already, in some degree, laid the foundation of commercial speculations that bid fair to obtain a considerable increase; in the encouragement of these, the navigation by the St. Francis into the St. Lawrence on the one hand, and through Lake Memphremagog and the rivers branching from it into the United States on the other, the main road by the St. Francis towards Three Rivers and Quebec, with several others leading into the different townships, will be greatly instrumental. At the forks of the St. Francis, and the foot of the great fall, are Hyat's mills, in a most convenient situation; a little below them, in the river, is a very singular high rock, on the pinnacle of which there is one solitary pine-tree of large dimensions, making together an appearance both extraordinary and uniuqe: the mills are a valuable property, belonging to Gilbert Hyat, to whom, with several associates, the township was originally granted, and who is at present the greatest landholder.

COMPTON is situated in the districts of Montreal and Three Rivers, and the counties of Richelieu and Buckingham; it joins Ascott on the north-west, Barnston and Barford on the south-east, Hatley on the south-west, and Clifton on the north-east: this township is in no respect inferior to Ascott. It has in various parts many wide spreading but gentle rises of most excellent land, thickly covered with pine, maple, and beech timber, of fine quality and large size. It is completely watered by the Coaticook and Moose rivers; the former connecting with Lake Tomefobi, and both with the St. Francis, besides many more inconsiderable streams, in whose vicinity there are some fine breadths of luxuriant meadow and pasture. An industrious population, though not much exceeding 700 souls, inhabits numerous settlements on the banks of the rivers, where most of the farms appear to be in a very thriving and excellent condition, generally producing crops of wheat of excellent quality, and in quantity far beyond the home consumption: many large patches of the land might be very beneficially employed in the culture of flax and hemp. The principal rivers work several mills of both sorts, and there are some manufactories of pot and pearl-ash. Through the most cultivated, parts of the township, roads have been opened and bridges thrown over the rivers, that are each kept in good repair, by which a communication is formed with the main road to Quebec, and with the state of Vermont. Among the inhabitants there are a few traders and artisans, who, in following their respective avocations, occasion something like the first rudiments of commerce, and confer a little importance upon this increasing settlement among the neighbouring ones. This township was erected by patent in 1802, when 26,460 acres were granted to Jesse Pennoyer, Esq., and several associates, much of which was immediately cleared, and is, in fact, the part that is now the best settled and cultivated; the greatest portion of this grant is at present held by various settlers, M. Pennoyer having retained no more than a sufficiency for his own use. In the year 1810, 13,110 acres in the easterly part were granted to Sir Rob. S. Milnes, Bart. Within this tract several lots are now in an advanced state of cultivation: indeed, from the general quality of the soil, by a little industry and good management, the whole might be turned to a very profitable account.

CLIFTON, in the county of Buckingham, joins Compton on the west, Auckland on the east, Eaton on the north, and Barford and Hereford on the south. The surface of the land is tolerably level, except in the vicinity of the rivers, where there is an easy rise and fall, that forms rather an agreeable diversity; the quality of it is unexceptionable, and would produce grain of every kind abundantly. Some swamps covered with cedar and black ash spread in different directions, but they are such as might be drained with the greatest facility. The timber is spruce, beech, ash, maple, birch, and basswood; the spruce greatly predominating. It is watered by two or three rivers, and numerous less considerable streams, all of which ultimately fall into the St. Francis; on the fifth range there is a small lake. Though large grants of land have been made in this township to several persons since the year 1799, they have attracted but few settlers; the inconsiderable cultivation that has taken place is toward the boundary of Compton. The population does not exceed 100 souls.

HEREFORD, in the county of Buckingham, has Clifton and Auckland on the north, Barford on the west, Drayton on the east, and the boundary of the province on the south. The greater part of this township may be called fair good land, and generally applicable to any kind of agriculture; the surface of it is un-

even, and as it approaches the Connecticut rather bearing a mountainous character: several
branches of that river, aided by many small
streams descending from the high lands, and
the lake called Leeches Pond, lying on the
American boundary, water it very well. The
timber is various, and in general good, consisting of maple, beech, oak, birch, pine, ash, besides cedar and spruce. In the year 1800 the
southern half of the township was granted to
James Rankin and others; but a very small
progress has been made towards its settlement:
there are indeed a few farms in tolerable good
condition, but a population of no more than
200 souls is not much calculated to increase
the number of them. Roads have been opened
leading southward into the state of Vermont,
and one to the township of Compton.

Eaton, in the county of Buckingham, lies
between Westbury and Clifton. The land in
this tract is of a uniform and favourable quality,
generously repaying the farmers, wherever any
part of it is under tillage. The timber is more
remarkable for its diversity of kind than excellence of quality; among it beech, maple, elm,
pine, birch, basswood, spruce, and hemlock
are plentiful. It is not watered by any stream
of magnitude, but it is intersected by numerous
small rivulets and brooks. The westerly half

of this township was granted in 1800, to Josiah
Sawer and others; of this a great part is now
settled. The farms by care and industry are
brought into good condition, and assume a
very flourishing aspect. Several corn and saw-
mills have been erected on some of the streams.
The inhabitants number about 600.

WESTBURY, in the county of Buckingham,
is a very small township of a triangular figure,
containing no more than 12,262 acres, exclusive
of the proportionate reserves, and lying between
Stoke, Eaton, Dudswell, and Bury. It was
granted in 1804, to the late Honourable Henry
Caldwell, receiver-general of Lower Canada,
and is now possessed by his son, John Caldwell,
Esq. The soil of the westerly part of this tract
is favourable to the encouragement of agriculture in most of its branches; but on the eastern
side is of a much inferior description, being
rough, uneven, and swampy. The timber, par-
taking of the quality of the land, consists, on
the first part, of very good beech, maple, pine,
and birch; inferior kinds only are produced on
the latter. The River St. Francis is here navigable for canoes and small boats, and by it the
logs felled in the adjacent woodlands are floated
singly down to the Eaton falls: numerous
streams of inconsiderable note fall into that
river. A few settlers on the river side have

got their farms into a very respectable state. The inhabitants of this township do not exceed 60, but its good situation is likely to increase the number.

DUDSWELL, in the county of Buckingham, has Westbury and Stoke for its south-west boundary, Weedon for the north-east, Wotton for the north-west, and Bury for its south-east. The land of this township, where it is level, is applicable to the culture of grain of all the species peculiar to the country; in some places it is uneven, and from the sixth range rises into a considerable mountain, that stretches westward into Wotton; the top of it is a flat table land, and from being wholly unclothed with trees or underwood derives its name of the Bald Mountain. In the timber there is a great variety, as beech, maple, birch, basswood, butternut, elm, some oak, pine, spruce, and cedar. The St. Francis with many small streams provide an ample and complete irriga-tion. Only one quarter of it has been laid out, which was granted to John Bishop and others; he is now the principal landholder: on this part some farms have obtained a very respectable state of prosperity. The popula-tion is about 90 souls.

. BURY, in the county of Buckingham, is irregular in its figure, bounded by Dudswell on the north, Lingwick on the north-east, Newport and Westbury on the north-west. One quarter of it is all that has been surveyed, but the land in general is of a moderately good soil, very susceptible of cultivation, and to all appearance would furnish good crops of grain of most sorts. The timber is butternut, maple, beech, ash, birch, cedar, and basswood. Many little streams water it. An intended road into the state of Vermont, striking off from Craig's Road, at a place called Kemps Bridge, in the township of Ireland, will pass through it; this route has been already marked and blazed in the field, and mile-posts fixed along the whole of its distance.

LINGWICK, in the county of Buckingham, has Bury on the south-west, and is surrounded on its other sides by the unsurveyed townships of Weedon, Stratford, and Hampden. This tract of land is very similar in quality to the level district of Dudswell: the timber upon it also answering nearly the same description. It is watered by several streams of tolerable size that flow into the St. Francis. The westerly half has been surveyed and granted to divers individuals, but not one of them has yet undertaken to break up the ground.

NEWPORT, in the county of Buckingham, is situated between Eaton and Ditton, having

Auckland on the south, and Bury to the northward. Although the land in many parts of
this tract is uneven, the general tendency of the
soil is good. Beech, maple, and birch, spruce,
basswood, and fir, are the prevalent sorts of
timber. A great number of rivulets descending into the St. Francis water it in almost
every direction. About one-half of it has been
granted; and on the south-west quarter some
progress has been made in cultivation, where
the land is found very productive in most species of grain, and congenial to the growth both
of hemp and flax. Several roads passing to
the adjacent settlements intersect it, as does
the intended new one from Craig's Road. The
inhabitants amount to about 160.

Ditton, in the county of Buckingham, is
bounded by Newport on the west, Marston
and Chesham on the east, Hampden on the
north, and Emberton on the south. The surface of this township is irregular, in several
places rising into large eminences; but yet, in
general, of a moderately good soil, timbered
with beech, birch, basswood, and maple. It
is intersected by some large streams that fall
into the St. Francis. The south-west quarter
has been surveyed and granted, but no part
thereof settled upon.

Auckland, in the county of Buckingham,

lies between Hereford, Drayton, and Newport, bounded by Clifton on the west, and Emberton on the east. The land is here uneven and rugged, in some places mountainous, and in others sinking into swamps; the level and dry tracts have a pretty good soil, that if brought under culture would answer moderate expectations: there are some patches in lower situations that appear fit for hemp. The timber is a mixture of most species that are found on the surrounding tracts. It is abundantly watered by a great number of streams and brooks, some of them flowing into the St. Francis, and others into the Connecticut river. The northerly half of the township has been granted, but no part whatever is settled. A sort of foot-path runs through it, by which the Indians frequently make their way to the River Chaudiere.

MARSTON, in the county of Buckingham, is well situated on the westerly side of Lake Megantick; the whole of it has been surveyed, but only one quarter of it granted, and no part thereof settled. The land is irregular, hilly, and frequently very stony, but mostly of a moderately good soil, that would answer very well for agriculture in general; many spots present eligible situations for the culture both of hemp and flax. The timber forms but an indifferent mixture of maple, fir, hemlock, cedar, and spruce. It is watered by several streams and small lakes, besides Lake Megantick that has a considerable expansion, being nine miles in length, and two upon the average in breadth, running deeply into the land in several bays, closing upon which, and around the lake generally, are some very excellent meadows. The scenery in the vicinity is beautifully picturesque, as the land rises gradually from its borders clothed with a rich verdure, and embellished by large groups of stately trees ranging above each other until they crest the summit, and exhibit a most enchanting variety of foliage. The waters abound with excellent fish, and the country around this sequestered and romantic spot is the resort of almost every species of game.

CLINTON, in the county of Buckingham, is a small tract, only equal in dimension to the quarter of a township; it is most agreeably situated at the southern extremity of Lake Megantick, joining Marston on the north, and in other directions surrounded by Chesham and unsurveyed wastes. In almost every respect the land is here marked by a superiority of character; the soil in general is of the very first quality, exhibiting many large patches of luxuriant pastures. The timber is pine, beech, maple, birch, fir, spruce, and cedar. It is watered by the River Arnold, and some other streams falling into the lake; the former derives its name from the American General Arnold, who in the year 1775 passed part of his troops down it, when conducting his army through an almost unknown country to besiege Quebec. No part of this township is settled, although it abounds with numerous excellent situations, where the land is fit for every species of agriculture.

HAM, in the county of Buckingham, lying between Wotton and Wolfestown, joins Tingwick and Chester on the north-west, and Weedon on the south-east. The complete outline of this township has been run, and one half of it granted among several individuals. The land is here of a quality that might be brought into cultivation with great advantage, and would produce wheat or any other species of grain natural to the country: many parts of it are fit for the growth of flax and hemp. The surface is diversified by many large swells of inconsiderable elevation, covered with the kinds of wood that denote them to be of a fine rich soil: in some few places in the valleys it is a little swampy. The timber is maple, beech, basswood, birch, hemlock, and cedar. It is watered by part of the River Nicolet, which here has its source in the beautiful little lake of the same name, situated on the borders of Weedon and Ham; it is about two miles and a half long and one broad, with several small islands scattered about it, which are the resort of vast quantities of wild-fowl. The surrounding country possesses every trait of wild romantic beauty; it is environed by rising grounds clothed with trees, in some places thickly clustered together, and in others irregularly dispersed over the acclivities: beyond the first heights are seen in the distance the softened and fantastic forms of a much more elevated chain. The intended road to communicate with Craig's Road passes on the south-east side of this lake.

WOLFESTOWN, in the county of Buckingham, lies between the townships of Ham and Ireland, is joined by Chester and Halifax on the north-west, and unsurveyed lands on the south-east. The north-westerly half of the township is moderately good, of which a part lying towards the north has been granted, and might be made to repay the trouble of cultivation; the timber upon it is pine, beech, basswood, cedar, and hemlock. The south-easterly half is a chain of rocky heights of which no part is arable, or indeed convertible to any use.

HALIFAX is in the districts of Three Rivers and Quebec, and the county of Buckingham;

it lies between Chester and Inverness, bounded
on the north-west by Arthabaska and Somerset, and on the south-east by Wolfestown and
Ireland. : The land is here excellent and fertile,
and would yield abundantly under almost any
system of agriculture; it presents many good
situations for hemp and flax : the north-easterly part, being low, has a few swamps, but
they might be easily reclaimed by ditching ;
in the opposite direction it is uneven, and rises
as it inclines towards the south : the soil almost
every where of the best quality. The kinds of
timber are nearly the same as are produced in
Wolfestown and Ham. It is watered by some
small rivers and streams, and the picturesque
little Lake Pitt of about five miles long and
half a mile broad, spreading across the seventh,
eighth, ninth, and tenth ranges, and communicating by a small channel with Lake William,
from whence the waters discharge into the
River Becancour. The south-easterly half of
the township has been laid out and granted,
but none of it is yet cultivated. Craig's Road
passing through a part of it, may be, perhaps;
the means of attracting some settlers to its
neighbourhood. The principal landholders are
the heirs of the late Joseph Frobisher, Esq.
and Mrs. Scott and family.

CHESTER, in the county of Buckingham,

lies between Tingwick and Halifax; bounded on the north-west by Arthabaska, and on the south-east by Ham and Wolfestown.' The land in this township has great advantages in point of locality, with a soil in every respect fit for all the purposes of agriculture, though still remaining unbroken by the plough. The timber is mostly beech, maple, pine, birch, elm, basswood, butternut, cedar, spruce, and hemlock. It is watered by large branches of the Nicolet and Becancour, that wind through it in various directions. Craig's Road crosses it diagonally. The south-east and north-west quarters have been surveyed and granted; they are both valuable tracts of land, well meriting attention. The proprietors of one quarter are the heirs of Joseph Frobisher, Esq. and the other belongs to various individuals.

WARWICK, in the county of Buckingham, joins Tingwick on the south-east, Stanfold on the north-west, Kingsey on the south-west, and Arthabaska on the north-east. This is a poor and rather sterile tract, that, excepting the three first ranges, is almost unserviceable, being rough, broken, and swampy,—defying all the art and labour of industry to give it any value. It is thickly covered with spruce and hemlock. The tract of waste lands adjoining it on the north-west is of the same description; in the spring it is deeply overflowed by several branches of the River Nicolet, and rendered impassable for a considerable distance. The south-east half of the township has been subdivided, and granted to various persons, but, as may be expected from its nature, no one has found sufficient inducement to attempt a settlement.

ARTHABASKA, in the county of Buckingham, is a triangular piece of land, situated between Chester and Halifax on the north-east, Bulstrode, Stanfold, and Somerset on the north-west, and Warwick on the south-west; containing a much less extent than a full township: one quarter of it is subdivided, and granted to John Gregory, Esq., who at present holds it. The land is much of the same nature as that in the townships of Halifax and Chester, but in some parts lower, and rather swampy. The timber is chiefly birch, beech, elm, and some pine, with much of inferior quality upon the swamps. Several branches of the Nicolet and Becancour run through it. No part thereof is settled.

STANFOLD, in the county of Buckingham, is situated on the south-east side of the River Becancour, that bounds it in front; it has Arthabaska on the rear, Nelson on the north-east, and Bulstrode on the south-west. From lying very low and being extremely swampy, not much of the land is fit for cultivation. It is traversed by some rivers and small streams that fall into the Becancour. One half of this township was granted to the Honourable Jenkin Williams, who is the present holder of it. No attempt has been made to clear it.

BULSTRODE, in the county of Buckingham, joins Stanfold on the north-east, Warwick in the rear, and waste lands of the crown on the west. The country hereabout is level and low, with many swamps and numerous *brulés*, particularly towards the middle of the township; near the river; and also inclining towards the limits of Warwick, the land rises a little, and is of a moderately good quality : the swamps and low lands are in some places of a sandy soil, and in others a black mould. On the highest situation the timber consists of beech, maple, and black birch; in the swamps cedar, hemlock, and tammarack. The main branch of the Nicolet, and several rivulets running into the Becancour, water it very well. Half of the township has been granted to the late Patrick Langan, Esq., and is now the property of his heirs. No settlements have yet been made.

ASTON, in the county of Buckingham, is situated in the rear of the seigniories of Becancour and Godefroi; bounded on the north-east by the

River Becancour, and on the south-west by waste lands of the crown. By the sides of the Becancour and River Blanche the land is pretty high, but a short distance from thence it descends into a low flat; the soil in general is good, and would no doubt prove highly productive if brought into cultivation. In situations near the rivers the timber is oak, elm, pine, beech, birch, and maple; in other directions it is either cedar, hemlock, or spruce. The Riviere Blanche and the Becancour, the banks of which are extremely picturesque, water it very completely. The whole township has been surveyed, and granted to various persons, but not one of them has yet undertaken to cultivate, or procured one single settler upon it.

MADDINGTON, in the county of Buckingham, is situated on the east side of the Becancour, opposite to Aston; bounded on the north-west by the seigniories of Becancour, Dutord, Cournoyer, and Gentilly; on the south-west and south-east by the River Becancour, and on the north-west by Blandford. In the surveyed parts of this township lying contiguous to the river the land is of the same nature and quality as in Aston, and like it is capable of being turned to good account in the hands of able farmers: in some places the soil would suit very well for hemp and flax.

On the superior grounds some excellent timber may be found, but on the lower parts only the indifferent assortment of cedar, hemlock, and similar kinds. The Becancour presents several eligible situations for the erection of mills. No part of this tract has yet been settled: the principal proprietor is the Honourable Jenkin Williams.

HUNTERSTOWN, in the county of St. Maurice, on the north side of the St. Lawrence, is situated in the rear of the seigniories of Rivière du Loup, Grand Pré, and Dumontier; is bounded on the east by the projected township of Caxton, and on the west by lands claimed by the late Charles Lanaudiere, Esq. as belonging to the seigniory of Maskinongé, and on the north-west by waste crown lands. This is a tract of very little value, being continued strata of rock lying very near the surface; toward the rear it rises into broken and almost mountainous ridges. Pine and maple are abundant, but cedar, spruce, and hemlock much more so. The Riviere du Loup with some small lakes and little rivulets water it very well. 24620 acres of this township were granted in 1800 to Mr. John Jones, the present proprietor. The unsurveyed or projected townships in this district are Caxton, Blandford, Wotton, Weedon, Garthby, Coleraine, Stratford, Hamp-

den, Gayhurst, Chesham, Emberton, and Drayton. In Weedon, Coleraine, and Garthby, is
situated Lake St. Francis, of considerable dimensions, forming two expanses of water that
are connected by a short river or channel. It
is surrounded in every direction by lofty wood-
covered mountains, approaching each other so
close on either side of the little river as almost
to cut off the communication of the waters between the two parts of the lake: these mountains contain iron ore in many places. On the
topographical map, Lake St. Francis is delineated by dotted lines, and laid down from the
reports of various persons who have penetrated
that country, and of the Indian hunters : it may
not therefore be correct in all its points ; but as
there never has been a survey of it made, such
authorities are all that afford any resources for
its description.

THE DISTRICT OF QUEBEC

Extends from the seigniory of Grondines,
whose western boundary joins the district of
Three Rivers, down the St. Lawrence on the
north side as far as the River St. John, on the
coast of Labrador; and on the south side
from the seigniory of Deschaillons as far down
as Cape Chat, where it is met by the district of

Gaspé; to the southward it is bounded by the
ridge of mountains already designated as the
north-easterly chain, and on the northward by
the 52d degree of north latitude. It contains
the counties of Cornwallis, Devon, Hertford,
Dorchester, Hampshire, Quebec, Orleans, and
Northumberland; eighty-seven seigniories, fourteen whole townships, four that are partly
within the district of Three Rivers, eighteen
projected townships, and forty-two parishes.
The quantity of land granted in *fief et seigneurie* amounts to 4,352,500 acres, or 5,109,319
French arpents: in free and common soccage,
561,234 acres. Of the old tenures, one third part,
or perhaps a little less, is under cultivation: in
the townships the proportion under tillage is
yet but small.

GRONDINES (the seigniory of, and its augmentation), in the county of Hants, on the
north side of the River St. Lawrence, is bounded on the south-west by the seigniory and augmentation of Ste. Anne, in the district of Three
Rivers, by La Tesserie on the north-east, and
by the unsurveyed township of Alton and waste
lands of the crown in the rear. It was granted
in three parts, viz. the western part, one league
in front by ten in depth, on the 20th March,
1638, to the Duchess d'Aiguillon; for *Les Dames
-Hospitalieres* of the Hotel Dieu of Quebec; the

eastern part, three quarters of a league in front by three leagues in depth, on the 3d November, 1672, to the poor of the said hospital; and the augmentation to the eastern part, two leagues in depth by three quarters of a league in front, on the 25th April, 1711, to Louis Hamelin: the whole is now the property of Mr. Moses Hart. Throughout the greater part of these grants the soil is of an indifferent character, being only a thin layer of poor earth upon a solid bed of stone: here and there a few patches of better quality may be found. A small ridge extends across the seigniory at a short distance from the front, and thence down to the borders of the river the space is principally occupied by very good meadow land. The timber is altogether of the most inferior sort. The principal settlements lie by the main road, passing just beneath the ridge, and upon the River Ste. Anne: taken in the aggregate, the soil and timber on this property are barely above mediocrity, yet it is not without some well cultivated farms upon it; they, however, owe more to the industry of their occupiers than to original fertility for that distinction. Somewhat more than a fourth part of these tracts are under culture. It is very well watered by the River Ste. Anne, the Batiscan, and a small river falling into the St. Lawrence; the latter turns a grist and a saw-mill. There is a church and a parsonage-house, but the service is performed by the curé of a neighbouring parish. The main road crosses the seigniory near its front: one ascends the Ste. Anne on each side, and another leads to the back concessions. In the St. Lawrence the extensive shoal, called Les Battures des Grondines, stretches along the front. There is a small fief called Francheville, within Grondines, which, by default of inheritance, has reverted to the crown.

LA TESSERIE (fief), on the north side of the St. Lawrence, in the county of Hants, is bounded on the south-west by Grondines, on the north-east by La Chevrotiere, in the rear by the township of Alton, and by the river in front; one league in breadth by three in depth: was granted November 3d, 1672, to Demoiselle de la Tesserie. In this grant the land greatly resembles that of Grondines, but perhaps has some little advantage over it as to the general quality of the soil; it is watered in the rear by the River Ste. Anne: by the main road there are a few well-cultivated concessions, but in other respects there is nothing meriting particular notice.

LA CHEVROTIERE (the seigniory of) is on the north bank of the St. Lawrence, in the

county of Hants, between La Tesserie and
Deschambault, bounded in the rear by waste
lands of the crown; one league in front by
three leagues in depth: the date of the grant
is uncertain, as the original title has never been
found among the records of the province; or
among the registers of fealty and homage;
but from the tenor of the grants of La Tesserie
and Deschambault, it appears to have been conceded sometime before the year 1652, to M.
Chavigny de la Chevrotiere: it is at this day
possessed by M. de la Chevrotiere, a lineal
descendant of the person who first received the
grant. Of the soil in this seigniory the generality possesses a good share of fertility, and is
well suited to the produce of wheat and all other
grain, though at this time not more than one
third of the land is under tillage. The surface
of it is uneven, and the same will be observed to
be the case more and more on approaching
Quebec from the westward; the banks of the
St. Lawrence also increase greatly in height,
and the beach becomes more rocky and irregular, with the battures or shoals running out to a
considerable distance from it. Beech, maple,
and some excellent pine-timber, are found
close to the river. The seigniory is watered
by many small streams besides the River Ste.
Anne, that crosses it near its rearward limit,

and the Chevrotiere, that winds along the middle about six miles, and then strikes off to the northward into the seigniory of Deschambault: this little river rolls its slender stream between two banks of considerable altitude, and after crossing the ridge in front descends through a valley into the St. Lawrence, in which by the side of the main road there are a dwelling-house, a grist and a saw-mill, most delightfully situated. On the west bank of this river the road is rather difficult, from its steepness and circuitous course; but on the opposite side the rise is gradual, and easy of ascent to the top of the eminence along which it passes onwards to Quebec: besides this road, which is the main one, there are several others running in different directions. On the summit of the elevation and each side of the highway many handsome farms, in a good state of improvement, present themselves to notice.

DESCHAMBAULT (the seigniory of), in the county of Hants, on the north side of the River St. Lawrence, is bounded by the barony of Portneuf on the north-east, by La Chevrotiere on the south-west, by the river in front, and by waste lands of the crown in the rear; one league in breadth by three in depth; granted March 1, 1652, to Demoiselle Eleonore de Grande Maison: it belongs at present to Louis de la Gorgendiere, Esq. and the Honourable Juchereau Duchesnay. This, in almost every respect, is a very valuable property, with a soil of unexceptionable quality; being a mixture of good clay with a little sand, a fine yellow loam, and in many places a rich black mould, which in the vicinity of Point Deschambault has a stratum of rock beneath it. The surface is uneven, and from being a fine level flat near the river, it rises in small ridges, mounting by gradations one above another nearly to the limits of the seigniory in the rear: from the westward also there is a gradual acclivity from the plain to the height of Point Deschambault. On this flat the land is every where fertile, and fit for the production of every article of the country, whether grain, fruit, or vegetables; the principal part of it is in an excellent state of cultivation, and the numerous farms on each side of the main road, with their substantial houses, and every requisite appendage, afford a pleasing evidence of the industry and good husbandry of the proprietors. On the different ranges of concessions towards the interior many of the lots display an equal share of good management, and which indeed is the case with nearly all the land under tillage, amounting to a full third of the whole seigniory. The timber is of a moderately good quality, though but of little diversity of species, being for the most part beech, maple, and pine; there is, however, wood of inferior descriptions. The Rivers Ste. Anne crossing the rear, La Chevrotiere, Belle-isle, and a few smaller streams, contribute to the luxuriant fertility of the soil. The Point of Deschambault has a considerable elevation, and stretches boldly into the river to the Richelieu rapid; the face of it appears a firm clay and sand, without any interposition of rock or stone. On this Point the church of Deschambault is built, and on the summit of the salient extremity is a very beautiful grove of pine-trees, remarkable rather for the regularity and equality of size than for their individual magnitude: a little below the church, on the sloping side of the Point, is the manor-house of Monsr. de la Gorgendiere. The River St. Lawrence forms a large curve between Cap Santé and Point Des-chambault, and either in ascending or descending the combination of objects that it presents is highly interesting and agreeable. The Point was formerly a sort of military post, as the French, in the year 1759, had a battery upon it, for the purpose of defending this pass of the river against any force that might have been sent upwards; indeed, this situation, and the superior height of Platon on the opposite side, might easily be fortified so as completely to

command the passage either way, and, together
with the difficulties of the Richelieu rapid,
would render any attempt to force it very disastrous to an enemy that should undertake the
enterprise.

PORTNEUF (the barony of), in the county of
Hants, has its front to the St. Lawrence, bounded on the south-west by the seigniory of Deschambault, on the north-east by that of Jacques
Cartier, and in the rear by Perthuis; one league
and a half in breadth by three leagues in depth:
was granted April 16th, 1647, to Sieur de Croisille; it now belongs to the convent of the
Hotel Dieu, at Quebec, but is let on a long
lease to Messrs. Coltman and Co. This is a
fine and valuable estate, the land fertile, and that
part of it that is under tillage in a good state
of cultivation: the soil is a light sandy earth
mixed with clay, and in many places a good
black mould upon a bed of clay. The timber
in the rear of the tract is a general mixture of
the middling sorts, but along the banks of
the River Portneuf some very good pine may
be collected. This river, that with several
small streams waters the property, is not navigable either for boats or canoes; it has its
source in a small lake within the seigniory of
Faussambault, and passing through Bourglouis, Neuville, Belair, and Jacques Cartier, it

flows into the St. Lawrence, near Deschambault. The banks on each side are high, and
very well wooded; the stream is precipitated
through so many rapids and along a broken
rocky bed with such violence, as to render it
impassable for any sort of boat, however light.
At the entrance into the river from the St.
Lawrence the land, for a short space, is
low, and extremely well cultivated on each
side. At a small distance up, on the western
side, are the valuable grist and saw-mills belonging to Messrs. Coltman and Co., most conveniently and agreeably situated in a hollow
near the main road, from whence the ground
rises almost in form of an amphitheatre; on
the gentle acclivities there are several fine settlements, and many good houses dispersed,
that greatly enliven a prospect naturally beautiful. From the mills the exportation of flour
is very great, and with the shipments of timber
almost continually carried on, the place generally presents a bustling scene of business:
the mercantile concerns of the proprietors
being very extensive, they have been induced
to establish a depot here for the collection of
all sorts of timber for exportation; and it is no
uncommon thing to see almost a small fleet of
vessels of various classes lying at anchor off
the mouth of the River Portneuf, receiving

384

their freights on board, besides those that usually anchor here in their passage up or down the
river, on account of the Richelieu rapid. Proceeding to the eastward from the mills, the
bank of the St. Lawrence takes a gradual rise
as far as the church at Cap Santé, and from
thence it almost immediately obtains an elevation of more than 150 feet above the level of
the river, by a very steep ascent up what is
called the Cote du Cap Santé. From the
front to the rear of this tract there are many
rising grounds, generally of a very good soil,
between which the hollows are in some places
swampy, and covered with cedar and hemlock.
The church of Cap Santé, standing nearly on
the point of the cape, is a handsome building,
usually attracting a stranger's notice by its exterior ornaments as well as interior decoration.
To vessels coming down the river the clump
of trees on Point Deschambault and this
church serve as sailing marks; the latter, by its
three spires, is distinguishable at a great distance.
Near the church is the parsonage-house, and a
group of others surrounding it, forming almost
a respectable sized village. Along each side
of the Quebec road the houses are numerous,
and being surrounded by neat gardens and extensive orchards, afford, particularly during the
spring, a most enchanting appearance. From

the main road, there are two that branch off to the
back concessions, and which continue as far to
the interior as any settlements have been made;
at different distances others take a transverse
direction towards the adjacent seigniories on
each side. From Cap Santé, the large shoal
called *Batture du Cap Santé* stretches almost
down to the entrance of Jacques Cartier River:
it is thickly beset with rocks that are uncovered
at low water.

· PERTHUIS (the seigniory of), in the county
of Hants, is situated immediately in the rear
of the barony of Portneuf; partly bounded on
the south-west by the lands forming the projected township of Alton, and partly on the
north-east by the seigniory of Jacques Cartier;
its other limits are closed upon by waste crown
lands; one league and a half in breadth, by
nine leagues in depth; was granted October
11, 1753, to Sieur Perthuis. From the boundary of Portneuf, the land rises in a broken
and irregular series of heights towards the rear,
where it falls in with the north-westerly ridge
of mountains: the soil, for a league, or two to
the interior, is a light loam or clay, sometimes
covered with a thick layer of fine black mould;
these spots, if brought under cultivation, would,
no doubt, prove very productive: of the quality further back nothing has yet been ascer-

c c

tained. No part of the grant is appropriated to agriculture. The timber is in general very good, and also abundant, consisting of the best species that are found upon a dry good soil, as maple, beech, ash, birch, and pine. The lower portion of the seigniory is watered by the River Ste. Anne, which runs across it, but in the other parts there are only a few small streams that break from the sides of the mountains.

JACQUES CARTIER (the seigniory of) is in the county of Hants, having its front on the River St. Lawrence, bounded on the south-west by the barony of Portneuf, by Belair and its augmentation on the north-east, and in the rear by waste crown lands; half a league in breadth by five leagues in depth; granted 29th March, 1659, to Dame Gaguier, widow of Jean Clement de Wauls, Chevalier and Seigneur de Monceaux. It is now the property of Messrs. de Lery, and Mr. Alsop. Although the surface is very irregular and broken, the land in general is of a moderately good quality; in some places the soil is light and sandy, in others a layer of black vegetable mould upon a stratum of lime-stone, and to the rear, where it becomes rather mountainous, a good light loam; each of these different kinds is sufficiently fertile, and several ranges of concessions are in an excellent state of cultivation, having among them many productive and valuable farms. The timber is various both in kind and quality, but there is good maple and birch, and along the banks of the different rivers some superior pine: the common species are very abundant. The Rivers Ste. Anne and Portneuf, already mentioned, cross this seigniory, but the principal one by which it is watered is the Jacques Cartier: to many it may be superfluous to mention the origin of its name, which was derived from the navigator who first examined the River St. Lawrence, and secured his vessels at the entrance of this river during the winter of 1536. It takes its source from several small lakes in the interior, near the parallel of 48° north latitude, and about 71° 20' of west longitude. After running a very circuitous course through a mountainous country that is but little known, it reaches the townships of Tewkesbury and Stoneham, passes through them, and flows on in a south-south-westerly direction, a distance of about forty-six miles, across the seigniories of St. Ignace, St. Gabriel, Faussembault, Neuville, Belair, and the fief Jacques Cartier, where it falls into the River St. Lawrence. From the townships its stream displays a character of great wildness, and is both grand and impetuous in its course, hurrying through valleys between the lofty mountains, and fre-

c c 2

quently dashing with violence over the precipices and immense fragments of rock that oppose its progress. The bed being extremely rocky, the great number of falls and rapids, and the vehemence of the torrent, particularly in the spring and after the autumnal rains, render it generally impassable for canoes or boats of any description. The banks are exceedingly high, and at intervals, for considerable distances, are formed of strata of limestone, or of granite rock that in many places are lofty, rugged, and majestic, partially displaying a few stunted pines in the interstices, or covered with creeping shubbery; but in many parts presenting only the frowning aspect of huge barren masses heaped perpendicularly one upon another. From the heights on each side of the river spread extensive forests, through which there are various paths traced out and kept open during all the changes of seasons by the Indians, and chiefly those of the village of Lorette, who consider the lands to an immense distance northwards as their hunting grounds. The general view along the course of the river is varied, picturesque, and extraordinary, presenting a thousand combinations of the grandeur, beauty, and wild magnificence of nature that stand unrivalled by that of any other country. In its course through the seig-

niory of St. Gabriel, it approaches within sixteen miles of Quebec; about nine miles before
it reaches the St. Lawrence is the new bridge
of Jacques Cartier. The stream is here precipitated over many large fragments of granite that
occasion a perpendicular fall of considerable
height, the effect of which is greatly increased
by the incessant roar of the torrent as it forces
its way through the hollows and excavations
that by the lapse of time it has wrought for
itself in the rocky bed and sides of the channel:
from hence it flows with the same impetuous
character, until its waters are lost in the current of the St. Lawrence. The River Jacques
Cartier, viewed with a military eye, forms a
most powerful natural barrier, and may be
termed one of the outworks to the city and
environs of Quebec; the velocity of the stream
would make it extremely dangerous to attempt
fording it; the height of the banks renders
them inaccessible, except in a very few places,
and those could only be ascended with much
difficulty by a small number of persons at a
time, which, with the numerous advantageous
positions along the whole range of the river for
posting a defensive force, would altogether constitute it a complete line of security; indeed,
the French, after they were expelled from Quebec in 1759, retired behind this river, and

manifested some intention of establishing themselves in force upon its western bank, where
they hastily threw up some works, under the
persuasion that they could there remain safe
for some time from the molestation of their
conquerors on the Plains of Abraham. On
the eastern side of the river, at a short distance
before its confluence with the St. Lawrence,
where the high bank receding considerably
from the margin, leaves a rather extensive flat
only a little elevated above the water's level,
are some corn-mills, and several stores belonging to the heirs of the late Mr. Allsop of Quebec. They are the remains of a much greater
and more valuable establishment that was
nearly destroyed some years ago by fire; a
large sum of money had been expended a
short time previous to the accident to render
it every way complete, and capable of carrying
on a very extensive concern, and in which a
flourishing progress had been made: since
that period none of the buildings have been
restored, consequently its importance is at this
time greatly diminished. The main road passes
along the front of the seigniory, and crosses the
Jacques Cartier by a ferry, of about 160 toises
broad, where, on account of the violence of
the stream, the boats are traversed from side to
side by means of hawsers stretched across; the

'charge for each person is three-pence, for a horse six-pence, a horse and carriage nine-pence, and fifteen-pence for a carriage and two horses. The road, as it passes in the vicinity of the river and winds up the lofty banks, is exceedingly steep ; but notwithstanding the difficulty and fatigue of it to passengers, it is much frequented, although there is another road from Quebec passing over Jacques Cartier bridge, that is something shorter in its distance, and by which almost all the inequalities of the ground are avoided. Less than one third of this seigniory is cultivated ; some of the best farms are near the road that passes by the St. Lawrence, and on the south-west side, by the road leading from the bridge to the barony of Portneuf.

BELAIR or LES ECUREUILS (the seigniory of, and its augmentation), in the county of Hants, joins Jacques Cartier. It has its front to the St. Lawrence, is bounded on the north-east by Pointe aux Trembles, and in the rear by D'Auteuil; half a league in breadth by one league in depth; was granted November 3d, 1672, to the Sieurs Toupin, father and son. The augmentation, of the same breadth as the seigniory, and two leagues in depth, was granted January 20th, 1706, to Marie Magdeleine Mézérai, widow of Jean Toupin. Though composed of a soil nearly similar to the front part of the seigniory of Jacques Cartier, Belair cannot vie with that property in fertility; but it is nearly all settled, and can show some neat, well-managed farms. The Jacques Cartier river crosses it diagonally, and it is otherwise watered by the Riviere aux Pommes, a pretty winding stream that flows into the former. The timber has been nearly all cleared off, and what little does remain is very inferior both in kind, and value. Several roads cross this grant, having one intersecting them at right angles, that runs from the banks of the St. Lawrence up to the Jacques Cartier. The augmentation is generally mountainous, but the land is not of a bad quality. It is only partially cultivated near where it joins the seigniory: it is tolerably well timbered with beech, ash, maple, pine, and birch, and watered by the River Portneuf and some of its branches. The road from Jacques Cartier bridge crosses it, on each side of which there are a few neat settlements.

D'AUTEUIL (the seigniory of), in the county of Hants, is immediately in the rear of the augmentation to Belair, bounded on the north-east by Bourglouis, on the south-west by Jacques Cartier seigniory, and on the north-west by waste crown lands; half a league in breadth by four and a half leagues in depth;

granted February 15th, 1693, to the Sieur d'Auteuil. This mountainous tract is still in a state of nature, and indeed likely so to remain. It produces some good timber, and judging from the different species thereof one would conclude that the land is above mediocrity.

NEUVILLE, or LA POINTE AUX TREMBLES (the seigniory of), in the county of Hants, is bounded by the St. Lawrence in front, Belair and its augmentation on the south-west, Desmaure, Guillaume Bonhomme, and Faussembault on the north-east, and by Bourglouis in the rear; two leagues and three quarters in front by four leagues in depth; was granted December 16th, 1653, to Jean Bourdon, and is at present the property of the Reverend Mr. Descheneaux, Grand Vicar. Viewing this seigniory as the possession of an individual, it must be estimated as one of great value, above two thirds of it being under cultivation and very productive in grain, as well as almost every other species of growth natural to the country. The surface, as is the case almost invariably within several leagues of Quebec, is very uneven, rising from the St. Lawrence in a series of irregular ridges to the elevated banks of the Jacques Cartier: beyond which it is mountainous and abrupt. The soil in front is a lightish mixture of sand and black friable

earth, but advancing to the north-west it becomes much stronger, and soon changes to a
fine loam, in some places pretty thickly strewed
with stones : large masses of granite lie about
in different directions as if rolled down from the
heights, although there is scarce any trace of
rock until reaching the bank of the Jacques
Cartier river. The timber is for the most part
very good ; but between the two rivers not
in great plenty, as the whole of that space is
laid out in fruitful settlements; further back,
beech, maple, pine, ash, and birch, are found
in abundance. It is watered by several
branches of the River Portneuf, the Riviere
aux Pommes, that traces a beautiful meandering course throughit, and the impetuous Jacques
Cartier, besides many rivulets descending from
the sides of the different ridges, the whole
amply providing for the irrigation, particularly
of the settled parts. Of the many roads that
intersect the seigniory, the one in front of the
St. Lawrence, one in the direct line from Quebec by the village of Capça to Jacques Cartier
bridge, and another, striking from the St. Lawrence, about midway between the village of
Pointe aux Trembles and Belair, to the same
place, are the principal; the others open a
convenient communication between the different concessions. The bridge itself deserves

notice for the easy lightness, and at the same
time solidity of its construction; the natural
high bank of the river on each side is finished
by masonry into solid piers, from whence the
arch, entirely of timber, forms a handsome
segment raised to more than the ordinary elevation above the stream; its appearance altogether is well calculated to attract attention:
near the west end of it is a small well-built
cottage most romantically situated, wherein
the collector of the bridge toll resides. The
village of Pointe aux Trembles, consisting of
about 25 houses, a church, parsonage-house,
and what is termed a convent, is exceedingly
well seated on a projecting point of the same
name, rising but a few yards above the level
of the St. Lawrence; it is backed by an amphitheatre of gently rising hills cultivated to
their very summits, embellished by farm-houses
mostly built of stone, surrounded by gardens
and extensive orchards, affording in every direction, but from the river particularly, a rich,
variegated, and pleasing *coup d'œil.* Many of
the houses in the village are of stone, their inhabitants industrious and wealthy, which is also
the case with most of the *habitans* of this seigniory. The convent is an establishment for
female education, conducted by two sisters of
the congregation of Quebec, who reside in it

as missionaries for disseminating religious and other useful knowledge. From the Point reaching nearly down to the seigniory of Desmaure runs a shoal called La Batture de la Pointe aux Trembles, thickly beset with rocks that are uncovered at low water.

BOURGLOUIS (the seigniory of), in the county of Hants, immediately in the rear of Pointe aux Trembles, is bounded on the south-west by D'Auteuil, on the north-east by Faussembault, and in the rear by waste lands; two leagues and three quarters in front by three leagues in depth; was granted May 14th, 1741, to Sieur Louis Fornel. This grant still remains in its natural state, no part whereof is cultivated, although the soil is tolerably good, being principally a strong loam. The timber is various, and among it is found ash, beech, birch, pine, and maple of good quality and large dimensions. It is watered by the River Ste. Anne towards the rear, and by many small streams that rise in the mountains southward of that river, and fall into the Portneuf.

DESMAURE, or ST. AUGUSTIN (the seigniory of), in the county of Hants, fronting the St. Lawrence, is bounded on the north-east by Gaudarville, on the south-west by Pointe aux Trembles, and in the rear by Guillaume Bonhomme and Faussembault. No official record has been found relative to this grant, consequently its original date and precise dimensions are not known. *Les Dames Religieuses* of the General Hospital of Quebec, to whom the property belongs, in performing fealty and homage on the 19th March, 1781, produced as their title an act of adjudication, dated September 22, 1733; but which was still indecisive of its dimensions, no notice whatever being taken of the extent. By the regulation of the parishes of the province, it is designated as containing two leagues and a half in breadth, by one and a half in depth. With a surface varied and uneven, this seigniory possesses a rich and fertile soil, which on the large swells and high lands is a lightish loam, but in the hollows and valleys lying between them is generally a good black mould; the situation for all works appertaining to agriculture is so favourable, that full three-fourths of the whole is under tillage; the farms, and indeed the major part of the concessions appear to great advantage, and display many favourable specimens of careful husbandry. In proportion to the increase of cultivation, the quantity of timber has greatly diminished, and at present but little of a superior quality is standing: nor are the common kinds in much greater abundance. It is watered by the Riviere du Cap Rouge, which has its source

among the heights near the back boundaries.
In the serpentine course it describes in passing
diagonally through the seigniory, it sends off
many small branches both to the right and
left; the banks are elevated, but the eminence
is attained by a very gradual slope, or it may be
said more correctly, that it flows through a
narrow valley abounding in natural beauties of
the most picturesque kind, and possessing all
the charms that can be looked for in the most
artful landscape composition. Lake Calviere,
about a mile and a half long, lying between
La Riviere du Cap Rouge and the St. Lawrence, will always obtain a large share of admiration when viewed from the surrounding
heights, where it presents a rich and diversified
prospect, the margin being charmingly varied
by cultivated lands, here and there broken by
small woods and numerous clumps of trees,
rising by gradations from the water's edge one
above the other. The land bordering the St.
Lawrence is the highest in the seigniory, from
whence there is an alternation of ridges and
valleys, the former diminishing in height as
they approach the rear boundary, composing
together a most agreeable undulation in the
perspective scenery. This property is very
conveniently crossed by roads in almost every
direction, and most of them kept in good re-

pair: the one along the front is called the post
road; another passing in the rear to Jacques
Cartier bridge, is denominated the stage road;
.on each side of the Riviere du Cap Rouge
a road leads to the seigniory of Pointe aux
Trembles, with several intermediary ones connecting the principals: by the sides of each of
them are many fine settlements, the houses
well built, and the farms showing every appearance of comfort and even affluence. The church,
seated on a point projecting into the St. Lawrence, a grist and a saw-mill upon a little branch
of Riviere du Cap Rouge, between two lofty
banks just where it discharges into the former,
compose a pleasing point of view either from
the Great River or the eminence just above the
mills. An extensive shoal, or rather reef of rocks,
bounds the whole front of the seigniory: the
Islets Donbour lie upon this reef, opposite the
south-west boundary..

GUILLAUME BONHOMME (the seigniory
of), is situated in the rear of Desmaure, bounded on the south-west by Pointe aux Trembles,
on the north-east by Faussembault, and on the
north-west by the River Jacques Cartier; one
league in breadth by two in depth; was granted November 24th, 1682, to Guillaume Bonhomme. This tract is uneven and mountainous; near Desmaure, which is the lowest and

most level part, the soil is a black mould, but
receding from thence toward the Jacques Cartier, a light-coloured loam prevails, a good
deal covered with loose stones: only a small
portion of the land is in cultivation. The timber is both abundant and good, particularly on
the high grounds towards the rear; but the irrigation is very sparing, as scarcely a stream or
rivulet traverses the interior.

FAUSSEMBAULT (the seigniory of), in the
county of Hants, is bounded on the north-east
by Gaudarville and St. Gabriel, on the south-west
by Guillaume Bonhomme, Pointe aux Trembles, and Bourglouis, on the south-east by Desmaure or St. Augustin, and on the north-west by
waste lands. From St. Augustin to the Jacques
Cartier it is only a narrow slip of land, three quarters of a league broad, and two leagues and a
half deep; but beyond that river it spreads to
a breadth of eight miles, with an additional
depth of three leagues: it was granted February 20th, 1693, to Sieur de Gaudarville, and is
now the property of Juchereau Duchenaye,
Esq. That part of the seigniory lying between
Gaudarville and Guillaume Bonhomme, though
rather mountainous, and particularly so towards
the river, is nevertheless of a good quality; the
land rising gradually affords many opportunities for cultivation; the soil is a middling sort

of loam, or else a layer of black earth, of no great depth, upon a stratum of sand: on the settled places the farms exhibit an appearance of good tillage, and are by no means defective in fertility. There is a tolerable variety of timber; the maple, beech, and birch, are particularly good : inferior wood is in great abundance. Several roads lead to the adjoining seigniories on each side, and one from St. Augustin up to the Jacques Cartier, but there is scarcely a stream to be met with until reaching that river ; from thence northward, it is a mountainous country, continually rising until it approaches the great north-westerly ridge ; it is very well clothed with timber, but generally incapable of cultivation. In the ravines there are some small lakes ; several of the little branches of the Portneuf have their sources on the skirts of the mountains.

GAUDARVILLE or GUARDARVILLE (the seigniory of), in the county of Hants, has its front on the St. Lawrence, is bounded on the north-east by St. Gabriel, on the south-west by St. Augustin and Faussembault, and in the rear by Faussembault also; it is forty-five arpens broad by four leagues in depth; was granted February 8th, 1652, to Louis de Lauson, Sieur de la Citiére. This grant consists of nearly the same species of soil as the preceding ones

D D

of Desmaure and the lower part of Faussembault, though superior in its fertility and good
cultivation. For a distance of nearly two
leagues and a half from the St. Lawrence, it is
entirely settled; but thence it becomes moun--
tainous; with scarcely any part of it under
tillage, though many patches appear to be tolerably good arable land. The front being thickly inhabited has but little timber standing; but
further on good beech, maple, and pine are
found in plenty. Its general fertility is aided
by several little streams that trace a mazy
course through it, and flow into the River St.
Charles, and also by the lower part of the Riviere du Cap Rouge, mentioned in the seigniory
of Desmaure, which still preserves its character
of being eminently beautiful and picturesque;
it feels the attraction of the ebb tide of the St.
Lawrence so strongly, that at low water its bed
is nearly dry, and can be crossed with the
utmost ease without the assistance of the ferry-
boat; but at high water boats of considerable
burthen can enter it and ascend as high as the
mill, about three quarters of a mile from the
St. Lawrence; at its mouth is an established
ferry where boats and scows are always ready,
though, as before observed, they are not always
necessary. On the west side of this river, near
its discharge, there is a gradual slope from the

high bank down to a delightful and well cultivated valley extending almost to the River St.
Charles, and joining the level tract of low land
that spreads for a great distance in the rear of
Quebec. This seigniory is intersected by numerous good roads in all directions; the main
one by the St. Lawrence ascends several steep
acclivities, especially in the vicinity of Cap
Rouge, of which travellers seldom fail to feel the
effect, particularly in the summer time.

SILLERY (the seigniory of), in the county of
Quebec, is bounded by the River St. Lawrence
in the front, Guadarville on the south-west,
part of St. Ignace and several small grants on
the north-east, and by St. Gabriel in the rear;
one league broad by about one league and a
half deep. This grant, originally forming part
of the concession of St. Gabriel, was ceded to
the King in 1664, and granted October 23d,
1669, to the Order of Jesuits: it is now the
property of the crown. The bank of the river
is very high; being the most elevated part of
the seigniory, from whence there is a plain, varied with a few rising grounds, reaching to the
road of Ste. Foi, northward of which for a short
distance is an easy declivity, terminated by a
steep descent into a valley that spreads nearly
to the boundary of St. Gabriel, where again
there is another gradual elevation. The soil is

very good near the St. Lawrence, consisting of a light reddish sandy earth intermixed with clay, in some places lying upon a bed of clay; in the vicinity of Ste. Foi there are many ledges of flat rock covered with a coat of excellent mould, but of no great depth; from the latter place on the slope already mentioned, it is a rich mould mixed with sand, with large quantities of loose stones strewed over its surface, and many massy fragments of granite lying about in various directions; in the valley, and on the rising ground towards La Vielle Lorette, there is some excellent meadow land: nearly the whole of the seigniory is cultivated, and extremely fertile in almost every variety of the productions of the country. Very little timber, of a superior quality is now remaining, or indeed much wood of any description, except what is found in Sillery Wood, and a few other patches that appear to have been left in various parts as much for ornament as for use. Part of the River St. Charles passes through, and it is also watered by several small streams that wind along the valley in a very pleasing manner.. At the place called Sillery Cove there is a plantation of hops, in a situation finely sheltered from every injurious wind, where the climate is friendly to their growth, and the soil admirably well adapted to their culture, which has been car-

ried on for some years with great success; the
'produce is not inferior to what is imported
from England.' Close by the plantation stand
a malt-house, a brewery, and a dwelling-house,
besides many other appendages, the property
of Mr. Hullett, to whom the hop-grounds belong; the two former are entitled to some respect as being the venerable remains of an ancient chapel and some other buildings, erected
in 1637 by the Jesuits, for the residence of a
mission employed in their favourite undertaking of converting the natives to Christianity;
the utter decay of these vestiges of zealous piety
has been for a while suspended, as a few years
since they were repaired and made applicable
to their present uses. Not far from this spot
the nation of the Algonquins had a village, and
it is somewhat remarkable that in Sillery Wood
there yet remains some of the *tumuli* belonging
to their burying-place, and what is still more
worthy of observation, some of their rude
mementos carved on the trees are at this day
sufficiently visible to be traced. In a hollow
a little to the westward of Sillery Cove, on a
gentle eminence now nearly overgrown with
brushwood and creeping shrubbery, are the
remains of a stone building, once the dwelling
of a few female devotees, who, in imitation of
the Jesuits, applied their religious enthusiasm

to convert and instruct the female savages.
On the high bank to the westward bounding
this cove is an elegant, well-built, stone house,
the property of Mr. M'Nider of Quebec; the
situation is commanding and agreeable: the
style both of the exterior and interior of the residence deserves notice.. Many roads in almost
every direction form an easy communication
with Quebec and all the surrounding seigniories;
of these, the one leading by the river side, one
by the church of Ste. Foi, and another by the
village of La Vielle Lorette, are the principal;
on either side of each there are many well-built
houses, with various plantations, and farms in
a very advanced state of improvement, and
strongly indicating the good circumstances of
the proprietors. The front of the seigniory is
indented by several coves, wherein, between
the high bank of the river and the high water
mark, there are level flats that afford most convenient situations for depositing, squaring, and
sorting timber, and staves of all descriptions
when prepared for exportation; and also
beaches for receiving the rafts as they are
brought down the river: these are called timber grounds. The principal of them is Sillery,
or as it is now called Hullett's Cove, that gentleman having obtained from government a
lease of the beach from Pointe à Puisseaux, up

to his present establishment. At a considerable distance from the high-water mark, a long reef of rocks forms a very convenient breakwater, and resists the strong set of the current from reaching the logs, which are otherwise prevented from drifting away, by means of booms secured at different places, either by anchors and grapnels, or to ringbolts in the rocks as most convenient. Westward of this place is another inlet called Ritchie's Cove, and to the eastward another spacious timber-ground called Atkinson's, in each of which there are convenient booms and other securities: the former has the appearance of a small village, from the numerous huts erected for the workmen, &c. To these timber-grounds the rafts intended for them are floated in at high-water through openings in the reef of rocks, and secured within the booms; they are then broken up, the timber sorted, and drawn ashore to proper spots either for seasoning, squaring, or reducing to standard dimensions for exportation.

SAINT GABRIEL (the seigniory of), in the county of Quebec, is bounded on the southwest by Gaudarville, Faussembault, and waste crown lands, on the north-east by St. Ignace, in the front by Sillery, and in the rear by waste crown lands; two leagues in breadth on the front, but as the lateral boundaries do not run parallel, its breadth in the rear is more than four leagues ; its depth is ten leagues ; granted April 16th, 1647, to Sieur Giffard, and is now the property of the crown. Of this tract two leagues and a half were granted March 13th, 1651, to the Hurons inhabiting the village of La Jeune Lorette, and the remainder transferred by donation on the 2d November, 1667, to the Order of Jesuits, by Sieur Giffard. The lower part of this seigniory is good fertile land, the soil in general a fine black mould ; near the first mountains, and in the vicinity of Lake St. Charles, it is a light loam ; the remainder, and much the largest portion of the grant, is so extremely rough and mountainous, as to be wholly unfit for agricultural purposes. Timber about the front is rather scarce, of inferior size and little value ; but on the sides of the rising grounds, and in the interior, beech, maple, and birch, are abundant, and some pine, and now and then a little good oak may be found. The River St. Charles bends a most picturesque course from south-east to north-west, for nearly two leagues along the lower part of the seigniory, and receives the waters of several small tributary streams that completely answer the purposes of irrigation. The Rivers Jacques Cartier, St. Anne, and Batis-

can, cross it at different points between the
mountains. To a distance of about six miles
from the front, all the land is in a flourishing
state of cultivation, every where interspersed
with well-built houses, good gardens and well
stocked farms: beyond this part a wilderness
spreads on every side, dreary and untrodden by
human beings, except the Indians in their
hunting excursions. The church and parsonage of St. Ambroise, the church of La Vielle
Lorette, the church and village of La Jeune
Lorette, one grist-mill and one saw-mill, are all
within this grant; roads in every direction
communicate with Quebec and the surrounding seigniories. The Indian village of La
Jeune Lorette is between eight and nine miles
from Quebec, situated on the eastern side of
the River St. Charles, upon an eminence that
commands a most interesting, varied, and extensive view; the city and environs of Quebec,
always beautiful in whichever way they are
seen together, form a prominent part of it, but
it extends widely over the southern shore, and
is terminated only by the softened forms of the
southern mountains. The number of houses is
between forty and fifty, which on the exterior
have something like an appearance of neatness;
they are principally built of wood, although
there are some few of stone. The inhabitants

are about 250, descendants of the tribe of the Hurons, once so formidable even to the powerful Iroquois, until by stratagem, in which consists much of the glory and self-applause of the savage, the latter, under the specious pretence of alliance, obtained the confidence of their opponents ; when, by an indiscriminate massacre, their whole race was nearly extirpated. The few who escaped with life fled towards the habitations of civilized man, and established themselves among the forests in the rear of Quebec, many hundred miles distance from the land of their ancient tribe on the borders of Lake Huron ; by the efforts of the Jesuits they were gradually drawn nearer to Quebec, and every exertion made to reclaim them from savage life. At present they nearly resemble the other tribes already mentioned, though perhaps in a small degree superior to them in some of the acquirements of civilized life ; but as a counterbalance of evil, their contiguity to the capital affords them numerous opportunities to indulge in many vicious propensities, that they are eager enough to avail themselves of. The Curé of St. Ambroise officiates as missionary among them, and has obtained a considerable influence in religious affairs. In their worldly concerns, as they speak the French language with tolerable fluency, they are sufficiently shrewd, and know how to take care of their own interests. The church of La Vielle Lorette is pleasantly situated on the western side of a little branch of the River St. Charles, on a rising ground, and nearly surrounded by a grove of small but handsome pine-trees. The parsonage-house is the residence of Mr. Deschenaux, the Grand Vicar, and Curé of the parish: this gentleman, who is well known and highly esteemed by a numerous circle of friends, both Catholic and Protestant, of the first rank, has exerted his well known good taste to great advantage upon the gardens and other embellishments of the place, which are on a scale of liberality quite in unison with the general hospitality of his character.

St. Ignace (the seigniory of), in the county of Quebec, is bounded in front by the River St. Charles, on the south-west by Sillery and St. Gabriel, on the north-east by L'Epinay and the township of Stoneham, and in the rear by the seigniory of Hubert; half a league in front by ten leagues in depth; was granted October 20th, 1652, to the community of the Hotel Dieu, to whom it still belongs. With respect to the quality of land and peculiarities of soil, there is a strong affinity between this and the seigniory of St. Gabriel; the lower part is rich, fertile, and well cultivated, for more than

two leagues towards the Lake St. Charles, in
which tract many farms are extremely productive in grain of all species. On some of the
lands flax is cultivated with great success; on
the River St. Charles the pastures and meadows
are so fine as scarcely to be rivalled by any in
the province: beyond the lake the country assumes a mountainous and barren character, affording no land upon which industry could be
exerted with any hopes of success in the way
of agriculture. On the lower part of the seigniory the little timber that remains is of inferior
dimensions, and confined to small woods and
patches here and there; but in the vicinity of
Lake St. Charles and further rearward, a great
abundance of the finest sort is produced. The
Rivers Jacques Cartier, St. Anne, and Batiscan, cross it in the intervals between the different ranges of mountains, while the cultivated
part is exceedingly well watered by the River
and Lake St. Charles, aided by many small
streams. The lake affords one of the most
exquisitely picturesque scenes in the whole
province; it is a narrow irregular figure, rather
more than four miles in length; about midway
a projecting point stretches nearly across, and
leaves only a narrow strait by which the almost
separated waters communicate: situated in a
low flat country, it is entirely surrounded by

hills of considerable elevation, covered with thick woods; these are again greatly over-topped by more distant mountains that rise very abruptly to the northward. The margin presents an appearance at once wild, romantic, and delightful; the devious course of the low banks forms numerous little bays and head-lands, where the trees to the water's edge com-plete, by the variety of their foliage and grada-tion of size as they rise upon the different slopes, one of the richest views that can delight an admirer who prefers a prospect adorned only by the hand of nature to one heightened by the devices of art. This charming panorama is rather more than four leagues from Quebec, and during the spring and summer is frequently visited on account of its arcadian beauty: the road leading to it passes all the way by the side of the River St. Charles, and by its embel-lishments greatly heightens the satisfaction of those who make the excursion, and from whence no one returns without ample gratification.

L'EPINAY (fief), in the county of Quebec, joins St. Ignace, is bounded by the River St. Charles in front, and the township of Stoneham in the rear; eleven arpens in breadth by four leagues in depth; was granted February 28th, 1626, to Louis Hebert.

D'ORSANVILLE (another fief), on the north-cast side of L'Epinay, is a small grant containing only a superficies of 3575 arpens; made —— May, 1675, by Letters Patent from the King to the *Religieuses* of the General Hospital of Quebec; and from whom it has never been alienated. The land in both these pieces is of the same character, being a light sandy earth intermixed with clay about the front part; proceeding inwards it changes to a black mould, and in the vicinity of the mountains it is a good yellow loam : from the River St. Charles the surface is uneven, and continues ridge above ridge to the rear, where it is more abrupt and broken. Near the river there are fine meadows and pastures in both grants; of the arable, about one half is in a state of very good culture, producing wheat and other grain abundantly, with garden vegetables in great quantity and variety for the consumption of the city. The lower parts are but scantily timbered; but on the rising grounds, and on the skirts of the mountains, there is a profusion of fine beech, maple, birch, and other woods of the best description. The little River Jaune, and several small streams, all flowing into the St. Charles, amply and conveniently water the cultivated lands.

HUBERT (the seigniory of), in the county of Quebec, is situated in the rear of the seigniories of St. Gabriel and St. Ignace, and from its remoteness entirely surrounded on the other sides by waste crown lands; two leagues in breadth by as many in depth; was granted June 10th, 1698, to Sieur Réné Louis Hubert. Being so far northward of all the cultivated lands, the quality or worth of this seigniory is wholly unknown; even the timber upon it seems never to have been deemed an object deserving enquiry.

NOTRE DAME DES ANGES (the seigniory of), in the county of Quebec, is situated between D'Orsanville and Beauport, bounded in front by the Rivers St. Charles and St. Lawrence, and in the rear by the township of Stoneham; one league broad and four leagues deep; was granted 10th March, 1626, to the Order of Jesuits; and like their other properties, now reverted to the crown. Within this seigniory the greater part of the land is of a superior quality, and equally pre-eminent for its fertility : about the front it is a good rich earth mixed with clay or sand; beyond this sort, and more to the interior, there is a fine black mould, much drier and more friable than the former; in the rear a good loam prevails; the surface is uneven, and from a fine flat near the river, rises into ridges by easy gradations to the back boundary; and, thereabouts, becomes broken, rough, and mountainous. Of the whole superficies, about two-thirds are in the best state of cultivation, and exceedingly well inhabited. The flat space near the river is called La Canardiere, and is wholly employed as meadows and pasture; the former produce abundant crops of hay of superior quality. The arable lands are very fruitful in grain of all kinds, besides which there is a considerable quantity laid out as garden ground, where vegetables of every description and great excellence are raised for the supply of the capital. The most cultivated parts are sparingly timbered, presenting only occasionally reserves of wood, where the trees are of inferior dimension and of little estimation, but they embellish the country agreeably enough; in the rear wood is abundant, and the land is conceded to the inhabitants in small portions for the purposes of fuel and other domestic uses, of which, exclusive of their own consumption, they continually supply large quantities for the use of Quebec. The beach of the St. Lawrence, in front of the seigniory, is occupied as timber ground, and furnished with extensive booms, and every necessary means of securing the timber. The village of Charlebourg is pleasantly situated on a rising ground of considerable eminence, about a league to the northward of Quebec,

and consists of about forty well-built houses,
mostly of a respectable appearance, with a
handsome church and parsonage-house. A
good garden and small orchard are the appendages of every dwelling. The elections of members of parliament for the county are always
held here. A little below the village, on the
skirts of a small rising ground on the north
side of a concession or cross road, stands
a small group of handsome houses, usually
called the Little Village, which does not yield
in beauty of situation to the other. Of two
roads leading from Dorchester bridge, the one
on the left hand is called Le Chemin de
Charlebourg, and the other La Canardiere, or
Le Chemin de Beauport; on the latter there
is a succession of good houses, excellent gardens, and farms in a high state of cultivation.
Two houses of superior elegance, belonging to
the Honourable P. Debonne, usually attract
notice, by the advantages of a good style of
architecture and excellence of situation, their
beautiful gardens, and surrounding shrubberies
and plantations. There is also a very spacious
house belonging to the Ecclesiastics of the
Seminary of Quebec, generally distinguished
by the appellation of La Maison des Prêtres;
it is retained in their own hands as a farm, and

E E

also serves as a place of recreation for all the members of the establishment once a week.

BEAUPORT (the seigniory of), in the county of Quebec, is bounded on the north-east by the Cote de Beaupré, on the south-west by Notre Dame des Anges, on the front by the St. Lawrence, and in the rear by the township of Stoneham; one league broad by four leagues deep; was granted December 31, 1635, to Robert Giffard, Sieur de Beauport; but by that concession its depth was limited to one league and a half; on the 31st March, 1653, the other two leagues and a half were added to it: it is now the property of Monsieur Duchesnaye. The surface of this seigniory embraces a variety similar to those that surround it, being intersected by ridges of different heights; between the first rise of the ground and the beach of the St. Lawrence, there is a level space ranging the whole breadth of the grant, occupied as meadows, pastures, or gardens; the soil is black mould intermixed with clay or marl: on this flat there are many large globular fragments of granite quite detached, and lying loosely on the surface. From hence, penetrating further to the interior, the soil varies considerably, almost as frequently as the inequalities of the land; on the front ridge, where the road passes, there

are flat ledges of rock, that in some places for
a considerable extent are quite bare, and in
others but very superficially covered with a
layer of earth; more inward these rocks disap-
pear, and are succeeded by a dark mould, or
else a yellowish loam, which continues to the
skirts of the mountains. On the fore parts of
the seigniory there remains but little wood; in
the interior, however, and on the heights, the
timber is of the best quality, beech, birch, and
maple. It is watered by the River Montmorenci on the north-east side, by the Petite Riviere de Beauport, and by many small streams
falling into the St. Lawrence, and forming rivulets along the beach at low water: about two
leagues from the front there is a small lake, and
at a short distance further on the River Jaune;
some small mountain streams flow between the
different ridges. The cultivated land extends
about six miles from the St. Lawrence, and is
for the most part in a state of excellent tillage,
producing all kinds of grain abundantly, vegetables, &c. &c. In various parts of the seigniory there are quarries of stone, that furnish an
excellent supply for the new buildings in the
city and in the neighbourhood; there are also
in many places indications of veins of coal, but
no attempt has yet been made to work them.
A large quantity of maple sugar is made here;

and indeed in all the adjoining seigniories; the process of obtaining it may be described in a few words. In the spring, when the sap begins to rise in the trees, the *habitans* repair to the woods, furnished with kettles, troughs, and all the necessary apparatus for carrying on the manufacture, where they form a temporary encampment: the mode of collecting the sap is by making an incision in the tree, into which is inserted a thin bit of stick to serve as a conductor, from whence, an hour or two after sunrise, the sap begins to trickle down into a trough placed to receive it; when a sufficient quantity of this liquor is obtained from several trees, it is put into an iron kettle and boiled, until it comes to the consistence of a thick syrup; it is then cooled, and afterwards subjected to another process of boiling and clarifying. When this is sufficiently performed in proportion to the degree of purity they intend to give it, it is put into vessels of different sizes to harden, containing from half a pound to eight or ten pounds. Its colour is of all shades between a dark and a light brown, according to the care that is taken in clarifying it; indeed, by a repetition of the process it may be rendered as white as common refined sugar. Being considered very wholesome, the use of it is general among the country people for all purposes, and the consumption of it is considerable in families of respectability for ordinary occasions; the price of it varies from three pence halfpenny to six-pence per pound. It is constantly to be had in the market of Quebec. The roads communicating with the adjacent grants are enlivened by houses and gardens at short intervals from each other, throughout nearly their whole distance. On the road leading to the capital, the populous village of Beauport is situated on a gently rising ground; it contains from sixty to seventy houses, many of them built of stone, and distinguished by great neatness in their exterior appearance: the church and parsonage-house are situated on the south side of the road; the former is much more observable for its solidity than for beauty or embellishment: regularity and neatness are prevalent through the whole village. On each side of the road also, the farm and other houses are so thickly placed, that they seem to be a prolongation of the place itself; the farm-lands and garden-grounds, all in a most flourishing state; the orchards and occasional clumps of trees, all combine to render it one of the most pleasant roads in the environs of Quebec. This village is the residence of many families of the first respectability, besides tradesmen, artizans, and farmers. Westward of the church, on the declivity of the hill, stands a manor-house, an ancient irregular stone building, designed originally for defence as well as residence: the extraordinary thickness and solidity of the walls, were it perceptible from the exterior, would attract notice; but its other advantages are not of a nature to solicit a passenger's observation. A little to the westward of this house, and on the bank of the River Beauport, are the distillery and mills, erected about twenty-five years ago by the Honourable John Young at a very great expense; they are seated on the western bank of the river, over which there is a bridge leading past them; the former belongs at present to Mr. Racy, and the latter to Mr. Mc Callum. The buildings and other appurtenances of the distillery form a hollow square exceeding two hundred yards on each side: in the middle of this square are several large stone buildings communicating with each other, and containing a still-house, malt-house, granary, machinery, &c. of every description for carrying on the whole process of distillation and rectifying to a very large extent. The River Beauport is navigable as high up as these premises, for small decked vessels that can come along the wharf adjoining. The gentleman who built these works was also proprietor of an extensive brewery at St. Roch's, in both of which concerns he gave employment for some years to several hundred persons; but they were found to have been undertaken upon too great a scale for the consumption of the province at that period. Mr. Young's abilities were of a superior class, and having attracted the notice of Lord Dorchester when Governor-General, procured for him the nomination to a seat in the executive council, wherein, as well as in the provincial government, of which for three or four sessions he was a distinguished member, his talents were always exerted in favour of measures calculated for the benefit and interest of the province. The mill is both extensive and complete, in a building three stories high; the water for working it is received from the Beauport into a large reservoir or dam above the road, from whence it is conveyed to the mill by an aqueduct. On an eminence to the north-eastward are two handsome stone dwelling-houses with gardens and summer-houses, surrounded by a wall; from their singularly beautiful situation, and the rich prospect they command over the basin of Quebec and surrounding distant objects, they obtain much notice: the Honourable H. W. Ryland is proprietor of both. The Falls of the Montmorenci present the most majestic spectacle of the neighbourhood, and indeed one of

the grandest in the province; they have been
frequently described, and with so much correctness, that a slight notice of them may now suffice.
The river, in its course through a country that
is almost a continued forest, rolls a stream of
very trifling consequence, unless when swelled
by the melting snow in spring, or autumnal
rains, over an irregular broken rocky bottom,
until it arrives at the precipice, where its breadth
is from sixteen to twenty yards. A little declination of the bed before it reaches this
point gives a great velocity to the stream,
which, in being impelled over the brink of a
perpendicular rock, falls in an extended sheet
of water, of a whiteness and fleecy appearance
nearly resembling snow, into a chasm among
the rocks two hundred and forty feet below.
An immense spray rises from the bottom in
curling volumes, which when the sunshine displays their bright prismatic colours, produce an
effect inconceivably beautiful. At the bottom
of the fall the water is restrained within a basin
formed by the rocks, from whence, after its
impetuosity is subdued, it flows in a gentle
stream into the St. Lawrence, a distance, perhaps, of two hundred and eighty or three hundred yards. The summer-house built by the
late General Haldimand, and mentioned by
Mr. Weld and others for its appalling situation

as projecting over the great precipice, still remains: if it be true that at the time of his visit the beams had begun to feel the gnawing tooth of time, they must be now in a very precarious state; indeed, it would be prudent to have it removed immediately, rather than allow it to fall by its natural decay; for while it keeps its present position, curiosity will attract many an unwary visitant, and perhaps ultimately produce a fatal catastrophe. The provincial parliament has recently passed an act for erecting a bridge across the Montmorenci. The houses, farms, &c. near the river, formerly the property of General Haldimand, now belong to —— Patterson, Esq. From Dorchester bridge, passing towards the falls, some traces yet remain of the field fortifications thrown up by the French in the memorable year 1759, as a defence against the British army. Along the beach there is a road at low water, which, when practicable, is always preferred by the country people, passing with their carts and sleighs to and from market, not only because it is rather shorter than the high road, but for the much more important reason of its saving the toll at Dorchester bridge.

The description of the various seigniories on the north side of the River St. Lawrence having brought us close down to Quebec, an account

of that capital may be appropriately introduced. Some notice has been taken already of
its situation and convenience as a sea-port, in
the observations that have been made upon
the River St. Lawrence; but it will perhaps be
excused, should the same points be again adverted to in giving a detailed description of the
city, &c. From the time that Cartier visited
Canada, up to the period that the concerns of
the colony came under the superintendance of
Champlain, (about seventy years), the French
settlers and adventurers were dispersed over
various parts of the sea-coast, or islands in the
Gulf of St. Lawrence, as each, or a few together, discovered convenient places to fix their
habitations in; during that time none of them
had attempted to settle on or near the Great
River. The selection of a situation and building a town, wherein the benefits and habits of
social life might be enjoyed, and from whence
the management of the trading intercourse
with the natives, and the government of the
colony, could be more advantageously carried
on than what they hitherto had been, was
reserved for Samuel de Champlain, Geogra-
pher to the King: acting under a commission
from the Sieur de Monts, (who a little while
before had obtained from the court of France
the exclusive privilege of trading between Cape

Raze in Newfoundland, and the fortieth degree of north latitude), he in 1608 made choice of the site of an Indian village called Stadaconé, upon the promontory, now named Cape Diamond, and there, in the month of July, laid the foundation of the metropolis of New France, which has through many vicissitudes risen into importance, and at the present day maintains a distinguished rank among those of the greatest consequence on the northern division of the new hemisphere.—No less difference of opinion has arisen as to the origin of its name, than about that of Canada; and the result of the disputes has not been more satisfactory in fixing its derivation: whether it comes from the Algonquin, Abenaqui, or Norman languages, to each of which conjecture has assigned it, we have not the means of verifying; nor is it indeed very material: it is enough to know that Champlain called his new town Quebec. The progress of its aggrandisement there is much reason to believe was slow; for the new settlers, and indeed Champlain at their head, were not only so impolitic as to encourage the prosecution of hostilities between the two neighbouring nations of the Algonquins and Iroquois, but even to join the former against the latter. This interference drew upon the French the hatred of the powerful Iroquois, and was the means of involving the whole colony in a long and most destructive warfare; which, at an early period, rendered some defensive fortifications necessary to protect Quebec from the enmity of her new, but implacable enemies. The defences were at first of the rudest description, being nothing more than embankments, strengthened with palisades. In 1629 it was in an untenable state against the English, and fell into their hands; but, with the whole of Canada, was restored to its former master in 1632. From this period some attention was paid to the increase of the town, until 1663, when the colony was made a royal government, and it became the capital. Its progress towards prosperity was then somewhat accelerated.

From its growing importance, the English were desirous to recover possession of the place that a few years before, there would scarcely have been started an objection against their retaining, and made an unsuccessful, because ill-timed attempt, in the latter part of the year 1690, to reconquer it, which was attended with a disastrous result, and a severe loss. As the place obtained consequence, and became an object of desire to other and far more powerful enemies than the native savages, it was in the last mentioned year fortified in a more regular manner by works according to the rules of art, built of stone, which, from that period,

have been carefully attended to, and by continual additions and rebuildings, are now improved into bulwarks that may stand in competition with some of the best constructed and
strongest fortifications of Europe. From 1690
the increase was gradual while it remained
under the French government; but since that
period its progress towards prosperity has been
much more rapid. The situation of Quebec is
unusually grand and majestic, in form of an
amphitheatre; it is seated on a promontory on
the north-west side of the St. Lawrence, formed
by that river and the St. Charles: the extremity
of this headland is called Cape Diamond, whose
highest point rises three hundred and forty-five
feet above the level of the water; it is composed
of a rock of grey granite mixed with quartz
crystals (from which it obtains its name), and
a species of dark-coloured slate; in many places
it is absolutely perpendicular and bare; in
others, where the acclivity is less abrupt, there
are patches of brownish earth, or rather a de-
composition of the softer parts of the stone, on
which a few stunted pines and creeping shrubs
are here and there seen; but the general aspect
of it is rugged and barren. From the highest
part of the Cape, overlooking the St. Lawrence,
there is a declination towards the north by
flattish ridges of a gradual decrease, as far as

the steep called Coteau Ste. Genevieve, from
whence the descent is more than one hundred
feet nearly perpendicular; at the foot of it the
ground is level, and continues so as far as the
River St. Charles, and in fact far beyond it. The
distance across the peninsula from one river to
the other, in front of the line of fortification, is
one thousand eight hundred and thirty-seven
yards; these fortifications may be called the *en-
ceinte* of the city, and the circuit within them
upon which it stands is about two miles and
three quarters; out of this space forty acres or
thereabouts on Cape Diamond are occupied by
or reserved for military works. From the Cape
in a north-easterly direction, there is an easy
diminution in the height of the rock of about
one hundred and fifteen feet to the Castle of
St. Louis and the grand battery, that crests a
perpendicular steep of two hundred and thirty
feet above the level of the river, overlooking
the lower town. This altitude and frowning
appearance continues with very little alteration
round the town as far as the entrance called
Palace Gate, where it sinks to the ridge already
mentioned at the foot of Coteau Ste. Genevieve, and continues its course at nearly the
same elevation, through the parish of St. Foi,
connecting itself with Cape Rouge, and forming between the River St. Lawrence, the valley

through which the St. Charles flows, and that
under Cape Rouge, an height of land about
eight miles long, rising above the general level,
like an island above the surface of the ocean.
The city, beside the distinction of Upper and
Lower Towns, is divided into domains and
fiefs, as the King's and Seminary's domains;
Fief St. Joseph; ground belonging to the Hotel
Dieu; the Fabrique, or church lands; and the
lands that formerly belonged to the Order of
Jesuits: these, with the military reserves, constitute the principal divisions, in which the suburbs are not included. In the year 1759 the
population of Quebec was estimated between
eight and nine thousand; at present, including
the suburbs, it is about 18,000. The public
edifices are the Castle of St. Louis, the Hotel
Dieu, the convent of the Ursulines, the monastery of the Jesuits, now turned into barracks,
the Protestant and Catholic cathedrals, the
Scotch church, the Lower Town church; the
court-house, the seminary, the new gaol, and
the artillery barracks; there are two market-
places, a place d'armes, a parade, and an
esplanade. Of these buildings the Castle of St.
Louis, being the most prominent object on the
summit of the rock, will obtain the first notice:
it is a handsome stone building, seated near the
edge of a precipice, something more than two

hundred feet high, and supported towards the
steep by a solid work of masonry, rising nearly
half the height of the edifice, and surmounted
by a spacious gallery, from whence there is a
most commanding prospect over the bason,
the Island of Orleans, Point Levi, and the surrounding country. The whole pile is one hundred and sixty-two feet long, by forty-five broad,
and three stories high; but in the direction of
the Cape it has the appearance of being much
more lofty: each extremity is terminated by a
small wing, giving to the whole an easy and
regular character: the interior arrangement is
convenient, the decorative part tasteful and
splendid, suitable in every respect for the residence of the governor-general. It was built
shortly after the city was fortified with solid
works, consequently had but little to recommend it to notice: for a long series of years it
was neglected so much as to be suffered to go
to decay, and ceasing to be the residence of
the commander-in-chief, was used only for the
offices of government until the year 1808, when
a resolution passed the provincial parliament
for repairing and beautifying it; the sum of
£7000 was at the same time voted, and the
work forthwith commenced. The money applied was inadequate to defray the expenses
upon the grand scale the improvements were

commenced, but an additional grant was
made to cover the whole charge; and in the
present day, as a residence for his Majesty's
representative, it is highly creditable to the
liberality and public spirit of the province:
Sir James Craig was the first who took possession of it. The part properly called the Chateau occupies one side of the square, or court-
yard; on the opposite side stands an extensive
building, divided among the various offices of
government both civil and military, that are
under the immediate control of the governor;
it contains also a handsome suite of apartments,
wherein the balls and other public entertain-
ments of the court are always given. During
the dilapidated state of the Chateau, this
building was occupied by the family of the
governors. Both the exterior and the interior
are in a very plain style; it forms part of the
curtain that ran between the two exterior bastions of the old fortress of St. Louis; adjoining
it are several other buildings of smaller size,
appropriated to similar uses, a guard-house,
stables, and extensive riding-house. The fortress of St. Louis covered about four acres of
ground, and formed nearly a parallelogram;
on the western side two strong bastions on each
angle were connected by a curtain, in the centre
of which was a sallyport; the other faces pre-

F F

sented works of nearly a similar description, but of less dimensions. Of these works only a few vestiges remain, except the eastern wall, which is kept in solid repair. The new guard-house and stables, both fronting the parade, have a very neat exterior: the first forms the arc of a circle, and has a colonnade before it; the stables are attached to the riding-house, which is spacious, and in every way well adapted for its intended purpose; it is also used for drilling the city militia. On the south-west side of the Chateau there is a most excellent and well stocked garden, one hundred and eighty yards long, and seventy broad; and on the opposite side of Rue des Carrieres there is another, one hundred and seven yards long by eighty-four broad, both for the use of the governor: the latter was ori-ginally intended for a public promenade, and planted with fine trees, many of which yet remain.

The court-house on the north side of St. Louis Street is a large modern stone structure, the roof of which is covered with tin; its length is one hundred and thirty-six feet, and breadth forty-four, presenting a regular handsome front, approached by a flight of steps leading to an arched entrance, from whence a vestibule on each side communicates to every part of the building. The ground floor apartments are disposed for holding the quarter sessions, and other inferior courts, offices of clerks of the different courts of law, &c. &c. Above stairs there is a spacious chamber, in which the courts of King's Bench and Common Pleas, the Court of Appeals, and the Admiralty Court are held, with separate offices for the high sheriffs and other magistrates, and a room for the occasional convening of militia courts-martial. In the same building is the hall and offices of the corporation of the Trinity-house of Quebec, established by an act of the Provincial Parliament in the 45th year of George the 3d. The embellishments of this edifice, both interior and external, are in a style of simplicity and neatness; the arrangements for public business methodical and judicious; the whole may be considered a great ornament to the city, and does honour to the liberality of the province, thus to provide for the easy and expeditious administration of justice. It occupies part of the site upon which stood an old monastery, church, and garden of the Recollets, destroyed by fire in the year 1796: it was at one time a very extensive establishment, covering the whole space between the parade, Rue des Jardins, de St. Louis, and de Ste. Anne; the order is now extinct in Canada.

The Protestant Cathedral is situated near the court-house; and parallel with Ste. Anne Street: it is one hundred and thirty-six feet long, by seventy-five broad, built of a fine grey stone, the roof covered with tin, which, being continually bright, gives a remarkable appearance of lightness and elegance to the whole structure; it occupies part of the ground of the Recollets, or Franciscans. This is, perhaps, the handsomest modern edifice of the city, and though not highly decorated, the style of architecture is chaste and correct; in the interior, a neat and unostentatious elegance prevails, wherein ornament is judiciously but sparingly introduced. There is a principal entrance at each end of the church, approached by a flight of steps: the fitting up of the inside is commodious and handsome, corresponding with the unassuming beauty of the whole. The organ is of a very superior power. The spire is lofty, light, and elegant, being covered with tin, and the church standing upon nearly the highest ground within the city, is a very conspicuous object at an immense distance; taken altogether, this is the most faultless structure in the place, or indeed within the whole province.

The Catholic Cathedral stands on the north side of Buade Street, fronting the market-

place, on ground belonging to the Fabrique, or
in other words, church-land. It is a lofty, spacious, plain stone edifice, two hundred and sixteen feet in length, by one hundred and eight
in breadth : the interior is divided by ranges
of arches into a nave and two aisles ; at the
upper end of the former is the grand altar,
placed in the middle of a circular choir, that
for the height of about sixteen feet is lined
with wainscot divided into square compartments, each including a portion of Scripture
history represented in relief; the spaces between the squares are wrought into different
devices. In the side aisles there are four
chapels, dedicated to different saints. Being
whitewashed, the interior has always the appearance of neatness and cleanliness. On the
outside, the solidity of the building may perhaps attract a spectator's notice ; but nothing
like taste in design, or graceful combination
of architectural embellishment, will arrest his
attention. The steeple is lofty, with an air of
lightness not altogether devoid of beauty, and
like the roof, is covered with bright tin ; but
for some cause, that perhaps could only be
traced to an affectation of singularity, it sets
the rules of art and symmetry at defiance, and
instead of springing from the roof, it is placed
on one side of the front. The church is dedi-

cated to Notre Dame de Victoire, and is sufficiently spacious to contain a congregation of
about 4000 persons.   A few years ago it was
not equal to the accommodation of the increased population; but the erection of galleries
has, for the present, remedied that inconvenience.   The organ is an excellent one.   The
presbytery is the residence of the curate and
four vicars of the cathedral, and has a covered
avenue leading from it to the church; there is
also a similar one between the church and the
seminary.

The extensive building called the Seminary
of Quebec stands near the cathedral, and is
within the precinct of the seminary's domain,
occupying with its attached buildings, court-
yard, gardens, &c. a large space of ground.   It
is a substantial stone edifice, principally two
stories high, though some portions of it have
been raised to three: it forms three sides of a
square, each about seventy-three yards in length,
with a breadth of forty feet; the open side is to
the north-west.   This establishment, originally
intended for ecclesiastical instruction exclu-
sively, was founded in the year 1663, by M.
de Petré, under the authority of letters patent
granted by the King of France; the early regulations have long been departed from, and
at present students of the Catholic persuasion,

intended for any profession, may enjoy the advantage of it. It is divided into two branches, distinguished as the Grand and Petit Seminaire. The studies of the superior department are conducted under the superintendance of M. Robert, who is himself professor of philosophy, three directors, and a competent number of professors in the different branches of literature and science. The ability and zeal of these gentlemen are sufficiently attested by the great number of pupils who have been dismissed from under their care, possessing every accomplishment of a learned, liberal, and polished education. M. Parent is director of the Petit Seminaire, which is exceedingly useful as a general school, wherein great numbers are educated free of expense, excepting only the trifling sum of five shillings per year as a compensation for fuel; boarders are also received on the very moderate pension of twelve pounds ten shillings per annum. The interior plan of this structure is judicious, and the arrangement very convenient: it contains all requisite domestic apartments, halls for the senior and junior classes, residences for the superior, directors, professors, and different masters. The situation is airy and salubrious; the house is surrounded by large productive gardens, enclosed by a wall, and extending in depth to the grand battery, where it overlooks the harbour : the length is one hundred and seventy-two yards, and the breadth two hundred. It is well laid out and ornamented by many handsome trees. In the year 1703, the whole of the buildings belonging to the seminary were destroyed by fire, and no time was lost in replacing them ; when, unfortunately, they again fell a sacrifice to a similar calamity in 1705. The Catholic Bishop of Quebec has fixed his residence in the seminary, where he lives surrounded and respected by his clergy, and not less esteemed by the laity of all persuasions for his learning, piety, and urbanity. The Hotel Dieu, including under that name the convent, hospital, church, court-yard, cemetery, and gardens, contains within its walls a space of ground extending from the French burying-ground, or Cimetiere des Picotés, to the Rue des Pauvres, or Palace Street, a length of two hundred and ninety-one yards by a depth of one hundred and ninety-six from Couillard Street to the rear wall. This establishment, for the reception of the sick poor of both sexes, was founded by the Duchess D'Aiguillon, in 1637, through whose charitable zeal some nuns were sent from France for the purpose of commencing it, and superintending its progress. The principal structure is three hundred and eighty-tree feet in length, by fifty in breadth; from the centre on the west side, a *corps de logis* ranges a length of one hundred and forty-eight feet, and of a proportionate breadth: the whole is two stories high, substantially built of stone, with more regard to interior convenience than attention to symmetry, and totally devoid of architectural decorations. It contains the convent, hospital, and nearly all the domestic offices. The church, about one hundred feet in length by forty in breadth, facing the Hotel Dieu Street, has nothing to recommend it to notice but the plain neatness of both its interior and exterior. The convent contains the residence of the superieure, and accommodations for all the sisters of the congregation. The hospital is divided into wards for the sick, wherein both sexes receive nourishment, medicine, and attendance, free of all expense. This charitable institution produces extensive benefit to the community, and continually affords relief to great numbers suffering under the accumulated oppression of disease and poverty; the funds by which it is supported are derived from landed property within the city, from whence it is entitled to all *lods et ventes;* also from the revenues of some seigniories that have been granted to it; and although these are considerable, yet, from the liberality and extensive nature of the disbursements, the expenditure so nearly balances the revenue, that it requires, and occasionally receives, grants of public money. The whole administration, care, and attendance of the establishment, are conducted by a superieure, La Reverende Mere Ste. Claire, (Venerande Melançon), and thirty-two sisters, to whose zeal in the offices of humanity must be attributed the state of comfort, cleanliness, and good arrangement, that invariably obtains the encomiums of every stranger who visits the institution.

The Ursuline Convent is situated a short distance to the northward of St. Louis Street, within the fief of St. Joseph, a property that belongs to it: it is a substantial stone edifice, two stories high, forming a square, whose side is one hundred and twelve feet; the building is forty feet broad, containing ample and convenient accommodation for all its inmates. The church of St. Ursula, connected with the convent, is ninety-five feet long by forty-five in breadth, very plain on the outside, but eminently distinguished for the good taste and richness of its interior ornaments; to the eastward of it are several detached buildings, forming part of the establishment. The surrounding ground, six hundred and forty-five feet long, and four hundred and thirty-six broad, is encircled by a lofty stone wall, and, with the exception of a space allotted to the court-yard, is laid out in fine productive gardens. This institution, for the purpose of extending the benefits of a careful and religious education to the females of the colony, owes its foundation in the year 1639, to Madame de la Peltrie, a lady residing in France: it consists of a superieure, La Reverende Mere Sainte Ursule, (Marguerite Marchand), and forty-five nuns, who are employed in the instruction of the pupils in the most useful branches of knowledge, besides embroidery, fine work, and other female accomplishments. The religieuses live very recluse, and are more rigid in their manner than any other in the province. The landed property of the institution is not very great, but the industry of the sisters is incessant, and the profits arising from it are all placed to the general stock, which thereby is rendered sufficiently ample: their embroidery is highly esteemed, particularly for ecclesiastical vestments, and church ornaments; their fancy-works are so much admired, that some of them obtain considerable prices; the produce of their gardens, beyond their own consumption, also serves to increase the revenue of the community. The building is exceedingly neat,

and some parts thereof tastefully decorated.
This establishment being well worth inspection, is usually visited by strangers; for which
purpose a permission or introduction from the
Catholic Bishop is necessary, and always will-
ingly granted upon an application being made.
The Monastery of the Jesuits, now converted
into a barrack, is a spacious stone building,
three stories high, forming a square, or rather
parallelogram of two hundred feet by two hundred and twenty-four, inclosed within a wall
extending more than two hundred yards along
Ste. Anne Street, and the whole of Rue de la
Fabrique. On the arrival of some of the order
in Canada in 1635, their first care was the
erection of a suitable habitation, which being
destroyed some years afterwards, made way
for the present structure: it was formerly surrounded by extensive and beautiful gardens;
but these, to the great regret of many, have
been destroyed since the house, in common
with the other property of the order, has reverted to the crown, and now form a place of
exercise for the troops; indeed, no one could
view without much reluctance the fall of some
of the stately and venerable trees, yet untouch-
ed by decay, that were the original tenants of
the ground at the first foundation of the city.
As a building, this is one of the most regular

of any in the place; when inhabited by its founders, it is said to have been planned with every attention to convenience they were so capable of bestowing upon it; but the nature of the arrangement for its present occupants being so well known to every one, they do not attract our notice.

The New Gaol is a very handsome building of fine grey stone, one hundred and sixty feet in length by sixty-eight in breadth, three stories high, having its roof covered with tin; it is situated on the north side of Ste. Anne Street, with the front towards Angel Street; standing on an elevated spot, it is airy and healthful; it has in the rear a space of ground one hundred feet in depth confined by a lofty wall, where the prisoners are allowed the benefit of exercise. The interior is most judiciously planned, as it respects the health, cleanliness, and safe custody of those who are so unfortunate as to become its inmates. The design and construction confer much credit upon the architect; and the commissioners under whose superintendance it was erected; it has been but recently finished, and was occupied only in 1814. The expense of the building, upwards of £15,000, was defrayed by the provincial legislature.

Opposite to the new gaol is the Scotch Church, a small building not distinguished for any thing deserving particular mention, but being new and very neat, it looks well.

The building denominated the Bishop's Palace has been a fine edifice, and standing on an elevated spot, it is very conspicuous; it is situated near the grand battery, extending in an easterly direction from the gateway, or communication to the Lower Town, along Mountain Street one hundred and eighteen feet, and then in a line running at right angles to the former, one hundred and forty-seven feet; its average breadth is thirty-four feet; on the south and east sides it is three stories high, but on the others no more than two; it was built for the residence of the Catholic Bishop of Quebec; it contained a chapel with every suitable convenience, and was by no means destitute of embellishment. An annuity has been granted by the government to the head of the Catholic faith in lieu of it. A very dilapidated state at present threatens a speedy dissolution; some of the walls are bad even to the foundation, and unless almost immédiate repairs are undertaken will not long support the fabric. The different divisions of the building are now occupied by many of the offices of government; the Legislative Council, the Executive Council, the House of Assembly, the Public Library, &c. &c. The chapel, sixty-five feet by thirty-six, the only part kept in thorough repair, is fitted up for the meetings of the House of Assembly; adjoining it are different committee rooms, library, &c.: above this part, that forms the north-west angle, is the apartment where the Legislative Council holds its sittings, and on the same floor are committee rooms, council office, &c. &c. dependant on that branch of the legislature. In the other angle are chambers for the Executive Council and various offices connected with it; at the further end of the building is the Public Library, below which are the offices of the adjutant-general of militia, surveyor-general of the province, the engineer department, secretary of the province, and some others. The vaults underneath the palace, excepting such as are appropriated to the secretary of the province and clerks of the court, and occupied as depositories of the archives and most of the public records, are in a ruinous state; indeed so much so under the chamber of the legislative council, where the session of parliament is always opened, that it is now hazardous to admit a large concourse of people, who usually attend that ceremony. The public convenience of this building for the various purposes to which it is now applied makes it a matter of surprise that the attention of government has not been directed towards giving it a substantial repair.

The Artillery Barracks form a range of stone buildings two stories high, five hundred and twenty-seven feet in length by forty in breadth, extending in a westerly direction from Palace Gate; they were erected previous to the year 1750, for the accommodation of troops, by which the garrison was reinforced, and were then distinguished as the *casernes nouvelles*: they are roughly constructed, but very substantial and well arranged: the east end of the range was for several years used as a common prison; but since the erection of the new gaol, this practice has been discontinued. Besides sufficient room for quartering the artillery soldiers of the garrison, there is an ordnance office, armoury, storehouses, and workshops. The armoury is very considerable, and occupies several apartments, wherein small arms of every description for the equipment of 20,000 men are constantly kept in complete repair and readiness for immediate use; the musquetry and other fire-arms are arranged so as to admit convenient access for the purposes of cleaning, &c.; the *armes blanches* of all classes are well displayed in various designs and emblematical devices, and present, on entering the room, a fanciful *coup d'œil*. In front of the barracks there is a good parade. The Union Hotel is situated near the Chateau, on the north side of the Grand Parade, and contributes greatly towards its embellishment; it is a capacious well-built stone house, two stories high, in a handsome style of modern architecture, eighty-six feet in length, by forty-four in breadth. It was erected about the year 1803, under an act of the provincial parliament, by a number of persons who raised a sufficient joint stock by shares, and who, by the act, were formed into a corporate body; the object was to have a commodious hotel of the first respectability, for the reception and accommodation of strangers arriving in the capital. The entrance is under a portico of good proportions and tasteful design, approached by a flight of steps. The interior is well planned, with much attention to regularity and convenience; the principal rooms are spacious and lofty, fitted up with great elegance, and continually kept in good order. The scheme that first gave rise to this undertaking did not obtain so much success as could be wished to so public spirited an enterprise: in fact, the shareholders find the speculation to be an unprofitable, and even a losing one. Should the property be disposed of, and diverted from its original intention, a circumstance by no means impro-

bable, it would be well worth the attention of
government to make the purchase, for the purpose of concentrating therein as many of the
public offices as accommodation could be found
for. The edifices that have been enumerated
are the principal ones, or at least those most
worthy of notice. The peculiar situation of
the city, as already described, occasions irregularity and unevenness in the streets; many of
them are narrow, but most of them are well
paved; the breadth of the principal ones is
thirty-two feet, but the others usually only from
twenty-four to twenty-seven. The greater proportion of the houses are built of stone, very
unequal in their elevation, with high sloping
roofs, principally of shingles, and sometimes
covered with tin or sheet iron. Great improvement has taken place of late years in the mode of
building and in the appearance of the dwellings,
as the old-fashioned methods of the country are
gradually superseded by a modern style. No
less amendment has taken place in paving the
streets. Mountain Street, where formerly the
ascent was so steep as to make it difficult for
a carriage, is now passable for all sorts of vehicles with the greatest ease. John Street,
Buade Street, Fabrique Street, and the greater
part of Palace Street, may be considered as the
mercantile part of the Upper Town, being in-

habited chiefly by merchants, retail traders, artizans, and abundance of tavern-keepers, and are certainly the greatest thoroughfare of any. St. Louis Street, running nearly parallel to St. John Street, is much more elevated, airy, and agreeable, and by far the pleasantest part of the town ; as such, most of the superior officers of the provincial government, and people of the first rank, reside there : many of the houses are modern and very handsome ; that belonging to the late T. A. Coffin, Esq., is now inhabited by the Protestant Bishop of Quebec, who, by his situation of Metropolitan, is member of the Legislative and Executive Councils of the Upper, as well as the Lower Province. The present Chief Justice, the Honourable Jonathan Sewell, occupies a very spacious and handsome house ; that of the late Chief Justice Elmsly, though not modern, is large and elegant. It is at present converted into a barrack for officers, who have the greatest reason to be satisfied with their quarters. On Mount Carmel there is the remnant of an old military work, near to which is agreeably situated a wooden building, usually occupied by the governor's military secretary. The market-place is one hundred and sixty-five feet long ; in front of the Jesuits barracks it is two hundred and fifty feet broad, but near the cathedral it is reduced to

one hundred and seventy-two. In the centre
stands the market hall, a circular building, one
hundred and twelve feet diameter, over which
there is a dome, whose dimensions are every
way so much at variance with proportion as to
warrant a supposition that deformity had been
studied instead of symmetry; it is, however,
no longer to remain a public mark of bad taste,
for the legislature has decreed its removal, to
make way for something more appropriate.
Underneath the hall is a large reservoir of
water, contrived to afford a speedy supply in
cases of fire. The accommodations of the
place have been considerably increased by the
removal of the Jesuits church, and appropriation of the ground it occupied to the wood-
market. On the side of Fabriqué Street is the
space allotted to the hay-market. Main streets
diverge from the different sides of the market
to the principal entrances into the city. The
market is held every day, and almost always
well stocked; but Saturday usually affords the
greatest abundance, when there is a good shew
of butcher's meat of all kinds, furnished both
by the butchers of the city, and the *habitans*,
who bring it from several miles round. The
supplies of poultry, fish, fruit, vegetables,
herbs, and indeed every article of consumption,
are brought by the country people in large

quantities from the different fertile seigniories round the capital. In fact, nothing is wanting to furnish the table, and that too at a moderate price, for every rank of society, from the humble labourer to the man of affluence, who can enjoy both the comforts and luxuries of life.

The Place d'Armes, or Grand Parade, in front of the Chateau, though not extensive, is handsome, and may be termed the court end of the town. Being surrounded by the most distinguished edifices in the capital, it affords an agreeable promenade.

The Esplanade, between St. Louis and St. John's Gate, has a length of two hundred and seventy-three yards, by an average breadth of eighty; except at the St. Ursula bastion, where it is one hundred and twenty yards; it is tolerably level, in some places presenting a surface of the bare rock. This is the usual place of parade for the troops of the garrison, from whence every morning the different guards of the town are mounted. The musters, and annual reviews of the militia belonging to the city, are held here.

The Lower Town is situated immediately under Cape Diamond, and by the continuation of merchants' stores and warehouses, reaches from L'Ance des Mères round the point of the Cape, as far to the north-west as the suburbs of St. Roch: it stands on what may be termed an

artificial ground, as formerly, at flood tide, the
waters of the river used to wash the very foot of
the rock : from time to time, wharf after wharf
has been projected towards the low-water mark,
and foundations made sufficiently solid to build
whole streets, where once boats, and even vessels
of considerable burden, used to ride at anchor.
The greatest breadth of this place is at Rue Sous
le Fort, where, from the Cape to the water's
edge, the distance is two hundred and forty
yards, but proceeding more to the northward,
this dimension is greatly reduced.   L'Ance des
Mères, or Diamond Harbour, is the southern
extremity of the Lower Town; it is immediately under the highest part of Cape Diamond,
having around its shore a continuation of extensive wharfs, stores, and workshops in full
activity, from which there is an uninterrupted
routine of business carried on with other parts
of the town.   A commodious dock for repairing vessels, and a yard for building, from
whence ships of large tonnage have frequently
been launched, contribute very much 'to increase the importance of the place.   From
L'Ance des Mères to Brehaut's Wharf, the road
passing by the foot of the Cape is very narrow,
and that the communication may be rendered
as direct as possible, it has been necessary in
many places to cut through the solid rock.
Near the wharf there is a landing-place, which

serves during the summer season as a sort of harbour for the gunboats and king's batteaux. From thence to the Cul de Sac is almost an uninterrupted succession of store-houses and wharfs, at the greatest part of which ships can lie without taking the ground at low water. At Dunn's Wharf are the large and valuable premises called the Cape Diamond Brewery, where an extensive business is carried on, not for the home consumption alone, but in porter and ale for exportation. The Cul de Sac is situated between the King's and Queen's Wharfs, forming an open dock, dry at every tide; ships can be there conveniently laid aground to receive any necessary repairs; in the winter, boats and small-decked vessels that navigate the river between Quebec and Montreal are also laid up in security from the ice. It spreads five hundred and forty feet in length, and about two hundred and forty in depth: all craft lying here for repair, or otherwise, must observe the rules and regulations prescribed by the Trinity-house, and are placed under the immediate superintendance of the assistant harbour-master. Between the Queen's and M'Callum's Wharf is the principal landing-place, about two hundred feet wide, where boats and canoes usually set their passengers on shore, but where much inconvenience is frequently occasioned by the numerous rafts of fire-wood that are brought down the river for the use of the city, and moored hereabout, sometimes to the complete obstruction of the passage. If the regulations of the harbour, properly enforced, be insufficient to prevent this public annoyance, it should be removed by legislative interference. The custom-house stands on M°Callum's Wharf, and during that part of the year when the navigation of the river is uninterrupted it presents the crowded scene of activity and business commonly met with at such establishments. A short distance from hence, and between the premises of the Honourable John Caldwell, the Receiver-General of the province, and those of Mr. Tod; passes the boundary line between the King's and Seminary's domains; a definition of the precise extent of the former would prove tedious, as it is presumed to include generally all ground in and about the city not disposed of by deed of concession, or letters patent, either to public bodies or individuals; such parts of it as may be deemed necessary are reserved for military and other public uses, and the remainder is usually conceded subject to the payment of *lods et ventes*. The Seminary domain was granted by Monsieur de Chauvigny, the governor of the province, to the seminary of Quebec, on the 29th October, 1686, by which concession the whole extent of beach in front, and reaching to the low-water mark in the River St. Charles, was confirmed to it. This grant is quoted by Le Maitre La Morille, Arpenteur Royal et Juré à Quebec, in his proces verbal, dated —— ——, 1758, wherein he minutely describes the boundaries of both domains, and also of the ground granted to the Hotel Dieu. As the limits of these grants are correctly delineated upon the plan of the city of Quebec on the Topographical Map, it may suffice here to give a sort of average or general outline of them, as they are met with in the course of the description of the city. The Seminary's domain is nearly as follows; beginning at the separation from the King's domain in the Lower Town, it passes between the houses of the Honourable Mr. Caldwell and Mr. Tod; from whence it extends in an easterly direction as far as the low-water mark. Returning to the first mentioned separation from the King's domain, it shapes nearly a west-south-west course as far as the presbytery, near the Catholic cathedral, where it takes a direction nearly north-westerly to the French burying-ground, or Cimetiére des Picotés, and from thence it ends by a line running north eleven degrees west by compass, to the low-water mark; dividing on this side the domain from the grounds of the Hotel Dieu. From Mc Callum's to Messrs. Munro and Bell's wharf the line is occupied by a continuation of waterside premises and wharfs, conveniently situated towards the St. Lawrence, and well calculated for the extensive shipping concerns of their respective owners. From the avenue leading down to Munro and Bell's, the Rue Sault au Matelot is prolonged in a westerly direction as far as La Canoterie, so close under the cliff as to admit of only one row of houses; and although by undermining and cutting away the rock so as to make it quite perpendicular, in order to render the street as convenient as the nature of circumstances will admit; yet in one place, with all these contrivances, it is no more than twelve feet wide. In the rear of these houses there is another line of wharfs, that can be reached by river craft at high-water only, or a little before. From the end of Rue Sault au Matelot there is a way communicating with the Upper Town, by Hope Gate. Proceeding westward through St. Charles and St. Nicholas Street, there is a range of spacious wharfs, the King's store-houses and wharfs, the batteaux-yard, and the jetty; the latter is no more than a rude pile of loose stones, that have been heaped together year after year since 1751, at which time it was in a better state, than at present; it had then a level surface

covered with a platform, and served as a public promenade. In the batteaux-yard the
boats and batteaux employed in the service
of government are built, repaired, and laid up
during the winter. On the western side of St.
Nicholas Street, and fronting that of St. Vallier, are the ruins of the intendant's palace, once
an edifice of much importance and no mean
share of grandeur, as the apartments were fitted
up with all the splendour that the times could
confer upon them, for the Council of the French
Government. After the conquest in 1759 but
little attention was paid to it, and in the year
1775 its ruin as a palace was completed; for
when the Americans, under Arnold, blockaded
the city, they found means to establish a body
of troops within it; but they were soon afterwards dislodged from their quarters by shells
thrown from the garrison, which set it on fire,
and nearly consumed the whole. Near the
ruins is a small building preserved in good
repair, and appropriated for the residence of
the chief engineer of the garrison; since the period of its demolition, a small part, that required
but little expense to restore, has been converted into government store-houses. The distinction of Le Palais is still applied to a part
of the Lower Town, in the neighbourhood of
the ruins. Between Le Palais and the beach

is the King's Wood-yard, occupying a large
plot of ground, wherein a sufficient quantity of
fuel for a year's consumption of the whole garrison is always kept in store. On the western
side of the wood-yard the suburb of St. Roch
commences, and extends in a westerly direction
to La Vacherie, a distance of seven hundred
and thirty-five yards, and from the Coteau Ste.
Genevieve to the River St. Charles, about
seven hundred and thirty yards. The streets,
though narrow, are regularly built and straight,
crossing each other at right angles : the greater
part of the houses are of wood, but a few of
those lately constructed are not destitute of a
showy exterior. The church of St. Roch is not
yet finished, and will, when completed, prove a
very handsome structure; the ground on which
it stands was a free gift from J. Mure, Esq.;
the work is now going on under the patronage
of the Catholic Bishop, who is also the protector
of a public school in this suburb, and another
in St. John's. A period of ten years has produced a very great increase in this part of the
town, as well in buildings as in population, and
there is all appearance of the same continuing
to a much more considerable degree. The
inhabitants of St. Roch are entitled to vote for
the representatives in parliament for the Lower
Town, which elects two. From the extremity of

the suburbs to the banks of the River St.
Charles, which winds beautifully through the
valley as before-mentioned, there is a large extent of fine meadow and pasture land, varied
at intervals by gardens, and intersected by the
road leading from the city to Dorchester bridge.
The beaches of the Rivers St. Charles and St.
Lawrence, in the neighbourhood of Quebec,
require a few words of particular observation,
as they are disposed of by specific grants, and
sometimes sold in portions at great prices, or
let at high rents, or for other valuable considerations. That of the River St. Charles from
Pointe à Carcy to Dorchester bridge is low,
flat, and generally sandy, with many groups
of rocks lying about it, but particularly between the Point and the Jetty, where they
almost edge the low-water channel; the space
that lies between a line prolonged from St.
Peter Street down to the low-water mark of the
St. Charles and the St. Lawrence has been
conceded by the seminary to Messrs. Munro
and Bell; and within its limits these gentlemen
have very extensive premises. On a wharf
that projects a great way into the river stands
a conspicuous large red store-house, well situated to be made a sailing mark, by which
directions might be laid down to prevent vessels in coming to their anchorage before the

town from keeping too much within the River
St. Charles, where, at half ebb, they would get
aground upon the reef that stretches nearly
across its mouth. From the same wharf down
to the edge of the St. Lawrence at low water
the distance is two hundred and thirty feet,
nearly all a reef of flat rocks; and in a north-
easterly direction, the Pointe à Carcy, a large
irregular ridge, runs about two hundred and
forty yards beyond the wharf; it leaves a small
opening for the channel of the St. Charles,
from whence another chain of rocks ranges in
different directions about the entrance of it,
which, at low water, is uncovered, and at high
water has about two fathoms and a half upon
it. From the Grand Battery on the cliff, a
little before the flood-tide makes, two distinct
reefs can be seen stretching across it, nearly
parallel to each other; the entrance into it is
close within Pointe à Carcy, where several
sand-banks form two or three different passages
between them. Opposite to Pacquette's Wharf
there is a large rock, and also a ledge lying off
Hunter's Wharf; if these were removed it would
greatly improve the convenience of the beach,
and might be effected without much difficulty; at half ebb these, the ledge before
Henderson's Wharf, and the large green plats
on the opposite side of the channel, begin to

be visible. At Henderson's there is a spacious building-yard, from whence have been launched some of the largest vessels built in Lower Canada. From the western boundary of the Seminary Domaine as far as the Jetty, or Stone Dyke, the beach belongs to the Hotel Dieu, and, with the right of fishery, was granted to it on the 21st March, 1648; but the greater part thereof has been conceded by that establishment to different persons, and is now occupied either as wharfs, dock-yards, or timber-grounds. From the Jetty, as far as St. Roch Street, the whole of the beach is reserved by government, beyond which the remaining portion, in front of St. Roch, has lately been granted by the crown to the Honourable John Richardson, of Montreal, in trust for the heirs of the late William Grant, Esq. It is now divided into several dock-yards, wharfs, and timber-grounds, and occupied by various persons; among the former, Goudie's yard is the most eminent and complete, where ship-building upon an enlarged scale has been carried on for many years. Campbell's Wharf projects so far into the river as to form rather a remarkable feature of it in looking toward Dorchester bridge: the large building formerly called Grant's Mill still remains upon it; within these premises there is a very extensive wet dock, or dam, for keeping timber.

afloat. From the line of La Vacherie, which
in fact is the western extremity of St. Roch's
suburb, the beach up to the bridge on either
side of the channel is generally used as timber-
grounds, and provided with extensive booms,
&c. The bed of the St. Charles is flat; at low-
water the two channels are narrow, winding,
and frequently divided by wide spreading shoals
of sand or mud; when the tide is out, the water
in them varies from eight to twenty-seven
inches, but at full flood the average is from two
to two fathoms and a half. Dorchester bridge is
six hundred and sixty feet in length, by twenty-
seven in width, built entirely of wood, and
supported upon piers of the same materials;
its elevation is fifteen feet above high-water.
From hence to the city the distance is about
a mile, and the road, particularly during the
summer-time, is much frequented. The prospect on every side from the bridge is agreeable and pleasing; the town, suburbs, and
the Cape, are seen to great advantage. It
is always kept in good repair, although the
toll is frequently avoided by passengers going
along the beach at low water: in winter
time, as soon as a solid track can be made
upon the ice, this evasion is almost general.
On each side of the river, below the bridge,
besides the established dock-yards, there are

several convenient places for building, where ships of large tonnage have been occasionally constructed.

.The suburb of St. John, above the Coteau Ste. Genevieve, is built on very uneven ground, with an elevation towards the Grande Allée, or road to Sillery. It occupies a mile in length by half a mile in breadth, and is increasing very fast in buildings as well as population; there are several parallel streets crossed by others at right angles, except George Street, which takes a diagonal direction across Richelieu and Olivier Streets, connecting this suburb with St. Roch, by the Cote d'Abraham, and communicates with the roads to Lorette, Charlebourg, and Beauport. St. John Street is the principal one, and from the end of it the road continues to Ste. Foi. In different parts of this suburb some well-built houses present themselves, several of which are of stone: on the south side of St. John Street is the Protestant burial-ground. In the elections for members of parliament, the inhabitants of St. John's are entitled to vote for the two who represent the Upper Town. On the Chemin de la Grande Allée, just beyond St. Louis Gate, is the house and garden belonging to Mr. Jones; further along the road, on the left hand side, is the building called Fergusson's

House, standing on the highest ground of the
celebrated plains of Abraham. It is calculated
to be three hundred and thirty feet above the
level of the river, and commands most of the
works on this side of the town, except those on
the very summit of Cape Diamond, which are
still higher by ten or fifteen feet. To diminish
the probability of this eminence being ever
seized upon as a point of offence against the
city, four Martello towers have been erected
some distance in advance of it, extending from
the St. Lawrence, across the peninsula, to Ste.
Genevieve, at between five and six hundred
yards distance from each other, and so posted
that they can sweep the whole breadth of the
plains; they are very solidly constructed, and
armed with guns of large calibre. Proceeding
along the Grand Allée westward, on the left
hand side are several large pieces of ground
belonging to the Hotel Dieu, and the Ursuline
Convent; on the opposite side, well cultivated
fields, and rich pastures, spread down to the Ste.
Foi road. The four meridian stones fixed in
1790 by the late Major Holland, then Surveyor-
General of Canada, are placed at convenient
distances from each other across the plains;
they represent a line astronomically north, and
were established for the purpose of adjusting
the instruments used in the public surveys of

lands. One of them that stood in the angle of
a field redoubt where General Wolfe is said
to have breathed his last, has been greatly
impaired by the pious reverence of *curious*
strangers, who, wishing to bear away a relic of
any thing from the spot consecrated by the hero's
death, have broken off pieces of the stone
placed there thirty years after that event. Beyond these stones are some open fields belonging to the Hotel Dieu, but retained by government for military uses. Further to the westward is a property belonging to Dr. Mountain,
Bishop of Quebec, that, from its fine and commanding situation, is admirably well calculated
for the erection of a country house and formation of pleasure grounds. Contiguous to this
property is the beautiful estate of the Honourable Mr. Percival, called Spencer Wood, formerly known by the name of Powel Place, and
which used to be the country residence of the
Governor-General. Woodfield, the property
of Mr. Bell, is another house and garden, which,
from its charming position, is very deserving of
notice. The beach directly under the height
upon which these houses stand is divided into
many valuable timber grounds, extending to
the westward as far as Pointe à Puisseaux,
which chiefly belong to Messrs. Patterson,
Dyke, and Co. Wolfe's Cove is the largest of
all the bays in the vicinity of the city, and

memorable as the landing-place of the English
army which achieved the conquest of the capital
in 1759. It is generally a scene of great activity
in the timber trade; during the summer season, numbers of ships are continually seen anchored in groups before the premises of the
different merchants: it is principally the property of Messrs. Grant and Greenshields. The
city, whose most vulnerable part is towards the
plains of Abraham, is fortified by a strong line
of regular works, from Cape Diamond to Coteau Ste. Genevieve, with ditch, covered way,
glacis, &c., strengthened by some exterior works
more recently erected, between St. Louis Gate
and St. John's Gate, well calculated to render
the approach to the town by the main roads exceedingly difficult, if not impracticable; but
from the ground rising a little towards the plain,
it has been deemed expedient to construct the
Martello towers before-mentioned, to prevent
any advantage being taken of its superior elevation. In its present state Quebec may rank
as a fortress of the first consequence: the citadel on the highest part of Cape Diamond presents a formidable combination of powerful
works, from whence a strong wall, supported by
small batteries in different places, runs to the
edge of the precipice, along which it is continued
to the gateway leading to the Lower Town,
which is defended by heavy cannon, and the

approach to it, up Mountain Street, both en-
filaded and flanked by many guns of large
calibre; thence a line of defence connects
with the grand battery, a work of great strength,
armed with a formidable train of twenty-four
pounders, and commanding the bason and passage of the river; from hence another line is carried on past the Hope and Palace Gates, both
protected by similar defences to those of the
Lower Town Gate, until it forms a junction
with the bastion of the Coteau du Palais.
The General Hospital stands on the bank of the
River St. Charles, about a mile distant from
the city, in a healthy, pleasant situation, surrounded by fine fields and meadows, having its
front towards the road called Chemin de l'Ho-
pital General; it was founded in 1693, by
Monsieur St. Vallier, Bishop of Quebec, for
the relief of sick and disabled poor of all descriptions; it is governed by a superieure, La
Reverende Mere St. Joseph, (Esther Chalou)
at the head of forty-four nuns.   It has a regular
handsome front, two hundred and twenty-eight
feet in length, and forms nearly a square; the
main body of the building is thirty-three feet
in breadth, but on the south-west side a range,
one hundred and thirty feet in length, projecting
from it, is fifty feet in breadth. Detached from
the principal edifice, and on the opposite side of

the road, are two houses belonging to it; one appropriated for the reception and treatment of persons labouring under insanity, and the other as a dwelling-house for servants, employed in a farm attached to the establishment. The interior arrangement and management of this excellent charity, with respect to accommodation, are very judicious; the patients are lodged in comfortable and spacious wards, men on the ground floor, and women on the floor above; for the superieure and the nuns there is ample room for residence, refectories, and apartments for carrying on different works in which they employ themselves, exclusive of their attendance on the sick: a spacious and neat church is attached to the convent. As this hospital administers succour to the afflicted under any of the diseases within the wide range of human calamity, it is most commonly nearly filled. Its support is drawn from the revenues of the landed property that has been granted to it, the sale of the works performed by the nuns, particularly of church ornaments, which they make and gild in great perfection, and by occasional grants of money from the provincial parliament.

To facilitate travelling in the lower province, and render it as expeditious as possible, there is a line of post-houses from Quebec to Mont-

real on one side, and by the southern shore of the
river down as far as Trois Pistoles, below the island of Bic, on the other; these houses are kept
under rules and regulations, established by authority of the parliament, and annually inspected
by a person who is appointed superintendant
of post-houses in the province, whose duty it is
to see that each station furnishes a sufficient
number of calashes in proper order, with good
horses for the public accommodation, and that
in each house the regulations are conspicuously
posted up, so that every traveller may have an
opportunity of knowing that no imposition is
practised upon him, or how to obtain redress in
cases of extortion : should these rules be devi-
ated from by any of the post-masters, they are
subject to a pecuniary fine. The expense of
travelling is generally one shilling a league during the summer time, or fifteen-pence in the fall
of the year with a calash and one horse; the
charges of tolls and ferries must be borne by
the travellers. The conveyance of the regular
mail, under the direction of the post-master
general, is a distinct concern from the post-
houses; it is sent by couriers who leave Quebec and Montreal every day at four o'clock.
Both convenience and comfort are now considerably increased by a stage-coach, that starts
from each city regularly, every day during the

year : in the summer time it is furnished with
four good horses quite in the English style; in
the winter the body of the coach is placed on
a sledge, and drawn by the same number of
horses, in which season it performs its journey
somewhat quicker; it conveys six passengers
inside, with a proportion of baggage, &c. The
charge by this conveyance is a trifle more than
by posting, but the accommodation is certainly
superior at the different stopping places, where
refreshments and other conveniences of an inn
are always to be obtained in a very good style.
Since the year 1812, two steam-boats have been
launched upon the St. Lawrence, and during
the summer time there are two of them constantly navigating between Quebec and Montreal; they are fitted up with great attention
to the ease and comfort of the public. A cabin
passenger, with sixty pounds of luggage, pays
£3 to Montreal; but from thence to Quebec
only £2 : 10s. : 0d., the expense of the table
therein included : steerage passengers pay 15s.
each way : extra luggage is paid for at the rate
of one penny a pound. The voyage down the
river is performed in forty-eight hours; but
going upwards it is some hours longer, on
account of the strong currents. The smallest
of these boats measures one hundred and ten
feet in length, by twenty-eight in breadth,

and commodiously accommodates fifty cabin passengers, with separate apartments for ladies, beds, &c.: the other is of greater capacity, being one hundred and forty feet by thirty-two. This mode of travelling is easy, and exceedingly pleasant: a liberal table is provided, with every other means of rendering the passage quite a party of pleasure. Mr. Moulson, of Montreal, is the person who has embarked a large capital in this undertaking, and it is pleasing to find that his enterprise has been productive of considerable profit to him; he has been countenanced in his plan by the provincial legislature, but has not obtained any exclusive privilege. On occasions of emergency, these boats have been used for the conveyance of troops, and have thereby greatly contributed to forward the public service. A courier with a mail leaves Quebec every week for Halifax and Nova Scotia, by the way of Fredericton, and St. John's, New Brunswick. As this communication across the portage of Timiscouata is one of considerable importance, it will be recurred to again, on speaking of the settlements thereabouts. Between the city and Point Levi, on the opposite shore of the St. Lawrence, a great number of ferry-boats are continually passing to and fro, the principal part of which belong to the inhabitants about the Point, as

they are all permitted, by regulation, to ply
with their boats, on condition of receiving no
more than the established rates, which are very
moderate; in almost any weather they will
cross in their canoes, which are large, and very
strong, being made from the trunk of a tree
hollowed out, or more frequently of two joined
together, and firmly secured on the inside;
they are managed with great dexterity, and
sometimes take as many as eight passengers
besides the three or four men who work them.
In the winter, when large masses of ice are
floating up and down with the tide, and often
when there is a strong breeze, impelled at the
rate of three or four knots an hour, this passage is singularly laborious, and to all appearance extremely hazardous, yet it is very rare
that a fatal accident has happened; in snow
storms, indeed, they have been frequently
driven several leagues out of their course,
either above or below the town, without knowing whereabouts they were, but have always
reached their place of destination sooner or
later. It is not an uncommon thing to see
several of these large canoes, laden with provisions for the market, crossing the river as nearly
in a line as they are able to keep: the cargoes
are generally secured by a strong lashing; they
are provided with strong poles having iron

hooks at the end for grappling hold of the ice,
and drag ropes. When large sheets of ice oppose their progress, the men, by means of the
poles and ropes, which they employ with an uncommon ability, get the canoe upon it, and by
main force drag it perhaps fifty or sixty yards,
or until they find a convenient opening to
launch it again among the smaller fragments;
and then, using their paddles, they proceed
until they are intercepted by another flat, upon
which it is again hoisted as before, continuing
thus in toilsome succession across the river.
Frequently, while they are forcing it over a sheet
of ice, their slippery foundation breaks beneath
them; but they mostly contrive to skip nimbly
into the canoe, and evade the difficulty. Often
in pursuing their course through a narrow vein
of water between two enormous masses, they
are suddenly closed upon; and, at the moment
when a stranger would imagine the canoe must
be ground to atoms by the collision, they skil-
fully contrive, by means of their poles, to make
the pressure of the two bodies act upon the
lower part of their vessel, and, with a little assistance of their own, heave it upon the surface,
over which it is pushed and dragged as before.
They are amazingly steady in this laborious
work, and long habit seems to have expelled
from their minds every sense of danger: thus

employed, they appear to be insensible to the severity of the cold; they are not encumbered with much clothing, which is as light and as warm as they are able to procure. If one of them happens to get an unlucky plunge, he is extricated by his comrades as expeditiously as possible; when a hearty *coup de rum* all round, with which they are never unprovided, is the usual remedy for such misfortunes. When they arrive at the landing before the market-place, sometimes the tide is low, and the ice forming the solid border perhaps ten or twelve feet above them; in this case they jump out as fast as they can, all but one man, and while the rest are getting a firm footing above, he fastens the drag rope to the fore part of the canoe, and immediately assisting his comrades, the whole is hauled up by main force out of the water, when the lading, consisting of poultry, carcases of sheep or pigs, of fish or other articles, is transferred without delay to the market-places. It has been said by many writers, that during the winter vegetables and milk in a frozen state are brought from distant places; this certainly used to be the case, but now these articles are furnished in the best state all the year round, from the farms and gardens in the vicinity. When the river *takes,* i. e. is frozen over from Quebec to Point Levi, which does not happen

every year, it is not only productive of much
amusement, but of great advantage to the city,
as well as to the inhabitants of the southern
shore, who can at that time bring their produce
to market in large quantities without inconvenience. Hay, fire-wood, and all bulky articles
of consumption are furnished in abundance, and
the consumers usually experience a great reduction in price in consequence of such an influx.
As soon as the surface is deemed sufficiently solid,
the road across it is immediately traced out, and
continues under the inspection of the *Grand
Voyer* of the district, who causes proper beacons
to be set up on each side, and at intervals where
they are required. When the river has *taken*
in the north channel between the Island of
Orleans and the Main, (the southern channel is
never frozen over) which is the case every year,
the markets of the city never fail to feel the
effect of it, as abundance of provisions of all
kinds, the growth of that fruitful spot, which
have been prepared for the approaching season,
are immediately brought in : considerable supplies are drawn from thence during the summer;
but such as do not spoil by keeping are commonly retained, until this opportunity admits
of their being sent with much less trouble and
expense. The summer scenery of the environs
of Quebec may vie in exquisite beauty, variety,

magnificence, sublimity, and the naturally har-
monized combination of all these prominent
features, with the most splendid that has yet
, been portrayed in Europe, or any other part
of the world.   Towards Beauport, Charlebourg,
and Lorette, the view is diversified with every
trait that can render a landscape rich, full, and
complete; the foreground shews the River St.
Charles meandering for many miles through a
rich and fertile valley, embellished by a succes-.
sion of objects that diffuses an unrivalled ani-
mation over the whole scene.   The three villages, with their respective churches, and many
handsome detached houses in the vicinity, seated·
on gently rising eminences, form so many distinct points of view; the intervals between
them display many of the most strongly marked
specimens of forest scenery, and the surrounding country every where an appearance of fertility and good cultivation upon which the eye
of the spectator wanders with ceaseless delight.
As the prospect recedes it is still interesting,
the land rising in gradation, height over height,
having the interval between succeeding elevations filled up with primeval forests, until
the whole is terminated by a stupendous ridge
of mountains, whose lofty forms are dimly seen
through the aerial expanse. The sense of vision
is gratified to the utmost, and the spectator

never fails to turn with regret from the contemplation of what is allowed to be one of the most superb views in nature. Nor is it on this side only that the attention is arrested; for turning towards the bason, which is about two miles across, a scene presents itself that is not the less gratifying for being made a secondary one: it is enlivened by the ever changing variety of ships coming up to and leaving the port. On the right hand, Point Levi, with its church and group of white houses, several other promontories on the same shore clothed with lofty trees; in front, the western end of the beautiful and picturesque island of Orleans, displaying charming and well-cultivated slopes down almost to the water's edge, backed by lofty and thick woods, and every where decorated by neat farm-houses, present altogether an interesting and agreeable subject to the observer: in fine still weather, the *reflects* of the different objects around the margin, in all their variety of colouring, are thrown across the unruffled surface of the water with an almost incredible brilliance. On the plains of Abraham, from the precipice that overlooks the timber-grounds, where an incessant round of activity prevails, the St. Lawrence is seen rolling its majestic wave, studded with many a sail, from the stately ship down to the humble fishing-boat;

the opposite bank, extending up the river, is highly cultivated, and the houses, thickly strewed by the main road, from this height and distance have the appearance of an almost uninterrupted village, as far as the eye can reach in that direction. The country to the southward rises by a very gentle ascent, and the whole view, which is richly embellished by alternations of water, woodland, and cultivation, is bounded by remote and lofty mountains, softening shade by shade until they melt into air. Whoever views the environs of Quebec, with a mind and taste capable of receiving impressions through the medium of the eyes, will acknowledge, that, as a whole, the prospect is grand, harmonious, and magnificent; and that if taken in detail, every part of it will please, by a gradual unfolding of its picturesque beauties upon a small scale.

The Island of Orleans, below Quebec, divides the River St. Lawrence into two channels; it is about twenty miles long and five broad; was granted as a seigniory on the 15th January, 1636, to the Sieur Castellon: it is at present divided into three distinct properties, belonging to Madame Drapeau, Monsr. Poulain, and Monsr. Le Comte Dupré; it also forms the county of Orleans. This island, next in size to that of Montreal, approaches it

in fertility and richness of soil more nearly
than any other part of the district of Quebec:
its western extremity is only four miles from
Cape Diamond. The shores slant gradually to
the beach, in some places there are a few
rocky cliffs, but not of great extent or elevation: from the foot of the slopes there are
large spaces of low meadow land, sometimes
intersected by patches of excellent arable.
Bordering the north channel the beach is flat
and muddy, with reefs of rocks running along
it; but on the southern side it is a fine sand,
with only a few pointed rocks sticking up
here and there. The highest part of the island
is by the church of St. Pierre, about four miles
from the western extremity, and almost fronting the falls of Montmorenci; and also just
above Patrick's Hole, nearly abreast of St.
Pierre, on the south side, on which is placed
the second telegraph of the chain from Quebec
to Green Island. The centre part is thickly
wooded, but without producing any timber of
superior growth. The soil is highly fertilized
in almost every part; on the high lands it is
commonly a light good earth, either mixed
with sand, or sand and clay; on less elevated
situations there is a fine black mould, which,
as it nears the shores, is likewise blended with
sand. This delightful spot is but scantily

watered by the little River Dauphin, the Rivulet Maheux, and a few more trifling streams,
all of which in summer-time fail of a sufficient
supply to work a couple of mills that are built
upon them. The parishes of St. Pierre and
St. Famille on the north, St. Laurent, St. Jean,
and St. Francois on the south, each of which
has its church and parsonage-house, embrace
the whole circuit of the island: St. Jean and
St. Famille are more populous than the others,
and their inhabitants wealthy and substantial
farmers. Four curates perform the clerical
duties of the five parishes, the incumbent of St.
Famille serving St. Francois: these gentlemen
have long been resident in their respective
curacies, and have made themselves generally
known and respected by their attention and
hospitality towards strangers who are attracted
by the beauties of this charming place. There
is a good road that encompasses the whole
island, and several others crossing it. The
churches of St. Laurent and St. Jean are situated close down upon the southern shore: the
distance between them is six miles; all the way
through excellent well cultivated lands, richly
diversified with orchards and gardens: the
ground rising with an easy slope from the road
displays the industry of the farmers to very
great advantage. Along the road side there

are houses at short intervals from each other throughout the whole distance. . Patrick's Hole, a little westward of St. Laurent, is a safe and well sheltered cove, where vessels outward-bound usually come to an anchor, to wait their final instructions for sailing. On the western point there is a group of very neat houses; at several of which the inhabitants furnish accommodations to the numerous persons who visit the island for amusement or curiosity, both in summer and winter. The fertility of this spot is so great, and the *habitans* reckoned such good cultivators, that large quantities of grain, and most sorts of provisions, are continually furnished for the consumption of Quebec: among the fruits, apples and plums attain a much greater degree of perfection than in any other place in the lower district; but still they do not equal the productions of Montreal. In St. Famille there is a large stone building, wherein several nuns reside, and keep a seminary for the education of females. The population of the island may be estimated at about 4000.

LAUZON (the seigniory of), on the south side of the St. Lawrence, in the county of Dorchester, is bounded by the river in front, La Martiniere on the east, St. Antoine, Gaspé, and St. Gilles on the west, and St. Etienne and Jolliett in the rear; six leagues in breadth by six leagues in depth; was granted January 15th, 1636, to M. Simon Le Maitre, and is now the property of John Caldwell, Esq. The soil throughout this extensive property is, generally speaking, of a superior description; it includes almost every variety, but the sort that predominates is a rich, lightish loam, and in situations lying rather low, a fine dark mould. In the front but little timber remains; in the interior, and towards the rear, beech, maple, birch, and pine are found in great plenty, besides some oak; of the inferior sorts, cedar, hemlock, and spruce, are very abundant. It is watered by the Rivers Chaudiere, the Beaurivage, falling into the Chaudiere, the Echemin, the Boyer, and several other inferior rivers and streams. The Chaudiere and Echemin traverse the seigniory in a south-easterly direction, and the Beaurivage by a south-westerly course. Neither of them are navigable for boats, or even canoes to any distance, on account of the great number of falls and rapids: their banks, but most particularly those of the Chaudiere, are lofty and steep, presenting in many places almost perpendicular rocky cliffs. The banks of the St. Lawrence are also high and steep, covered with trees of a small growth on some spots, but cleared and cultivated in others: the

beach below them is sandy, a good deal encumbered by rocks, with almost a regular reef
stretching along the low water line; from the
top of the bank the land rises by ridges and
small hillocks (many of which are rocky) gradually to the rear. There are two extensive
domains, and several small fiefs within the
seigniory; three churches dedicated to St.
Joseph, St. Nicholas, and St. Henry; three
grist-mills, and several saw-mills. The cultivated land, which amounts to one-third of the
whole, is divided into ranges of concessions,
bearing the names of St. Joseph, Trompe
Sourri, Arlaca, Brise Culotte, Pin Tendre, St.
Jean Baptiste, St. Charles, Premier Rang,
Grillade, St. Gervais, Jean Guerrin nord-est,
Jean Geurrin sud-ouest, Bois Claire, St. Anne,
St. Joachim, Plaisance, Bellaire, Ste. Augustin, Beauliece, Liverpool, St. Jean, St.
Dennis, Ste. Anne on the Beaurivage, Terrebonne, Grande Village St. Nicholas, Viveresse,
&c., besides five ranges of concessions in woodlands, towards the rear. The most thickly
settled and best cultivated parts of this valuable property are situated along the front, in
the parishes of St. Joseph and St. Nicholas,
and for several concessions towards the interior; throughout which may be seen a succession of fine arable land under a very good sys-

tem of husbandry, rich meadows, good gardens and orchards; but the produce of the latter is not of a very superior kind. The farm and other houses are neat and substantially built. In the remaining concessions, the state of agriculture is not so far advanced; on the Chaudiere, the best lands lie at some distance from the banks; nearly the same is the case with those on the Echemin, the margins of both being generally flat rock, with only a shallow covering of soil upon them. Almost every one of the ranges are intersected by roads: the main ones, or those on the bank of the St. Lawrence, the one leading from Pointe Levi Mills to St. Henri, and thence to the River Chaudiere, the route St. Gilles from St. Nicholas, along the south-west bank of the Beaurivage, and thence communicating with Craig's Road, are very good, and maintained in excellent repair. Nearly opposite to Quebec, and on a little river which there discharges itself into the St. Lawrence, are the extensive and valuable premises called the Pointe Levi Mills, and further westward, at the mouth of the Echemin, the no less important establishment called the Echemin Mills, from both of which large exportations of flour annually take place. From Pointe des Peres to the Chaudiere River, the beach is almost wholly 'occupied as timber-grounds; the principal of them is New Liverpool Cove, latterly named New Glasgow, the property of Messrs. Hamilton and Co.; it is a fine sandy bay, sheltered from the north-east by a rocky point, on which there is a long wharf, where ships lie to take in their cargoes. The situation, shores, depth of water, &c. render it very convenient for ship-building; and in consequence, there is a very good dock for repairing, as well as the construction of vessels, surrounded by numerous dwelling-houses for persons employed therein. At the entrance of the Chaudiere there is another wharf, with store-houses for the shipment of flour. From Pointe des Peres, and other parts in front of the seigniory, there are ferries to Quebec. Lauzon is very populous: its quota of militia is large, and well disciplined: during part of the winter of 1813, assisted by a detachment of the division from the Island of Orleans, it performed garrison duty in Quebec, with a cheerfulness and alacrity that were highly exemplary. The River Chaudiere, that traverses this seigniory, and falls into the St. Lawrence, about two leagues above Quebec, is of considerable magnitude; and although not navigable for boats or even canoes, owing to its numerous rapids, falls, and other impediments, yet maintains a character of some importance, and merits a few observations. It takes its source from Lake Megantic, flowing northerly forty-one miles, as far as the seigniory of Aubert Gallion; from thence north-westerly, it winds through the seigniories of Vaudreuil, St. Joseph, Ste. Marie, St. Etienne, Jolliett, and Lauzon, to the St. Lawrence, a distance of sixty-one miles, making the whole course one hundred and two from Lake Megantic to its estuary; in breadth it varies from four hundred to six hundred yards. The stream is frequently divided by islands, some of them containing many acres, and covered with timber-trees: the banks in general are high, rocky, and steep, pretty thickly clothed with wood of an indifferent growth; the bed rugged, and much contracted by rocks jutting from the sides, that occasion violent rapids. The descent of the stream over the different shelves occasions falls of considerable height; the most noticeable are those called the Chaudiere, about four miles before the river discharges itself into the St. Lawrence. Narrowed by salient points extending from each side, the precipice over which the waters rush is scarcely more than one hundred and thirty yards in breadth; the height from which they descend is about as many feet. Huge masses of rock rising above the surface of the current, just at the break of the fall, divide the stream into three portions, forming partial cataracts, that unite before they reach the basin which receives them below. The continual action of the water has worn the rock into deep excavations, that give a globular figure to the revolving bodies of brilliant white foam as they descend, and greatly increase the beautiful effect of the fall: the spray thrown up, being quickly spread by the wind, produces in the sunshine a most splendid variety of prismatic colours. The dark hued foliage of the woods, that on each side press close upon the margin of the river, forms a striking contrast with the snow-like effulgence of the falling torrent; the hurried motion of the flood, agitated among the rocks and hollows as it forces its way towards the St. Lawrence, and the incessant sound occasioned by the cataract itself, form a combination that strikes forcibly upon the senses, and amply gratifies the curiosity of the admiring spectator. The woods on the banks of the river, notwithstanding its vicinity to the capital, are so impervious as to render it necessary for strangers who visit the falls to provide themselves with a competent guide. Although of no utility as a water communication, yet the Chaudiere is entitled to a few remarks, because it traces out a route whereby an easy access may be had into the American territories, and from them into Canada, during the whole year. From Quebec along the eastern bank, there is an excellent road for about fifty miles, and thence a tolerably good one in continuation, as far as the River du Loup, on which the Canadian settlements at present terminate. The first settlements on the River Kennebec, within the American frontier, are seventy miles distant from those on the River du Loup: the country between them is mountainous, intersected by rivers and small streams, and every where in a state of nature. The chain of mountains is not so closely connected as to render it impracticable, or even difficult to open a road through the passes between them, that would afford a free intercourse from the state of Massachussetts to Lower Canada. Previous to the late war, the legislature of that state had nominated commissioners, for the purpose of making a route from the settlements on the Kennebec, up to the height of land dividing the two territories. If this plan be carried into execution, there will then remain no greater distance than about twenty miles to the English settlements on the River du Loup. The facility with which this line of communication may be made, and the completion of it on the American side, should be viewed with serious attention by the British Government, particularly when it is accompanied by the consideration, that by such a road the distance from Hallowell on the Kennebec, from whence the navigation for vessels of large burthen is uninterrupted to the sea, up to Quebec, is no more than two hundred miles; and from Boston to the same place, only three hundred and seventy miles. The views of the United States with respect to Canada have been too unequivocally demonstrated to leave a shadow of uncertainty as to their ultimate object; and as the preservation of this valuable colony has always been deemed worthy of our strenuous efforts, we cannot be too much on our guard against the slow working policy by which that government endeavours to compass its ends, or too heedful in adopting precautionary measures to avert a threatening danger, however remote it may at first appear.

TILLY, or ST. ANTOINE (the seigniory of), on the south side of the St. Lawrence, and in the county of Buckingham, is bounded on the east by Lauzon, on the west by Desplaines, in front by the river, and in the rear by the seigniory of Gaspé; a league and a half in breadth by a similar depth: it was granted October 29th, 1672, to Sieur de Villieu, and is now the property of ——— Noel, Esq.

GASPE' (the seigniory of), in the rear of Tilly, has the same lateral limits as that seigniory, and is bounded in the rear by St. Gilles; it is a league and a half in breadth by the same quantity in depth; was granted March 25, 1738, to Dame Angeleque Legardeur, widow of Aubert Gaspé.

MARANDA (fief), having its front to the St. Lawrence, is a small piece of thirty arpens in breadth, and one hundred in depth, lying between the seigniories of Tilly and Bonsecours; was granted in equal moïties to the Sieurs Duquet, father and son, November 3d, 1672.

DESPLAINES (the seigniory of), in the county of Buckingham, is bounded by Tilly and Gaspé on the east, Bonsecours and Ste. Croix on the west, and St. Gilles in the rear; was granted in two parts, the first, three-quarters of a league in front by three leagues in depth, from the rear of fief Maranda, to Demoiselle Charlotte Legardeur, on the 4th January, 1737; and the second, about seventy-four arpens in front, by one league sixty arpens in depth, being the space between the preceding grant and the seigniory of Ste. Croix, to the same-person; the whole intended to form only one seigniory.

BONSECOURS (the seigniory of), between Desplaines and Ste. Croix, is bounded in the rear by the former; contains about a league and a half in breadth by two leagues in depth ; was granted July 1st, 1677, to Francois Bellanger. Of these five grants only a very small portion is in a state of cultivation, which is confined to the road leading by the River St. Lawrence, through Tilly, Maranda, and Bonsecours : in this direction the soil is good and fertile, and the farms generally in high condition. Gaspé cannot produce an acre of tillage. The banks of the river are high; but the rise is gradual. The whole tract is abundantly furnished with timber of good quality, of which large quantities are felled every year, and sent to Quebec. St. Antoine has a church and parsonage-house. Throughout the whole of these properties there is scarcely a stream of water to be met with.

. St. Gilles (the seigniory of), in the county of Buckingham, is bounded in front by the seigniories of Gaspé and Desplaines, on the east by Lauzon, Ste. Etienne, and Ste. Marie, on the west by Ste. Croix and the township of Leeds, and in the rear by the township of Broughton; two leagues and three quarters broad by six leagues deep; was granted April 1st, 1738, to Rageot de ———. The heirs of the late Judge Davison are the present proprietors. In this seigniory, although it may be termed a valuable property, there is only a small proportion under tillage. The soil is a good black mould, varied with yellow and dark loams; the surface is irregular, and towards the south-west lies so low as to occasion swamps, that are thickly covered with cedar and black ash; the other parts produce a mixture of good timber of all kinds. It is very well watered by the river Beaurivage, and many small streams falling into it. The cultivated lands lie on each side of the Beaurivage, and are pretty thickly settled, with many of the farms in excellent condition. On the western bank of that river there is a good road leading from St. Nicholas, on the St. Lawrence, into the township of Leeds, where it falls into Craig's Road. As this is a great thoroughfare, it excites some surprise, considering the goodness of the land, that more of it is not under cultivation.

STE. CROIX (the seigniory of), on the south side of the St. Lawrence, in the county of Buckingham, is bounded in front by the river, on the east by Bonsecours, Desplaines, and St. Gilles, on the west by Lotbiniere, its augmentation, and the township of Nelson, and in the rear by the township of Leeds. The original title of this concession has not been found; but it appears from the registers of fealty and homage, a declaration has been exhibited by a notary, that "the Dames Religieuses Ursulines possessed the seigniory of Ste. Croix, containing one league in front by ten in depth, which was granted to them on the 16th January, 1637, and confirmed by M. Lauzon, the Governor, on the 6th March, 1652 :" it still remains the property of the convent. On the high and steep bank of the river in front the soil is a light-coloured loam, greatly improved by a very superior style of cultivation. Receding from thence, the land decreases in height, and the soil changes to a rich dark mould, which continues for some miles, and then declines into extensive swamps, covered with cedar, hemlock, black ash, and spruce fir: with the exception of the wet lands, the whole range of the seigniory, from front to rear, is abundantly clothed with fine timber of all sorts. No stream of magnitude is to be met with throughout the whole tract.

LOTBINIERE (the seigniory of), with its augmentation, situated on the south side of the St. Lawrence, in the county of Buckingham, is bounded in front by the river, on the east by Ste. Croix, on the west by Deschaillons and its augmentation, and in the rear by the townships of Somerset and Nelson. This seigniory was granted in several parcels as follows, viz. November 3d, 1672, half a league in front

by a league and a half in depth, on the western
side near Deschaillons, to the Sieur Marsolet.
On November 3d, 1672, two leagues and a half
in front by two in depth, adjoining Ste. Croix,
to Sieur de Lotbiniere. On April 1st, 1685, half
a league in front by two in depth to M. de
Lotbiniere; being the vacant space between
the two former grants. The augmentation;
three leagues and a half in front by four in
depth, on the 25th March, 1693, to Monsieur
de Lotbiniere. The whole, being three leagues
and a half in front by six deep, is now the
property of the Honourable M. E. G. A. Chartier de Lotbiniere, a lineal representative of
the original grantee, in whose family it has
always remained. The generality of the soil
over all this extensive tract is excellent; and
so advantageously varied, that every production of the country may be raised upon it.
It is well stocked with fine elm, ash, maple,
beech, plane, merisier, and other timber: the
banks of the Rivers du Chêne, Huron, and
Boisclere, produce pine of first rate growth.
It is very well watered by these three rivers:
the former is navigable at all times as far as
the place called the *portage*, distant about two
miles from the St. Lawrence; but the two
latter only during the rise of the waters in
spring and autumn. Notwithstanding the su-

périor fertility of the soil, about an eighth part only of the grants are settled upon. There are seven ranges of concessions parallel to the St. Lawrence, and one perpendicular to it, which contain five hundred and eighty lots, of three acres in front, by thirty in depth; of this number, four hundred and five, under the management of an industrious tenantry, who are good cultivators, yield abundant crops of grain, and indeed of every other article. Near the middle of the front of the seigniory stand a handsome stone church and parsonage-house, and near to them a few neat and well-built houses; indeed, this is the characteristic of the major part of the dwellings; the number of them is considerable, as the population ascends to 3400 souls. On the eastern side, near the St. Lawrence, is a small domain of only twelve acres, wholly uncultivated, but thickly clothed with timber-trees of a superior description: in it is situated the seignorial mill. On the different streams there are six saw-mills, and five manufactories of pot-ash. The main road passing by the St. Lawrence, as well as all the others throughout the seigniory, is always kept in excellent repair.

DESCHAILLONS, ST. JEAN DESCHAILLONS, or RIVIERE DU CHENE (the seigniory of and its augmentation), in the county of Bucking-

K K

ham, joins Lotbiniere on the north-east, Livrard, or St. Pierre les Becquets, and the township of Blandford on the south-west, and is
bounded in the rear by a small piece of waste
crown lands, that separates it from the townships of Somerset and Stanfold. The seigniory, in dimensions two leagues square, was
granted April 25th, 1674, to Sieur de St. Ours;
the augmentation, two leagues in breadth, by
four leagues and a half deep, was granted
January 25th, 1752, to Roc de St. Ours, and
Sieur Deschaillons: they are now the property
of Charles de St. Ours, Esq. In general, the
soil of this seigniory is of a favourable quality,
being either a good yellow loam, or else a fine
black mould; but notwithstanding these advantages, cultivation has made but an indifferent, progress. On the bank of the St. Lawrence there are two ranges of concessions, containing together about one hundred and fifty
farm lots, of which the majority appear to be
under respectable management: their produce
of wheat and almost all sorts of grain is commensurate thereto, and of a good quality.
Both the original grant and the augmentation
are thickly clothed with wood of various species, better calculated for firewood than any
other purposes; and from whence great quantities are supplied to the garrison and city of

Quebec. The Little Riviere du Chêne, which crosses it diagonally, and falls into the St. Lawrence, a little below Cap à la Roche, is the only stream that waters this tract. It is not navigable at any season for any thing larger than a canoe. About half a mile above the discharge of this river there is a good grist-mill: the augmentation has scarcely any means of irrigation. A little distance upwards from Cap à la Roche a very neat church is seated on the bank of the St. Lawrence, which, along the whole front, is a good deal elevated. The houses of the tenantry, about one hundred and twenty in all, are dispersed among the concessions, by the side of the main road that passes close to the river. They are mostly built of wood, and have a very neat appearance.

St. Etienne (the seigniory of), in the county of Dorchester, is situated in the rear of Lauzon, bounded on the north-east by the River Chaudiere, on the south-west by St. Gilles, and on the east by Ste. Marie: its demensions are three leagues by two, granted on the 7th October, 1737, to François Etienne Cugnet.

Jolliet (the seigniory of) is also in the rear of Lauzon, separated from St. Etienne by the Chaudiere, and bounded on its other sides by the townships of Frampton and

Buckland, and the seigniory of Ste. Marie. It is of an irregular figure, its greatest length being about three leagues, and its utmost depth nearly the same: it is now the property of —— Taschereau, Esq. Both these grants, with respect to the kinds of soil and species of timber found in them, bear a great affinity to the rear part of the adjoining seigniory of Lauzon; in each of them, a little removed from the rocky banks of the Chaudiere, there are some ranges of settlements where the land is tolerably fertile, and has the appearance of being well managed, through which some good roads pass. About the middle of the grant, the main road from Quebec to the new townships crosses the Chaudiere at the ferry. Jolliet is also partially watered by the river Echemin.

STE. MARIE (the seigniory of), is in the counties of Buckingham and Dorchester, bounded on the north-west by the township of Frampton, and seigniory of Jolliet, on the south-west by St. Gilles, on the west by St. Etienne and Jolliet, and on the east by St. Joseph, three leagues deep, by four leagues broad; was granted 23d September, 1736, to Sieur Taschereau, in whose family it still remains.

St. Joseph (the seigniory of) touches the

rear boundary of Ste. Marie, is between the
townships of Frampton and Broughton, and
has Vaudreuil on the east; three leagues in
depth, by four in breadth ; was granted September 27th, 1736, to Sieur Rigaud de Vaudreuil;
it is now the property of Monsieur Taschereau.
The surface of these two grants is uneven,
rocky in several places, with an irregular ridge
of, broken heights passing in a south-westerly
direction over the rear part of Ste. Marie; yet
the land is tolerably good, and in general very
productive where it is under culture. Timber
of almost every description is found in great
plenty. The River Chaudiere passes through
both grants, dividing them nearly in equal
proportions. On each side of it there are settlements a little withdrawn from the bank,
where agriculture has been carried on with
good success. Besides these tracts, there
are, in different parts of the interior, a few
concessions that have also made considerable
progress. The farm-houses by the road side,
on each bank of the river, are numerous,
neat, and substantial, with every appearance
of ease and comfort among their occupants.
In either grant there is scarcely any stream
but the main river: there is a church and
parsonage-house belonging to each. At the
lower part of St. Joseph are the valuable mills

belonging to the heirs of the late —— Taschereau, Esq., Grand Voyer of the district.

VAUDREUIL (the seigniory of), in the counties of Buckingham and Dorchester, is situated
in the rear of St. Joseph, and bounded on the
north-east by the township of Cranbourne, on
the south-west by the township of Tring, and
in the rear by the seigniories of Aubert Galleon
and Delisle; its dimensions are precisely the
same as St. Joseph; granted September 23d,
1736, to Sieur Fleury de la Gorgendiere: it
belongs now to Monsieur de Lery. The surface of this property is uneven and broken,
and although a good deal encumbered with
rocks, that in many places are only thinly
covered, the soil is not of an inferior quality;
the cultivated parts lie on each side of the
Chaudiere, and vary, from a quarter to half a
mile in depth; they contain about one hundred
and seventy concessions, many of them in a
flourishing state. The timber consists of a
general assortment of the best quality. Besides the Chaudiere, it is watered by several
other streams, of which the Bras de Sud Ouest,
falling into the Chaudiere, is the largest; it is
supplied from several small lakes in the township of Tring, and is generally passable in
canoes, but not with boats. Within the seigniory there are a church and a parsonage, a

grist-mill, four saw-mills, and altogether about
two hundred and twenty houses, chiefly built
of wood ; the population is between one thousand four hundred and one thousand five hundred. The Chaudiere may be crossed at two
or three fords; but these, after a couple of
days rain, are too much swollen to be safe to
venture a carriage through them.

AUBERT GALLION, and DE L'ISLE (the
seigniories of), in the counties of Buckingham
and Dorchester, are the two last settlements
on the River Chaudiere, and separated by it
from each other, both in the rear of Vaudreuil.
The former is bounded on the south-west by the
township of Shenley, and on its eastern side by
unsurveyed crown lands; it is two leagues
square; granted September 24th, 1736, to
Dame Aubert, and is now the property of Mr.
Jacob Pozer. The latter is bounded by unsurveyed lands, except on the side towards
Vaudreuil. It is of the same dimensions as
Aubert Gallion, and was granted on the same
day to Sieur Gabriel Aubert de L'Isle: it now
belongs to M. de Lery. The land in both
grants is of a good quality, and on the Chaudiere thickly settled; but the farms neither
exhibit much care or good management: nor
do the inhabitants bear that character of industry, or possess the attendant comforts, that

are so visible in many other parts of the district. The timber found here is generally of a good quality, and in profusion. In addition to the Chaudiere, De L'Isle is watered by Rivieres du Loup and la Famine; in the vicinity of the former there are many extensive tracts of excellent meadow land.

La Martiniere (fief), on the south bank of the St. Lawrence, in the county of Hertford, is bounded on the south-west by Lauzon, on the north-east by Mont-à-Peine, and in the rear by the township of Buckland; its breadth is only ten arpens, but its depth is six leagues; granted August 5th, 1692, to Sieur de la Martiniere, and now belongs to ———— Reid, Esq., of Montreal.

Mont-a-Peine (fief) joins the above, and is bounded on the north-east by St. Michel, in the rear by St. Gervais; it was granted in two parts; the first, ten arpens broad by forty deep, to Sieur de Vitré, on the 24th September, 1683; the augmentation, of the same breadth, and completing the depth of the whole to six leagues, was granted June 18th, 1749, to Claude Antoine de Berment; it is now the property of Féréol Roy, Esq. These two fiefs possess a soil nearly similar to the seigniory of Lauzon, and are in a forward state of cultivation, two thirds of the whole

being under hand. The most flourishing settlements are near the St. Lawrence, and on
each side of the River Boyer. The timber is
various, but that of an inferior kind is most
prevalent. Both fiefs are well watered by the
River Boyer, and some inferior runs of water.
The former turns a grist-mill in La Martiniere.

VINCENNES (the seigniory of), in the county
of Hertford, has Mont-à-Peine on the south-
west, Beaumont on the north-east, the St.
Lawrence in front, and Livaudiere in the rear,
seventy arpens in front, by one league in
depth; was granted November 3d, 1672, to
Sieur Bissot. Féréol Roy, Esq., is the present
proprietor. The land in this grant lies rather
high towards the river, and is, on the most
elevated parts, of a lightish sandy earth; in
other places a good dark mould, couched upon
a substratum of rock, is prevalent. The greatest
portion of the grant is under a very respectable
state of culture, and produces fine crops of
grain, &c. The timber has been greatly reduced;
and what now remains is but of indifferent
quality. Several small streams falling into the
St. Lawrence provide rather a scanty irrigation; one of them works a grist-mill seated in
a cove under the lofty bank of the river. There
are many good farm-houses and other dwellings

by the side of the several roads that intersect the seigniory.

LIVAUDIERE (the seigniory of), in the county of Hertford, lies behind Vincennes, and is bounded by Beaumont and its augmentation on the north-east, Mont-à-Peine on the south-west, and in the rear by St. Gervais; it has about three quarters of a league in front, by three leagues in depth; granted September 20th, 1734, to Sieur Pean de Livaudiere. Upwards of one-third of this tract is in a very high state of cultivation; the soil, rich and fertile, produces large crops of grain, and almost every article peculiar to the district; the surface is somewhat uneven, but not to such a degree as to cause serious impediments to agriculture, until approaching the rear boundaries, where the elevation is abrupt. There is a great deal of beech, birch, and maple; from the latter, considerable quantities of sugar are made by the inhabitants every year. The seigniory is well watered by the River Boyer, each side of which presents some of the best cultivated land in the different concessions: towards the boundary of Vincennes there are also many specimens of very good husbandry. The church of St. Charles, and its parsonage, are seated on the north-west bank of the Boyer.

Roads, generally kept in thorough repair, pass through the seigniory to the main road on the River Echemin.

BEAUMONT (the seigniory of and its augmentation), is in the county of Hertford, between Vincennes and La Durantaie, having its front upon the St. Lawrence, and bounded in the rear by St. Gervais; about three quarters of a league in breadth, by a league and a half in depth; was granted November 3d, 1672, to Sieur des Islets de Beaumont: the augmentation was granted April 10th, 1713, to Sieur de Beaumont, and is of the same dimensions as the original grant: they now belong to Féréol Roy, Esq. This tract presents generally, rather a light and sandy soil; it rises to a considerable elevation on the bank of the river, but preserves a tolerably level surface when compared with the adjacent grants; nearly one half of the seigniory and a considerable portion of the augmentation are under a flourishing state of cultivation. Adjacent to the St. Lawrence there remains but little timber, though, penetrating further into the interior, much may be found of first rate quality; several small streams water it very plentifully: the augmentation is intersected by the Rivers Boyer and du Sud. The church and parsonage-house are seated on the bank of the river in front, and a grist-mill on the Riviere du Sud : the seigniory is crossed by several roads leading into the adjacent grants.

LA DURANTAIE (the seigniory of and its augmentation), in the county of Hertford, fronts the St. Lawrence : it is bounded on the south-west by Beaumont, on the north-east by Berthier, and in the rear by the township of Armagh, and the seigniory of St. Gervais; two leagues in breadth by two in depth; was granted October 29th, 1672, to Sieur de la Durantaie : the augmentation, of the same dimensions, was granted to Sieur de la Durantaie, May 16th, 1693. The grant and augmentation are now divided in equal proportions into the two seigniories of St. Michel and St. Vallier.

ST. MICHEL contains six ranges of concessions parallel to the River St. Lawrence, divided into one hundred and eighty-five lots that are in a forward state of cultivation, and about forty-five others entirely of wood-land. Near the river the soil is light and sandy; receding from thence about a mile, there is a fine loam of very excellent quality, but towards the rear the land grows poor and steril; consequently none of it is occupied. On the best grounds an advantageous system of husbandry is pursued, and the crops of wheat and other grain are in general abundant. The houses, amounting to about two hundred and thirty in all, are neatly built; the farms are well stocked, and bear every appearance of industry and care. In the back part of the grant some very good timber is produced; the best kinds are maple, birch, and beech, with some pine; but towards the St. Lawrence only a very few patches of wood remain among the concessions. The Rivers Boyer and Le Bras, besides a few small rivulets, water it; the two rivers rise considerably during the freshes of spring and autumn, though they are not of use at any time as navigable rivers. A bridge has been built of wood over each of them. There are a church and parsonage-house, surrounded by about a dozen other dwellings, occupied principally by artizans and workmen: the telegraph station, No. 3, is not far from the church. Of three saw-mills, the work is limited to spring and autumn, owing to the very scanty supply of water during the summer. Many roads pass through the seigniory in almost all directions, and are, the concession as well as the main ones, kept always in good repair. According to the size of this grant, the population is considerable, being upwards of 1700 persons.

ST. VALLIER, the property of ———— Delanaudiere, Esq., is, as nearly as possible, the counterpart of St. Michel; the species and quality of the soil, and the varieties of the timber differ only in a very slight degree; but the bank of the river is much lower, and the rear part somewhat broken and rugged. The greater part of the land is in an excellent state of culture; it is divided into about one hundred and eighty or one hundred and ninety lots, the best and most flourishing of which are situated on the St. Lawrence, and along both banks of the Riviere du Sud; these, with the Belle Chasse and Boyer, and a few small streams, water it very well: each of the rivers have bridges over them. The church of St. Vallier is pleasantly situated close to the St. Lawrence; the parsonage and a few other houses surround it; at a short distance to the eastward of it is the telegraph No. 4. This grant is intersected by numerous roads, in addition to the main one by the river, all of which, as well as the bridges, are well kept up; it has two grist-mills and several saw-mills. The augmentation is cultivated only to a very trifling extent; the surface of it is irregular, and in the rear quite mountainous, but it produces very fine timber almost of every description.

St. Gervais (the seigniory of), in the county of Hertford, is situated in the rear of Livaudiere, and the augmentations of Beau-

mont and La Durantaie, bounded on the north-
east by the township of Armagh, in the rear by
Buckland, and on the south-west by Mont-à-
Peine; two leagues and a half in breadth, by
the same in depth; was granted September
20th, 1750, to Sieurs Michel, Jean Hugues,
and Pean de Livaudiere. Only a very partial
settlement has yet taken place in this seigniory,
and the cultivation of it is very insignificant,
as the irregularity and mountainous nature of
its surface are both inimical to the exertions of
industry, although the soil itself is not bad,
being principally a light-coloured loam. It
abounds in timber of the best species, and is
watered by the Riviere du Sud, and some small
streams. The few inhabitants of this seigniory
obtain a living with difficulty; one of their
principal occupations during the spring is the
manufacture of maple-sugar, of which they contrive to send considerable quantities to market.

BERTHIER (the seigniory of), in the county
of Hertford, having the River St. Lawrence in
front, St. Vallier on the south-west, St. Thomas
on the north-east, and the Riviere du Sud
in the rear, is two leagues in front by as much
in depth; was granted October 29th, 1672, to
Sieur Berthier; it is now the property of ——
Denechaud, Esq. This seigniory is bounded
on the map according to a private survey; the

irregularity of it arises from a cession that the
proprietor of it made to the Seignior of Riviere
du Sud, on the 22d January, 1728. A light
sandy earth, varied with a mixture of yellowish
loam, is the prevalent kind of soil; it is fertile,
and highly productive of grain of all kinds; the
largest proportion of the land is under culture,
and the general system of husbandry seems to
have obtained a great degree of improvement.
Many of the farms are in a flourishing condition, of which those on the Riviere du Sud,
and the bank of the St. Lawrence, are perhaps
the best and most conspicuous. Along the
front the ground is rather low, but it gradually
rises to a small ridge about a mile from the
shore, from the summit of which a very interesting prospect unfolds itself; the river, between eleven and twelve miles across, is beautifully varied by the groups of islands, lying off the
west end of Crane Island. The eastern end of
the island of Orleans, with all its rich diversity
of scenery, and the lofty mountains rising behind Cape Tourmente complete the distant
view; the descent from the crest of the ridge
down to the shore is a continuation of well
cultivated fields, enriched with almost every
object that can make a landscape perfect;
these, with the addition of the church, and a
small cluster of houses charmingly seated al-

most close to the water's side, on the edge of a
little cove called Le Trou de Berthier, when
viewed from the main road, are well calculated to give a stranger an exalted idea of the
picturesque beauty of the country. Another
chain of heights, somewhat more elevated than
the one just mentioned, rises between it and
the Riviere du Sud, on which there is some
fine timber; in other parts of the seigniory
wood is not abundant. The Rivieres du Sud,
à la Caille, and Belle Chasse, provide an ample
and complete irrigation for every part. Near
the Riviere du Sud stands the church of St.
François; and a short distance from it a grist-
mill, worked by a little rivulet flowing into the
river. Numerous good roads intersect every
part of the seigniory; the main or post-road is
on the bank of the St. Lawrence.

ST. THOMAS (the seigniory of), in the county
of Devon, with its front to the St. Lawrence,
is bounded on the south-west by Berthier, on
the north-east by Fournier, and in the rear by
L'Epinay, a league and a half in breadth by
four and a half in depth; was granted May
5th, 1646, to the Sieur de Montmagny. The
original dimensions of this seigniory have been
the subject of much litigation, and were at
length fixed by an order from the Court of
King's Bench of the province, according to

L L

the line of boundary traced upon the Topographical Map, giving an average depth of about
a league and a half: it is now the property of
Monsr. Couillard.   In proportion to its extent,
this is one of the most valuable possessions in
the whole province; it lies generally low, with
the exception of a small ridge or two that separate the settlements on the St. Lawrence from
those on the Riviere du Sud.   The soil is so
rich and highly productive, particularly in grain
of all species, as to obtain for it the distinguishing epithet of the granary of the Lower District.
As may be supposed, no part of so good a soil
is neglected, and the whole is actually under a
state of cultivation not surpassed by any grant.
Owing to the great extent of agriculture, very
little timber remains.   It is advantageously
watered by the Riviere du Sud, a large branch
of the same called Bras St. Nicholas, the Riviere à la Caille, and many rivulets.   The first
mentioned is a beautifully winding stream that
has its source in the mountains, about the rear
of the seigniory of St. Gervais.   Another principal branch of it descends from the heights
much further in the interior.   From the confluence of this branch with the main stream in
the seigniory of St. Vallier, it meanders through
a fine plain in a north-easterly direction to the
village of St. Thomas, where it forms a large

basin before it discharges into the St. Lawrence; its course is much impeded by shoals,
and not navigable for any thing but canoes; a
little below the village its breadth is one hundred and fifty yards; the level of its bed is
twenty feet above the St. Lawrence, which occasions a fall, that from the latter has a very
beautiful effect. On each side of it, just at the
break of the descent, are two saw-mills, in situations most advantageously chosen for ensuring
a continual supply of water. The basin is
spacious, and well sheltered; at high water
vessels from twenty to twenty-five tons may
run in for security against a gale, by taking
care to avoid a muddy flat at its entrance: the
channel, however, is not difficult. The branch
called Bras St. Nicholas has its source in the
high lands, in the rear of the seigniories of
Bonsecours and Islet, and flows parallel to
the St. Lawrence, but in an opposite direction,
until it falls into Riviere du Sud, at the village
of St. Thomas. At its confluence, a handsome
bridge, called Prevost Bridge, was erected in
1812 by Jacques Morrin; it is one hundred
and twenty feet in length, eighteen in breadth,
and fifteen above the level of the water. Over
the Riviere du Sud there is a much handsomer
one, called the Regent's Bridge, built in 1813
by François Frichette; this is three hundred

feet long, twenty in breadth, and fifteen above
the water's level. It is built of wood, and supported by substantial neat stone piers; on the
top there is a very handsome railing: the two
being nearly together, and almost at right
angles with each other, have a very light and
pretty appearance. In every part of the seigniory, but particularly by the St. Lawrence,
and on each side of the Riviere du Sud, there
are many good houses in the midst of fertile
well stocked farms, surrounded by fine gardens
and good orchards, that convey an imposing
idea of the affluent circumstances of their
owners. Several excellent roads pass in different directions through the seigniories, particularly by the sides of the rivers. It contains
two churches, one in the village, dedicated to
St. Thomas, and another to St. Peter, on the
south side of Riviere du Sud. A small chapel,
called La Chapelle de St. Pierre, is seated on
an eminence, from whence a most agreeable
prospect of the St. Lawrence and the surrounding country opens itself. On the different
streams there are two grist-mills, and several
saw-mills. The village of St. Thomas contains
about ninety houses, exclusive of store-houses
and granaries, with a population of five hundred
persons; it is most delightfully situated at the
confluence of the two Rivers du Sud and St.

Lawrence. The houses are nearly all built
of wood, generally whitewashed, and disposed
into streets with something like regularity;
most of them have gardens and orchards attached, and in many instances form desirable
residences. There are several shop-keepers
and artizans, with some inns as they are called,
though they have no great claim to distinction
for the good accommodation they afford to
travellers. A few highly respectable families
have fixed their habitations here, and form
among themselves a select and pleasant society.

L'Epinay (the seigniory of), in the county
of Devon, lies in the rear of St. Thomas, three
leagues in breadth, by a league and a half in
depth, on an average; it was granted April
7th, 1701, to Sieur de L'Epinay. The soil in
this seigniory is of good quality, being in some
places a yellowish loam, and in others a good
black earth; in front the surface is rather
irregular, and as it recedes towards the rear
becomes mountainous. The part adjoining
St. Thomas is thickly settled, and there cultivation has made considerable advances; but
this portion is but of small dimensions, in
comparison to the whole extent of the seigniory. The timber consists of maple, birch,
and beech in profusion, with some very good

pine, besides a great plenty of inferior sorts.
It is watered by a few small streams, that de-
scend from the mountains, and flow into the
Riviere du Sud.

FOURNIER (fief), in the county of Devon,
fronting the St. Lawrence, is bounded on the
south-west by St. Thomas and L'Epinay, on
the north-east by Gagné and Ste. Claire, and
in the rear by waste lands of the crown; thirty
arpens in breadth, by two leagues in depth;
granted November 3d, 1672, to Sieur Fournier.

GAGNE' (fief) joins the north-east side of
Fournier, and bounded in the rear by Ste.
Claire; ten arpens in front, by one league in
depth; granted September 3d, 1675, to Sieur
Louis Gagné.

CAP ST. IGNACE (fief), next to Gagné, is
half a league in front, by a league in depth; it
is the property of Monsr. Vincelot. No docu-
ment relating to this grant has been found
among the records lodged in the surveyor-
general's office.

STE. CLAIRE (fief), in the rear of Gagné
and Cap St. Ignace, two leagues in depth, by
nearly one league in breadth; was granted
March 17th, 1695, to Réné Le Page. Of
these fiefs, the three first possess a tolerably
rich and productive soil, and are in a very

good state of cultivation, particularly along
the bank of the St. Lawrence, where the surface is smooth and level, but the back part of
them is rugged and mountainous. In St. Ignace very little timber remains; but Fournier
produces a great deal of all sorts. Excepting
Ste. Claire, they are all well watered by the
Bras St. Nicholas, and some rivulets that flow
into the St. Lawrence. Ste. Claire is still in its
natural state: the land is very uneven, but
moderately good; the timber in great variety
and superior quality.

VINCELOT (the seigniory of) and its augmentation, in the county of Devon, is bounded
on the north-east by Bonsecours, on the south-
west by Cap St. Ignace and Ste. Claire, and in
the rear by waste lands; it is one league square,
and was granted November 3d, 1672, to the
widow Amiot. The augmentation is one league
in breadth by two in depth, and was granted
February 1, 1693, to Sieur de Vincelot. Towards the river the land is low, the soil a light
sandy earth with clay or marl; in the rear there
is a light-coloured loam as it approaches the
mountains; the greatest part is under cultivation: it is rather bare of timber. The Bras
St. Nicholas and some small streams water it
very well. The front is indented by a large
bay, near to which is situated the church and

parsonage-house, and the telegraph station No. 6. Several roads by the St. Lawrence, and on the side of the Bras, communicate with the adjoining seigniories. The augmentation is neither remarkable for the goodness of its soil nor quality of the timber; it is mountainous, and wholly uncultivated.

·Bonsecours (the seigniory of), in the county of Devon, fronts the St. Lawrence, and is bounded on the north-east by Islet, on the south-west by Vincelot and its augmentation, and by waste lands in the rear; one league and a half in front by two in depth; was granted July 1; 1677, to Sieur François de Bellanger. This seigniory differs but little from the preceding one, as far as respects the nature of the soil, and timber growing thereon; about one half of it may be estimated under cultivation, and is very well inhabited; the system of agriculture is good, and well adapted to the land, which towards the river lies low, with the exception of a trifling ridge that runs nearly from one side to the other, but in the rear it is rough and mountainous. Some good timber, particularly pine, is produced in the back part of the grant. It is principally watered by the Bras St. Nicholas, the other streams being very insignificant.

Islet de St. Jean (the seigniory of), in

the county of Devon, is bounded by the river
in front, by Lessard in the rear, and lies between Bonsecours and St. Jean Port Joli; one
league in breadth by two in depth; granted
May 17th, 1677, to Demoiselle Génevieve
Couillard. The front of this grant is low, but
receding from the river towards the mountains
the land rises gradually; the soil in general is
good, producing grain of all kinds; in the rear
it is a light-coloured loam that continues up to
the high lands. About one-third of it may be
estimated to be under hand, and is pretty well
managed, as well as thickly inhabited. It is
watered by a continuation of the Bras St.
Nicholas, and several small runs of water.
Beech, birch, and maple, are the prevailing
kinds of timber, but there is likewise some pine
of very good growth. The church and parsonage are situated close to the St. Lawrence,
near a point of land, upon which is placed the
telegraph station No. 7. At high water this
point is completely isolated, from which circumstance it derives its name of Islet de St.
Jean.

LESSARD (the seigniory of) is situated in
the rear of Islet, and encompassed on three
sides by waste crown lands; it is one league
square, and was granted June 30th, 1698, to
Pierre Lessard. As this tract lies considerably

southward of the ridge of mountains, it is but little known. It is very well clothed with timber, but no attempt at cultivation has yet been made.

St. Jean Port Joli (the seigniory of), in the county of Devon, with its front to the St. Lawrence, bounded on the north-east by Reaume, on the south-west by Islet, and in the rear by waste crown lands; two leagues and a half in breadth by as much in depth; granted May 25th, 1677, to Noel L'Anglois: it is now the property of —— Gaspé, Esq. In front the land is somewhat low, but the uniformity of it is varied by a trifling ridge, and a few rising grounds: drawing towards the rear it is mountainous and rugged. The soil is a mixture of light sandy earth and clay; about the high lands it is poor and indifferent. About one-third of the tract, however, is in a moderate state of cultivation; and the settlements, generally speaking, have been brought, by industry, into a very respectable condition. Beech, birch, maple, and pine timber are in great plenty, as well as most of the inferior species. The Riviere des Trois Saumons, and River Port Joli, have their sources in the mountains at the back of the seigniory, and descending in a westerly direction, water it very well: there are a few other streams of inconsiderable note.

The church and parsonage-house are situated close to the St. Lawrence, by which the main road passes; there are also several other roads to the adjacent grants on each side. At the mouth of Riviere des Trois Saumons the valuable mills and distillery belonging to Mr. Harrower are very eligibly placed : the latter is an establishment of considerable magnitude, with every convenience for carrying on an extensive business ; at high water decked vessels of twenty tons may come up to the premises. Over the river there is a good bridge. The beach at the discharge of Riviere des Trois Saumons is flat, and thickly covered by detached rocks that run a good way out. From the St. Lawrence the view of the mills and surrounding objects, heightened by the pleasing natural scenery of the environs, is very agreeable.

REAUME (fief) is a small strip of land, between St. Jean Port Joli and St. Roch des Annais, half a league broad by two leagues deep; was granted March 16th, 1677, to Demoiselle de la Combe. In this property the same species of soil and timber are found as in St. Jean Port Joli; about one-third of it is well cultivated and thickly inhabited. A few trifling rivulets supply a very scanty irrigation.

The main road crosses it, besides which there are some concession roads.

ST. ROCH DES ANNAIS (the seigniory of), in the county of Devon, is bounded in front by the River St. Lawrence, on the north-east by Ste. Anne, on the south-west by Reaume, and in the rear by the unsurveyed township of Ashford; three leagues in breadth by two in depth; granted April 1, 1656, to Nicholas Juchereau de St. Denis: it is now the property of Chevalier Duchesnaye, Esq. In the vicinity of the river the land is low, and intersected by some broken ridges of no great elevation, but about the rear boundaries the mountains form a close chain of considerable height. Near the front the soil is excellent, consisting of a fine light earth, with a good deal of marl in various parts: on the higher lands a yellow loam is prevalent. One-third of the seigniory is in cultivation, and exhibits every appearance of fertility and good management, especially near the St. Lawrence. On the land under culture very little timber is left, but the other parts are well stocked with the best kinds, and among them some pine of a valuable size. Several small rivers and other streams water it very well, and also work two or three mills. The church and parsonage-house, with a small group of other dwellings surrounding them, stand on a pleasant site close to the Point. of St. Roch, from whence stretch the extensive shoals, that, by greatly narrowing the deep water channel, form the traverse mentioned in a former part of this work for the difficulty of its navigation. A little westward of the church. is the telegraph station No. 8. Many roads branch off in. almost every direction through the seigniory, but the one passing close.to the river is the main post road: they are kept in good order, as well as the different bridges.

STE. ANNE, or LA POCADIERE (the seigniory of), in the county of Cornwallis, lies between St. Roch des Annais and the seigniory of River Ouelle, with its front to the St. Lawrence, and bounded in the rear by the unsurveyed township of Ixworth; one league and a half in breadth by as much in depth; was granted October 29th, 1672, to Demoiselle de la. Combe: it is now the property of Monsr. Schmidt. So great a similarity reigns through several grants hereabouts, that a description of one may almost serve for the whole: the soil in. this one is very fertile, and produces grain of all sorts; most of the concessions are under a. good system of agricultural management, and thickly inhabited: the land approaching the mountains is, of good quality, but none of it under tillage. Among a variety of fine timber, abundance of capital pine is produced: it is watered by Le Grand Ruisseau, and several other streams that turn both grist and sawmills. It contains a church that is surrounded by several houses, very pleasantly situated on the bank of the river. Besides the main road, there are some others branching off in different directions into the seigniories of Riviere Ouelle and St. Roch, all of which are in good order.

RIVIERE OUELLE (the seigniory of), and its augmentation, in the county of Cornwallis, is bounded on the south-west by Ste. Anne, on the north-east by St. Denis, in front by the St. Lawrence, and on the rear by the unsurveyed township of Ixworth; two leagues in breadth by one and a half in depth; was granted October 29th, 1672, to Sieur de la Boutellerie. The augmentation, two leagues in front by two in depth, was granted October 20th, 1750, to Dame Génévieve de Ramzay, veuve de Sieur de Bois Hebert: they are now the property of ——— Casgrin, Esq. This is a very valuable and productive tract of country, the greater part of it being a plain, of which the soil is both rich and fertile, being a fine dark mould, interspersed with clay and good marl: the equality of surface is here and there varied by a few small swells and perpendicular rocks of granite, covered at top with creeping shrubbery. The greater part of the land bespeaks a superior state of husbandry; the arable yields grain of all sorts in abundance, and of a quality scarcely surpassed by any other seigniory in the province: the meadow and pasture lands are very luxuriant, and the produce of the dairies forms no inconsiderable portion of the farmer's wealth. The farm-houses and other dwellings are generally accompanied by well stocked gardens and good orchards, their inhabitants enjoying, from all appearance, every comfort that industry can procure among a people wholly cultivators. Although the lands in occupation are generally good, yet a little superiority is perceptible among those on each side of River Ouelle, on the plain stretching north-eastward from thence, and on the main road in the vicinity of the St. Lawrence. In the front part of the seigniory there is but little timber; in the rear, however, there is a profuse variety of the best kinds. It is admirably watered by the River Ouelle, many small streams, and the Lake St. Pierre. The source of the former is in the north-east range of mountains, from whence it winds a serpentine course down to the St. Lawrence: it feels the effect of the tide for some distance up, and is so far navigable for

vessels of twenty-five tons burthen, many
of which are constantly employed in transporting to Quebec the produce of this excellent tract, consisting of grain, butter, poultry, live-stock, and a coarse species of woollen
cloth manufactured here. Where the post-
road arrives at this river there is a ferry, with
scows and canoes always in attendance. In
so populous a seigniory it is strange that a
bridge has not been built; the want of one has,
however, been so much felt, that such a measure
is said to be in contemplation. A handsome
church and parsonage stand on the eastern
bank of Riviere Ouelle, by the side of the main
road, and almost opposite is the manor-house:
at the mouth of the river is the telegraph station No. 9. In the St. Lawrence, about the
entrance of River Ouelle, a porpoise fishery is
carried on; but, either from less attention
being paid to it, or the fish not frequenting the
spot so much as formerly, it is not now so productive as it used to be.

St. Denis (fief), in the county of Cornwallis, lies between River Ouelle (seigniory) and
Camouraska, and is bounded in the rear by
the unsurveyed township of Woodbridge; it
has about a league in breadth by four in
depth; granted May 12th, 1679, to Sieur de
St. Denis, for, and in the name of, Joseph Ju-

chereau, his son. The soil in this fief is not much inferior to that of the preceding seigniory, but its surface is more overspread by small detached ridges; it is crossed by the high chain of mountains near the middle of its depth. About a quarter of the grant is under culture, and produces good wheat and other grain. The timber is excellent and plentiful, among which there is pine of a fine growth. Part of Lake St. Peter and a few small streams are the only means of irrigation. The best cultivated lands are by the sides of the roads that cross the seigniory. On a rising ground, close by a little inlet called St. Denis Cove, is the telegraph station No. 10.

CAMOURASKA (the seigniory of), on the south bank of the St. Lawrence, in the county of Cornwallis, is bounded by St. Denis on the south-west, Granville on the north-east, and the unsurveyed township of Woodbridge in the rear; three leagues in breadth by two in depth; was granted July 15th, 1674, to Sieur de la Durantaie: it is now the property of ———— Taché, Esq. This is another of the very valuable and productive seigniories of the Lower District. In the vicinity of the river the land is rather low, and forms an extensive plain, here and there marked by a few singular hillocks, or rather rocks, covered about the top

by a few dwarf pines and low underwood. The
soil is excellent, being either a rich black mould,
a yellow loam, or a mixture of clay and sand :
towards the rear it loses some of its goodness
and fertility, as it becomes mountainous.—
About one half of the grant is under cultivation, and agriculture has made great progress
in a very productive system : wheat and all
kinds of grain seldom fail of abundant harvests;
but these are not the only dependence of the
farmer, as there are within the seigniory some
of the best dairies in the province, from whence
large quantities of excellent butter are continually sent to Quebec, where it is more esteemed
than any other kind brought to the market. Except the mountainous parts, where fine beech,
birch, maple, basswood, and pine, are produced,
there is not much timber to be found. It is
watered by the Riviere du Domaine, which in
its course works a grist and a saw-mill, and by
a variety of other small streams falling into the
St. Lawrence. Several roads leading into the
adjoining grants, and many others, open a communication with the different concessions : on
both sides of them there are many farm-houses,
situated in the midst of fields of most luxuriant
fertility, that from spring to autumn present all
the beautiful variety of an interesting country.
The church and parsonage are pleasantly seated

on the main road, near the St. Lawrence : close
to the former, and running south-west on each
side of the road, is the village of Camouraska,
consisting of forty or fifty houses, the greater
part of them built of wood; but there are some
few of stone, in a much superior style to the
others : some families of great respectability
have fixed their residence here, also some very
reputable shopkeepers' and artisans; it can
likewise boast of one or two inns, where travellers may be comfortably lodged and well
entertained. During the summer time this
village is enlivened by numerous visitants, who
come hither to recruit their health, as it has the
reputation of being one of the healthiest spots
in all the Lower Province; it is also the *water-
ing-place*, where many people resort for the
benefit of sea-bathing. The manor-house,
which is the residence of M. Taché, is eligibly
situated near the river, at a short distance from
the village. The islands of Camouraska, in
front of the grant, are appendages thereto :
being almost bare rocks, they are scarcely of
any value, but they are of great utility as affording a safe shelter to small vessels, of which
great numbers are always passing to and from
the numerous coves hereabouts; on one of
them, called Isle Brulée, stands a telegraph.

The Camouraska schooners are well known at Quebec for the large quantities of provisions they are laden with, such as grain, live-stock, poultry, butter, maple-sugar, &c., besides considerable freights of deal planks and other timber. The general aspect of the country in this part of the district of Quebec will always attract the notice of attentive observers. From the bank of the river, which is not much elevated, a plain that, generally speaking, is very level, stretches almost to the foot of the north-east range of mountains: the even surface of this tract is, in various parts, singularly embossed with abrupt masses of solid rocks of granite, destitute of any thing like a covering of soil. From the crevices in them spring a few dwarf pine-trees, rising a little above a thick foliage of creeping shrubbery, issuing from the same places, and spreading over nearly their whole summits: in circumference, some of them cover from three to perhaps half a dozen acres, and vary from twenty to about thirty yards of perpendicular height. From the position, appearance, and exact resemblance of these *terra firma* islands to those of Camouraska, between which and the shore the bed of the river is almost dry at low water, a naturalist will be strongly excited to believe that what is now the continent was, at some period or other, submerged beneath the wide-spreading wave of the St. Lawrence, and that .the elevations in question formed islands, or rocks, exposed to the action of the waters. The progressive diminution of the river; and its withdrawing into the comparative narrow channel that it now occupies, would become an interesting subject for the researches of the geologist; but as it does not fall within the province of the topographer, the enquiry may be dispensed with here.

GRANVILLE (the seigniory of) is bounded by Camouraska on the south-west, Islet du Portage on the north-east, the St. Lawrence in the front, and the unsurveyed township of Bungay in the rear; one league in breadth by three in depth; granted October 5th, 1707, to Marie Anne de Granville, widow of Sieur de Soulange.

ISLET DU PORTAGE (the seigniory of) lies between those of Granville and Lachenaye, bounded in the rear by waste crown lands; one league in front along the river, and one in depth; granted October 29th, 1672, to Sieur de Granville.

GRANVILLE and LACHENAYE (the seigniory of), in the county of Cornwallis, having its front to the river, is bounded on the south-

west by Islet du Portage and the unsurveyed
lands of Bungay, on the north-east by the seigniory of Riviere du Loup, and in the rear by
Bungay and waste lands; two leagues in
breadth by three in depth; granted June 2d,
1696, to Sieurs de Granville and Lachenaye.
In these three seigniories there are some very
fertile patches of land, but as the north-easterly
chain of mountains draws closer upon the river,
a great part of them is very mountainous; a
small portion of each has been cultivated, but
none of it is at present in a very flourishing
condition. The best farms, however, in each
grant, are found near the main road that passes
close to the river. Timber is sufficiently plentiful, and some of it of the best kinds. They
are but sparingly watered by a few small
streams that descend into the St. Lawrence.
In Granville there is a grist-mill. Islet has a
church dedicated to St. Andrew; but Granville and Lachenaye possesses nothing at all
worth notice: there are indeed ranges of concessions marked out, and bearing the names of
St. André, Bouchetteville, Marie Louise Ade-
laide, Ste. Rachel, and St. Theodore; of these
St. André only is in a good condition; in the
others the ground has scarcely been broken.
A grist-mill is seated on the Riviere des Caps,

at its junction with the little stream called
Fouquet. ¡The four islands called the Pilgrims
lie about a mile and a half off the front of the
seigniory, stretching nearly its whole breadth;
they are only piles of rock covered with low
brushwood and a few small trees: the westerly
one is the station of the telegraph No. 12.

RIVIERE DU LOUP (the seigniory of), in the
county of Cornwallis, fronts the Saint Lawrence,
joining Granville and Lachenaye on the south-
west, and the seigniory of Isle Verte on the
north-east: in the rear it is bounded by waste
crown lands. It has nearly five leagues in
breadth by two in depth; granted April 5th,
1689, to the Sieurs Villerai and Lachenaye:
Alexander Fraser, Esq. is the proprietor. The
general appearanc of this seigniory is uneven
and mountainous, but it contains some extensive patches of good arable and very fine
meadow land; these are divided into several
ranges of concessions, bearing the names of St.
André Riviere du Loup, St. Patrick Riviere
du Loup, Fraserville, Nouvelle Ecosse, St.
George, or Cacona, St. Anthony, St. Andrew,
and St. Jacques: the first, a great part of the
second, and a little of the third, are in a very
good state of cultivation and well inhabited.
The whole seigniory is abundantly timbered

with beech, maple, birch, and large quantities
of pine. It is watered by several streams, but
the principal one is Riviere du Loup, which
rises in the high lands, and flows in nearly a
northerly course into the St. Lawrence; on
both sides of it the banks are high, until approaching within about three quarters of a mile
of its discharge, where they become low and
flat: vessels of twenty-five tons may ascend it as
high as the bridge, a little more than half a
mile from its mouth. Fraser Lodge, the residence of the owner of the seigniory, is situated
on the north side of the entrance of the
river. The main road passes close to the
River St. Lawrence, except near the church
of St. Patrick, where it makes a *detour* by a
rising ground, up to the bridge over Riviere
du Loup, and afterwards descends again to
the bank of the St. Lawrence, and so continues
through the remainder of the grant. By the
side of this road there are many ranges of well
cultivated fields, that yield abundant crops of
all kinds of grain; numerous farm-houses, with
large and substantial outbuildings, besides a
great many dwelling-houses. Through the
whole of this extensive property there is but
one church; however, in the concession of St.
George, near Cacona, there is a chapel for

those to whom distance denies a regular attendance at the former. Cacona is almost an island, being separated from the main land by a salt marsh, that in the spring always presents a luxuriant pasturage: on the point of Cacona there are several inhabitants. About four miles and three quarters eastward of the Riviere des Caps is the commencement of the Timiscouata portage, which, as being the only route by land from Quebec to Halifax, a distance of six hundred and twenty-seven miles altogether, is of great importance, and a particular description of it therefore will perhaps be acceptable. It was first opened in the year 1783, by General Haldimand, then Governor, but was at that time, considered by many as so intricate, and to present so many difficulties, as to make it impracticable to establish a regular road by it; perseverance, however, with the few attentions it has received from time to time, have clearly shewn the contrary; and it is at this time a route (susceptible indeed of very great improvement) by which the communication may be kept up all the year round: the British mail is always conveyed by it, when landed from the packet at Halifax. From the main road of the St. Lawrence, where the portage road branches off, to Long's Farm on the bank of Lake Timiscouata, the distance is thirty-seven miles : the direction of the road is generally to the eastward, but it has numerous turns and windings to avoid ascending several very lofty and rugged hills, or crossing deep swamps; as it is, about twenty-four miles of the distance is over a succession of mountains, many of them rough and very steep. However, none of the formidable impediments exist that were formerly considered so insurmountable ; and indeed a little exertion, with an expense not very considerable, would render this road as good and convenient for travelling as can be reasonably expected in a wild and unsettled country. From the bank of the St. Lawrence, up to Coté's Ferry, on the Riviere du Loup, a distance of about five miles, the road is as good as can be desired, and by which carriages of burthen may proceed to the ferry, or to Ballentine's Mills, a little to the left: the remainder of the way to Lake Timiscouata has been much improved by *corvées* of several hundreds of militia men, who were employed in mending it in the year 1813, under the superintendence of the *Grand Voyer*, Captain Destimauville. In many parts where the bottom was unsound and swampy, causeways were formed with logs. Though much has been

done, more is yet wanting to complete the
work; cutting trenches on each side of the
road would be serviceable in draining off the
water, and rendering the base of it more solid.
Bridges should be erected over the different
streams, instead of the inconvenient *make-shift*
now resorted to, of placing three logs across
them; a contrivance very awkward and unsafe
for a horse to pass, and much too narrow for a
cart. In a few years these defects will unquestionably be remedied, as the government
is desirous of keeping open this line of communication, and rendering it as commodious
as circumstances will permit: and in consequence of orders given for that purpose, several soldiers of the 10th Royal Veteran Battalion, with their families, were settled in 1814
upon lands allotted to them at convenient intervals, under the personal direction of the
Surveyor-General of the province. These few
settlers are not, however, sufficient wholly to
answer the intended purpose, and most probably others will hereafter be placed on proper
places, of which many may be found, where
there are large portions of good land, and some
extensive *brulés*, that might very speedily be
brought into a state of moderate fertility: at
present there are only a few sheds at different

intervals, where travellers may pass the night under shelter from the weather; but as they are uninhabited, nothing further is to be expected from them. Two of the veteran soldiers (Clifford and Gardner) who are settled on the River St. François, about midway along the portage, have got good and comfortable cottages, the accommodations of which they are always ready to afford to passengers, and it rarely happens that any one goes by who is not eager to accept them. The principal mountains over which the road runs are the St. François, Cote de la Grande Fourche, Jean Paradis, La Montagne de la Riviere Verte, and du Buard; the rivers are Du Loup, Riviere Verte, and Trois Pistoles, that flow into the St. Lawrence, and the Riviere St. François, that falls into River St. John. At Long's Farm the traveller cannot fail to be pleased with a beautiful and picturesque prospect of Lake Timiscouata, twenty-two miles in length by the average breadth of three quarters of a mile, encompassed in all directions by lofty mountains covered with thick wood almost down to its margin: several large rivers lend the aid of their powerful streams to swell the waters of this romantic and secluded expanse. In this spot, so far removed from the habitations of man and the pleasures of society, the farm, though but an humble one, becomes an object of considerable interest; it consists only of a cottage, a barn, and two or three small out-houses, surrounded by a few cultivated fields and a garden. In summer time the scenery around it is various, and uncommonly pleasing, but it can hardly compensate for the dreary solitude of winter. Long, the proprietor of it, has a large family: himself and his sons are the ferrymen of the lake, and have always bark canoes ready to take passengers from one side to the other. From this place to the entrance of the Madawaska river the distance is fifteen miles; and five miles further on is Birch river, where there are two other settlers of the Veteran Battalion (Serjeant Smith and Simpson): twenty-three miles beyond this place are the little falls of St. John. There is a house kept by Simon Hébert, about a mile below these falls, on the westerly side of the river, where something like the accommodations of an inn may be obtained; and if they are not of the best description, the traveller is in general too pleased, in availing himself of them, to descant upon their deficiencies. At this place the Madawaska settlement begins, and continues by intervals on each side of the River St. John for about

twenty-five miles; it consists of about two
hundred families of Canadians and Acadians.
The cottages are for the most part neatly built,
and both fields and gardens well cultivated:
on the eastern side of the river, at the beginning
of the settlement, there is a church and parsonage-house; there are also two grist-mills in it.
From the termination of this little colony to
the Great Falls of River St. John the distance
is fifteen miles, where there is a military post,
or more properly speaking a few old houses
occupied by a non-commissioned officer and a
few privates, detached from some of the corps
serving within the province of New Brunswick:
from this post down to Presqu'ile is fifty-two
miles, where a similar establishment is kept.
From Long's House to Presqu'ile the total
distance is one hundred and thirty-five miles, of
which there can be said to be only thirty-five
of road already made. To keep the communication free and convenient throughout the
year, it will therefore be necessary to form
about one hundred miles more, but of this
distance the length of the Madawaska settlement may be considered as nearly done already.
This task, arduous as it may at first appear,
would not be very difficult to complete,
and might be performed on the west side of

the St. John and Madawaska rivers, following nearly the route taken by the 8th and 104th regiments, that, in the winter of 1813-14, marched from Presqu'ile to Long's, round Lake Timiscouata in nine days. From Presqu'ile to St. John's in the Bay of Fundy, one hundred and thirty-six miles, the roads are tolerably good on both sides of the river. During the summer season the water communication from Lake Timiscouata to St John's is easy, being interrupted only by the Little and Great Falls: at the former there is a portage of about sixty yards, and at the latter another of about a quarter of a mile. From St. John's, the packet-boat crosses the Bay of Fundy to Annapolis; from thence down to Halifax (one hundred and thirty-three miles) the road is very good, along which travellers may always obtain moderately good accommodation.

Isle Verte (the seigniory of), in the county of Cornwallis, is bounded in front by the River St. Lawrence, on the south-west by Riviere du Loup (seigniory), on the north-east by Dartigny, and in the rear by waste lands; two leagues in breadth by two in depth; granted April 27th, 1684, to Sieurs Dartigny and La Cardoniére.

Dartigny (the seigniory of) joins the north-east side of Isle Verte (seigniory); is two leagues broad and two deep: no record of this grant has been found, even the date of the concession is unknown.

TROIS PISTOLES (the seigniory of), in the county of Cornwallis, is bounded by Dartigny on the south-west, on the north-east by Richard Rioux, and in the rear by waste lands; two leagues in breadth by two in depth; granted January 6th, 1687, to Sieur de Vitré.

RICHARD RIOUX, now a part of Trois Pistoles, is an extensive grant, fronting the St. Lawrence, and nearly encompassed on the other sides by waste lands; it is six leagues in length by four in breadth; granted April 6th, 1751, to Sieur Nicholas Rioux. From the seigniory of Riviere du Loup, along the banks of the St. Lawrence eastward, agriculture has kept but a very unequal pace with the other parts of the district, and the land under cultivation is insignificant in quantity; in many places it is very good, but situation and climate are both unfavourable to tillage: little therefore remains to be said of the few remaining settlements in the lower part of the district of Quebec. The four seigniories just recited are nearly throughout their whole extent mountainous and rugged; the great north-easterly ridge ranges so close to the river as to leave only a narrow slip between it and the shore. This space possesses a moderately good soil, upon which there are a few settlements under a respectable state of husbandry; there are also several patches of good land more in the interior, lying in the hollows between the ridges. Close by the river side there is a very good road extending as far as Bic, and indeed to some distance below it. Isle Verte is much better settled, and in proportion to its extent far more productive than either of the others. It is watered by Riviere Verte, which has its source in the mountains south of Timiscouata portage, and flows in a northerly direction into the St. Lawrence; it has a ferry over it at the main road. Isle Verte, or Green Island, lying off the front of this seigniory, is six miles and a half in length by the extreme breadth of one mile: the soil on this spot is good, and yields fine pasturage for a large quantity of cattle; there is also some pretty good timber upon it. The light-house on the north-east point has been already noticed; the keeper of it, Mr. Hamilton, with his family, and one other family, are the only inhabitants. The island is an appendage to the Riviere du Loup, and belongs to the same proprietor. Dartigny and Richard Rioux are very scantily watered, but very well covered with timber of various species, and very good growth. Trois Pistoles is intersected by a large river of the same name, whose current is supplied from several small lakes among the mountains that surround the end of Lake Timiscouata. Timber of all sorts may be had here in great abundance.

BIC (the seigniory of), in the county of Cornwallis, next below Richard Rioux, has two leagues in breadth upon the St. Lawrence, and two in depth; was granted May 6th, 1675, to Monsr. de Vitré, together with the Island of Bic, lying in front of it, nearly three miles in length by three quarters of a mile in breadth.

RIMOUSKI (the seigniory of) joins Bic; it has two leagues in front along the river, and two in depth; granted April 24th, 1688, to Sieur de la Cardoniere. The island St. Barnabé, lying off this seigniory, is also included in the grant.

ST. BARNABE' (the seigniory of) extends from the north-east boundary of Rimouski, down to and comprising Pointe aux Peres, about a league and a quarter in breadth by two leagues in depth; granted March 11th, 1751, to Sieur Le Page de St. Barnabé.

LESSARD (the seigniory of) is next in succession to St. Barnabé, containing a league and a half along the St. Lawrence, by two leagues in depth; was granted March 8th, 1696, to Pierre Lessard.

Le Page (the seigniory of) follows Lessard; it is about three leagues in front by one in depth; granted November 4th, 1696, to Sieurs Louis Le Page and Gabriel Tibiérge. An augmentation to it of two leagues in depth was granted to the same persons, May 7th, 1697.

Pachot (the seigniory of), lying next to Le Page, consists of the River Metis, from its discharge into the St. Lawrence for one league upwards, and a tract of land along the St. Lawrence, of one league in breadth by one league in depth; granted January 7th, 1689, to Sieur Pachot.

De Peiras or Metis (the seigniory of) follows Pachot, and contains two leagues in front along the river by two in depth; granted May 6th, 1675, to the Sieur de Peiras. The general surface of these seigniories is mountainous, and broken along the front, affording but little good soil for the purposes of agriculture. In the interior, and by the sides of the rivers that water them, a few patches of tolerable land, with some meadows and pastures, present themselves. In Bic, Rimouski, and St. Barnabé, there are some settlements in as favourable a condition as the soil and climate will admit of; but in the others only a few scattered farms are now and then visible. The timber is abundant, and of very good quality in all of them. An indifferent road leads from a little below Bic down to Pointe aux Peres, where there is a little settlement consisting of a few houses, that are inhabited by pilots, surrounded by some cultivated fields and gardens. In the river, near these seigniories, there are one or two banks, where fishing might be very profitably carried on, as they abound with fine ling, cod, salmon, and other fish. Crane Island, and Goose Island, were originally appendages to the seigniory of Riviere du Sud, being granted with it on the 5th. May, 1646; but they have since been dismembered from it, and are now the property of Mr. McPherson. They are connected with each other by a marsh, and altogether make four leagues in length: they are inhabited by about forty families, and well cultivated, producing wheat much beyond their own consumption. The marshes are peculiar for the abundance of fine hay they produce, and their pastures, which are sufficient for three thousand head of cattle.

LAC METIS (the seigniory of) consists of the lake, and one league of land surrounding it on every side; was granted February 10th, 1693, to Sieur Louis Rouer.

LAKE MATAPEDIACH (the seigniory of) is a grant of the preceding description, made

May 26th, 1693, to Sieur Nicholas Joseph
Damour. Neither the lakes nor the surrounding
land have been yet surveyed; consequently,
no correct account of them has been yet obtained.

Cote de Beaupré (the seigniory of), on
the north side of the river, in the county of
Northumberland, joins the seigniory of Beauport on the south-west, and reaches to the Rivière du Gouffre on the north-east, a distance
of sixteen leagues by a depth of six leagues;
was granted January 15th, 1636, to Sieur
Cheffault de la Regnardiere, and is now the
property of the ecclesiastics of the Seminary
of Quebec. This very extensive seigniory is
more mountainous than any other in the province, yet it contains a large proportion of rich
and fertile land. The nature of the soil varies
a great deal, as may be readily conjectured, in
so vast a space; but the general character of
such as is fit for cultivation is nearly the following, viz. on the low grounds along the
front of the seigniory, from Beauport to Cape
Tourmente, is a dark-coloured mould of good
quality, here and there mixed with sand and
clay, and some marl; on the higher lands there
is for the most part a strong black earth,
which, as it approaches the mountains, gives
place to a yellowish loam. Among the timber,

beech, maple, birch, pine, hickory, and basswood, are very abundant, as also the inferior
species of cedar, sprucefir, hemlock, &c.
From the north-eastern extremity of the seigniory of Beauport to Cape Tourmente, a dis-
stance of rather more than twenty-two miles,
there is a strip of land ranging in breadth from
half a mile to a mile, and bounded to the
northward by an eminence of considerable elevation : the part of this space not under tillage
is very excellent meadow land : the outer margin of the whole of it, at low water, is a continued marsh of not much less than a mile in
width, on which, during the spring and autumn,
the sportsman is sure to meet with excellent
game, as it is visited by wild-ducks, snipes, and
plover, in amazing quantities. Beyond the
boundary of this level the ground continues to
rise by gradations, until it reaches the lofty
mountains in the rear. Cape Tourmente is a
bold bluff point, rising more than one thousand
eight hundred feet above the river, forming a
very prominent object in the view of the north
shore, either from the eastward or the westward. From hence to Cape Maillard, another
bold promontory about five leagues down the
river, there is a continuation of capes and projecting points, varying greatly in their size and
height, but all of them rising abruptly from the

beach. At their bases is the route called Le
Chemin des Caps, which is the only means of
communication between the two places, and
not passable at high water. From Cape Maillard to Cap de la Baie, a distance of nearly
three leagues, there is a narrow space between
the river and the rising ground in the division
called La Petite Riviere, similar to that on the
westward of Cape Tourmente, and which is
very well cultivated. Proceeding by the Bay
of St. Paul and the Riviere du Gouffre, the
country is exceedingly mountainous; but the soil
is good, thickly inhabited, and well cultivated.
The seigniory is watered by a great many
streams flowing into the St. Lawrence and the
Riviere du Gouffre; the chief of them are the
Montmorenci, Riviere du Sault à la Puce, Riviere au Chien, Riviere Ste. Anne, that receives
the little rivers à la Rose and des Roches; Riviere du Domaine, flowing from two lakes in
the rear of Cape Tourmente, that are at least
eight hundred feet above the level of the St.
Lawrence; Riviere du Sault au Cochon, Bras
du nord-ouest du Gouffre, Riviere des Mares,
Riviere Remus, &c. &c. It is divided into the
six parishes of Ange Gardien, Château Richer,
Ste. Anne, St. Joachim, Baie de St. Paul, and
La Petite Riviere; in each of which there is a
church and parsonage-house, besides a grist-

mill and several saw-mills. The best cultivated and most populous divisions of the seigniory are Ange Gardien, Chateau Richer, Ste.
Anne, St. Joachim, and the settlements about
St. Féréole. Between the latter and those of
La Petite Riviere there intervenes a barren
tract of five leagues in length, that has always
proved most seriously inimical to the progress
of the settlements about St. Paul's Bay, there
not being a single road through it, or other
means of communication between the two settlements, except by water, and the uncertain
one of Le Chemin des Caps, as already mentioned. This great inconvenience will, most
probably, soon be remedied; for a road has been
traced from St. Féréole to the Bay of St. Paul,
to pass in the rear of the mountains, pursuant
to an act of the provincial parliament, which
likewise provides a sum of money to defray the
expenses of the work. Ange Gardien is populous, and well settled; the main road, passing
along the eminence almost fronting the river,
presents a number of very good houses on each
side of it, and which, with those that appear
among the concessions upon the rising grounds
more in the interior, have a most pleasing effect
to the eye. As the county of Northumberland
extends from Beauport to the extremity of the
province at the River St. John, on the coast of

Labrador, when an election takes place for its members of parliament, it is held at Ange Gardien for the western part of it, and when finished there the candidates repair to St. Paul's Bay, where the votes for the eastern district are collected, and from whence the members are declared duly elected. The Riviere Sault à la Puce is a small stream, descending from the high lands in the rear of Chateau Richer: it winds through a mountainous and woody country, and is entitled to notice for two or three very romantic falls, where its stream is precipitated from the declivity of one ridge to the level of another; and for the beautiful and truly sylvan scenery that decorates its banks, and, in the fall of the year particularly, presents a most extraordinary combination of various foliage. In Chateau Richer are the ruins of a Franciscan Monastery, that was built at the beginning of the last century, upon a little rocky promontory, on the bank of the St. Lawrence. Its destruction took place at the time the British army, under General Wolfe, was encamped on the eastern side of the River Montmorenci: the priests of the order at that period, paying more attention to temporal than to spiritual concerns, exerted themselves so much in preventing the country people from supplying any provisions to the troops, that

the general found it expedient to dislodge
them from their house, which they had so
strongly barricaded as to require the aid of a
few pieces of artillery in bringing them to sub-
jection; in consequence, the monastery was
destroyed; and there now remain only some of
the exterior walls, and part of an adjoining
tower. On a rising ground, in the rear of these
ruins, stands the parish church, rather a handsome structure with two spires: from this spot
a wide-spreading and beautiful prospect unfolds itself, comprehending a large portion of
the river, Cape Tourmente, the Island of Orleans and Cape Diamond, with all the intermediate scenery of the well-cultivated tracts of
the surrounding country, the whole bounded
by distant mountains both to the northward
and the southward. The parish of St. Joachim
is thickly inhabited; the lands in it are of good
quality, and in high cultivation, producing
wheat and other grain very plentifully; it contains also some very luxuriant pasturage. Within
this parish, delightfully situated on a rising
ground, a short distance from Cape Tourmente,
is a country residence, with a chapel and various outbuildings, belonging to the Seminary of
Quebec, and whither many of the superiors
retire every year during the fine season. The
settlements of St. Féréole range along the

western bank of Riviere Ste. Anne for about six miles. From the increased elevation of this part, and its great exposure to the severity of the climate, agriculture often experiences powerful checks, and the crops sometimes sustain serious injury; however, great industry among the inhabitants, who are altogether estimated at between five and six hundred, supplies them abundantly, and leaves something to spare of all the necessaries and many of the comforts of life. The road through the settlement of La Petite Riviere is, for the space of about six miles, well settled on each side; the houses neat, and the farms in a respectable state of tillage. The road continues to La Martine, a settlement about three miles in the interior, from whence it goes on through Cote St. Antoine and Cote St. Gabriel, as far as Riviere Remus, a distance of about ten miles and a half; at short intervals through this route there are houses and farms in a flourishing state of agriculture. In St. Paul's Bay, and along the Riviere du Gouffre, the settlements are girt by a lofty range of mountains stretching northward from the St. Lawrence, and enclosing a valley of about thirteen miles in length, and from a mile to a mile and a half in breadth; the greatest part of which is numerously inhabited, and very well cultivated, notwithstanding the land is in many places very rocky and uneven : several spots on the sides of the hills, though difficult of access from their elevated and precipitous situation, are tilled by manual labour, and are extremely fertile in grain of most sorts. On this tract the houses of the inhabitants are nearly all of stone, very well built and whitewashed on the outside, which greatly adds to the gaiety of the general prospect of the settlement, as well as to the neatness of their individual appearance. Several small streams descend from the mountains, and after serpentizing through the valley fall into the Riviere du Gouffre, turning in their way several saw and grist-mills. The main road passes at the foot of the bounding heights to the extremity of the cultivated land in Cote St. Urbain, and on each side presents many neat and interesting farms and settlements, in a very improved state. The church of St. Pierre is situated on the bank of the Riviere du Gouffre, near its discharge into St. Paul's Bay.

LE GOUFFRE (the seigniory of), in the county of Northumberland, is bounded on the westward by the Riviere du Gouffre, on the eastward by the seigniory of Les Eboulemens, and in the rear by waste crown lands; it extends about half a league on the River St. Lawrence by four leagues in depth, along the

Riviere du Gouffre; granted December 30th, 1682, to Pierre Dupré: it is now the property of Madame Drapeau. This seigniory, on the easterly side of the river, is nearly the counterpart of the opposite settlement in Cote du Beaupré, possessing almost the same kind of soil, and cultivated in a similar manner. The Capes Corbeau and La Baie, projecting into the St. Lawrence, are of great height, and rise abruptly from the water's edge: they are connected with the chain of mountains that ranges along the Riviere du Gouffre, far into the interior; diverging at first a short distance from it, leaving an intermediate tract of good land, but afterwards drawing quite close upon its bank. The first concession, bordering upon St. Paul's Bay, and coasting the river, shows a range of settlements where agriculture has obtained no small degree of improvement: some trifling degree of amelioration has also obtained in the rear of this range. The Bay of St. Paul is about three miles in depth, and rather more than two miles at its entrance, from the capes on each side; it receives the waters of Riviere du Gouffre, which is a stream of considerable size, flowing from some lakes in the second range of mountains in the interior. From the capes that form the exterior points of the bay on either side, the ridges of high lands describe a circuit before they close upon the river: their lofty and craggy summits form a grand amphitheatric back ground to the picturesque and highly romantic situation, generally known as the St. Paul's Bay Settlement.

LES EBOULEMENS (the seigniory of), in the county of Northumberland, fronting the St. Lawrence, lies between the seigniories of Le Gouffre and Murray Bay, bounded in the rear by waste crown lands; three leagues in breadth by two in depth. No record of this grant has been preserved, but it appears from an act of fealty and homage performed April 3d, 1723, by Pierre Tremblay, then proprietor, that he produced a concession of the land in question made to Pierre Lessard, but the date thereof was not quoted: it is now the property of M. de Sales La Terriere. The face of this seigniory is excessively mountainous; but the soil is not inferior to that about St. Paul's Bay, and is in many parts equally productive. The shore of the St. Lawrence is very lofty, especially about Cap aux Oies; but the edges of the bays, between the different projecting points, afford some good patches of meadow and pasture land: from the elevated bank of the river the ground continues to rise ridge over ridge until it reaches the mountains in the rear. In the concessions called Godefroid,

Dorothée, St. Joseph, and St. George, some very good settlements, that are in an improved condition, present themselves on the slopes of the high lands, and in the intervals between them: the whitewashed cottages and farm-houses, frequently embosomed in thick clumps of trees, have an appearance singularly pic-turesque. The seigniory is watered by several streams, but principally by les Russeaux du Moulin, du Mouton, de L'Eglise, and du Cap aux Oies, that descend from the rear, and wind between the different ridges in a manner truly decorative. On the first mentioned, near its discharge into the St. Lawrence, are seated an excellent grist-mill and saw-mill; at a short distance from which stands the manor-house, a large and substantial stone building, with numerous appendages. There are several roads leading along the St. Lawrence, where the ground is practicable for them, and in other places over the ridges: they are in general tolerably good, but frequently obliged to ascend some very long and fatiguing hills. The fief of Madame Drapeau, of twenty-nine arpens in front, and running the whole depth of the seigniory, is taken from the western extremity of it. From the situation of this settlement, and those of Le Gouffre and St. Paul's Bay, being denied access by land with other seig-

niories, owing to the intervention of the barren
tract of Cote de Beaupré before alluded to,
the principal part of their disposable produce
is transported to Quebec by water, in which
trade many schooners are almost continually
employed during the season of navigation;
their cargoes consist chiefly of grain, live cattle, and poultry, besides large quantities of
pine planks. In one or two of the bays there
are some good banks for fishing, on which a
great abundance of excellent fish of various
species is caught, and large quantities of herrings during the season for them.

ISLE AUX COUDRES (the seigniory of) lies in
the St. Lawrence, about two miles from its
northern shore, nearly opposite to the Bay of
St. Paul, and forms part of the county of
Northumberland: it is about six miles in
length; its greatest breadth is three miles, but
the eastern extremity of it terminates in a
point; granted October 29th, 1687, to the ecclesiastics of the Seminary of Quebec, to whom
it still belongs. Compared with the neighbouring mainland, the island is low, though
about its centre there are some few rising
grounds: the shore in one or two places rises
abruptly from the water, and is covered with
thick creeping shrubbery, but in general the
ascent of it is gradual and easy. The soil

·throughout is of a good prolific quality, and nearly 'all under tillage, producing grain of all sorts far beyond its own consumption: there are a few meadows 'and pasture grounds. The concessions are separated into two divisions, distinguished as the Cote du Cap à la Branche, and Côte de la Baleine; these are very little watered by streams of any description. A small quantity of wood of very inferior kinds still remains on the high ground; about the middle of the island. There is one parish, a church, and a parsonage-house; the inhabitants are reckoned between two and three hundred persons, living in neat well-built houses on each side of a road that makes the complete tour of the island. The battures and shoals surrounding it are very productive fishing-banks; the little bays are ·the rendezvous of numerous small craft, employed in transporting to Quebec the surplus produce of the island, and the opposite seigniories.

MURRAY BAY, or MALBAY (the seigniory of), in the county of Northumberland, is one of the only three grants *en fief et seigneurie*, that have been made by the British government; it extends from the seigniory of Eboulemens along the river St. Lawrence, as far as Malbay, a distance of four leagues by three leagues in depth; was granted April 27th,

1762, to John Nairn, Esq., Captain in His Majesty's 78th regiment of foot: it belongs at present to Mrs. Nairn.

. MOUNT MURRAY (the seigniory of) is an-other British grant *en fief et seigneurie*, (the third of the same description is Shoolbred, in the district of Gaspé); it reaches from the north side of the River of Malbay, along the bank of the St. Lawrence, as far as the River Noire, by three leagues in depth; granted April 27th, 1762, to Lieutenant Malcolm Fraser, of His Majesty's 78th regiment of foot, and is now the property of Malcolm Fraser, Esq. These two seigniories are separated from each other by Malbay river, and contain only a very small proportion of cultivated land, in comparison to their dimensions. The general surface of both is mountainous, but in some places the soil is moderately good: timber of all kinds is plenti-ful and very fine, particularly pine. The lands under the best state of improvement are those that range along each side of Malbay river for about six miles. A tolerably good road passes through these settlements to the extremity of them, upon which there are many farm-houses and neat dwellings. Murray Bay has a church and parsonage-house, two grist-mills, and some saw-mills: there is also a well-built manor-house, belonging to the proprietor of the seigniory. In Mount Murray the best settlements are on the borders of Malbay river, and stretch as far as those on the opposite shore. The manor-house belonging to Colonel Fraser, called Mount Murray, is very well situated at the entrance of the bay on the east side, and surrounded by a large tract of well-cultivated lands. Both grants are watered by several streams, neither of which are more than sufficient to work the mills.

HARE ISLAND lies nearly in the middle of the St. Lawrence, abreast of the seigniory of Riviere du Loup; it is nearly eight miles in length by the average breadth of about half a mile, low and flat, extending in a direction nearly parallel to the shores of the river: the soil is good, but wholly uncultivated; at each extremity there are long and dangerous shoals stretching off from it. On the south-east side lie the three small islands called the Brandy Pots, already noticed in speaking of the navigation of the river: on the westerly one is placed the telegraph No. 13, the last in the chain from Quebec.

The RIVER SAGUENAY, which discharges itself into the St. Lawrence, at Pointe aux Allouettes, is the largest of all the streams that pay their tribute to the Great River; it draws its source from Lake St. John, a collection of

waters of considerable expanse, lying in 48°
20' of north latitude, and 72° 30' of west longitude, receiving many large rivers that flow
from the north and north-west, from an immense distance in the interior, of which the
Piekouagamis, the Sable River, and the Pari-
boaca are the principal ones. At its eastern
extremity two large streams, one called the
Great Discharge, and the other the Kinogami
Land River, issue from it; which, after flowing
about fifty-seven miles and encompassing a
tract of land of the mean breadth of twelve
miles, unite their waters, and become the irresistible Saguenay; from which point it continues its course in an easterly direction, for
about one hundred miles down to the St. Lawrence. The banks of this river throughout its
course are very rocky, and immensely high,
varying from one hundred and seventy even to
three hundred and forty yards above the stream:
its current is broad, deep, and uncommonly ve-
hement; in some places, where precipices inter-
vene, there are falls from fifty to sixty feet in
height, down which the whole volume of the
stream rushes with indescribable fury and tremendous noise. The general breadth of the
river is from two miles and a half to three
miles, but at its mouth this distance is contracted to about one mile. The depth of this

enormous stream is also extraordinary. At its discharge, attempts have been made to find the bottom with five hundred fathoms of line, but without effect; about two miles higher up, it has been repeatedly sounded from one hundred and thirty to one hundred and forty fathoms; and from sixty to seventy miles from the St. Lawrence, its depth is found from fifty to sixty fathoms. The course of the river, notwithstanding its magnitude, is very sinuous, owing to many projecting points from each shore. The tide runs about seventy miles up it, and on account of the obstructions occasioned by the numerous promontories, the ebb is much later than in the St. Lawrence; in consequence of which, at low water in the latter, the force of the descending stream of the Saguenay is felt for several miles. Just within the mouth of the river, opposite to Pointe aux Allouettes, is the harbour of Tadousac, which is very well sheltered by the surrounding high lands, and has good anchorage for a great number of vessels of large size, where they may lie in perfect safety. On the northern shore of the St. Lawrence, and at many places on the Saguenay, there are stations for trading with the Indians in peltry, and for carrying on the whale, seal, porpoise, and salmon-fishery; these are known by the name of King's Posts,

and are now let, with all their privileges, to the
North-West Company at Quebec, on a lease,
at one thousand and twenty-five pounds per
annum.   An establishment is maintained at
Tadousac, at Chicoutami on the Saguenay, at
Lake St. John, at Les Isles de Jeremie, near
Betsiamitis Point, at the Seven Islands, beyond Cap des Mont Pélés, and at Cap des
Monts: at those towards the sea the fisheries
are pursued during the summer, and at the
interior ones the fur trade is carried on with
the Indians during the winter.   About the
trading post at Chicoutami the land is tolerably
fertile, and the timber of a superior quality;
in the little agriculture that is here paid attention to, it has been observed that grain ripens
sooner than it does in the vicinity of Quebec,
although the situation is much further to the
northward: another of the many anomalies
that distinguish the climate of Canada.

MILLE VACHES (the seigniory of), in the
county of Northumberland, situated near the
River Portneuf, ten leagues below the Saguenay; it extends three leagues along the
bank of the St. Lawrence by four leagues in
depth; was granted November 15th, 1653, to
Robert Giffard.

TERRA FIRMA OF MINGAN (the seigniory
of) extends from Cape Cormorant, along the

northern shore of the Labrador Channel, to Goynish River; was granted February 25th, 1661, to Sieur François Bissot. From Cape Cormorant to St. John's River is the only part now contained in the province of Lower Canada. In both of these tracts the land is very indifferent and wholly uncultivated, indeed unfit for agriculture. The group of islands lying off the shore of the latter, called the Mingan Islands, are advantageously situated for carrying on the fisheries.

TOWNSHIPS.

The townships in the district of Quebec are, generally speaking, so much inferior to those of the other districts in the quality of the soil, and so far behind them in the quantity of settlements and state of agriculture, that the description of them will prove but little more than a recapitulation of uncultivated lands.

NELSON and SOMERSET are two irregular townships in the county of Buckingham, joining each other, and situated in the rear of the seigniories of Deschaillons and Lotbiniere. Somerset is bounded by Stanfold on the southwest; and is partly in the districts of Three Rivers and Quebec. Nelson is bounded on

the north-east by the seigniory of Ste. Croix.
They were granted in April, 1804, to officers
and privates of the Canadian militia. The
land in these two townships' lies rather low,
but is of a tolerably good quality, and fit for the
production of most kinds of grain: in many parts
it is well suited for the growth of hemp and
flax. Towards the south-east end of Nelson
there are some rising grounds, of a soil much
superior to the parts lying adjacent to Lotbiniere. The timber on both these townships
is chiefly beech, maple, birch, and pine; on
the low and moist grounds, basswood, cedar,
spruce, and hemlock, are prevalent. They are
very well watered by the Rivers Becancour, du
Chêne, and numerous small streams, that after
winding through almost every part of them,
fall into the two rivers. None of the land has
yet been brought under culture.

HALIFAX, in the county of Buckingham,
lies in the two districts of Three Rivers and
Quebec, and is situated between Chester and
Inverness; bounded on the north-west by Somerset and Arthabaska, and on the south-east
by Wolfestown and Ireland. The land in this
township is principally of a good quality, and
capable of being turned to account in growing
most species of grain; the northern part of it
is rather low, and in some places runs into

swamps. No portion of it is yet settled upon, nor has any attempt been made to bring it into cultivation, although it might be done with almost a certainty of success. There is a great supply of beech, elm, maple, butternut, birch, and basswood, besides abundance of cedar and spruce fir in the low lands. It is watered by Lake Pitt, and several small runs of water that fall into the Becancour. The south-easterly part has been surveyed, and granted to the late Mathew Scott and Benjamin Jobert: the present proprietors are Mrs. Scott and family, and the heirs of the late Mr. Frobisher.

Inverness, in the county of Buckingham, lies between Halifax and Nelson, bounded on the north-west by Somerset and part of Nelson, and on the south-east by Leeds. No part of this tract is cultivated, although it contains lands in the southerly quarter of a superior quality, eligible for almost any description of cultivation; and the remainder is generally above mediocrity, except an extent of swamp of about eight thousand acres to the northward, which is covered with hemlock, spruce fir, and cedar. On the dry lands, timber is in great abundance and of an excellent description. It is watered by Lake William, which discharges itself by a small stream into the Becancour, and by another is connected with Lake Pitt, besides several small rivulets. The south-west part was granted to the late Joseph Frobisher, Esq., and now belongs to his heirs.

IRELAND, in the county of Buckingham, joins Halifax and Inverness on the north-west, is bounded by Wolfestown on the south-west, and by Leeds and Thetford on the north-east. The north-west part of this township consists of land of an unexceptionable quality, and fit for the growth of grain of all kinds, hemp, flax, and every other purpose of agriculture. The south-east part is not arable, being only a series of rugged mountains running to a considerable distance, with many small lakes and swamps in the intervals between them. The north-west quarter, the only one that has been surveyed and granted, now belongs to the heirs of Joseph Frobisher, Esq.: this is a fertile spot, and inhabited by a few families forming what is called Lord's Settlement. Beech, maple, birch, and many other sorts of timber, are found in great abundance in this township. It is watered by several rivulets, and Trout Lake, which is connected by a little stream with Lake Pitt. Craig's Road passes through it, and crosses the Becancour at Kemp's Bridge. In Lord's Settlement there is a saw-mill, which is found of great utility in this interior part of the country.

LEEDS, in the county of Buckingham, is an

irregular tract, situated between the seigniory
of St. Gilles and the township of Ireland,
bounded on the north-west by Inverness, Nelson, and St. Croix, and on the south-east by
Thetford and Broughton. Except the north-
west quarter, where the land is poor and very
stony, the generality of this township is of excellent quality, fit for the growth of all kinds
of grain, flax, hemp, and other general purposes of agriculture. It is well stocked with
timber of many sorts, as beech, birch, maple,
basswood, elm, ash, ironwood, spruce fir, and
hemlock; and very well watered by the Becancour, which divides itself into several branches,
and by many other small streams. Cultivation
has made but very small progress here, although
some settlements have been attempted, particularly along the line of Craig's Road, where it
might be reasonably inferred that better success would have attended them. This road
was originally devised to open a direct communication between Quebec, the townships on
the frontiers, and the adjacent American States;
but its completion has been retarded by many
difficulties, more apparently originating in a
want of determined enterprize, than in any natural impediments. It was originally traced out
by Mr. Joseph Kilborne, Deputy Provincial
Surveyor, in 1800, at the expense of Joseph Fro-

bisher, Esq., and other landholders in the
townships through which it passes: it extends
from the bank of the St. Lawrence through the
seigniory of St. Gilles, to the township of Shipton, from whence a road had already been
made to the river St. Francis, and thence to
the boundary line. The enterprise did not
succeed very well, as Lord's Settlement, in the
township of Ireland, was the only one that was
attempted. In 1809, during the administration
of Sir James Craig, a fresh attempt was made
to render the route from Quebec to the frontiers commodious and easy; detachments of
troops were employed in clearing and making
the road, and in erecting bridges of timber
over the rivers wherever they were found necessary. The object in view was so far obtained
as to enable a stage to travel with tolerable dis-
patch, though not without inconvenience to
those who availed themselves of its conveyance,
from the want of proper places to stop at, and
houses for the refreshment of travellers; as there
is no accommodation of that kind from the
last settlement on the River Beaurivage to the
township of Shipton, a distance of about sixty
miles. At Kemp's Bridge, Palmer's inn was
at one time opened; but it neither answered
the expectations of the public, nor produced
benefit to the proprietor. Notwithstanding the

inducements held out to encourage settlers, by granting them a patent for any lots they might occupy, on condition of clearing a certain portion of land, and building a house (of timber) of given dimensions contiguous to the road; these terms were accepted only in two or three instances, and even these were of no utility in advancing the work, or of advantage to the individuals who undertook them. At the commencement of the late war very little progress had been made, and since that period no means have been used to preserve from decay that portion of the road that was completed, so that at present it is obstructed by fallen trees, and many other impediments, which render it almost as impracticable as if it still remained a wilderness. The several bridges over the rivers are named after the military officers who commanded the detachments employed on this service: they also obtained lands adjacent to the road; but military men have seldom the leisure or the means of becoming permanent cultivators. Such a communication would undoubtedly be of immense advantage to this part of the province, and it is to be hoped that, notwithstanding the hitherto unpromising results, the attempt may be again renewed under the immediate sanction of the legislature. One quarter of the township of

Leeds was originally granted to Isaac Todd, but at present that tract belongs to the heirs of Joseph Frobisher, Esq. Several individuals have obtained grants, and George Hamilton, Esq., of Quebec, holds eight thousand acres by purchase from government, as lands were sold for the purpose of defraying some of the expenses incurred in constructing the road.

THETFORD, in the county of Buckingham, lies between Broughton and Ireland, bounded by Leeds on the north-west, and Adstock on the south-east. This township, though generally mountainous, has a few intervals of good land fit for cultivation, wherein grain, hemp, and flax might be raised: the south-east part is very indifferent, and covered with a thick moss, beneath which there is a bed of stone, with not more than five or six inches of poor exhausted earth upon it. The timber generally is not bad, and consists of beech, elm, birch, and maple, with plenty of hemlock, spruce fir, &c. It is watered by two large lakes, a few moderate sized rivers, and many inferior streams. One half of it is the property of Doctor North.

BROUGHTON, in the county of Buckingham, though somewhat mountainous, contains much land of a good quality; many of the inferior swells, if cultivated, would produce wheat and

other grain; some parts of it are well calculated
for hemp and flax, and many others are naturally tolerably good grass lands. It is well
stocked with beech, maple, birch, elm, and
other useful timber, besides abundance of
wood of inferior quality. It is watered by several branches of the Becancour, by some rivulets flowing into the Chaudiere, and by one
or two small lakes. The north-west half was
granted to H. Jenkins and William Hall, and
is now the property of the latter, who has made
some progress in forming a settlement and cultivating a part of it: he has also erected some
mills. From the settlement to the seigniory of St.
Joseph, on the Chaudiere, there is a moderately
good road, and another to Craig's Road.

TRING, in the county of Buckingham, joins
the seigniory of Vaudreuil on the north-east,
and lies between Broughton and Shenley. This
tract of land is, for the greatest part, of a favourable quality and fit for tillage; it would
produce grain, and in many places appears to
be well adapted to the culture of flax and
hemp. The timber is equally good as the
land, and much of the best kinds might be
collected. It is watered by a chain of five
beautiful lakes, that abound with excellent
fish; they discharge their waters into the River
Chaudiere, through a stream called the Bras
du Sud-Ouest. One half of the township has

been granted to individuals, but no progress
has been made in clearing it.

SHENLEY, in the county of Buckingham,
is an irregular tract lying between Dorset
and Tring, bounded on the north-east by
the seigniory of Aubert Gallion and the
River Chaudiere, and on the south-west by
vacant lands. The surface is irregular, in some
places low and swampy, but in others possessing
a moderately good soil, that would doubtless
be sufficiently fertile if brought under the
plough. On the dry lands the timber consists
principally of beech, maple, and birch; on the
others there is scarcely any thing else but
cedar, and spruce fir. It is not very well watered.
One quarter of the township was granted to
the late James Glenny, but no part thereof is
cultivated.

DORSET, in the county of Buckingham, is
situated on the westerly side of the River
Chaudiere, joining Shenley on the north, and
encompassed on the other sides by unsurveyed
lands. This is a large township, consisting
chiefly of fine rises of good land, very fit for
tillage, and almost every where favourable for
the culture of hemp and flax, though no settlements have hitherto been made in it; the
most inferior part of it is along the rocky bank
of the River Chaudiere. It is well stocked
with basswood, birch, maple, beech, and elm

timber: some of the swamps are covered with cedar and hemlock. It is admirably well watered by three large lakes, and a number of rivers that wind through it and fall into the Chaudiere: on their banks are found some fine breadths of excellent meadow land. The whole of it was granted to Mr. John Black, but now belongs to the heirs of the late Simon M'Tavish, Esq.

FRAMPTON is situated partly in the counties of Dorchester and Hertford; it lies in the rear of the seigniories of St. Joseph and Ste. Marie, on the River Chaudiere, and is bounded by Buckland on the north-east, by Jolliet on the south-west, and by Cranbourne on the south-east. A soil for the greatest part favourable to agriculture, though a good deal diversified with hill and dale, is the general character of this township, but a few of the low lands incline to be marshy. Beech, birch, and maple, thickly clothe the rising grounds, but cedar and spruce fir are most prevalent on the other parts. It is watered by the principal branch of the River Echemin, and some inferior rivers, on which there are some excellent situations for mills. Only a very small portion of this township is yet cultivated. The south-westerly half has been surveyed and granted to P. E. Debartzch, Esq., and to other persons; that gentleman,

P P

however, and —— Pyke, Esq., of Quebec, are the principal landholders.

BUCKLAND, in the county of Hertford, is an irregular township, situated in the rear of the seigniory of St. Gervais, and the fiefs La Martiniere and Mont-à-Peine; it joins Jolliet and Frampton on the south-west, and is bounded on the other sides by waste lands of the crown. The surface of this tract is much varied, in many places rising into considerable swells, the intervals between which are rather swampy, but the soil is in general excellent; even the wet lands are by no means of a bad quality. Every species of grain and grass, besides hemp and flax, might be produced upon it in great abundance. It is principally timbered with beech, birch, maple, ironwood, basswood, and elm, with a great deal of cedar, spruce fir, and black ash. It is completely watered by several large streams and branches of the Echemin, with many rivulets, on nearly all of which there are very eligible situations for mills, and much good meadow land along their borders. Large quantities of maple-sugar are made here by the inhabitants of St. Gervais. Only one quarter of the township has been surveyed, which is now the property of William Holmes, Esq., of Quebec.

IXWORTH, in the county of Cornwallis, is an

irregular tract lying in the rear of the seigniory
of Ste. Anne, and the augmentation to the
River Ouelle. Of this township no more than
one thousand two hundred acres have been surveyed, and granted to Matthew Omara, the
whole of which is most excellent land: it joins
Ste. Anne, and some part of it is in a very forward state of cultivation: on the remainder
there is a large quantity of excellent pine timber, much of which is transported by the River
Ouelle to the St. Lawrence, and thence to
Quebec.

STONEHAM and TEWKESBURY, two townships on the north side of the St. Lawrence, in
the county of Quebec, except a small part of
the latter which is in the county of Northumberland; they join each other, and are situated
in the rear of the seigniories of Cote de Beau-
pres, Beauport, and Notre Dame des Anges.
The general face of the land throughout these
tracts is mountainous and rocky; the largest
part of it barren and unfit for cultivation,
though here and there some scanty patches of
arable land lie in the vallies, where the soil is
moderately good, and would bear tillage. Some
little exception, however, may be made in
favour of that part of Stoneham from the front
of it to the River Jacques Cartier, where the
land is chiefly arable, and of a yellow loamy

nature. They are watered by the large rivers
St. Anne, Jacques Cartier, and Batiscan, flowing majestically between the lofty ridges of
mountains, by several of inferior magnitude,
and by some small lakes. The timber consists of beech, maple, birch, and pine of good
dimensions. The most valuable part of Stoneham was originally granted to Kenelm Chandler, Esq. and is now the property of Mrs.
Brydon.

THE DISTRICT OF GASPE',

The eastern extremity of the province on the
south side of the St. Lawrence, lies between the
parallels of 47 degrees 20 minutes, and 49 degrees 10 minutes of north latitude; and between the 64th and 66th degrees 30 minutes of
longitude west from Greenwich. It is bounded
on the west by the district of Quebec, on the
east and north-east by the River and Gulf of
St. Lawrence, and on the south by the province
of New Brunswick and the Bay of Chaleurs.
It forms one county, called Gaspé, and sends
one member to the provincial parliament. Less
in size, it is also inferior in every respect
to either of the three preceding districts; the
north-easterly ridge of mountains, that terminates only at Cape Roziere, divides it nearly in
two, from the north-west side of which, down

to the shore of the. St. Lawrence, the whole tract is rough and unfertile, being covered with almost impenetrable forests, except a few spots on the river, where grants have been made of land that is supposed eligible to culti-vation. There is not much difference on the south-east side of the ridge, until approach-ing pretty close to the shore of the Bay of Chaleurs, where, bordering on the sea and for some distance inland, there are in several places portions of land upon which agriculture might be successfully carried on to a much greater extent than it is at present. The line of coast from Cape Chat in the St. Lawrence round by Cape Roziere to the River Ristigouche, at the bottom of the Bay of Chaleurs, is about 280 miles: from Gaspé bay, near the latter cape, to Ristigouche bay, the coast is divided into townships called Carleton, Maria, Richmond, Hamilton, Coxe, Hope, and Nos. 7, 8, and 9, each from eight to twelve miles in breadth, and intended to be nine miles in depth. In the tract extending from Richmond to the eastern boundary of Hopetown there are several patches running at least eight miles back, that are likely to prove fertile and productive: in Coxe town-ship the depth of the moderately good arable land is estimated to exceed 18 miles. The dis-tance from Richmond to Hope township is about forty-two miles, and excepting the space of Ironbound shore, lying between Richmond and Bonaventure, the front line of concessions is nearly all settled upon. The front of Maria and Richmond forms an open bay, but the anchorage, even for vessels of the smallest burthen, is a mile from the shore, on account of the shoals at low water. In Carleton such lands as are capable of being cultivated are already occupied, but they amount to one or two concessions only. Between Cape Roziere and Cape Chat the coast is mountainous and barren, having only three or four houses throughout the whole distance, besides a small settlement of a few families at Mont Louis, in the vicinity of which there happens to be some land fit for culture, although there are five seignioral grants of land within that space. The whole population of the district in 1808 amounted to 3200 souls, exclusive of three to four hundred fishermen, who sojourn in it during the fishing season, but quit it on the approach of winter: since that period it has probably not much increased. The industry of the inhabitants is chiefly employed in the fisheries, which are regulated by an act of the provincial parliament of the forty-seventh year of George the Third, and carried on to a considerable extent, as the quantity ex-

ported amounts, *communibus annis*, to about
35,000 cwt. of codfish, 5000 of salmon, and from
10 to 12,000 of herrings, pilchards, and mackarel;
to this may be added the produce of some
whales caught in Gaspé Bay, a trifling trade in
peltry, and the building of one ship and three
or four small vessels annually. The fisheries
are sedentary, but the exportations and im-
portations usually employ eight or nine square-
rigged vessels, and about thirty-five small ones.
Agriculture meets with only a secondary attention, and the produce of it at present does not
much, if at all, overbalance the consumption.
The timber consists of spruce fir, white and
black birch, beech, elm, and pine, fit for mast-
ing of small dimensions, with some oak of a
very inferior quality. The town of New Carlisle, the principal one, is situated in Coxe
township, and laid out in a manner that hereafter it may become a compact and regular
little place : the position of it is nearly central
from each extremity of the Bay of Chaleurs ; and
the number of houses is from forty to fifty, all
of wood : it has a church, a court-house, and a
gaol ; the two latter are now building, under the
superintendance of commissioners appointed
by an act of parliament. The situation is very
healthy, and the surrounding lands some of the
most fertile of the district. From the town nu-

merous settlements extend on each side, occupying nearly the whole front of the townships
of Coxe and Hope, and, including the town
itself, may be estimated to contain nearly one
half of the whole population. These settlements are in a much more improved state than
any of the others. The want of grist-mills is
seriously felt by the inhabitants of this place,
and indeed all over the district, and greatly
retards the progress of agriculture : there are
good situations for them on a river that takes
its source from a small lake within the township
of Coxe, and from its proximity to the settlement would be a very eligible place for constructing one. In front of these townships there
is an excellent beach, where the fish is cured
and dried. Percé, the next place in importance to New Carlisle, is situated on a rising
ground that forms the southern point of Malbay, contains twenty-five or thirty houses,
principally inhabited by fishermen, and like
the chief town is honoured with a court-house
and gaol : in front of it the beach is very good
for curing fish, and lying off are some of the
best banks in the bay for catching them. The
island of Bonaventure lies about a mile and a
half from the shore, opposite to the point; it is
little better than a barren rock, but yet a few
persons are hardy enough to winter there for

the sake of retaining possession of the fishing
places they have occupied during the summer.
Very near the southerly point of Malbay there
is a remarkable rock rising about two hundred
feet out of the water, and of about twelve hundred feet in length, in which there are three
arches completely wrought by nature; the centre one is sufficiently large to admit a boat
under sail to pass through it with ease: from
this rock, round Malbay to Point Peter, there
is an excellent beach for fishing, part of which
is named La Belle Ance, or Lobster Beach:
close to this place is the house of the late Governor Coxe. Gaspé Bay lies between Cape
Gaspé and Whale Head; it runs about sixteen
miles into the land, and is about five miles
broad: from the extremity of it two other inlets, called the north-west and south-west
arms, penetrate a considerable distance into
the interior, and receive the waters of several
streams that flow from the mountains: the bay
itself is deep and well sheltered, and capable
of affording protection to a large number of
ships from bad weather; the shores are lofty,
and the settlers upon them are nearly all fishermen. Douglass town, or rather the situation
for it, as there are only five or six houses yet
built, is at the entrance of the River St. John;

on the south side of the bay; on the opposite
shore of the river is the site of the intended
town of Haldimand. At Pabos Bay, about
midway between Cape Despair and Point
Maquereau there is a small village on the
western side, and on the opposite side, on a
projecting point, stand the summer habitations
of the fishermen, as they are usually termed :
several streams descend into this bay from a
numerous chain of small lakes to the north-
westward. A little to the westward of Pabos
is a small snug inlet called Port Daniel. Bonaventure is a small place, containing about
twenty-five houses and a church, situated on
the western side of the harbour of the same
name, in the township of Hamilton : the land
surrounding it is level and pretty good, but its
whole dependence is the fishery. On the north
shore of Ristigouche Bay the country presents
a great deal of luxuriant meadow land; from
Megoacha Point there is a tract of about sixteen miles in length and about a mile and a
half in breadth, granted in *fief and seigneurie*
on the 4th July, 1788, to John Shoolbred, Esq.
and although several parts of it claim notice as
being well adapted for settling upon, it yet
remains without a single individual, from the
object of the proprietor not being any partial

concession, but the disposal of the whole of it, probably only at a future period. A little beyond this grant, upon the northern bank of the River Ristigouche, is a small village of domiciliated Indians of the Micmac tribe, which is superintended by a missionary, who resides at Tracadigash or Bonaventure. The communication from Gaspé to Quebec may be kept up by three different routes: one by pursuing the coast of the Gulf and River St. Lawrence; the second is by following the course of the River Ristigouche as far as the River Matapediach, and continuing along the side of it as far as Lake Matapediach; from thence there is an Indian footpath for nearly thirty miles to the River Mitis, the course of which is pursued until it reaches the St. Lawrence near about where the settlements begin; the third route is by proceeding along the Ristigouche River nearly up to its source, from whence there is an Indian footpath or portage road of eleven miles to the Grand River, which flows into the River St. John, fifteen miles above the Great Fall, from whence the traveller proceeds in the road of the Temiscouata portage; this is the least difficult of the three, and the distance by it from New Carlisle to Quebec is three hundred and ninety miles; this may be shortened by eighteen or twenty miles, by a road that has been blazed from the River Waganitz to the Rivière Verte, that descends into the River St. John in the Madawaska settlement. With the description of Gaspé the topographical account of the whole of the province of Lower Canada closes.

UPPER CANADA.

SINCE the year 1791 the Province of Upper Canada has been bounded in the following manner; viz. on the east by Lower Canada, on the north-east by the Grand or Ottawa River, which in that direction separates it from the Lower Province; on the north by the territory of the Hudson's Bay Company; on the south and south-east by the United States of America, or rather by an imaginary line, beginning at the village of St. Regis, on the parallel of the forty-fifth degree of north latitude, from whence it passes up the middle of the River St. Lawrence, Lake Ontario, the Niagara River, Lake Erie, and continuing thence through the middle of the Water Communication into Lakes Huron and Superior, the Long Lake, and along the middle of the chain of lakes and water communication up to the north-west angle of the Lake of the Woods, and from thence due west to the

River Mississippi ;* on the west and north-west
no limits have been assigned to it, therefore it
may be supposed to extend over the vast regions
that spread towards the Pacific and the Northern
Oceans. The separation between it and the
United States is so vague and ill defined, and
the prolific source of so many disagreements
between the two powers, that it has long called
for the revision which is now about to be performed in fulfilment of the fourth and fifth articles of the treaty of peace of 1815. The
interior divisions are eight districts, viz. the
Eastern, Johnstown, Midland, Newcastle, the
Home, Niagara, London, and the Western;
these are again subdivided into 23 counties, viz.
Glengary, Stormont, Dundas, Prescott, Russel,
Grenville, Leeds, Carleton, Frontenac, Lenox,
Addington, Hastings, Prince Edward, Northumberland, Durham, York, Norfolk, Oxford,
Middlesex, Lincoln, Haldimand, Kent, and
Essex. These contain one hundred and fifty-
nine townships, exclusive of Indian lands, and
certain other large portions that are reserved for
the crown, and the maintenance of the Protestant clergy. The townships, taken one with
another, will average about 61,600 acres; making

* This boundary was fixed by the treaty of 1783, but is
erroneous, inasmuch as a line drawn due west from the Lake
of the Woods will not strike the Mississippi at all.

the aggregate quantity of 9,694,400 acres, that may be arranged under the following heads; about 3,000,000 of acres are granted in free and common soccage, 2,769,828 are reserved for the crown and clergy, and 3,924,572 still remain to be granted. The extent of country thus laid out reaches from Pointe au Baudet along the north shore of the river St. Lawrence, Lake Ontario, Lake Erie up to Lake St. Claire and the communication between it and Lake Huron, a distance little less than one hundred and ninety leagues. Through this range, wide as it is, and for a depth that varies from forty to fifty miles, the soil for the most part is scarcely excelled by any portion of the continent of North America; it is so happily varied in its nature as to present situations where agriculture may be successfully carried on in all its numerous branches; but perhaps the particular species that most prevails is a fine dark loam mixed with a rich vegetable mould. A sameness of appearance overspreads almost the whole country, from which very little deviation is perceptible. Between Pointe au Baudet and the Bay of Quinté, comprising the eastern, Johnstown, and midland districts, the land presents an almost uniform level of exquisite beauty, rising only a few feet from the bank of the St. Lawrence, finely intersected, and admirably

well watered in almost every direction by numerous streams, several of which are navigable
for boats and canoes, and obstructed only by a
few falls that occasion short portages ; they offer
hundreds of the most convenient situations for,
erecting mills, while their banks are with few
exceptions very desirable for the formation of
new settlements. From the bay of Quinté
along the edge of Lake Ontario to its western
extremity, there runs a ridge of heights, of no
great elevation, and extending only a short distance in breadth or to the northward, but from
which the land soon descends again to its former
level; the interior of this tract is intersected
by a chain of lakes, that by means of a short
portage or two are connected with Lake Simcoe,
and thence with Lake Huron. Along the northern
part also of the Niagara district runs a ridge
called the Queenstown Heights, stretching across
the river Niagara, and away eastward into the
state of New York; the altitude of this range
in any part of it does not exceed one hundred
and sixty yards above the surface of the lake.
This space, containing the Newcastle, the Home
and Niagara districts, is watered by a great
number of streams both large and small, that
greatly contribute to its fertility : in the latter
district is the Welland, formerly called the
Chippewa, a beautiful river flowing through a

remarkably fertile country, for about forty
miles, and wholly unobstructed by falls; also
the Ouse or Grand River, a stream of much
greater magnitude, rising in the interior of the
country, towards Lake Huron, and after winding a long and picturesque course, falls into
Lake Erie; across its mouth there is a bar, but
always with eight feet water upon it: it is navigable for small vessels from the Lake many
miles upwards, and for boats to a much greater
distance. The land through the whole of this
last mentioned district is uncommonly rich and
fertile, with a considerable portion of very
flourishing settlements upon it. From the
river Ouse, proceeding along the shore of Lake
Erie, up to the Lake and River St. Claire, the
whole space is extremely even, with scarcely a
league of it but what displays excellent situations for settlements, and in spots where the
land is already under tillage, finer crops or more
thriving farms are not to be met with in any
part of either province. The portion of the
western district lying between Lake Erie and
Lake Ste. Claire is perhaps the most delightful
spot of all the province; the fertility of the
soil, the richly diversified and luxuriant beauties
that every where court the view, the abundant
variety of excellent fish that teem in the rivers,
and the profusion of game of different species

that enliven the woods, the thickets, and the meadows, combine to insure a preference to this highly favoured tract for the establishment of new settlements. From the Ouse to Lake Ste. Claire the space is occupied by the London and Western districts; it is watered by many small streams falling into Lake Erie, besides the River Chenail Ecarté and the exquisitely picturesque River Thames, formerly called the Rivière à la Tranche; it rises far in the interior, about the township of Blandford, and after pursuing a serpentine course in a direction nearly south-west, discharges itself into Lake St. Claire. It is navigable for vessels full twenty miles from its mouth, and for boats and canoes nearly up to its source, but little less than one hundred miles. The River Chenail Ecarté runs almost parallel to the Thames, at about ten miles from it, and falls into Lake St. Claire. The portions now described are those only that are more or less settled upon; in the rear of the townships are large tracts of land, stretching far to the northward, covered with immense forests, and little known except to the Indians; but it has been ascertained that there are many wide spreading extents of rich and fertile soil, particularly bordering on the south-west bank of the Ottawa River. Through these regions, as yet unexplored by civilized man, there are many

streams, and some of great size, that flow both
into Lake Huron and into the Ottawa River,
but none of them have been sufficiently traced
to admit of being delineated on any map.
Timber in almost every variety is found in the
greatest profusion; the oak, beech; walnut,
ash, hickory, maple, elm, pine, sycamore, birch,
and many other sorts, are of peculiar excellence,
and of capital dimensions. The climate is so
particularly salubrious, that epidemic diseases,
either among men or cattle, are almost unknown;
its influence upon the fertility of the soil is more
generally perceptible than it is in Lower Canada, and supposed to be congenial to vegetation in a much superior degree. The winters
are shorter, and not always marked with such
rigour as in the latter; the duration of the frost
is always accompanied with a fine clear sky and
a dry atmosphere; the spring opens, and the resumption of agricultural labours takes place
from six weeks to two months earlier than what
it does in the neighbourhood of Quebec; the
summer heats rarely prevail to excess, and the
autumns are usually very friendly to the harvests, and favourable for securing all the late
crops. In fact, upon so good a soil, and under
such a climate, industry and an increase of population are only wanting to render this colony
flourishing and happy. In reviewing the popu-

lation of this province, an important increase
will be found to have taken place of late years;
in 1783, the utmost amount that could be estimated did not exceed ten thousand souls, and
of these the numerous frontier posts and gar-
risons constituted by much the greater part.
After that period a great accession was made
by the settlement of loyalists and disbanded
soldiers, and which was considerably increased
by the emigration of many people who soon grew
tired of the newly acquired independence of the
American States; in addition to the natural
increase of the numbers thus acquired, they
have been gradually augmented by emigrations
from Great Britain, Ireland, Scotland, the
United States, and many other places, so that
in the year 1814 it was taken in round numbers
at ninety-five thousand souls, and which may
be trusted to as a tolerably exact statement, or
at least considering the difficulty that must be
experienced in collecting the returns, as nearly
so as can well be obtained. Of the three millions of acres already stated to have been
granted, the quantity now under tillage will be
found to approach pretty near to two hundred
and ninety thousand acres, dispersed over the
different districts. The most populous and improved part of the colony is undoubtedly that
from Pointe au Baudet to the head of the Bay

of Quinté, a range of one hundred and seventy miles, in which are contained the towns of Kingston, Johnstown, and Cornwall ; Fort Wellington, the Mohawk village, Brockville, and several smaller villages ; besides a continuation of houses, (many of them spacious and well built) and farms by the side of the main road, as well as the other roads that lead to the interior settlements. Great industry and attention to improvement are displayed upon most of the lands throughout this tract ; the roads that were formerly made have been gradually rendered sound and good, and many new ones constructed ; bridges have been thrown across the rivers, and various communications both by land and water opened to the interior ; indeed various indications of a flourishing and accelerated progress are apparent in almost every direction. Of the towns just mentioned, Cornwall, lying about five miles above St. Regis, and Johnstown, three miles east of Fort Wellington, contain each from sixty to seventy houses, built of wood, with a church, courthouse, &c.; they stand close to the River St. Lawrence ; the ground planned out for each is a mile square. Fort Wellington, formerly called Prescott, is situated directly opposite to the American town and fort of Ogdensburgh, or Oswegatchie, as it used to be named ; between them the river is no more than one thousand six hundred yards broad; during hostilities shot were repeatedly exchanged betweeen them, particularly on the passing of brigades of boats up the river. The town of Kingston, the largest and most populous of the Upper Province, is very advantageously seated on the north side of the River St. Lawrence, or rather at the eastern extremity of Lake Ontario; it is in lat. 44°. 8′. north, and in long. 76°. 40′. west from Greenwich. On the ground upon which it is built formerly stood Fort Frontenac, an old French post. Its foundation took placē in 1784, and by gradual increase it now presents a front of nearly three quarters of a mile, and extending in depth about six hundred yards. The streets are regularly planned, running at right angles with each other, but not paved : the number of houses may be estimated at about three hundred and seventy ; some of them are well built of stone, but the greater number are of wood; many of them spacious and commodious. The public buildings are a government-house, a court-house, a Protestant and a Catholic church, a market-house, a gaol, and hospital, besides the garrison, block-houses, government magazines and stores. For the last fifteen years the town has obtained consi-

A TABLE of DISTANCES
from
KINGSTON,
to
MONTREAL.

	Kingston	Gananoqui	Petit Detroit	Brocks Ville	Fort Wellington	New Johnston	Pointe des Gallops	Pt. Iroquois	to upper end Rapid Plat	Grand Remous	Hooples	Shicks	Cornwall	Rt. au Raisin	Pt. au Baudet	The Traverse	to McDonals	Coteau du Lac	Village of Cedars
Gananoqui	21																		
Petit Detroit	35	14																	
Brocks Ville	55	34	20																
Fort Wellington	67¼	46¼	32¼	12¼															
New Johnston	70¼	49¼	35¼	15¼	3														
Pointe des Gallops	74¼	53¼	39¼	19¼	7	4													
Pt. Iroquois	80¼	59¼	45¼	25¼	13	10	6												
to upper end Rapid Plat	86¾	65¾	51¾	31¾	19½	16½	12½	6½											
Grand Remous	99¾	78¾	64¾	44¾	32½	29½	25½	19½	13										
Hooples	103¾	82¾	68¾	48¾	36½	33½	29½	23½	17	4									
Shicks	110¾	89¾	75¾	55¾	43½	40½	36½	30½	24	11	7								
Cornwall	116¾	95¾	81¾	61¾	49½	46½	42½	36½	30	17	13	6							
Rt. au Raisin	126¾	105¾	91¾	71¾	59½	56½	52½	46½	40	27	23	16	10						
Pt. au Baudet	147¼	126¼	112¼	92¼	80	77	73	67	60½	47½	43½	36½	30½	20½					
The Traverse	151¾	130¾	116¾	96¾	84½	81½	77½	71½	65	52	48	41	35	25	4½				
to McDonals	158¾	137¾	123¾	103¾	91½	88½	84½	78½	72	59	55	48	42	32	11½	7			
Coteau du Lac	176¾	155¾	141¾	121¾	109½	106½	102½	96½	90	77	73	66	60	50	29½	25	18		
Village of Cedars	181¾	160¾	146¾	126¾	114½	111½	107½	101½	95	82	78	71	65	55	34½	30	23	5	
Montreal	197¼	176¼	162¼	142¼	130	127	123	117	110½	97½	93½	86½	80½	70½	50	45½	38½	20½	15½

derable mercantile importance; wharfs have been constructed, and many spacious warehouses erected, that are usually filled with merchandize: in fact, it is now become the main entrepôt between Montreal and all the settlements along the lakes to the westward. From the commencement of spring until the latter end of autumn, great activity prevails; vessels of from eighty to nearly two hundred tons, employed in navigating the lake, are continually receiving and discharging their cargoes, as well as the batteaux used in the river. The harbour is well sheltered and convenient, accessible to ships not requiring more than three fathoms water, with good anchorage close to the north-eastern extremity of the town; the entrance to it is defended by a battery on Mississaga Point, and another on Point Frederick, which, with the shoal stretching from the former, with only five feet of water upon it, are quite sufficient for its protection. In the rear of the town, upon a rising ground, some temporary field-works have been thrown up for its defence upon that side; but from the growing importance of the place these cannot be deemed sufficient, and permanent works ought to be constructed in their stead. Opposite to the town, and distant about half a mile, is a long low peninsula, forming the west side of Navy

Bay; the extremity of it is called Point Frederick: Point Henry is the extremity of another
peninsula, but of higher and more commanding
ground, that forms the eastern side of it. This
is the principal depot of the royal navy on
Lake Ontario, and where the ships are laid up
during the winter; the anchorage is good, but
somewhat exposed to south and south-west
winds; it is very well defended by batteries
and block-houses on Point Frederick, and by a
strong fort on Point Henry. On the western
side of Navy Bay are the dock-yard, large store-
houses, slips for building the men of war, naval
barracks, wharfs, and several dwelling-houses
for the master builder and other artificers,
for whom, since their occupations have been so
unremitting, it has been found necessary to erect
habitations on the spot. In this yard the ships
composing the present British Ontario armament were built and equipped: the construction
of the St. Lawrence, a first-rate, mounting one
hundred and two guns, will sufficiently prove
that the power of this fleet may hereafter be
increased to a vast extent. As a rival station
to the American one of Sacket Harbour, Navy
Bay is entitled to every consideration, and as
long as it becomes an object to maintain a
naval superiority on the lake, the greatest attention must be paid to this establishment;

particularly when we observe with what care our rivals complete such of their ships as were begun during the war, and also the measures they are adopting generally to be enabled to contend against us, at a future period, with numerical strength in their favour; and, in fact, the methods they pursue are well calculated to obtain the object they steadily keep in view. The conduct of an enterprising enemy should always be narrowly observed, and a countervailing power be prepared, commensurate to the means of aggression. The Americans build their ships much faster than we do on our side, and for this reason, strength is the chief object with them, and if that be obtained they care but little about beauty of model or elegance of finishing; in fact, they receive no other polish than what is given them by the axe and the adze. On the other hand, we employ as much time upon ours as we should in the European dock-yards: they are undoubtedly as strong as the Americans, they are handsomer and much better finished, but they are far more expensive, and will not endure a longer period of service. When we reflect that ships built on this lake will not last more than five, or at most six years of actual service, it may be a subject not unworthy of consideration, whether we cannot, with some advantage to ourselves, adopt the methods of our opponents; and if we have a fleet as strongly built, equal in number and size to theirs, and capable of keeping up the unrivalled splendour of our national banner, be satisfied with it, although it be not a rival in beauty and splendid decorations to that which has awed every enemy into submission. The situation of the town of Kingston is convenient and very well chosen; the soil in its vicinity is very fertile by nature, and much improved by cultivation for a great distance all round; roads lead from it to the westward, to the eastward, and to the interior; with the latter there is a good water communication by means of the rivers Rideau and Petite Nation, and some lakes that are connected by short portages. In the lapse of time, as the townships become settled, this will prove of great advantage in facilitating the transport of their produce, either to Kingston or to Montreal, as both the Rideau and Petite Nation discharge themselves into the Ottawa. Fronting the harbour of Kingston is Wolfe Island, or Grand Isle, twenty miles in length and about six in extreme breadth; it is uncultivated, but very well clothed with oak, elm, ash, and pine timber, and where large quantities are continually felled for the use of the dock-yard: on the south side of it a deep bay runs in so far as to leave an isthmus of no more than one mile in breadth; up this bay is the general route from the south side of the St. Lawrence to Kingston; at the entrance of it lies Carleton Island, which has a good harbour, and was in the year 1775 the naval depot, but at present it is seldom occupied by more than a non-commissioned officer's detachment of troops. The approach to Kingston harbour is made by three different channels: the first, called the Batteaux Channel, is between Wolfe Island and Forest Island, and is generally used by small craft only, having in several places hardly two fathoms and a half water; the next is the South Channel, formed by Forest Island and Snake Island, a small spot with an extensive bank spreading from it; here also, in the fair way, the water shoals from three to two fathoms and a half: the third and best is the North Channel, between Snake Island and the main land, which, although it increases the distance a little, is by far the safest, having from four to ten fathoms water in it. A little to the westward of Kingston is the bay of Quinté, very singularly formed between the irregular peninsula of Prince Edward county on the south and the main land of the midland district on the north; the length, through the various crooked turns it makes, is little short of

fifty miles, and its breadth varies between six
and twelve miles; the isthmus formed between
it and Lake Ontario, in the township of Murray, is not more than three furlongs broad, over
which there is a portage; this inlet affords to
vessels safe shelter from the heavy gales frequently experienced on the Lake. The peninsula on every side is indented by numerous
small bays and coves. Several rivers fall into
the bay, of which the largest are the Appannee,
the Shannon, the Moira, and the Trent; the
latter, flowing from Rice Lake, is the channel
by which the waters of a chain of shallow lakes
in the Newcastle district are brought into Lake
Ontario. On the south side of the Trent, in the
township of Percy, are several springs highly
impregnated with salt, and from which that article is made, but does not answer the purpose
of curing provisions; being found, by repeated
experiments, not to possess the preservative
qualities of sea salt. The townships on the
borders of the bay and on the peninsula are
thickly inhabited, and in a prosperous state of
cultivation; their produce of wheat and other
grain is very abundant, the soil being extremely
rich and very easily tilled: among the timber
there is some fine oak, pine, elm, and hickory.
A very short distance westward of the isthmus
of the bay of Quinté there is another small in-

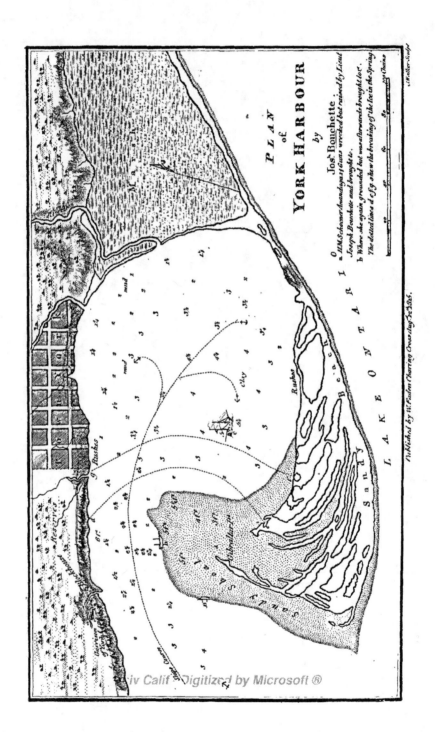

PLAN
of
YORK HARBOUR
by
Jos.h Bouchette.

0   a H.M.Schooner Onondaga 14 Guns wrecked but raised by Lieut.
I   Joseph Bouchette and brought to.
II   b Where she again grounded but was afterwards brought to.
        The dotted lines d e f g shew the breaking of the Ice in the Spring.

LAKE ONTARIO

Published by W. Faden Charing Cross Aug.t 1.st 1815.

let now called the harbour of Newcastle, but
formerly Presqu'ile, which is sheltered from
every wind, and has good anchorage for vessels. As the prosperity of the colony obtains
increase, and towns and villages are built, this
place will not go unnoticed, as it offers a most
excellent situation for a small town and port.
At a place called Duffin's Creek, in the township of Pickering, there is a fishery both for
salmon and sturgeon, that yields a large supply and of a pretty good quality, considering
the great distance it is from the sea. The
front part of all the townships from Kingston
to York are, with few exceptions, well settled;
roads lead through them, from which, in many
places, others branch off to the interior; at intervals, rather distant indeed from each other,
there are a few small villages, or it may be
rather more correct to say groups of houses;
but single dwellings and farms are continually
presenting themselves all the way. On the
lands that are occupied great progress has
been made in agriculture; the houses, generally speaking, are well built and strong; and
the inhabitants appear to be possessed of all
the necessaries as well as most of the comforts
that a life of industry usually bestows. The
town of York, the infant capital of Upper Canada, is in lat. 43°.33'. north, and in long. 79°.20'.

west, exceedingly well situated in the township of the same name, on the north side of
an excellent harbour. It is very regularly laid
out, with the streets running at right angles, and
promises to become a very handsome town.
The plot of ground marked out for it extends
about a mile and a half along the harbour,
but at present the number of houses does not
greatly exceed three hundred, the greatest part
of which are built of wood, but there are however many very excellent ones of brick and
stone. The public edifices are a government-
house, the house of assembly for the provincial
parliament, a church, a court-house, and a gaol,
with numerous stores and buildings for the various purposes of government. The garrison is
situated to the westward of the town, at a mile
distance; it consists of barracks for the troops
usually stationed here, a residence for the commanding officer, now most frequently occupied
by the lieutenant governor of the province, a
battery and two blockhouses, which together
protect the entrance of the harbour; the space
between the garrison and the town is wholly reserved for the use of government. The harbour
of York is nearly circular, and formed by a very
narrow peninsula stretching from the western
extremity of the township of Scarborough in an
oblique direction, for about six miles, and ter-

minating in a curved point nearly opposite the garrison; thus enclosing a beautiful basin about a mile and a half in diameter, capable of containing a great number of vessels, and at the entrance of which ships may lie with safety during the winter. The formation of the peninsula itself is extraordinary, being a narrow slip of land, in several places not more than sixty yards in breadth, but widening towards its extremity to nearly a mile; it is principally a bank of sand with a very little grass upon it; the widest part is very curiously intersected by many large ponds, that are the continual resort of great quantities of wild fowl; a few trees scattered upon it greatly increase the singularity of its appearance; it lies so low that the wide expanse of Lake Ontario is seen over it: the termination of the peninsula is called Gibraltar Point, where a block-house has been erected. The eastern part of the harbour is bounded by an extensive marsh, through part of which the river Don runs before it discharges itself into the basin. No place in either province has made so rapid a progress as York: in the year 1793 the spot on which it stands presented only one solitary Indian wigwam; in the ensuing spring the ground for the future metropolis of Upper Canada was fixed upon, and the buildings commenced under the immediate super-

intendance of the late General Simcoe, then
lieutenant governor; in the space of five or six
years it became a respectable place, and rapidly.
increased to its present importance : it now contains a population of two thousand five hundred
souls. The parliament of the province annually holds its sittings here, as do all the courts
of justice. Considerable advances have also
been made in the commerce, general opulence,
and consequent amelioration of its society :
being the residence of the chief officers of government both civil and military, many of the
conveniences and comforts of polished life are
to be met with. A newspaper is printed once
a week, and indeed at Kingston also. The
lands of the adjacent townships for several miles
round are in a high state of cultivation, so that
the market of the town is always well supplied.
The pressure of the late war has been considerably felt here, as it was captured by the
American army on the 27th April, 1813; they
held it, however, but a few days, but in that
time the government-house, and all the public
buildings and stores, were burnt, after removing
so much of their contents as could be conveniently carried off. Immediately in the rear of
the town there is a very good road, called Yonge
street, that leads to Gwillimbury, a small village
thirty-two miles to the northward, and thence

five miles more to Cook's Bay, from which by Lake Simcoe there is a communication to Lake Huron. This being a route of much importance, has of late been greatly improved by the North-west Company, for the double purpose of shortening the distance to the Upper Lakes, and avoiding any contact with the American frontiers; the land on each side of it, for a considerable depth, is very fertile, and many settlements are already formed, where some of the farms are in a good state of cultivation. The advantage of this communication will be in some degree shewn by the following recapitulation of it. From York to Cook's Bay, on Lake Simcoe, the distance is thirty-seven miles; the navigation through that Lake and the River Matchedash up to the old trading post on Matchedash Bay, is seventy-seven miles more, making together one hundred and fourteen. A shorter route even than this is likely to be formed very soon, by a road which has been already traced at the expense of the North-West Company, from Kempenfelt Bay on Lake Simcoe, to Penetengushene harbour, opening into Gloucester Bay on Lake Huron; this line of road being only twenty-nine miles, will reduce the distance from York to Lake Huron to eighty-eight miles, going by water from Cook's Bay into Kempenfelt Bay; another small reduction

might still be made, by opening a road from
Holland river up to the last-mentiòned bay.
By pursuing this route the distance from York
to St. Mary's Rapid, between Lake Huron and
Lake Superior, is about four hundred miles,
whereas by the circuitous one of Lake Erie and
the River Ste. Claire it is full seven hundred;
the importance of the communication is therefore obvious. From York to the westward there
is another good road, called Dundas-street, leading to Coot's Paradise, at the extremity of Lake
Ontario, and from thence nearly in a straight
line to the township of New London upon
the River Thames, altogether upwards of one
hundred miles, by which an inland communication with the western district is maintained.
On each side of this road there are many settlements scattered here and there, some of them
very well cultivated and thickly inhabited;
there are also several inns for the accommodation of travellers. The River Thames winds
through a fine level country, highly fertile, and
rich in every requisite for new' settlements;
its banks present many fine plains and large
patches of excellent meadow land; the soil is
principally a light sandy earth, interspersed with
marl and reddish clay: the oak, pine, maple,
walnut and beech growing in its vicinity, are of
very superior quality. There are already roads
formed along its course, and on each side of it

numerous scattered settlements down to Lake
St. Claire; the Delaware Indian village, and
another of Moravian settlers, are situated on it.
This last is about thirty-five miles from the
mouth of the river; it is under the superintendance of missionaries from the society of
Moravian United Brethren, who maintain a
chapel here; there are many Indian converts
residing in it, whose peaceable conduct and
general demeanour show some of the benefits
derived from civilization; the village is surrounded by thriving corn fields, and tillage
has made a considerable progress in its neighbourhood. About twenty miles further down
the river is a small place called Chatham, very
desirably seated at the junction of a large
stream with the Thames; it is in a very centrical
situation, and likely, as the population of the
province increases, to become a town of much
note. A dock-yard might be advantageously
established on the point of land formed by the
two rivers, from whence vessels might be conveniently launched. The Thames is deep enough
for ships of any size: a bar across its entrance
into Lake Ste. Claire is certainly some draw-
back, but as there is at all times sufficient water
upon it to float small craft perfectly equipped,
the resources of art would very easily pass those
of a much larger rate; camels, for instance,

might be used, or even common lighters dexte-
rously managed would prove adequate to the
service. The British bank of the Niagara River
is generally high, and exhibits a well-cultivated
and thickly inhabited country, with roads leading along its course, from which others strike off
to almost every part of the district; in this portion of the province agriculture and new settlements have been carried to a great extent, and
the amount of its population is surpassed only
by the three eastern districts. By the side of
the roads that coast the extremity of Lake Ontario there is a continual succession of houses,
and many excellent farms. The town of Newark
is conveniently and very pleasantly situated at
the entrance of the River Niagara from Lake
Ontario, and almost fronting Fort Niagara on
the American side; it was begun in 1792, and
had increased to about two hundred neat and
well-built houses, with a church, court-house,
and one or two other public buildings; but all
of these, with the greatest part of the dwelling
houses, were destroyed by the Americans in the
month of December, 1813, when they evacuated
Fort George, which stands on the bank of the
river, a little above Navy Hall, and had been
captured by them a few months before. A few
huts are the only remains of this once thriving
town, that from its defenceless state had never

been able to make any opposition to the enemy's force: its destruction was as cold-blooded
as it was unjustifiable, and betrayed a depraved
ferocity not often portrayed in modern annals,
but which was afterwards dearly expiated in
the course of the war. From Newark to Queenstown the distance is seven miles by the road
along the river: this is a place of much note,
exceedingly well situated under the ridge called
Queenstown Heights ; it has a harbour capable
of receiving vessels of all descriptions; the
number of houses is about one hundred and
fifty, with a good church, court-house, stores for
government and for the Indian department,
wharfs, and barracks for the troops always
stationed here: much commercial activity takes
place during the season of navigation, as all the
goods sent to the north-west country are landed
here from the vessels which bring them from
Kingston, and returns made in peltries, provisions, and other commodities; from hence there
is a portage or road to Chippewa Creek, by
which the goods are transported in waggons on
account of the Great Fall. Queenstown suffered very much during the war ; in its vicinity
was fought the action by which our country
was deprived of the valuable services of that
gallant and able soldier General Brock. About
three miles from Queenstown, on the road
leading towards the head of the lake, is the vil-

lage of St. David's, very pleasantly situated on a stream called the Four-mile Creek, and surrounded by land in a very high state of cultivation: previous to feeling the severities of American warfare it contained forty houses, but now it is much short of that number. Between Queenstown and Fort Erie there is only the village of Chippewa, containing a few houses, many storehouses, and two or three taverns; it is on the eastern bank of the River Welland, and near it a small military post called Fort Chippewa. Bordering the road throughout the whole distance, at short intervals, there are houses and farms in a very flourishing state, many of them beautifully and romantically situated on the bank of the river, and surrounded by some of the most picturesque scenery in nature: between Newark and Chippewa a stage coach travels regularly. Fort Erie stands on a little rising ground close to the entrance into the Niagara River from the Lake Erie. During the war it was considerably strengthened and connected by a chain of field-works with a strong battery on Snake Hill, about eleven hundred yards distant. The northern shore of Lake Erie is not remarkable for any strong traits of nature; all the townships are watered both by large and small streams in abundance; they increase very fast in the number of their settlements and the quantity of land brought under culture; in many parts they are naturally. but scantily timbered, and almost unencumbered with underwood, circumstances materially contributing to this increase. Along the shore there are several convenient harbours for small craft, and two or three for the armed vessels that have occasionally navigated it. Long. Point, or the North Foreland, is a narrow slip of land, or rather a sandy beach, projecting eastward from the township of Walsingham, little less than twenty miles, and not greatly exceeding one hundred and eighty yards in breadth; it forms the deep nook called Long Point Bay, at the head of which there is a portage across the neck of land to the lake, that from its lowness is sometimes so much overflowed as to be passable for boats. At Turkey Point, projecting from the main land within the foreland, a spot has been surveyed and planned out for a dock-yard. From this spot to Amherstburgh nothing intervenes to break the uniformity of the coast: this town is situated about three miles up the eastern side of Detroit River, and contains about one hundred and fifty houses, a church, court-house, gaol, &c. It was a frontier post and naval depot, but the military works, dock-yard, and stores, were destroyed by the English in 1813, when they were forced to evacuate it by an overwhelming American force: there is a very safe and convenient harbour, with good anchorage, in 3½ fathoms. Fourteen miles beyond Amherst-burgh, pursuing the course of the river, stands the town of Sandwich, containing about one hundred houses, a church, distinguished by the appellation of the Huron church, a court-house, and gaol : there are some wharfs along the river side, where vessels may be safely laid up during the winter. From Sandwich to Lake Ste. Claire the bank of the river is every where in a high state of culture, with houses thickly placed all along the road; good gardens, and almost invariably an orchard, are attached to them : no part of the province can rival this in luxuriance of soil or picturesque beauty, nor can any one be easily conceived more agreeable than it is in the spring of the year. Beyond this valuable tract there is no cultivated land, except in small quantities round the different stations of the North-West Company in the in-terior. In reviewing the American frontier op-posed to Upper Canada, it is found to extend from the village of St. Regis, on the parallel of the forty-fifth degree of north latitude, along the south bank of the St. Lawrence and the Great Lakes, up to the north-west angle of the Lake of the Woods, a distance of about 1570 miles : on this line many military stations and trading posts are established. Upwards of six hundred miles of it are extremely well cultivated, thickly peopled, and divided into districts, counties, and townships. The state of New York presents by far the most interesting front along the Great River, Lake Ontario, and part of Lake Erie, comprising the counties of St. Lawrence, Jefferson, Oneida, Onondaga, Cayuga, Seneca, Ontario, Genesee, and Niagara; the counties of Erie and Crawford are within the state of Pensylvania; thence westward, the counties of Geauga, Cayahoga, Huron, and the Miamis Country as far as the southerly line of the Michigan Territory, are in the state of Ohio; the Michigan Territory is divided into the districts of Erie, Huron, and Michilimackinac, composing the county of Wayne and the Chippewa country. The rapid progress of population and agriculture in this extent of six hundred miles is surprising, and perhaps stands without precedent in the annals of colonisation. In the year 1796 the whole of it was literally a wilderness, excepting only in the vicinity of the forts and trading establishments, and a very few settlements on the Genesee River. So different is the face of the country in the present day, that if a traveller were to view it who had witnessed the state of it at the time mentioned, he would with difficulty trust to the evidence of his own senses. The part of New York bordering the waters possesses a soil equal in fertility to almost any district of North America, abound-

ing with timber of first rate quality and finest
sorts, and watered in a most singularly convenient manner, by numerous large rivers, and an
extraordinary number of minor streams; many
of the former have their sources from forty to
fifty, and as much as ninety miles in the interior,
and descend into the St. Lawrence or Lake
Ontario; added to these are the Lakes Oneida,
Cayuga, Seneca, Crooked Lake and Chatanque.
Of the principal rivers may be mentioned the
Oswego, Genesee, Black River, Oswegatchie,
Grass River, Rackett River, St. Regis River,
and Salmon River; the Tonnewonta Creek,
Buffalo Creek, Oak Orchard Creek, and many
others: on their banks are many extensive levels
of fine arable; and abundance of luxuriant
meadow land. In no part of the United States
has the progress of industry been so eminently
conspicuous as here, and perhaps in no part of
the universe have numerous villages and towns,
convenient and good roads, grounds clothed
with harvests, and pastures covered with domestic cattle of every description, so suddenly
emerged from the depths of forests and a wilderness of matted thickets. From St. Regis to
the extremity of Lake Erie there are not less
than twenty principal roads striking off to the
interior, of which several lead by the shortest
route to Washington, Albany, New York, Phi-
ladelphia; and even to Boston. Between St.

Regis and the village of Hamilton, a distance of
thirty-three miles, there is a good road; the
latter stands on a rising ground close by the
river side, and consists of about thirty very well
built houses : at this place there is a ferry over
to the Canadian side, and roads diverging from
it to the southward, and to the settlements on
Lake Champlain. Nineteen miles further westward are the town and fort of Ogdensburgh.: the
former numbers about seventy houses, a church,
&c.; the latter is a strong work, presenting a
powerful front to the river, immediately opposite
to Fort Wellington. From Ogdensburgh good
roads lead parallel with the river, but there is
no place of note until arriving at Sacket Harbour, a distance of fifty-nine miles. This place
has risen into consequence from its rivalship to
Kingston, and attracted much public attention
by some ephemeral successes, that are not
likely to recur if the trident of Britain be hereafter grasped with its characteristic determination. It is situated on the south-east side of
an expansion of the Black River, near where it
flows into Hungry Bay, bearing from Kingston
south by east, distance twenty-five miles, but
by a ship's course thirty-five miles; as an harbour it is convenient, but rather small, with sufficient water for the large ships, and well sheltered from every wind, being nearly surrounded
by high lands. A low point of land runs out

from the north-west, upon which is the dock-yard, with large storehouses, and all the requisite buildings belonging to such an establishment. Upon this point there is a very powerful work called Fort Tompkins, having within it a strong block-house, two stories high; on the land side it is covered by a strong picketing, in which there are embrasures; twenty guns are mounted, besides two or three mortars, with a furnace for heating shot. At the bottom of the harbour is the village, that contains from sixty to seventy houses, and to the southward of it a barrack capable of accommodating two thousand men, and generally used for the marines belonging to the fleet. On a point eastward of the harbour stands Fort Pike, a regular work, surrounded by a ditch, in advance of which there is a strong line of picketing; in the centre of the principal work there is a block-house two stories high: this fort is armed with twenty guns. About one hundred yards from the village, and a little to the westward of Fort Tompkins, is Smith's Canton-ments or barrack, strongly built of logs, forming a square with a block-house at each corner; it is loop-holed on every side, and capable of making a powerful resistance: 2500 men may be accommodated in it. A little further west-ward another large fort presents itself, built of earth, and strongly palisaded, having in the centre of it a block-house one story high; it

mounts twenty-eight guns: midway between
these two works there is a powder magazine,
enclosed within a very strong picketing. By
the side of the road that leads from the village
to Henderson's Harbour stands Fort Virginia,
a square work with bastions at the angles, covered with a strong line of palisades, but no ditch;
it is armed with sixteen guns, and has a block-
house in the middle of it. Fort Chauncey is a
small circular tower, covered in with plank, and
loop-holed for the use of musketry, intended for
a small-arm defence only: it is situated a small
distance from the village, and commands the
road that leads to Sandy Creek. In addition
to these works of strength, there are several
block-houses in different situations, that altogether render the place very secure, and capable of resisting a powerful attack; indeed, from
recent events, the Americans have attached
much importance to it, and with their accustomed celerity have spared no exertions to
render it formidable. The strength of the
American armament lying in this port in the
summer of 1814 is given in a subjoined table,
as well as a statement of the English squadron
at Kingston. The country round Sacket Harbour is neither much cleared, nor in a very high
state of cultivation; but there are moderately
good roads leading to Brownville, and in various
directions into the state of New York. From

Brownville a road leads to a place called Kingston Ferry, on the St. Lawrence, from whence
over to Kingston, through the Bay of Wolfe
Island, the distance is twelve miles, making the
whole from Sacket Harbour by this route
thirty-four miles; but in the winter season it
may be shortened several miles by crossing the
lake upon the ice, almost in a straight line. Beyond Sacket Harbour, the River Oswego furnishes an easy and very convenient communication from Lake Ontario to the Mohawk
River, and thence into the Hudson River. The
Oswego has its source very near the head of the
Mohawk; it passes through Lake Oneida, and
in its course to Lake Ontario receives the Seneca
River, besides the waters of several less streams
and many small lakes, that in the spring and
fall of the year greatly swell its current. At the
mouth of the river there is a safe and good harbour with two fathom water, but a little way up
the stream the depth increases to four or five;
the entrance is narrowed by a large flat on each
side, covered with round stones, that are continually rolling with the flux and reflux, and occasion a sort of shifting bar, on which during the
summer there is seldom more than six or seven
feet water, but in the spring and fall this depth
is increased about three feet. The channel is
completely commanded by a well-built strong
fort, situated upon an eminence on the shore of

the lake, eastward of the river; on its western
bank stands the town of Oswego, consisting of
about one hundred houses, and laid out with
much regularity. From this place to the town
of Albany, on the Hudson River, besides the
communication by water, there are very good
roads leading through a flourishing well-settled
country, which have long constituted one of the
principal approaches to Upper Canada; and
although many others have been opened within
the few last years, the line will always remain
one of primary consequence, as being the most
direct. Between Sacket Harbour and Oswego
a road passes through Ellisburgh, and near the
mouth of Salmon River, from which places
there are others leading to Utica. Sixteen
miles westward of Oswego is a bay called the
Great Sodus, about four miles across, and two
deep: the entrance to it is narrow, being
formed by two projecting points; that on the
westward is high, and near to it is the deepest
water: a sandy bar stretches across the mouth
of the bay, on which there is generally six
feet water, but under the western point seven
and eight; within it there are several fathoms:
on the eastern side there is a small island: this
place forms a very good station for building
vessels: round the bay there are some settlements from whence roads strike off to Canan-
dagua. Irondiquet Bay is another large open-

ing that runs considerably inland, but the entrance to it is obstructed by a sandy bar with
no more than three or four feet water upon it :
in the vicinity are the settlements of Northfield,
from which a road leads to the Mohawk River,
and thence continues to the town of Bristol.
Tracing the shore of the lake, beyond Irondiquet Bay is the Genesee River, that has its
rise in the county of Porter, within the state of
Pensylvania, and winds through a country both
fertile and well inhabited; the entrance to it
from Lake Ontario is narrow, with no more
than six or seven feet water in the channel, but
within it there is sufficient depth for vessels of
two hundred tons. Hartford, Genesee Town,
and Williamsburgh, are principal places upon
it, and have roads in almost every direction
from them to the town of Batavia and the
interior of the state. The tract called the Genesee country is remarkable for the luxuriant
fertility of its soil; it is every where thickly inhabited, and in a very high state of cultivation;
the produce of wheat is unusually great, and
the grain of a very superior quality; in many
parts the land is congenial to the culture of
hemp and flax, and of each article large quantities are raised every year. Braddock's Bay is
large, but almost unserviceable, from the shallowness of the water. From the settlements at
Fish Bay there are roads to the town of Ba-

tavia. On sweeping round the extremity of
Lake Ontario the large fort of Niagara presents itself, on the eastern bank, at the entrance of the river: it was originally built by
the French in 1751, taken by the English in
1759, ceded to the United States by the treaty
of 1794, and delivered up to them in 1796,
with several other frontier posts. It was at
one time esteemed the key to the upper lakes,
from being a strong place and commanding
the entrance of the river, which from point
to point is about 1000 yards across. Among
the events of the late war it made a principal
figure, having been taken by the English on the
19th December, 1813, by assault, in a very distinguished manner, and held by them until the
peace, when it was returned to its former masters. On the bank of the River Niagara a very
good road, with a few settlements interspersed,
runs as far as Fort Schlosser. Lewistown, opposite to Queenstown, on the English side, a
pretty little village of forty or fifty houses, was
burnt by the British troops, immediately after
the capture of Niagara, as a measure of retri-
bution for the unnecessary and unprovoked
cruelties inflicted by the Americans upon the
unoffending town of Newark. From Lewistown
a fine road goes to Batavia, from whence others
branch off through the states of Pensylvania and

s s

New York, as well as almost every part of the frontier. At Black Rock and Buffalo Creek, at the eastern extremity of Lake Erie, were military posts, with a few houses and settlements around them, but they were destroyed at the same time and for the same reason as Lewistown; since that time, however, the Americans have been indefatigable in restoring the forts. From Buffalo up to Detroit, near Lake Ste. Claire, the shore of Lake Erie is generally low, except near the portage of Chataughque, where for a short distance it is rocky and lofty; and between Cleveland and the Reneshoua River, where the cliffs rise almost perpendicular nearly twenty yards above the water's level, and so continue until they approach almost close to the River Huron. Along this side of the lake there are but few points meriting particular notice: the entrance of Cataragus Creek affords a good harbour for boats, from whence there is a road to the interior. Presqu'ile harbour is situated opposite to the North Foreland, or Long Point, and formed by a sandy beach or narrow peninsula stretching a great distance, and covering it from the lake; in form it bears so strong a resemblance to York harbour on Lake Ontario, that the same description would apply almost equally well to both places, with the difference; that the latter opens to the south-west and the former to the north-east: the breadth of it is about a mile and a half, but it runs inward nearly three miles; the entrance is not more than half a mile wide, with a bar across it, on which there is in general not more than six or seven feet water. The town of Erie is seated on the south side of the harbour: it is of a respectable size, well laid out, and the streets regular; the houses altogether amount to two hundred, with a church, court-house, and a public prison: eastward of the town stands a strong battery, and on the point of the peninsula a large blockhouse, which combined completely defend the harbour. At this town there is a dock-yard, with storehouses, wharfs, &c. forming the American naval depot on this lake, and at which they have built and equipped brigs mounting twenty guns. A road leads from it by Fort Le Bœuf to Meadsville and Fort Franklin, on the Allegany River, and another by the margin of the lake to Buffalo. A little south-west of Erie is the small village of Litchfield, from whence a road continues by the lake side to Ralphsville, and by the Ashtabula River down to Jefferson and Austinburgh, from whence another proceeds to the towns of Warren and New Lisbon. From a small settlement called Newmarket, on the east side of Grand River, a road goes to Cleveland, and thence turns off to New Lisbon, and continues

s s 2

on to Fort M'Intosh on the Ohio river. From
Cleveland there is a very good road to Sandusky, that proceeds on to the old Fort Miami,
now almost in ruins: half a mile beyond it is
Fort Meggs, a place of some strength, and
mounting eighteen guns. The two bays of
Sandusky and Miami afford good anchorage
and shelter, as do most of the islands at the
west end of the lake. In Cunningham's Island
there is a fine harbour called Put-in-Bay,
open to the north, and very well sheltered,
with excellent anchorage: it is nearly of a
circular form, and the entrance to it not more
than a quarter of a mile wide, having on the
western side a narrow rocky point about forty
feet high, but where it joins the island the
isthmus is so low as to be generally overflowed;
from the point a block-house and strong battery
defend the harbour. The English ships Queen
Charlotte and Detroit were carried in here after
their capture, when the British squadron was
defeated by an American one of much superior
force. Without exception this is the best and
most convenient harbour on Lake Erie. From
Miami there is a road by French Town and
Brownville to Detroit, a considerable place on
the side of the river, and almost opposite to
Sandwich: the town consists of about two
hundred houses, a Protestant and a Catholic
church, a few public buildings, belonging to

the government, and wharfs in front of it: among the inhabitants there are many old Canadian settlers. The fort and military works at this place are very strong; they were taken by the British forces under General Brock in 1812, when General Hull surrendered himself and his army prisoners of war. The land about the town of Detroit and on the bank of the river is highly fertile, thickly inhabited, and under a very thriving state of culture: the settlements continue closely connected with each other along the western border of Lake Ste. Claire for about twenty miles. On both sides of the River Huron, at its embouchure in the lake, there are a few good settlements, distant about thirty-five miles from Detroit. The west bank of the River Ste. Claire is moderately good land, and settlements have been carried as high up as the Belle Riviere, about fifteen miles above the lake, as far as which there is a road all the way from Detroit. Beyond this point cultivation has not been extended, except a little at the different places where military or trading establishments are maintained. The government of Upper Canada is administered by a lieutenant-governor (who is almost always a military officer), a legislative council, an executive council, and a house of assembly. The legislative council, according to the act of the British parliament, is to consist of not less

than seven members, of which the chief justice
of the province is president; and wherein the
bishop of Quebec has a seat: the members
are appointed by mandamus from the king,
and hold their seats, under certain restrictions,
for life. The executive council is composed of
six members; the chief-justice is president, and
the bishop of Quebec likewise has a seat in it.
The house of assembly is composed of twenty-
five members, who are returned by the twenty-
three counties; they meet once a year, and the
session is opened and prorogued by the lieutenant-governor; the duration of this assembly
is limited by law to four years, at which period new elections take place; but the governor may, upon occasions that seem fit to him,
dissolve it at any time, by the authority vested
in him. The functions of this house are exactly similar to those of the parliament of the
lower province; it votes the annual supplies
for the militia, and all monies raised for the
service and improvement of the colony. The
civil and criminal law is administered by a
chief-justice and two puisne judges. There
is a court of king's bench, common pleas, and
a court of appeal: the laws of England, with
the rights and liberties granted by its constitution, are in force in Upper Canada in their
fullest extent, and without the slightest variation. There are also an attorney and solicitor

general, a surveyor-general, and several other officers of the crown; but the amount of their salaries, and indeed the whole civil list, is defrayed by Great Britain, without the smallest encumbrance to the province. For the defence of this extensive country detachments of regular troops are stationed in it, assisted by a sedentary militia, enrolled in the same way as that of Lower Canada, and which, upon paper, amounts to 11,000 men: from among these the battalions of incorporated militia, when ordered to be embodied, are filled up by ballot; but, spread over so wide a space as they are, it is rare that, upon cases of emergency, more than a few hundreds have been brought together at one time; the chief reliance, therefore, must be placed upon the former, and the navy on the lakes. Of the troops no permanent number can be mentioned, being augmented or reduced, as circumstances require, or the amicable relations with our neighbours will permit. The defence of this large and rapidly improving colony becomes, in the present day, a subject of much importance, and demands more than ordinary attention. If the actual state of this country and that part of the United States bordering upon it be critically examined, and taking into consideration the superior population of the latter, with the easy means of access by the large rivers that fall into the St. Law-

rence and the lakes; and combining these circumstances with the ardent desire shewn and
openly avowed by the American government
of obtaining possession of Upper Canada, we
shall not be misled by a belief that the present
means of defence are adequate to its preservation; in the event of another rupture between
the two powers. A war, undertaken for the ex-
press purpose of dismembering these provinces
from the British dominion, has been recently
terminated, in which the invader was overwhelmed with disgrace, and beaten back from
the territory he attempted to subjugate, by a
force that, reckoning its numerical strength
only, was never competent to stand before
him. This success may be attributed to two
causes; in the first place, to the patient fortitude and invincible bravery of our troops; in
the next, and certainly more adventitious one,
to the want of discipline and military talent
in their enemies. Upon the former we may
always rely with the most unshaken confidence, but not so with the latter; for even
defeats following quick upon each other have
before now taught the conquered to become in
their turn the victors. At the time the American declaration of war was known in Upper
Canada, and which reached Amherstburgh on
the afternoon of July 2d, 1812, there were not
more than 2000 British troops distributed all

over it, and none of the militia organised; in
the following year, when strengthened by every
man that could be spared from the lower province and the dependent governments, the campaign was made with 7000 men, against armies,
or rather collections, of much superior numbers; and it was not until the middle of 1814
that sufficient reinforcements arrived to place
it in a state of security.   On Lake Ontario the
preponderance of naval strength was latterly
with the English, but in the early part of the
war it was most decidedly on the enemy's
side; and to the co-operation of which he was
indebted for the advantage he obtained in
the few attacks that he made with success.
True it is, that he never gained any victory
that was eminently useful to him, even at the
time when the number of regular troops in the
province was at the lowest, for in nearly every
one of his attempts his plans were developed
and his armies overthrown by the bravery of
mere handfuls of well disciplined soldiers; but
the recurrence of a similar chain of fortunate
events is not to be presumed upon. In the
outset of the war a few hundreds of English
troops found it an easy task to bear away the
palm of victory from double, treble, and even
quadruple their number of opponents; but towards its termination a material difference was
observable; numerous disasters had taught the

Americans caution; frequent defeats brought
them better acquainted with tactics; and dear-
bought experience in the business of an active
campaign, enabled them to take the field with
many essential qualifications of good soldiers;
consequently the different actions were more
obstinately contested, and the side to which
victory would incline rendered more dubious.
The principal affairs that took place during
the two first campaigns were the following, and
while they prove that nothing but the uncommon firmness and heroic devotion of the different corps saved the country, will also shew that
such a result was hardly to be expected. Immediately after the declaration of hostilities,
General Hull, with a large force, crossed the
River Detroit, and made an incursion upon the
Canadian frontier, but retired almost immediately afterwards to his own side, and strengthened himself at Fort Detroit, where he was
attacked on the 16th August, 1812, by 700
regulars and militia, under the command of
General Brock, assisted by 600 Indians, and
so completely vanquished that he surrendered
himself and all his army of 2500 men prisoners
of war. On the night of the 12th October another American corps of 1500 men crossed the
Niagara River near Queenstown, and on the
morning of the 13th, soon after day-break,
were defeated by a body of 650 men under

General Brock, who unhappily for his country
received a mortal wound shortly after the action commenced. On the 22d January, 1813,
a detachment under General Winchester was
defeated and captured at Riviere aux Raisins,
on which occasion there was nearly a similar
disparity of force. On the 27th April, an
American force under General Dearborn, consisting of 2500 men, supported by Commodore
Chauncey's squadron of ten armed vessels, carrying altogether fifty guns, effected a landing,
and captured the town of York, which at that
period was protected only by two companies of
the 8th regiment, two weak companies of the
Newfoundland regiment, 40 men of the Glengary riflemen, 220 militia, and 40 Indians,
all under the personal command of General
Sheaffe. An action took place, but it only
served to gain time for destroying a new ship
on the stocks, and some public stores; when
after having sustained the loss of 130 brave
men in obstructing the enemy's advance, a retreat was effected with the remainder, and the
capital of Upper Canada for the first time received a conqueror, but who soon re-embarked,
after destroying such of the public buildings as
fell into his hands. The superiority of their
fleet gave the Americans the advantage of
choosing their points of attack, and on the
24th and 25th of May Chauncey's squadron,

in conjunction with Fort Niagara, bombarded Fort George, on the opposite side of the river, and in the two days nearly destroyed its defences. On the morning of the 27th the fleet received on board 4000 troops, under the command of General Lewis, which were immediately after landed between Mississaga Point and Two Mile Creek, under cover of a lively fire from the ships, and succeeded, after as much opposition as could be offered by the few troops it was possible to assemble, in capturing the fort. On this occasion the whole number of English troops did not amount to one tenth of the enemy's: when resistance was no longer of use, this small body effected a retreat unmolested, under the command of Brigadier General Vincent, to Queenstown, and subsequently to Burlington heights, where a position was taken up, and some reinforcement obtained. After his victory General Lewis moved forward with intent to attack this new post, but General Vincent, penetrating the design, determined to attempt a surprise; and with 280 men of the 8th, and 450 of the 49th regiment, before day-break on the 6th June fell upon his opponents in their camp near Stoney Creek, with such vigour that they were totally routed with great slaughter: in this affair the force of the enemy was 3500 infantry, with seven field-pieces; Brigadier-Generals

Chandler and Winder, 5 field-officers and captains, and upwards of 100 men, with 4 of the
guns, were taken. While these events were
taking place at the western extremity of Lake
Ontario, an attack was made by the English
upon Sacket's Harbour, before day-break on
the 29th May, but was not attended with the
desired success. In this encounter the numbers
of the enemy were treble those of the assailants;
adverse winds prevented the co-operation of the
large ships of the British squadron, and the fire
of the gun-boats being incapable of producing
much effect against the batteries, it was deemed impracticable to carry the place by assault;
the troops were therefore withdrawn and re-embarked without opposition, taking with them
four American officers and 150 soldiers prisoners, and occasioning the enemy to set fire to
some of their naval store-houses, lest the place
should fall into the hands of the English. The
principal feature of the campaign of 1813 was
the defeat of part of General Wilkinson's army on
the 11th November, near Chrystlers Farm, as it
entirely overthrew the plan of operations agreed
upon between him and General Hampton, and
which was the most formidable of any that was
concerted for the invasion of the lower province.
Wilkinson had collected 10,000 men at Grena-
dier Island, in Lake Ontario, from whence, on
the 30th October, he descended the St. Law-

rence in small craft, with a view to act in con-
cert with General Hampton; during the night
of the 7th November he passed Fort Wellington, but his intention being previously observed,
he experienced a very heavy and destructive
fire during the whole of the time he was within
reach of its guns. A corps of observation under
Lieutenant Colonel Morrison, of the 89th, consisting of part of the 49th regiment, the 2d battalion of the 89th, three companies of voltigeurs,
and some Indians, in all about 800 men, and two
field pieces, with a division of gun-boats, followed the American army, and closely watched
its movements. About two o'clock on the afternoon of the 11th, a detachment of two brigades
of infantry, a regiment of cavalry, and some
field-pieces, under the command of Brigadier
General Boyd, in all 4000 men, attacked the
British advanced guard, which gradually fell
back upon the position occupied by the main
body; half an hour afterwards the action became general, when several efforts were made
by the enemy to turn the British left flank, and
as often frustrated by spirited manœuvres; after
two hours contest, and being charged in his turn,
he gave way at all points from a formidable
position, and precipitately retired. After this
essay, in which he lost one gun and 800 men,
killed, wounded, or prisoners, General Wilkinson immediately re-crossed the St. Lawrence to

his own shores, and soon afterwards quitted the command of an army he had so unsuccessfully conducted. The year 1813 closed with two other defeats of the enemy, and both on his own territory: the first took place on the 19th December, when Fort Niagara was carried by the brilliant assault of a body of troops under Colonel Murray; and the second on the 30th of the same month, by detachments from the Royal Scots, the 8th, 41st, 89th, and 100th regiments, amounting to 1000 men, under the command of General Riall. The American general's force, upwards of 2000, was strongly posted at Black Rock; but after a sharp attack he was driven to Buffalo, where, in another good position, he endeavoured to retrieve his fortune, but with no better success, and after a short resistance fell back to Eleven Mile Creek on Lake Erie: the result of this enterprise was seven field pieces, four sloops and schooners, a considerable quantity of ordnance and other valuable stores, and 70 prisoners; the forts at Black Rock and Buffalo, with all the public buildings, and the four vessels, were burnt; after which the detachment withdrew, without interruption, to the Canadian shore. The events of the campaign of 1814 were not so numerous, but they evidently proved that the British troops must look forward to contend against opponents who had greatly profited by the experience of the two preceding years, as well as being far superior in numbers. Had the means employed by the Americans been more judiciously used, every impartial person must believe that their designs would have been realised, notwithstanding the heroism of the English soldiers. The incorporated militia, when it was organised and brought into action, always behaved nobly, and made good a title to the admiration of the country, for its bravery and loyalty; but still its support, had the invasion been conducted with skill and prudence, would not have made the defensive force sufficiently strong to avert the threatened danger. That the subjugation of both provinces hath been, and will continue to be, a favourite object with the Americans, is not to be doubted; in the late attempt upon them they sustained a loss of no less than 47,000 men, in killed, wounded, and prisoners; but this has not abated the keenness of their desires, and if appearances may be credited, or any judgment formed from the opinions of ruling men among them, the same sacrifices three or four fold would not be deemed too exorbitant a price to pay for the much envied possession. Great Britain cannot permit so valuable a part of her dominion to be wrested from her without a strife as obstinate as the richness of the jewel to be contended for demands.

APPENDIX.

=====

Extrait des Titres de Concessions de Terres octroyées en Fiefs dans la Province du Bas-Canada.

=====

ANCE DE L'ETANG.

CONCESSION du 20me Septembre, 1697, faite par *Louis de Buade,* Gouverneur, et *Jean Bochart,* Intendant, au Sieur *François Hazzeur* et *Denis Riverin,* de *l'Ance de l'Etang,* située au bas du fleuve *St. Laurent,* six lieues au dessous de la *Vallée* des monts de *Notre Dame,* avec une demi lieue de front de chaque côté de la dite Ance, sur une lieue de profondeur.

Régistre d'Intendance, N° 5, *folio* 18.

ANTAYA.

Concession du 29me Octobre, 1672, faite par *Jean Talon,* Intendant, au Sieur *de Comporté,* d'une demi lieue de terre de front, sur une lieue de profondeur, à prendre sur le fleuve *St. Laurent,* bornée d'un côté par la concession du Sieur *Dautré,* tirant sur le fleuve et descendant vers les terres non-concédées ; avec l'*Isle au Foin* et islets situés entre la terre ferme de son front et la dite *Isle au Foin.*

Régistre d'Intendance, N° 1, *folio* 20.

ARGENTEUIL.

Pierre Louis Panet, Ecuyer Propriétaire du Fief et Seigneurie d'*Argenteuil,* produisit un Acte de Foi et Hommage du 7me Mars, 1725, rendu par Dame *Louise Denis,* Veuve de *Pierre d'Aillebout,* Ecuyer, Sieur d'*Argenteuil,* faisant mention " d'une promesse (*sans octroi régulier*) de la part du Gouvernement François, à Mr. d'*Aillebout* et autres personnes, d'une étendue de terres qui se rencontreront au côté du Nord, *la Rivière du Nord* comprise, depuis le bas du *Long-Sault* jusqu'à deux lieues en descendant du côté de *Montréal,* (avec les Isles, &c.) sur quatre lieues de profondeur." Aussi un Arrêt du Conseil, d'où il paroit que cette Seigneurie joint celle du *Lac des deux Montagnes* et que les rumbs de vent du front et de la ligne qui termine la profondeur doivent être Est, quart de Sud-est et Ouest quart de Nord-ouest ; et que les rumbs de vent des lignes qui bornent la largeur de chaque côté seront (pour la

B

ii

Seigneurie du *Lac des deux Montagnes* aussi bien que pour celle d'*Argenteuil*,) Sud quart de Sud-ouest et Nord quart de Nord-est.

Régistre des Foi et Hommage, N° 76. *Page* 346, 21*me Mars*, 1781.
Cahiers d'Intend. 10 à 17, *folio* 576.

AUBERT GALLION.

Concession du 24me Septembre, 1736, faite par *Charles Marquis de Beauharnois*, Gouverneur, et *Gilles Hocquart*, Intendant, à Dame veuve *Aubert*, de deux lieues de terre de front et de deux lieues de profondeur, du côté du Sud-ouest de la riviére du *Sault de la Chaudiére*, en remontant, à commencer à la fin de la concession accordée au *Sieur de la Gorgendiére*, ensemble les isles et islets qui se trouveront dans la dite riviére dans l'etendue de deux lieues, et des deux côtés d'icelle, lesquels isles et islets seront partagées par égale portion entre la dite veuve *Aubert* et le Sieur de l'*Isle*, auquel nous avons accordé aujourd'hui pareille concession du côté du Nord-est de la dite riviére.

Régistre d'Intendance, N° 8, *folio* 11.

BAIE ST. ANTOINE OU LEFEBVRE.

Concession du 4me Septembre, 1683, faite par *Lefebvre de la Barre*, Gouverneur, et *de Meulles* Intendant, au Sieur *Lefebvre*, des terres nonconcédées, d'environ deux lieues de front, joignant au Nord-est la terre du Sieur *Cressé*, d'autre au Sieur de la *Lussaudiere*, au Sud-ouest, au Nord-ouest sur le lac *St. Pierre*, sur pareille quantité de profondeur, à prendre dans le bois vis-à-vis la dite largeur, avec les isles, islets, et prairies qui se rencontreront sur le dit espace.

Insinuations du Conseil Supérieur, lettre B. *folio* 31.

BATISCAN.

Concession du 23me Mars, 1639, faite par Monsieur *de la Ferté*, pour la Compagnie, aux révérends peres Jésuites, du fief de *Batiscan*, joignant d'un côté un quart de lieue au delà de la riviére de *Batiscan* au Nordest, et d'autre côté au Sud-ouest, un quart de lieue au delà de la riviére *Champlain* en la largeur, sur vingt lieues de profondeur.

Cahiers d'Intendance, N° 2 à 9, *folio* 29.

VILLECHAUVE OU BEAUHARNOIS.

Concession du 12me Avril, 1729, faite par sa Majesté au Sieur *Charles Marquis de Beauharnois*, et au Sieur *Claude de Beauharnois de Beaumont* son frere, de six lieues de front sur six lieues de profondeur, Nord-est et Sud-ouest; joignant la Seigneurie de *Chateaugay* le long du fleuve *St. Laurent*, avec les isles et islets adjacentes.

Insinuations du Conseil Supérieur, lettre F. *folio* 129.

BEAUPORT.

Concession du 31me Décembre, 1635, faite par la Compagnie à *Robert Giffard*, Sieur de *Beauport*, de la Seigneurie de *Beauport*, contenant une lieue de terre, à prendre le long de la côte du fleuve *St. Laurent*, sur une lieue et demie de profondeur dans les terres, à l'endroit où la riviére appelée *Notre Dame de Beauport* entre dans le dit fleuve, icelle riviére comprise. De plus, prolongement du 31me Mars, 1653, par Mr. *Lauzon*, Gouverneur, de deux lieues et demie de profondeur, laquelle, avec la concession ci-dessus, forme une lieue de front sur quatre de profondeur.

Le *Régistre des Foi et Hommage*, N° 16. Folio 78, 2me Février, 1781, dit que la Seigneurie de *Beauport* s'étend en front depuis la rivière de *Notre Dame* jusqu'au Sault de *Montmorency*.

Régistre d'Intendance, N° 10 à 17, *folio* 655.

BEAUJEU OU LACOLLE.

Concession du 8me Avril, 1733, faite par *Charles Marquis de Beauharnois*, Gouverneur, et *Gilles Hocquart*, Intendant, au Sieur *Louis Denis de la Ronde*, de deux lieues de terre de front sur trois lieues de profondeur, bornée du côté du Nord par la Seigneurie nouvellement concédée au Sieur *Chaussegros de Léry*, et sur la même ligne ; et au Sud par une ligne tirée Est et Ouest du monde ; sur le devant par la rivière *Chambly*, et sur le derrière à trois lieues joignant aux terres non-concédées, et en outre la petite isle qui est audessus de l'isle aux *Têtes*.

Cette concession est accordée de nouveau au Sieur *Daniel Lienard de Beaujeu*, par titre daté 22me Mars, 1743. Voyez Reg. d'Intend. No. 9, folio 10.

Régistre d'Intendance, N° 7, *folio* 16.

BEAUMONT.

Concession faite au Sieur *Des islets de Beaumont*, le 3me Novembre, 1672, par *Jean Talon*, Intendant, de la quantité de terre qui se trouvera sur le fleuve *St. Laurent*, entre le Sieur *Bissot*, et Mr. *de la Durantaie*, sur une lieue et demie de profondeur.

Régistre d'Intendance, N° 1, *folio* 31.

AUGMENTATION DE BEAUMONT.

Concession du 10me Avril, 1713, faite par *Philippe de Rigaud*, Gouverneur, et *Michel Begon*, Intendant, au Sieur *de Beaumont*, fils, d'un terrein non-concédé contenant une lieue et demie en profondeur, et sur le front et largeur de la Seigneurie de *Beaumont*, entre la Seigneurie de *la Durantaie* et celle des héritiers du Sieur *Bissot*.

Sur la carte cette Seigneurie est couchée a quatre lieux de profondeur, au lieu de trois lieux ; l'autre lieue ayant été après accordée au Sieur *Jean*, dans le titre de *St. Gervais*.

Régistre d'Intendance, N° 6, *folio* 31.

BECANCOUR.

Concession du 16me Avril, 1647, faite par la Compagnie au Sieur *de Bécancour*, située au Sud du fleuve *St. Laurent*, contenant deux lieues et un quart de front sur pareille profondeur ; tenant du côté du Nord-est au fief *Dutort* et du côté du Sud-ouest au fief *Godefroi*; par devant le fleuve *St. Laurent*, et par derrière les terres non concédées ; avec les isles, islets et battures qui se trouvent tant dans la rivière de *Bécancour* que dans une autre rivière appelée la rivière *St. Paul* qui se décharge dans le dit fleuve.

Cahiers d'Intend. 10 à 17, *folio* 414.

BELAIR OU LES ECUREUILS.

Concession du 3me Novembre, 1672, faite par *Jean Talon*, Intendant, aux Sieurs *Toupin*, Pere et Fils, d'une demi lieue de front, sur une lieue de profondeur, à prendre sur le fleuve *St. Laurent*, moitié au dessus

et moitié au dessous de la pointe *Bouroila*, (*aux Ecureuils*) aboutissant des deux côtés aux terres non-concédées.
Régistre d'Intendance, N° 1, *folio* 39.

AUGMENTATION DES ECUREUILS.

Concession du 20me Janvier, 1706, faite par *Philippe de Rignud*, Gouverneur, et *François de Beauharnois*, Intendant, à *Marie Magdelaine Mezerai*, veuve de feu *Jean Toupin*, d'une demi lieue de terre de front sur deux lieues de profondeur derrière la Seigneurie de *Bélair*, le front à prendre immédiatement à une lieue du fleuve *St. Laurent*.
Régistre d'Intendance, N° 5, *folio* 41.

BELŒIL.

Concession du 18me Janvier, 1694, faite par *Louis de Buade*, Gouverneur, et *Jean Bochart*, Intendant, au Sieur *Joseph Hertel*, de deux lieues de terre de front, avec une lieue et demie de terre de profondeur, à prendre du côté du Nord-ouest de la rivière *Richelieu*, à la Seigneurie de *Chambly*, en descendant icelle rivière, vers les terres non-concédées.
Régistre d'Intendance, N° 4, *folio* 16.

AUGMENTATION A BELŒIL.

Concession du 24me Mars, 1713, faite par *Phil. de Rigaud*, Gouverneur, et *François de Beauharnois*, Intendant, au Sieur *de Longueuil*, le long de la rivière de *Richelieu*, d'une lieue de terre de front sur une lieue et demie de profondeur, en lieu non-concédé, à prendre depuis la Seigneurie de *Belœil*, qu'il posséde, en tirant du côté du Sud-ouest, derrière la Seigneurie de *Chambly* pour le front, et pour la profondeur dans les terres en allant au Nord-ouest.
Régistre d'Intendance, N° 6, *folio* 3.

BELLEVUE.

Concession du 3me Novembre, 1672, faite par *Jean Talon*, Intendant, au Sieur *de Vitré*, d'une demi lieue de front sur une lieue de profondeur, à prendre depuis les terres *de Contrecœur*, en remontant vers les terres non concédées.
Régistre d'Intendance, N° 1, *folio* 31.

BERTHIER.

Concession du 29me Octobre, 1672, faite par *Jean Talon*, Intendant, au Sieur *Berthier*, de deux lieues de terre de front sur pareille profondeur, à prendre sur le fleuve *St. Laurent*, depuis l'ance de *Bellechasse* incluse, tirant vers la rivière du Sud, icelle non comprise.
Cette Seigneurie est bornée sur la carte suivant un arpentage particulier. L'irregularité de ce terrein provient d'une cession que firent les propriétaires de cette Seigneurie à ceux de la rivière du Sud, par une transaction du 22me Janvier, 1728.
Régistre d'Intendance, N° 1, *folio* 7.

BERTHIER.

Concession du 27me Avril, 1674, faite à Mr. *Berthier*, de trois quarts de lieue ou environ de front sur deux lieues de profondeur, à prendre sur le fleuve *St. Laurent*, depuis la concession du Sieur *Randin* en descendant, jusqu'à la riviére *Chicot ;* ensemble une Isle d'une lieue en superficie étant audessous et joignant presque l'isle *Randin,* vis-a-vis l'*Isle Dupas ;* aussi l'isle qui est au bout d'enbas de l'*Isle au Castor,* accordée à Mr. *Berthier,* le 25 Mars, 1675.

Ou les deux concessions sont accordées par un seul titre. Cahiers d'Intend. where both these concessions are granted by one title.

Régistre des Foi et Hommage, Nº 9, *folio* 38. *le* 26*me Janvier,* 1781.

Derriere Antaya, Randin, Berthier et Chicot.

AUGMENTATION DE BERTHIER.

Concession du 31me Décembre, 1732, faite par *Charles Marquis de Beauharnois,* Gouverneur, et *Gilles Hocquart,* Intendant, au Sieur *Pierre* l'*Etage,* de trois lieues de terre de front, si telle quantité se trouve entre la ligne qui sépare le fief de *Dautré* d'avec celui ci-devant appelé de *Comporté* (aujourd'hui *Antaya,*) et celle qui sépare le fief du *Chicot* d'avec le fief *Masquinongé;* à prendre le dit front au bout de la profondeur et limites des dits Fiefs d'*Antaya* et du *Chicot* entre lesquels se trouve le fief de *Berthier ;* sur trois lieues de profondeur, avec les riviéres, ruisseaux et lacs qui pourront se rencontrer dans la dite étendue de terre, pour être la dite concession unie et jointe au dit fief de *Berthier.*

Régistre d'Intendance, Nº 7, *folio* 4.

LE BIC.

Concession du 6me Mai, 1675, faite par *Louis de Buude, Gouverneur,* au Sieur *de Vitré,* de deux lieues de front, le long du fleuve *St. Laurent,* du côté du Sud, à prendre du milieu de la largeur de la riviére appelé *Mitis,* et qui s'appellera dorénavant la riviére ———en montant le dit fleuve, et deux lieues de profondeur, ensemble l'isle du *Bic* qui est vis-a-vis.

En 1774, dispute s'étant élevée entre les propriétaires du *Bic* et de *Rimousky,* la Cour des Plaidoiers Communs rendit un jugement, confirmé en appel en 1778, qui détermina, que le milieu de l'embouchure de la riviére *Hatté* seroit la borne entre les dites deux seigneuries.

Insinuations du Conseil Supérieur, let. B. *folio* 14.

BLEURY.

Concession du 30me Oct. 1750, faite par le Marquis *de la Jonquiére,* Gouverneur, et *François Bigot,* Intendant, au Sieur *Sabrevois de Bleuri,* de trois lieues de terre de front sur trois lieues de profondeur, le long de la riviére *Chambly,* bornée du côté du Nord par la Seigneurie du Sieur *Hertel,* et sur la même ligne; du côté du Sud à trois lieues de la dite Seigneurie par une ligne tirée Est et Ouest du monde; sur le devant par la riviére *Chambly* et sur la profondeur à trois lieues joignant aux terres non-concédées.

Régistre d'Intendance, Nº 9, *folio* 72.

BONAVANTURE.

Concession du 23me Avril, 1697, faite par *Louis de Buade,* Gouverneur, et *Jéan Bochart,* Intendant, au Sieur *de la Croix,* de la riviére de *Bonavanture,* avec deux lieues de terre de front, savoir : une demi lieue d'un côté de la dite riviére au Sud-ouest, en allant vers *Kiscabériac,* et une lieue et demie de l'autre au Nord-est, tirant vers *Paspébiac*, sur quatre lieues de profondeur, avec les isles, islets et battures qui se trouveront dans la dite étendue; le tout situé dans le fond de la *Baie des Chaleurs*.

Régistre d'Intendance, N° 5, *folio* 14.

GUILLAUME BONHOMME.

Concession du 24me Novembre, 1682, faite par *Lefebre*, Gouverneur, et *de Meulles*, Intendant, à *Guillaume Bonhomme*, des terres qui sont au bout de celles de Mr. *Juchereau de la Ferté*, tirant vers la riviére *Jacques Cartier*, bornées d'un côté, au Sud-ouest, de Mr. *Dupont*, Conseiller, et de l'autre à Mr. *de Mesner*, Greffier, au Nord-est; d'un bout, sur le dit Sieur *de la Ferté* au Sud; et de l'autre au Nord-ouest à la dite riviére : la dite terre contenant environ une lieue de front avec deux lieues ou environ de profondeur dans les dites terres.

Insinuations du Conseil Supérieur, Lettre B. *folio* 26.

BONSECOURS.

Concession du 16me Avril, 1687, faite par *Jacques de Brisay*, Gouverneur, et *Jean Bochart*, Intendant, au Sieur *Villeneuve*, de la quantité de soixante et quatorze arpens de front sur le fleuve *St. Laurent*, du côté du Sud, sur deux lieues de profondeur, en cas qu'elle ne soit concédée à d'autres. Les dits soixante et quatorze arpens tenant d'un côté aux terres des Dames Religieuses Ursulines et d'autre côté à la veuve *Duguet*.

Cahiers d'Intendance, 2 à 9, *folio* 295.

BONSECOURS.

Concession du 8me Août, 1702, faite au Sieur *Charon*, par *Hector de Coliére* Gouverneur, et *Jean Bochart*, Intendant, de deux lieues de terre ou environ de front, sur pareille profondeur, le long de la riviére *Yamaska*, icelle compris à prendre vis-à-vis celle accordée au Sieur *René Fézeret*, bourgeois de *Montréal*, tirant d'un côté à la Seigneurie du Sieur *Petit*, et de l'autre aux héritiers du feu Sieur *Bourchemin*, avec les isles, islets, prairies et battures adjacentes.

Régistre d'Intendance, N° 5, *folio* 35.

BONSECOURS.

Concession du 1er Juillet, 1677, faite par *Jacques Douchesnaux*, Intendant, au Sieur *François Bellanger*, des terres qui sont le long du fleuve *St. Laurent*, du côté Sud, entre celle qui appartient à la Demoiselle *Genevieve Couillard*, en remontant le dit fleuve, jusqu'à celle de la Demoiselle veuve *Amiot*; contenant le tout une lieue et demie, ou environ, de front, avec deux lieues de profondeur.

Insinuations du Conseil Supérieur, lettre B. *folio* 88.

BOURCHEMIN.

Concession du 22me Juin, 1695, faite par *Louis de Buade*, Gouverneur, et *Jean Bochart*, Intendant, au Sieur *Jacques François Bourchemin*, d'une lieue et demie de terre de front de chaque côté de la riviére *Yamaska*, icelle comprise, à prendre une demi lieue au-dessous du ruisseau dit *Salvayle*, et une lieue au-dessus, en lieu non-concédé, sur pareille profondeur, courant Nord-ouest et Sud-est, avec les isles, islets et prairies adjacentes.

Régistre d'Intendance, N° 4, *folio* 27.

BOUCHERVILLE.

Concession du 3me Novembre, 1672, par *Jean Talon*, Intendant, au Sieur *Boucher*, de cent quatorze arpens de front sur deux lieues de profondeur, à prendre sur le fleuve *St. Laurent*, bornée des deux côtés par le Sieur *de Varennes*; avec les isles nommées Percées.

Cahiers d'Intendance, N° 4, *folio* 153.

BOURGLOUIS.

Concession du 14 May, 1741, faite par le *Marquis de Beauharnois*, Gouverneur, et *Gilles Hocquart*, Intendant, au Sieur *Louis Fornel*, de deux lieues et trois quarts, ou environ, de terre, sur trois lieues de profondeur, derrière la Seigneurie de *Neuville*, appartenant au Sieur *Deméloise*, bornée sur le front par la ligne qui sépare la dite Seigneurie de *Neuville* des terres non-concédés, au Nord-est par la ligne de profondeur du fief *St. Augustin* prolongée au Sud-ouest par une ligne parallèle à la précédente, à prendre sur la ligne du fief de *Bélair* aussi prolongée, et par derrière aux terres non-concédées.

Régistre d'Intendance, N° 9, *folio* 8.

BOURG-MARIE, DE L'EST.

Concession du 1er. Août, 1708, faite par Messieurs *de Vaudreuil*, Gouverneur, et *Raudot*, Intendant, à *Marie Fezeret*, étant un reste de terre non-concédé d'environ cinquante arpens de front sur deux lieues, moins un arpent, de profondeur sur la rivière *Yamaska*, tirant au Nord-ouest, dans la profondeur, joignant au Sud-ouest la ligne de la Seigneurie *Bourgchemin*; au Nord-est la ligne des terres concédées au Sieur *Charon*; et au Nord-ouest les profondeurs de la Seigneurie de *Sorrel*, dans l'étendue de la dite concession.

Régistre des Foi et Hommage, N° 112, *folio* 64.
Cahier d'Intend. 2 à 9, *folio* 235.

BOURGMARIE DE L'OUEST.

Et aussi au Sud-est de la dite rivière un autre reste de terre non-concédé d'environ soixante arpens de front sur une lieue et demie de profondeur, tirant au Sud-est aux terres non-concédées, joignant au Sud-ouest le fief *St. Charles*, appartenant au Sieur *Fezeret*, son pere, et au Nord-ouest la Seigneurie de *Lavallière*.

Régistre des Foi et Hommage, N° 112, *folio* 64.

CAP DE LA MAGDELAINE.

Concession du 20me Mars, 1651, faite par Mr. *de la Ferté*, aux révérends pères *Jésuites*, contenant deux lieues le long du fleuve *St. Laurent*, depuis le Cap nommé des *Trois-Rivières*, en descendant sur le grand fleuve, jusqu'aux endroits où les dites deux lieues se pourront étendre, sur vingt lieues de profondeur du côté du Nord, et compris les bois, rivières et prairies qui sont sur le dit grand fleuve et sur les dites *Trois Rivières*.

Régistre d'Intendance, N° 2 à 9, *folio* 131.

CAP ST. MICHEL OU LA TRINITÉ.

Le titre de cette Concession n'a pas été trouvé dans le Secrétariat. Par un acte de Foi et Hommage, rendu le 3me Août, 1676, devant Mr. *Duchesneau*, alors Intendant, il paroit que ce fief doit avoir une lieue de front sur une lieue et demie de profondeur, situé sur le fleuve *St. Laurent*, entre les concessions de Mr. *de Varennes* et *Laurent Borney*, Sieur *de Grandmaison*, avec deux petites isles vis-a-vis de sa devanture.

Régistre des Foi et Hommage, N° 27, *folio* 182, *le* 10me *Février*, 1781.

CARUFEL.

Concession du mois de Mars, 1705, faite par *Philippe de Rigaud*, Gouverneur, et *François de Beauharnois*, Intendant, au Sieur *Jean Sicard*, Sieur *de Carufel*, de l'espace de terre qui reste dans la rivière de *Masquinongé*, dans le lac *St. Pierre*, depuis celle qui a été ci-devant accordée au Sieur *Legardeur*, jusqu'au premier sault de la dite rivière, ce qui contient deux lieues ou environ de front sur pareille profondeur.

Régistre d'Intendance, N° 5, *folio* 40.
Cahiers d'Intend. more authentic.

CHAMPLAIN.

Concession du 22me Septembre, 1664, faite par Mr. *de Mézy*, à *Etienne Pezard*, Sieur *de Latouche*, d'une lieue et demie de terre de front à prendre sur le grand fleuve *St. Laurent*, depuis la rivière *Champlain* en montant sur le dit fleuve, vers les *Trois Rivières*, sur une lieue de profondeur dans les terres ; la dite rivière *Champlain* mitoyenne, avec ceux qui occuperont les terres qui sont de l'autre côté d'icelle, avec tous les bois, près, rivières, ruisseaux, lacs, isles et islets, et généralement de tout le contenu entre les dites bornes.

Les Jesuites ayant par leur titre anterieur de Batiscan, un quart de lieu au Sud-ouest de la rivière *Champlain*, cette Concession ne pouvoit s'etendre jusques-là, mais avant l'année 1721, ils cedèrent à M. *Latouche Champlain*, ce quart de lieue compris entre leurs borne et la dite rivière ; et c'est ainsi que la Seigneurie est actuelment bornée.

Insinuations du Conseil Supérieur, Régistre B. folio 7.

AUGMENTATION DE CHAMPLAIN.

Concession du 28me Avril, 1697, faite par *Louis de Buade*, *Comte de Frontenac*, Gouverneur, et *Jean Bochart*, Intendant, à Madame *de Latouche*, de trois lieues de terre en profondeur, joignant la derrière de sa Seigneurie de *Champlain*, sur tout la largeur d'icelle ; tenant d'un côté au fief de *Batiscan*, et de l'autre au fief du Sieur *Hertel*.

Hertel n'est qu'un arrière fief, concédé par les révérends Peres Jésuites dans leur Seigneurie du *Cap de Magdeleine*.

Régistre d'Intendance, N° 5, *folio* 16.

CHAMBLY.

Concession du 29me Oct. 1672, faite par *Jean Talon*, Intendant, au Sieur *de Chambly*, de six lieues de terre de front sur une lieue de profondeur, à prendre sur la rivière *St. Louis* (*Chambly*) savoir trois lieues au Nord de la dite rivière (deux lieues en deçà du Fort que y est bâti et une lieue au delà) et trois lieues au Sud de la dite rivière.

Régistre d'Intendance, N° 1, *folio* 10.

CHATEAUGAY.

Concession du 29me Septembre, 1673, à Mr. *Le Moine*, Sieur *de Longueil*, de deux lieues de terre de front, à commencer dix arpens audessous de la riviére *du Loup*, en montant dans le lac *St. Louis*, du côté du Sud ; et de profondeur trois lieues, ensemble l'isle *St. Bernard* qui est à l'embouchure de la dite riviére.

· *Foi et Hommage*, N° 48, *folio* 214, *le 27me Février*, 1781.
Cahiers d'Intend. N° 10 à 17, *folio* 425.

CHICOT.

Concession du 3me Novembre, 1672, faite par *Jean Talon*, Intendant, au Sieur *Dupas*, de l'*Isle Dupas* et adjacentes, ensemble un quart de lieue audessus et un quart au dessous de la riviére de *Chicot*, sur un lieue et demie de profondeur, supposé que cette quantité ne touche pas à celle accordée à Mr. *Legardeur*, fils.
· *Régistre d'Intendance*, N° 1, *folio* 35.

CLORIDON.

Par Acte de Foi & Hommage rendu le 8me Juin, 1736, par *Jean Claude Louet*, au nom d'*Anne Morin* son épouse, veuve de *Réné d'Eneau* et au nom du Capitaine *Réné d'Eneau*, son fils, pour le fief d'*Eneau* il paroit qu'il exhiba une ordonnance de Mr. *de Champigny*, Intendant, du 28me Mars, 1691, annexée à une requète, faite par feu le dit Sieur d'*Eneau*, exposant que ses titrés lui avoient été enlevés par les Anglois, et demandant d'être maintenu dans sa possession de la riviére *Ristigouche* avec huit lieues de terre de front sur pareille profondeur, le long de la dite riviére, et les isles et battures qui se trouveront devant de la dite étendue, avec droit de chasse, pêche, &c. La susdite Ordonnance accordant le contenu de cette requète, sauf seulement les oppositions que pourra faire Mr. *de Fronsac*, Seigneur de *Miramichi*. De plus un accord entre les héritiers du dit feu Sieur *Réné d'Eneau* et Mr. *de Fronsac*, par lequel *Cloridon* fut borné comme suit, savoir, *commençant à l'entrée de la riviére au Porc-épic, qui tombe dans celle de* Ristigouche, *en montant la dite riviére* Ristigouche ; *et que les rumbs de vent des terres du dit Sieur* d'Eneau *soient Nord-est et Sud-ouest pour la profondeur, conformément à ceux du dit Sieur* de Fronsac, *et à l'égard du front ou largeur Sud-est et Nord-ouest.*
Ins. Con. Sup. lettre D. *folio* 53.

CONTRECŒUR.

· Concession du 29me Octobre, 1672, faite par *Jean Talon*, Intendant au Sieur *de Contrecœur*, de deux lieues de terre de front sur autant de profondeur ; à prendre sur le fleuve *St. Laurent*, depuis les terres du Sieur *de St. Ours*, jusqu'à celles du Sieur *de Villeray*.
Cahiers d'Intend. 2 à 9, *folio* 190.

COTE DE BEAUPRE'.

Concession du 15me Janvier, 1636, faite par la Compagnie, au Sieur *Cheffault de la Régnardiére*, située du côté du Nord du fleuve *St. Laurent*, contenant l'étendue de terre qui se trouve depuis la borne du côté Sud-ouest du dit fief, qui le sépare d'avec celui ci-devant appartenant au Sieur *Giffard*, en descendant le dit fleuve *St. Laurent*, jusqu'à la riviére du *Gouffre*, sur six lieues de profondeur dans les terres; avec les isles du cap brulé, l'islet rompu et autres islets et battures au devant de la dite Seigneurie.

Régistre d'Intendance, N° 10 d 17, *folio* 667.

COURNOYER.

Situé au Sud du fleuve *St. Laurent*, contenant une demi lieue de front sur trois lieues de profondeur, tenant du côté du Nord-est au fief de *Gentilly* et du côté du Sud-ouest au fief de *Dutort*, appartenant aux héritiers de feu Sieur *Linctot*.

Par le reglement des paroisses fait par le Gouverneur et l'Intendant, cet fief est cité pour avoir deux lieues de front sur trois de profondeur.

Régistre du papier Terrier, folio 204, *le* 2me *Mars*, 1725.

COURNOYER.

Concession du 1er Mars, 1695, faite par *Louis de Buade*, Gouverneur, et *Jean Bochart*, Intendant, au Sieur *de Cournoyer*, de deux lieues de terre de front sur pareille profondeur du côté du Nord de la riviére *Richelieu*, à commencer à la Seigneurie du Sieur *Joseph Hertel*, en descendant la dite riviére.

Régistre d'Intendance, N° 4, *folio* 19.

COURVAL.

Concession du 25me Septembre, 1754, faite au Sieur *Cressé*, par le *Marquis Duquesne*, Gouverneur, et *François Bigot*, Intendant, de deux lieues de front sur trois lieues de profondeur, située au bout de la profondeur de la Seigneurie vulgairement nommée la *Baie St. Antoine* ou *du Febvre*, au bord du lac *St. Pierre*, laquelle Seigneurie à deux lieues ou environ de front, que deux lieues seulement de profondeur, et se trouve enclavée entre le fief du Sieur *Cressé* pere, au Nord-est, et un autre fief appartenant au Sieur *Lussaudiére* au Sud-ouest.

Régistre d'Intendance, N° 10, *folio* 19.

DERRIERE LA CONCESSION DU SIEUR NEVEU AU SUD-OUEST.

Concession du 6me Oct. 1736, faite par *Charles, Marquis de Beauharnois*, Gouverneur, et *Gilles Hocquart*, Intendant, au Sieur *Jean d'Aillebout d'Argenteuil*, d'une lieue et demie de terre de front sur quatre lieues de profondeur, derriére la Seigneurie de *Lanauraie*, laquelle sera bornée pour la devanture par la rive du Nord de la riviére de l'*Assomption*; du côté du Sud-ouest par la ligne de la continuation de la Seigneurie de *Lavaltrie*; d'autre côte, au Nord-est par une ligne parallèle, tenant aux terres non-concédées, et dans la profondeur par une ligne parallèle à la devanture; joignant aussi aux terres non-concédées.

Régistre d'Intendance, N° 8, *folio* 14.

PARTIE EST DE DAUTRE.

Concession du 16me Avril, 1647, par la Compagnie, au Sieur *Jean Bourdon*, d'une demi lieue de terre, à prendre le long du grand fleuve *St. Laurent*, du côté du Nord, entre le Cap l'*Assomption* et les *Trois Riviéres*, à l'endroit où le dit Sieur *Bourdon* habitue, suivant pareille concession à lui ci-devant faite, en 1637, et de proche en proche icelle, sur pareille profondeur, revenant l'une et l'autre à une lieue de front sur deux lieues de profondeur.

Régistre d'Intendance, N° 10 à 17, *folio* 437.

PARTIE OUEST DE DAUTRÉ.

Concession du 1er Decembre, 1637, faite par la Compagnie ; au Sieur *Jean Bourdon*, du fief *Dautré*, contenant une demi lieue de terre ; à prendre sur le fleuve *St. Laurent*, sur deux lieues de profondeur en avant dans les terres ; à prendre en lieu non-concédé.
Régistre d'Intendance, N° 10 à 17, *folio* 435.

D'AUTEUIL.

Concession du 15me Février, 1693, faite par *Louis de Buade*, Gouverneur, et *Jean Bochart*, Intendant, au Sieur *D'auteuil*, d'un reste de terre non-concédé, qui a pour front la ligne de profondeur du Sieur *Toupin Dusunlt ;* au Nord-est la ligne du Sieur *Dupont*, au Sud-ouest celle du fief du dit Sieur *D'auteuil ;* et au Nord-ouest la ligne qui sera tirée au bout de quatre lieues et demie ; ensemble les riviéres et ruisseaux et tout ce que s'y trouvera compris.
Régistre d'Intendance, N° 4, *folio* 10.

DEGUIR.

Concession du 23me Septembre, 1751, faite par le *Marquis de la Jonquière*, Gouverneur, et *François Bigot*, Intendant, au Sieur *Joseph Deguir*, dit *Desrosiers*, de deux lieues de terre de front ou environ, sur deux lieues de profondeur, à prendre au bout de la profondeur de la Seigneurie *St. François*, bornée d'un côté, au Nord-est, à la riviére *St. François*, au Sud-ouest à la Seigneurie de la Dame *Petit*, sur le devant au trait quarré de la dite Seigneurie de *St. François*, et dans la profondeur aux terres non-concédées, ensemble la riviére *David* qui se trouve dans l'étendue du dit terrein.
Régistre d'Intendance, N° 9, *folio* 82.

DE LERY.

Concession du 6me Avril, 1733, faite par *Charles, Marquis de Beauharnois*, Gouverneur, et *Gilles Hocquart*, Intendant, au Sieur *Chaussegros de Léry*, de deux lieues de front le long de la riviére de *Chambly*, sur trois lieues de profondeur ; les dites deux lieues de front à prendre depuis la borne de la Seigneurie du Sieur *de Longueuil*, qui va au Nord-ouest, en remontant vers le lac *Champlain*, à une ligne tirée est et ouest du monde, et joignant la profondeur aux terres non-concédées.
Régistre d'Intendance, N° 7, *folio* 13.

DE L'ISLE.

Concession du 24me Septembre, 1736, faite par *Charles, Marquis de Beauharnois*, Gouverneur, et *Gilles Hocquart*, Intendant, au Sieur *Gabriel Aubin, De L'Isle*, d'un terrein de deux lieues de front sur deux lieues de profondeur, du côté du Nord-est de la riviére du *Sault de la Chaudiére*, avec les isles et islets qui sont dans la dite riviére du côté du Nord-est ; à commencer à la fin d'autres trois lieues concédées au Sieur *Joseph Fleury de la Gorgendiere* et finir aux terres non-concédées.
Régistre d'Intendance, N° 8, *folio* 12.

DERRIERE DAUTRÉ ET LANAURAIE.

Concession du 4me Juillet, 1739, faite par *Charles, Marquis de Beauharnois*, Gouverneur, et *Gilles Hocquart*, Intendant, au Sieur *Jean Bap-*

tiste Neveu, d'un terrein non-concédé, à prendre depuis la ligne qui borné la profondeur des fiefs de *Lanauraie* et *Dautre,* jusqu'à la riviére de l'*Assomption,* et dans la même étendue en largeur que celle des dits fiefs; c'est-à-dire borné du côté du Sud-ouest par la ligne qui sépare la Seigneurie de *Lavaltrie* et du côté du Nord-est par une ligne parallèle, tenant aux prolongations de la Seigneurie d'*Antaya ;* lequel terrein ne fera avec chacun des dits fiefs de *Lanauraie* et *Dautré* qu'une seule et même Seigneurie.

Registre d'Intendance, N° 8, *folio* 29.

DERRIERE LA CONCESSION DU SIEUR NEVEU, AU NORD-EST.

Concession du 7me Octobre, 1736, faite par *Charles Marquis de Beauharnois,* Gouverneur, et *Gilles Hocquart,* Intendant, à Dame *Geneviéve de Ramzay,* veuve du feu Sieur de *Boishébert,* d'une lieue et demie de terre de front sur quatre lieues de profondeur, bornée sur la devanture par la rive du Nord de la riviére de l'*Assomption,* du côté du Sud-ouest par la ligne de la concession nouvellement accordée au Sieur d'*Argenteuil ;* d'autre, au Nord-est par une ligne parallèle, tenant aux prolongations de la Seigneurie d'*Antaya ;* et dans la profondeur par une ligne paralléle à la devanture, joignant aussi aux terres non-concédées.

Régistre d'Intendance, N° 8, *folio* 15.

DESMAURE OU ST. AUGUSTIN.

L'Enregistrement de cet octroi n'a pas été trouvé jusqu'ici au Sécrétariat de la Province. Les Dames religieuses de l'Hôpital, qui possédent actuellement ce fief, en rendant Foi et Hommage le 19me Mars, 1781, n'ont produit qu'un Acte d'adjudication en date du 22me Septembre, 1733, dans lequel ni les dimensions ni le nom du concessionnaire de cette concession ne sont mentionnés.

Par le reglement des paroisses de cette province, l'etendue de cette Seigneurie se determine a deux lieues et demie de front, sur une et demie de profondeur.

Régistre des Foi et Hommage, N° 64, *folio* 168, *lc* 19me *Mars,* 1781.
Ins. Con. Sup.

DE PEIRAS.

Concession du 6me Mai, 1675, faite par le Comte *de Frontenac,* Gouverneur, au Sieur *de Peiras,* de deux lieues de front le long du fleuve *St. Laurent* du côté du Sud, à prendre du milieu de la largeur de la riviére appelée *Mitis* et qui s'appellera dorénavant la riviére————en descendant le dit fleuve, et deux lieues de profondeur, ensemble les trois isles et islets appelées *St. Barnabé.*

Régistre d'Intendance, N° 2 *à* 9, *folio* 370.
Ins. Con. Sup. B. folio 3.

DE RAMZAY.

Concession du 17me Octobre, 1710, faite au Sieur *de Ramzay,* de l'étendue de trois lieues de terre de front sur trois lieues de profondeur, savoir, une lieue et demie audessous de la riviére *Scibouet,* qui tombe dans la riviére *Yamaska,* et une lieue et demie au dessus, courant du Nord-est au Sud-ouest, avec les isles et islets qui se trouveront dans la

dite riviére, vis-à-vis de la dite concession : et donnant à la dite concession le nom de *Ramzay*.

Régistre des Foi et Hommage, N° 96, *folio* 62, *le 2me Janvier*, 1781.
Cahiers d'Intendance, N° 2 à 9, *folio* 358.

DESCHAMBAULT.

Concession du 1er Mars, 1652, faite par Mr. *de Lauzon* à Demoiselle
Eleonore de Grandmaison, située au Nord du fleuve *St. Laurent*, contenant une lieue de front sur trois lieues de profondeur, tenant du côté du
Nord-est au fief de *Portneuf*, appartenant au Sieur *Croisille*, et du côté
du Sud-ouest au fief de la Chevretiére.

Régistre d'Intendance, N° 10 à 17, *folio* 592.

PARTIE NORD-EST DE DESPLAINES.

Concession du 4me Janvier, 1737, faite à Demoiselle *Charlotte Lagar-
deur* par le Marquis de *Beauharnois*, Gouverneur, et *Gilles Hocquart*, Intendant, de trois quarts de lieue de terre de front à la côté du Sud du
fleuve *St. Laurent*, sur trois lieues de profondeur, à prendre au bout des
profondeurs du fief *Maranda* ; bornée d'un côté, au Sud-ouest, à la Seigneurie de *Bonsecours*, d'autre au Nord-est à celle de *Tilly*, et par derriére
aux terres non-concédées.

Régistre d'Intendance, N° 8, *folio* 19.

PARTIE SUD-OUEST DE DESPLAINES.

Concession du 26me Mars, 1738, faite par le Marquis *de Beauharnois*,
Gouverneur, et *Gilles Hocquart*, Intendant, à Demoiselle *Charlotte Legardeur*, d'une augmentation de terrein d'environ soixante et quatorze
arpens de front, qui se trouve non-concédé, et enclavé entre la concession à elle faite le 4me Janvier, 1737, et la Seigneurie de *St. Croix*,
tenant par devant au fief de *Bonsecours* et *Amiot*, et par derrière aux
terres non-concédées, sur une lieue et soixante arpens de profondeur,
pour les dits soixante et quatorze arpens ajoutés ne faire avec sa premiére concession qu'une même Seigneurie.

Régistre d'Intendance, N° 9, *folio* 2.

DUMONTIER.

Concession du 24mé Octobre, 1708, faite au Sieur *Dumontier*, d'une
lieue et demie de terre de front sur trois lieues de profondeur, à prendre
au bout de la profondeur de la Seigneurie de *Grosbois*, bornée de chaque
côté aux terres non-concédées.

Régistre des Foi et Hommage, N° 10, *folio* 52, *le 26me Janvier*, 1781.
Cahiers d'Intendance.

DUSABLE'.

Concession du 15me Août, 1739, faite par *Charles Marquis de Beauharnois*, Gouverneur, et *Gilles Hocquart*, Intendant, au Sieur *Louis
Adrien Dandonneau Dusablé*, d'une étendue de terrein d'environ une lieue
de front sur trois lieues de profondeur ; laquelle sera bornée pour la devanture au bout de la profondeur de la concession accordée par Mr. *Talon*, au Sieur *Jean Baptiste Legardeur*, le 3me Novembre, 1672, appartenant aujourd'hui au Sieur *Petit Bruno* ; au Nord-est par les terres concédées par le dit Sieur *Talon*, le 29me Octobre, 1672, aux Sieurs *Pierre
et Jean Baptiste Legardeur*, dont le dit Sieur *Petit* est aussi propriétaire,

et par la ligne de la Seigneurie du Sieur *Sicard de Carufel;* au Sud-ouest au fief du *Chicot,* et continuation du dit fief; et par derrière aux terres non-concédées.

Régistre d'Intendance, N° 8, *folio* 30.

DUTORT.

On n'a pu trouver le titre de cette Concession ni dans le Secrétariat ni dans le bureau du Papier Terrier, de sorte qu'on ne connoit ni l'étendue de son front ni le nom du concessionaire originaire. Elle est placée sur la carte d'après les lumières qu'on a pu tirer des titres des concessions voisines.

Par le reglement de l'etendue des paroisses fait par le Gouverneur et l'Intendant, cet fief paroit avoir un quart de lieue du front du precedent fief de Becancour qui devoit avoir deux lieues et trois quart de front.

LES EBOULEMENS.

Le titre de cet octroi n'a pas encore été trouvé au Bureau du Sécrétariat, mais il paroit par un Acte de Foi ét Hommage, rendu le 3me Avril, 1723, par *Pierre Tremblay,* alors propriétaire de ce fief, qu'entr'autres titres il produisit une concession faite à *Pierre Lessard,* portant que toutes les terres en Seigneuries qui se trouvent depuis la Seigneurie, du Sieur *Dupré,* jusqu'à celle du Sieur *de Comporté,* nommée la *Malbaie,* demeureront et appartiendront à l'avenir au dit *Pierre Lessard,* (*Pierre Tremblay,* probablement.)

Reg. Foi et Hommage, folio 55, *April* 3, 1723.
Cahiers d'Intend. N° 2 à 9, *folio* 3, *April* 5, 1683.

BELAIR OU LES ECUREUILS.

Concession du 3me Novembre, 1672, faite par *Jean Talon,* Intendant, aux Sieurs *Toupin,* Pere et Fils, d'une demi lieue de front, sur une lieue de profondeur, à prendre sur le fleuve *St. Laurent,* moitié au dessus et moitié au dessous de la pointe *Bouroila* (*aux Ecureuils*) aboutissant des deux côtés aux terres non-concédées.

Régistre d'Intendance, N° 1, *folio* 39.

AUGMENTATION DES ECUREUILS.

Concession du 20me Janvier, 1706, faite par *Phillipe de Rigaud,* Gouverneur, et *François de Beauharnois,* Intendant, à *Marie Magdelaine Mezerai,* veuve de feu *Jean Toupin,* d'une demi lieue de terre de front sur deux lieues de profondeur derrière la Seigneurie de *Bélair,* le front à prendre immédiatement à une lieue du fleuve *St. Laurent.*

Régistre d'Intendance, N° 5, *folio* 41.

L'EPINAY.

Concession du 7me Avril, 1701, faite par *Hector de Calliére,* Gouverneur, et *Jean Bochart,* Intendant, au Sieur *de l'Epinay,* du peu de terrein qui se trouve entre la Seigneurie de *Jean de Paris* et celle de la riviére du *Sud,* près de *Québec,* lequel terrein se termine en triangle au fleuve *St. Laurent,* et tient d'un bout aux terres non-concédées, et de l'autre par la pointe au dit fleuve; ensemble que le dit terrein sera borné à la hauteur de la concession du dit *Jean de Paris,* par une ligne parallèle

qui sera tirée Nord-est et Sud-ouest jusqu'à celle de la petite rivière
du Sud.

Régistre d'Intendance, N° 5, *folio* 32.

FAUSEMBAULT.

Concession du 20me Février, 1693, faite par *Louis de Buade*, Gouverneur, et *Jean Bochart*, Intendant, au Sieur *de Gaudarville*, de trois lieues
de profondeur au derrière du fief de *Gaudarville*, ensemble toutes les
terres attenantes qui sont derrière les fiefs des Sieurs *Desmaures* et *Guillaume Bonhomme*, et jusqu'à la profondeur de la même ligne du Nord-
est au Sud-ouest, qui terminera les dites trois lieues, ensorte que tout ce
qui est compris en la présente concession sera borné d'un bout, par devant, au Sud-est, par les lignes qui terminent les profondeurs des dits
fiefs de *Gaudarville*, *Bonhomme* et *Desmaure*, et par derrière au Nord-
ouest par une ligne courant aussi Nord-est et Sud-ouest qui terminera la
profondeur des dites trois lieues par derrière le dit fief de *Gaudarville*,
et sera prolongée droit jusqu'au fief de *Neuville*, et par un côté au Nord-
est, d'une partie des terres du fief de *Sillery*, d'une partie de celles de
Gaudarville, et des terres du dit *Bonhomme*; et de l'autre côté, au Sud-
ouest, bornée des terres du fief de *Neuville*.

Régistre d'Intendance, N° 4, *folio* 11.

FOUCAULT.

Concession du 3me Avril, 1738, faite par *Charles*, *Marquis de Beauharnois*, Gouverneur, et *Gilles Hocquart*, Intendant, au Sieur *Foucault*,
de deux lieues de terre de front, bornées du côté du Nord par la Seigneurie nouvellement concédée au Sieur *de Noyan*, et sur la même ligne,
et du côté du Sud à deux lieues de la dite ligne par une ligne parallèle
tirée Est et Ouest du monde; sur le devant par la rivière *Chambly*, et
sur la profondeur par la Baie de *Missisquoui*.

Régistre d'Intendance, N° 7, *folio* 9.

FOURNIER.

Concession du 3me Nov. 1672, faite par *Jean Talon*, Intendant, au
Sieur *Fournier*, de trente arpens de terre sur deux lieues de profondeur,
à prendre sur le fleuve *St. Laurent*; tenant d'un côté au Sieur *de l'Epinay*, et d'autre aux terres non-concédées.

Régistre d'Intendance, No. 1, *folio* 28.

GASPÉ.

Concession du 25me Mars, 1738, faite par le Marquis *de Beauharnois*,
Gouverneur, et *Gilles Hocquart*, Intendant, à Dame *Angelique Legardeur*, veuve du Sieur *Aubert de Gaspé*, d'une lieue et demie de terre de
front, derrière la Seigneurie de *Tilly*, appartenant aux Héritiers de feu
Sieur *Legardeur*; à prendre le front au bout de la profondeur et limite
de la dite Seigneurie de *Tilly*; tenant d'un côté à la Seigneurie de *Lauzon*, et d'autre à celle accordée à Demoiselle *Legardeur* sa Sœur, par
concession du 4me Janvier, 1737, et par derrière aux terres non-concédées.

Régistre d'Intendance, N° 9, *folio* 1.

GATINEAU.

Concession du 3me Novembre, 1672, faite par *Jean Talon*, Intendant, au Sieur *Boucher*, fils, de trois quarts de lieues de terre de front sur une lieue de profondeur, à prendre sur le lac *St. Pierre*, depuis la concession du Sieur *Boucher* son père, jusqu'aux terres non-concédées.
Régistre d'Intendance, N° 1, *folio* 37.

AUGMENTATION A GATINEAU.

Concession du 21me Octobre, 1750, faite par le *Marquis de la Jonquiére*, Gouverneur, et *François Bigot*, Intendant, à Demoiselle *Marie Josephe Gatineau Duplessis*, de quatre lieues de profondeur derrière le fief *Gatineau*, situé sur le lac *St. Pierre*, et sur le même front d'icelui.
Régistre d'Intendance, N° 9, *folio* 71.

GAUDARVILLE.

Contenant quarante cinq arpens de front sur quatre lieues de profondeur; tenant du côté du Nord-est au fief de *Sillery*, appartenant aux révérends pères Jésuites, et du côté du Sud-ouest au fief de *Desmaure*, appartenant au Sieur *Aubert*.
Cette Concession a pour date le 8 de Février, 1652, et fut accordée au Louis de Lauson, Sieur de la Citiere.
See Cahiers d'Intendance, N° 10 à 17, *folio* 638.

GENTILLY.

Concession du 14me Août, 1676, faite par *Jacques Duchesneau*, Intendant, à *Michel Pelletier*, Sieur *de la Perade*, de la Seigneurie de *Gentilly*, contenant deux lieues et demie de front sur le fleuve *St. Laurent*, à prendre aux terres du Sieur *Hertel* en descendant, et deux lieues de profondeur.
Régistre d'Intendance, N° 2, *folio* 11.

GODEFROI.

Concession du 31me Août, 1638, faite par *Charles Huot de Montmagny*, au Sieur *Godefroi*, de trois quarts de lieues de terre le long du fleuve *St. Laurent*, sur trois lieues de profondeur dans les terres; et sont les dites terres bornées du côté du Sud-ouest d'une ligne qui court Sud-est et Nord-ouest, au bout de laquelle, du côté du Nord, a été enfouie une grosse pierre avec des briquetons auprès d'un sicomore, sur laquelle une croix a été gravée, le tout pour servir de marque et témoignage, et du côté du Nord-est de la rivière nommée la rivière du lac *St. Paul*, sans néanmoins que le dit *Godefroi* puisse rien prétendre en la propriété du tout ou de partie de la dite rivière, et icelle y étant, ni du lac *St. Paul*, encore bien que la dite ligne s'y rencontrasse.
Cahier d'Intendance, N° 2 à 9, *folio* 151.

LE GOUFFRE.

Concession du 30me Décembre, 1682, faite par *Lefebre de la Barre*, Gouverneur, et *de Meulles*, Intendant, à *Pierre Dupré*, d'une demie lieue de terre de front sur quatre lieues de profondeur ;joignant douze arpens de terre qui sont depuis la borne de Monseigneur l'Evêque de *Québec*, en descendant vers le cap aux *Oies* ; le tout concédé a titre de fief et Seigneurie, avec le droit de chasse et de pêche ; pour la dite concession et les douze arpens plus haut mentionnés (à lui concédés par Mr. *de Frontenac*) ne faire qu'une seule et même Seigneurie.

Insinuations du Conseil Supérieur, Lettre B. folio 19.

GRAND PABOS.

Concession du 14me Novembre, 1696, faite par *Louis de Buade*, Gouverneur, et *Jean Bochart*, Intendant, au Sieur *Réné Hubert*, de la rivière du *Grand Pabos*, autrement dite la rivière *Duval*, située dans la *Baie des Chaleurs*, avec deux lieues et demie de front du côté de l'Est de la dite rivière, et demi lieue du côté de l'Ouest, en tirant vers la rivière du *Petit Pabos*, icelle comprise sur pareille profondeur.

Régistre d'Intendance, N° 5, *folio* 3.

GRANDPRE.

Concession du 30me Juillet, 1695, faite par *Louis de Buade*, Gouverneur, et *Jean Bochart*, Intendant, à *Pierre Boucher*, Sieur *de Grandpré*, d'une lieue de terre de front dans le lac *St. Pierre*, tenant d'un côté aux terres concédées de la rivière *Yamachiche*, et de l'autre à celles de la *Rivière du Loup* ; ensemble les isles, islets et battures adjacentes.

Régistre d'Intendance, N° 4, *folio* 18.

GRANDE RIVIERE.

Concession, du 31me Mai, 1697, faite par *Louis de Buade*, Gouverneur, et *Jean Bochart*, Intendant, au Sieur *Jacques Cochu*, de la *Grande Rivière*, située dans la *Baie des Chaleurs*, avec une lieue et demie de terre de front sur deux lieues de profondeur, à prendre depuis la Seigneurie du *Grand Pabos*, appartenant au Sieur *Réné Hubert*, en tirant du côté du Cap *Espoir*, vers l'isle *Percée*.

Régistre d'Intendance, N° 5, *folio* 18.

GRANDVILLE.

Concession du 5me Octobre, 1707, faite à Dame *Marie Anne de Grandville*, veuve du Sieur *de Soulange*, d'une lieue ou environ de front sur le fleuve *St. Laurent*, à commencer joignant le Sieur *de Foulon*, dont la concession commence à deux lieues au dessus de la rivière de *Kamouraska* et finit une lieue au dessous, et en descendant au Nord-est, joignant son ancienne concession, avec les isles et islets, bancs et batures qui se trouveront vis-à-vis icelle, laquelle sera incorporée et jointe avec la dite ancienne concession, pour des deux n'en faire qu'une.

Régistre des Foi et Hommage, N° 107, *folio* 107, *2me Août,* 1781.
Cahiers d'Intendance, 10 à 17, *folio* 584.

GRANDVILLE ET LACHENAIE.

Concession du 2me Juin, 1696, faite par *Louis de Buade*, Comte de *Frontenac*, Gouverneur, et *Jean Bochart*, Intendant, au Sieur *de Grandville* et de *la Lachenaie*, de deux lieues de terre de front, sur trois lieues de profondeur en lieux nonconcédés, joignant d'un côté la terre du dit Sieur *de Grandville* nommée l'islet *du Portage*, et de l'autre la Seigneurie de *Terrebois*, appartenante au dit Sieur *de Lachenaie*, représentant *Dautier*,

D

situées les dites concessions sur le fleuve *St. Laurent*, du côté du Sud, audessus de la riviére du *Loup*.

Régistre d'Intendance, N° 5, *folio* 1.

GRANDE VALLE'E DES MONTS.

Concession du 23me Mars, 1691, faite par *Louis de Buadé*, Gouverneur, et *Jean Bochart*, Intendant, au Sieur *François Hazzeur*, d'une étendue de terre de deux lieues de front, au lieu appelé la *Grande Vallée des Monts Notre Dame*, dans le fleuve *St. Laurent*, du côté du Sud, à deux lieues de la riviére *Magdelaine*, et quatre lieues de *l'Etang*, en descendant vers *Gaspé*, avec la riviére qui se rencontre à la dite *Vallée des Monts*, qui sera dans le milieu des dites deux lieues de front sur trois lieues de profondeur dans les terres, avec les isles et islets qui pourront se trouver sur la devanture des dites deux lieues, et dans la dite riviére sur la profondeur des dites trois lieues.

Régistre d'Intendance, N° 4, *folio* 3.

PARTIE OUEST DES GRONDINES.

Concession du 20me Mars, 1638, faite par la Compagnie, à Dame *Duchesse d' Aguillon*, pour les Dames Hospitaliéres de l'Hôtel-Dieu de *Québec*, de la Seigneurie des *Grondines*, contenant une lieue de terre en largeur sur le grand fleuve *St. Laurent*, sur dix lieues de profondeur : savoir : est, depuis la pointe de l'ance des *Grondines*, du côté du Nord-Est, un quart de lieue audessous de la dite pointe, en tirant vers le Cap de *Lauzon*, borné par une route qui court Sud-est et Nord-Ouest ou environ ; et d'autre côté au Sud-Ouest trois quarts de lieue, borné aussi par une route qui court Sud-Est et Nord-Ouest, d'un bout au Nord-Ouest par une route qui court Sud-Ouest et Nord-Est.

Régistre des Foi et Hommage, *folio* 47.
Aussi *Reg. d'Intendance, et Cahiers d'Intendance*.

PARTIE EST DES GRONDINES.

Concession du 3me Novembre, 1672, faite par *Jean Talon*, Intendant, aux Pauvres de l'Hôpital, de trois quarts de lieues de terre sur trois lieues de profondeur, à prendre sur le fleuve *St. Laurent*, au lieu dit les *Grondines*, tenant d'un côté à la Concession appartenante aux religieuses du dit Hôpital, de l'autre aux terres non-concédées ; tirant en descendant le fleuve vers *Chavigny*.

Régistre d'Intendance, N° 1, *folio* 34.

AUGMENTATION A LA PARTIE EST DES GRONDINES.

Concession du 25me Avril, 1711, faite par *Raudot* Gouverneur, et *Vaudreuil*, Intendant, à *Louis Hamelin*, de la continuation de deux lieues de profondeur sur le front de trois quarts de lieue non-concédé, étant au bout des trois quarts de lieue de front sur la profondeur de trois lieues, en quoi consiste l'étendue de la dite Seigneurie des *Grondines* ; borné d'un côté aux terres du Sieur *de la Chevrotiére* et d'un côté à celles du dit Sieur *Louis Hamelin*.

Régistre des Foi et Hommage, *folio* 47.

GUILLAUDIERE.

Concession du 3me Novembre, 1672, faite par *Jean Talon*, Intendant, à *Laurent Borney* Sieur *de Grandmaison*, de trente arpens de front sur une lieue de profondeur, à prendre sur le fleuve *St. Laurent*, depuis les terres du Sieur de *St. Michel*, en descendant vers les terres non-con-cédées.

Régistre d'Intendance, N° 1, *folio* 28.

HUBERT.

Concession du 10me Juin, 1698, faite par *Louis de Buade*, Gouverneur, et *Jean Bochart*, Intendant, au Sieur *René Louis Hubert*, fils, de deux lieues de terre de front sur pareille profondeur, située au derriére des seigneuries nommées *St. Gabriel* et *St. Ignace*, appartenant aux péres Jésuites et aux religieuses Hospitaliéres de *Québec*: le dit terrein tirant au Nord-ouest, borné d'un bout des dites Seigneuries, d'autre bout et des deux cotés des terres non-concédées.

Régistre d'Intendance, N° 5, *folio* 23.

ISLET ST. JEAN.

Concession du 17me Mai, 1677, faite par *Louis de Buade*, Comte de *Frontenac*, Gouverneur, à Demoiselle *Genevieve Couillard*, d'une licue de terre de front le long du fleuve *St. Laurent*, du côté du Sud, à commencer depuis les deux lieues promises à *Noël Langlois*, en remontant le dit fleuve, vers celle qui appartient à la Demoiselle *Amiot*, avec deux lieues de profondeur, ensemble un islet étant dans le fleuve, au devant de la dite licue de front, contenant quatre à cinq arpens ou environ.

Insinuations du Conseil Supérieur, Let. B. *folio* 39.

ISLET DU PORTAGE.

Concession du 29me Octobre, 1672, faite par *Jean Talon*, Intendant, au Sieur *de Granville*, de l'Isle nommée du *Portage* sur le fleuve *St. Laurent*, avec une demi lieue de terre en deça et une autre au delà de la dite Isle, sur une lieue de profondeur.

Régistre d'Intendance, N° 1, *folio* 14.

ISLE VERTE.

Concession du 27me Avril, 1684, faite par *le Febvre de la Barre*, Gouverneur, et *de Meulles*, Intendant, aux Sieurs Dartigny et de la Cardonniere, dépuis au Sieur Dartigny seul, contenant deux lieues de terre, prés et bois, de front sur le fleuve *St. Laurent* sur deux lieues de profondeur dans les terres ; à prendre depuis une rivière qui est vis-à-vis *l'isle Verte*, du côté du Sud de la dite isle, icelle rivière comprise, jusqu'à deux lieues en descendant le dit fleuve, ensemble les isles, islets et battures qui se rencontrent vis-à-vis les dites deux lieues, jusqu'à la dite isle *Verte*, icelle même comprise.

Régistre d'Intendance, Let. B. *folio* 22.

ISLE PERROT, AU DESSUS DE MONTREAL.

Concession du 29me Octobre, 1672, faite par *Jean Talon*, Intendant, de l'isle *Perrot* et autres adjacentes, comprises l'isle de la *Paix*, l'isle aux *Pins*, l'isle *Ste. Geneviéve* et l'Isle *St. Gilles*.

Régistre d'Intendance, N° 1, *folio* 5.

ISLE BIZARD, AU DESSUS MONTREAL.

Concession du 24me et 25me Octobre, 1678, faite par le *Comte de Frontenac*, Gouverneur, et *Duchesneau*, Intendant, au Sieur *Bizard*, de l'isle *Bonavanture*, (*Bizard*) ensemble les isles, &c. adjacentes.

> *Régistre des Foi et Hommage*, N° 18, *folio* 90. *le 3me Fevrier*, 1781.
> *Cahiers d'Intendance*, N° 4, *folio* 141.

ISLE ST. PAUL, AU DESSUS DE MONTREAL.

Confirmation du 23me Avril, 1700, par le Roi, d'une concession faite à Mr. *le Ber*, des deux tiers de l'isle de *St. Paul*. Plus, concession de l'autre tiers fait à *Claude Robutel*, Sieur de *St. André*, le 18me Juillet, 1676.

> *Cons. Cahiers d'Intend.* 2 à 9, *folio* 282, *et Rat. d'Ins. Cons. Sup. Lettre B. folio* 131.
> *Cahiers d'Intend.* 2 à 9, *folio* 331.

ISLE DE MONTREAL.

Lettres patentes, en forme d'Edit, données par sa Majesté très Chretienne, en Juillet, 1714, qui confirment la concession de la Seigneurie de l'isle de *Montreal*, isles *Courcelles* et dépendances, à titres onéreux d'amortissement des dites terres, accordées à Messieurs du Séminaire de *St. Sulpice*, par lettres patentes du mois de Mai, 1677, avec les droits d'échange.

> *Régistre des Foi et Hommage* N° 17, *folio* 81. *le 3me Fevrier* 1781.
> *Cahiers d'Intendance*, 10 à 17, *folio* 535.

ISLE JESUS.

Concession du 23me Octobre, 1689, faite par *Hector de Calliere*, Gouverneur, et *Jean Bochart*, Intendant, à l'*Evéque de Québec* et Messrs. du *Séminaire*, de *l'isle Jésus*, des *isles aux Vaches* et autres adjacentes,

> *Régistre des Foi et Hommage*, N° 62, *folio* 289, *le 19me Mars*, 1781.

ISLE BOUCHARD VIS-A-VIS BOUCHERVILLE.

Concession du 3me Novembre, 1672, faite par *Jean Talon*, Intendant, au Sieur *Fortel*, des isles contenues dans la carte figurative que le Sieur *de Becancour* a donnée et qui sont cottées A, reservant de disposer en faveur de qui il plaira au Roi de celles cottés B.

> *Régistre d'Intendance*, N° 1, *folio* 23.

ISLE ST. THERESE, AU BOUT D'ENBAS DE L'ISLE DE MONTREAL.

Concession du 3me Novembre, 1672, de l'isle *St. Thérèse* avec les isles et islets adjacens, par *Jean Talon*, Intendant, au Sieur *Dugué*, sauf le droit de Mr. *Repentigny* pour celles qu'il peut légitimement prétendre, et qui seront adjugées à celui des deux auquel il sera estimé à propos de les concéder.

> *Régistre d'Intendance*, N° 1, *folio* 18.

ISLE BOURDON.

Concession du 3me Novembre 1672, faite par *Jean Talon*, Intendant, à Mr. *de Repentigny*, des deux isles dites *Bourdon*.

> *Régistre d'Intendance*, N° 1, *folio* 36.

ISLES BEAUREGARD.

Concedées le 17me Aoust, 1674, par le *Comte de Frontenac*, Gouverneur, au Sieur *de Beauregard*, dont l'une est audevant du bout de la Seigneurie du Sieur *de Verchéres*, en montant, et les deux autres étant sur la ligne qui regarde les isles appartenantes au Sieur *de Grandmaison*.

Régistre d'Intendance, Let. B. *folio* 1.

ISLES ET ISLETS DANS LE LAC ST. PIERRE.

Concession du 19me Octobre, 1694, faite par *Louis de Buade Comte de Frontenac*, Gouverneur, et *Jean Bochart*, Intendant, au Sieur *Redisson* des isles, islets et battures non-concédées qui se trouvent au haut du lac *St. Pierre* audessus des isles concédées au Sieur *Sorel*, jusqu'au chenail du milieu appelé le chenail de l'isle *Platte*, lesquelles isles, islets et battures contiennent environ trois quarts de lieue de large sur autant de profondeur.

Régistre d'Intendance, N° 4, *folio* 18.

ISLE MORAN, A L'EMBOUCHURE DE LA RIVIERE NICOLET.

Concession du 29me Octobre, 1672, faite par *Jean Talon*, Intendant, au Sieur *Moran*, de l'isle dite *Moran*, qui se trouve à l'embouchure de la rivière *Nicolet*, au bord du fleuve *St. Laurent*.

Régistre d'Intendance, N° 1, *folio* 16.

ISLE DU LARGE.

Concession du 6me Avril, 1697, faite par *Louis de Buade, Comte de Frontenac*, Gouverneur, et *Jean Bochart*, Intendant, à la veuve du Sieur *de Lanaudiere*, des isles qui se trouvent devant sa terre de *Ste. Anne*, et à l'entrée de la rivière et entr'autres celle où est son moulin, appelée l'*Isle du Large*.

Régistre d'Intendance, N° 5, *folio* 12.

ISLE D'ORLEANS.

Lettres d'affranchissement et de règlement de la Seigneurie de *Beauprœ* et de l'*Isle d'Orléans*, du 28me Mars, 1674, rapportant une concession du 15me Janvier, 1636, de l'isle d'*Orléans*, au Sieur *Castillon*.

Régistre des Foi et Hommage, N° 100. *folio* 80, *le* 15me *Juin,* 1781. *Cahiers d'Intend.* 10 d 17, *folio* 758, 750.

ISLE AUX REAUX.

Concedée le 20me Mars, 1638, par Mr. *de Montmagny,* aux revérends péres Jésuites.

Cahiers d'Intend. 2 d 9, *folio* 71.

ISLE STE. MARGUERITE.

Concession du 5me Novembre, 1698, faite par *Louis de Buade,* Gouverneur, et *Jean Bochart*, Intendant, au Sieur *de Grandville*, d'une terre située près des isles *aux Oies,* appelée les isles *Ste. Marguerite,* consistant en quarante arpens de front sur cinq de profondeur, avec trois petites isles du côté du Sud, et la batture joignant les dites isles.

Régistre d'Intendance, N° 5, *folio* 25.

ISLE AUX COUDRES.

Concedée le 29me Octobre, 1687, par le *Marquis de Brisay*, Gouverneur, et *Jean Bochart* Intendant, au *Séminaire de Québec*, avec les battures qui sont autour d'icelle.

Régistre d'Intendance, N° 3, *folio* 11.

ISLE D'ANTICOSTI.

Concedée en Mars, 1680, par *Jacques Duchesneau*, Intendant, au Sieur *Jolliet*.

Régistre d'Intendance, N° 10 à 17, *folio* 619.

ISLES ET ISLETS DE MINGAN.

Concedés le 10me Mars, 1677, à Messrs. *de Lalande fils* et *Louis Jolliet*.

Régistre des Foi et Hommage, N° 78, *folio* 365, *le 28me Mai*, 1781.

JACQUES CARTIER.

Concession du 29me Mars, 1659, faite par la Compagnie, à Dame *Gagnier*, veuve de feu *Jean Clement de Wauls*, Chevalier, Seigneur de *Monceaux*, d'une demi lieue de large sur le bord du fleuve *St. Laurent*, avec cinq lieues de profondeur de terre en tel endroit qu'il plaira à Mr. *Daillebout*, Gouverneur.

Ensuite de cette concession est une copie d'un certificat du Sieur *Bourdon*, du 25me Octobre, 1659, que la Dame de *Monceaux* lui ayant remis la concession ci-dessus, par ordre de Mr. *Daillebout*, lors Gouverneur, pour prendre par la dite Dame possession de la dite demi lieue; avec demande de lui accorder la dite concession depuis la riviere *Jacques Cartier*, jusqu'à la concurrence de la dite demi lieue, descendant en bas, par lequel certificat il lui donne acte de diligence, comme elle prenoit le dit lieu pour l'emplacement et le choix de sa dite concession.

Papier Terrier, Page 96, *15me Juin*, 1781.
Cahiers d'Intendance.

JOLLIET.

Concession du 30me Avril, 1697, faite par *Louis de Buade*, Gouverneur, et *Jean Bochart*, Intendant, au Sieur *Louis Jolliet*, des islets qui sont dans la riviere des *Trechemins*, au dessus du premier sault, contenant trois quarts de lieue ou environ, avec trois lieues de terre de front sur pareille profondeur à prendre demi lieue au dessous des dits islets en montant la dite rivière, tenant d'un côté à la Seigneurie de *Lauzon*, et de l'autre aux terres non-concédées.

Régistre d'Intendance, N° 5, *folio* 15.

KAMOURASKA.

Concession du 15me Juillet, 1674, faite par le Comte *de Frontenac*, Gouverneur, au Sieur *de la Durantaie*, qui contient trois lieues de terre de front, sur le fleuve *St. Laurent*, savoir deux lieues au déssus de la riviére appelée *Kamouraska* et une lieue audessous, icelle comprise, avec deux lieues de profondeur dans les terres; ensemble les isles étant audevant des dites trois lieues.

Régistre d'Intendance, *Let*. B. *folio* 30 et 31.

LABADIE.

Concession du 3me Novembre, 1672, faite par *Jean Talon*, Intendant, au Sieur *Labadie*, d'un quart de lieue de front sur une demi lieue de profondeur, à prendre sur le fleuve *St. Laurent*, depuis la concession de Mr. *Severin Haineau*, tirant vers celle du Sieur *Pierre Boucher*.
Régistre d'Intendance, N° 1, *folio* 27.

LAC DES DEUX MONTAGNES.

Concession du 17me Octobre, 1717, faite par *Philippe de Rigaud*, Gouverneur, et *Michel Bégon*, Intendant, aux Ecclésiastiques du Séminaire de *St. Sulpice*, établi à *Montréal*, d'un terrein de trois lieues et demie de front, à commencer au ruisseau qui tombe dans la grande baie du *Lac des Deux Montagnes*, et en remontant le long du dit *Lac des Deux Montagnes* et du fleuve *St. Laurent*, sur trois lieues de profondeur.
Régistre d'Intendance, N° 6, *folio* 9.
Cahiers d'Intend. Rat. de la Concession.
Un brevet de ratification de l'octroi immédiatement suivant, en date du 1er Mars, 1735, accorde une augmentation de trois lieues dans les terres faisant ensemble six lieues de profondeur pour cette Seigneurie.

AUTRE AUGMENTATION AU LAC DES DEUX MONTAGNES.

Concession du 26me Septembre, 1733, faite par *Charles Marquis de Beauharnois*, Gouverneur, et *Gilles Hocquart*, Intendant, aux Ecclésiastiques du Séminaire de *St. Sulpice*, de *Paris*, d'une étendue de terre non concédée, entre la ligne de la Seigneurie appartenante aux représentans les feus Sieurs *de Langloiserie* et *Petit*, et celle de la Seigneurie du *Lac des Deux Montagnes*, appartenante au dit Séminaire sur le front d'environ deux lieues sur le *Lac des Deux Montagnes*, le dit lac aboutissant à un angle formé par les deux lignes ci-dessus, dont les rumbs de vent ont été réglés savoir, celle de la Seigneurie du *Lac des Deux Montagnes*, Sud quart de Sud-ouest et Nord quart de Nord-est par arrêt du Conseil Supérieur du 5me Octobre, 1722 ; et celle des Sieurs *Langloiserie* et *Petit*, Sud-ouest et Nord-ouest qui est le rumb de vent reglé pour toutes les Seigneuries situées sur le fleuve *St. Laurent*, par reglement du dit Conseildu 26me Mai, 1676, Art. 28 ; avec les isles et islets non concédés et battures adjacentes à la dite étendue de terre.
Régistre d'Intendance, N° 7, *folio* 22.

LA CHENAYE.

Concession en date du 16me Avril, 1647, faite par la Compagnie, à *Pierre Legardeur*, Sieur *de Repentigny*, de quatre lieues de terre à prendre le long du fleuve *St. Laurent*, du côté du Nord, tenant d'une part aux terres ci-devant concédées aux Sieurs *Cherrier* et *Leroyer*, en montant le long du dit fleuve *St. Laurent*, depuis la borne qui sera mise entre les dites terres des Sieurs *Cherrier* et *Leroyer* et celles-ci à présent concédées, jusqu'au dit espace de quatre lieues, auquel endroit sera mise une autre borne ; la dite étendue de quatre lieues sur six lieues de profondeur dans les terres.
Cahiers d'Intend. N°. 10 à 17, *folio* 414.

CHEVROTIERE.

On n'a pu trouver le titre de cette concession au Bureau du Sécrétaire, ni dans le Régistre des Foi et Hommage. Il paroit seulement par les concessions voisines de *Deschambault* et de la *Tesserie*, qu'elle fut faite avant mil six cent cinquante-deux, à un Mr. *Chavigny de la Chevrotiére*, qui, ou ses ayant-causes, la céda au propriétaire de *Deschambault*, à laquelle elle est restée réunie sous le nom de cette derniere. Suivant les arpentages que nous avons de cette partie, ces deux concessions réunies occupent deux lieues de front sur trois lieues de profondeur.

LAC MATAPEDIACH.

Concession du 26me Mai, 1694, faite par *Jean Bochart*, Intendant, au Sieur *Nicholas Joseph Damour*, du lac appelé *Matapediach*, avec une lieue de terre tout autour d'icelui.
Régistre d'Intendance, N°. 4, *folio* 17.

LAC MITIS.

Concession du 10me Février, 1693, faite par *Louis de Buade*, Gouverneur, et *Jean Bochart*, Intendant, au Sieur *Louis Rouer*, du lac appelé *Mitis*, avec une lieue de profondeur tout autour d'icelui, qui est éloigné environ douze ou quinze lieues du fleuve *St. Laurent*.
Régistre d'Intendance, N°. 4, *folio* 9.

LA DURANTAIE.

Concession du 29me Octobre, 1672, faite par *Jean Talon*, Intendant, au Sieur *de la Durantaie* de deux lieues de terre de front sur autant de profondeur, à prendre sur le fleuve *St. Laurent*, tenant d'un côté à demi arpent au delà du Sault qui est sur la terre du Sieur *Desislets*, et de l'autre le canal *Bellechasse*, icelui non compris, par-devant le fleuve *St. Laurent*, et par derriére les terres non-concédées.

Le canal de *Bellechasse* étoit si peu connu au tems de cette concession, que les parties y intéressées ne pouvant convenir de leurs bornes, des experts nommés par la Cour déterminèrent que la pointe de *Bellechasse* sépareroit les deux Seigneuries de la *Durantaie* et de *Berthier*.
Régistre d'Intendance, N°. 1, *folio* 7.

AUGMENTATION DE LA DURANTAIE.

Concession du 1er. Mai, 1693, faite au Sieur *de la Durantaie*, par *Louis de Buade* et *Jean Bochart*, Intendant, de deux lieues de terre de profondeur à prendre au bout et où se termine la profondeur de son fief de *la Durantaie*, sur pareille largeur du dit fief, qui a environ trois lieues de front, borné d'un côté au Sud-ouest aux terres de *Beaumont* et au Nord-est aux celles de *Berthier*.

La Durantaie différe, quant au front de celui de l'augmentation? ce front, est sur le terrein de deux lieues cinquante arpens. Par ordre de la Cour cette Seigneurie avec son augmentation a été divisée en deux parties égales connues aujourd'hui, savoir, celle du Sud-ouest sous le nom de *St. Michel*, et celle du Nord-est sous celui de *St. Valier*.
Régistre d'Intendance, Lct. D. *folio* 13.

LA FRESNAY.

Concession du 3me Novembre, 1672, faite par *Jean Talon*, Intendant, aux Sieurs *Gamache* et *Belleavance*, d'une demi lieue de terre sur une lieue de profondeur, à prendre sur le fleuve *St. Laurent*, depuis la concession de la Demoiselle *Amiot*, tirant vers celle du Sieur *Fournier*.
Régistre d'Intendance, N°. 1, *folio* 26.

LA MARTINIERE.

Concession du 5me Aout, 1692, faite par *Louis de Buade*, Gouverneur, et *Jean Bochart*, Intendant, au Sieur *de la Martiniere*, de l'espace de terre qui se pourra trouver, si aucun il y a non concédé, entre la Seigneurie de *Lauzon* et celle de *Mont-a-peine*, ou le fief du Sieur *Vitré*, sur la profondeur semblable à la Seigneurie de *Lauzon*, si personne n'e est propriétaire.
N. B. Ce fief sur les lieux a trente-deux arpens de front.
Régistre d'Intendance, N° 4, *folio* 7.

LANAUDIERE.

Concession du premier Mars, 1750, faite par le *Marquis de la Jonquiere,* Gouverneur, et *François Bigot*, Intendant, au Sieur *Charles François Tarieu de Lanaudiére* de deux lieues ou environ de front, à prendre au bout du fief *Carufel*, sur la profondeur qui se trouve jusqu'au lac *Masquinongé*, le dit lac compris dans toute son étendue, avec les isles, islets et batures qui se trouveront en icelui.
Régistre d'Intendance, N° 9, *folio* 48.

LA NORAYE.

Concession du 7me Avril, 1688, faite par *Jacques de Brisay*, Gouverneur, et *Jean Bochart*, Intendant, au Sieur *de La Noraye*, de l'étendue de terre de deux lieues de front, sur le fleuve *St. Laurent*, et deux lieues de profondeur ; à prendre entre les terres du Sieur *Dautré* et celles du Sieur *de Lavaltrie*, tirant vers *Montréal*.
Régistre d'Intendance, N° 3, *folio* 16.

LA PRAIRIE DE LA MAGDELAINE.

Concession du 1er Avril, 1647, faite par le Sieur *de Lauzon* aux révérends péres Jésuites, de deux lieues de terre le long du fleuve *St. Laurent*, du côté du Sud, à commencer depuis l'isle *Ste. Héléne* jusqu'à un quart de lieue au delà d'une prairie dite *de la Magdelaine*, vis-à-vis des isles qui sont proches du Sault de l'isle de *Montreal*, espace qui contient environ deux lieues le long de la dite riviére *St. Laurent,* sur quatre lieues de profondeur dans les terres, tirant vers le Sud.
Régistre d'Intendance, N° 2, à 9, *folio* 125.

LA SALLE.

Concession du 20me Avril, 1750, faite par le Marquis *de la Jonquiere*, Gouverneur, et *François Bigot* Intendant, au Sieur *Jean Baptiste Le Ber de Senneville*, d'un terrein non concédé, situé au bout des profondeurs des Seigneuries du Sault *St. Louis* et *Chateauguay*, et qui se trouve enclavé entre la Seigneurie de *Villechauve* et celle de la *Prairie de la Magdelaine*, sur une lieue et demie de profondeur.
Régistre d'Intendance, N° 9, *folio* 58.

E.

LA TESSERIE.

Concession du 3me Novembre, 1672, faite par *Jean Talon*, Intendant, à Demoiselle *de la Tesserie*, de la quantité de terre qui se trouvera entre la concession faite aux pauvres de l'Hôpital de *Québec*, jusqu'à celle de *Chavigny*, sur pareille profondeur que celle du dit *Chavigny*.
Régistre d'Intendance, N°. 1, folio 35.
Régistre Foi et Hommage.

LA VALTRIE.

Concession du 29me Octobre, 1672; faite par *Jean Talon*, Intendant, au Sieur *de Lavaltrie*, d'une lieue et demie de terre de front sur pareille, profondeur; à prendre sur le fleuve *St. Laurent*, bornée d'un côté par les terres appartenantes au Seminaire de *Montréal*, et de l'autre par celles non concédées ; par devant par le dit fleuve et par derrière par les terres non-concédées, avec les deux islets qui sont devant la dite quantité de terre, et la riviére *St. Jean* comprise.
, Régistre d'Intendance, N° 1, folio 6.

AUGMENTATION A LAVALTRIE.

Concession du 21me Avril, 1734, faite par *Charles, Marquis de Beauharnois*, Gouverneur, et *Gilles Hocquart*, Intendant, au Sieur *Marganne de Lavaltrie*, d'une lieue et demie de terre de front sur deux lieues et demie de profondeur, à prendre le dit front au bout de la profondeur et limite de la lieue et demie de profondeur du Fief de *Lavaltrie*; pour, être la dite prolongation en profondeur unie et jointe au fief de *Lavaltrie*, et ne faire qu'une même Seigneurie, laquelle, par ce moyen, se trouvera être d'une lieue et demie de front sur quatre lieues de profondeur.
Régistre d'Intendance, N° 7, folio 24.

LAUZON.

Concession du 15me Janvier, 1636, faite par la Compagnie, à Mr. *Simon Lemaitre*, de la côte de *Lauzon*, contenant l'étendue de terre ainsi qu'il suit savoir; la riviere *Bruyante*, (*Chaudiére*) située au pays de la *Nouvelle France*, avec six lieues de profondeur dans les terres et trois lieues à chaque côté de la dite riviére.
Régistre d'Intendance, N° 2, folio 37.

LESSARD.

Concession du 30me Juin, 1698, faite par *Louis de Buade*, Comte de *Frontenac*, Gouverneur, et *Jean Bochart*, Intendant, à *Pierre Lessard*, d'une lieue de terre de front, sur pareille profondeur, située sur le fleuve, *St. Laurent*, proche l'Islet *St. Jean*, au derriére de la Seigneurie de Mademoiselle *Dutartre* ; tenant d'un côté à la terre du Sieur *de la Chenaie*, et de l'autre à celle de *François Bellanger* ; d'un bout à la Seigneurie de dite Demoiselle *Dutartre*, et de l'autre aux terres nonconcédées.
Régistre d'Intendance, N° 5, folio 23.

LESSARD.

Concession du 8me Mars, 1696, faite par *Louis de Buade*, Gouverneur, et *Jean Bochart*, Intendant, à *Pierre Lessard*, d'une lieue et demie de terre de front sur deux lieues de profondeur, située au lieu dit le *Bic*, le dit front à prendre depuis la pointe aux *Peres*, appartenant au Sieur *René Lepage*, à cause d'un échange fait avec le Sieur *de la Cardonière*, et continué le dit front au Nord-est en allant le long du fleuve *St. Laurent*, tant que la dite lieue et demie pourra s'étendre.

    Régistre d'Intendance, N° 4, *folio* 28.

LEVRARD OU ST. PIERRE LES BECQUETS.

Concession du 27me Avril, 1683, faite par les Sieurs *Lefebvre de la Barre*, Gouverneur, et *de Meulles*, Intendant, au Sieur *Levrard*, d'une étendue de terre de deux lieues ou environ de front sur le fleuve *St. Laurent*, du côté du Sud, et généralement tout ce qui se rencontre entre la Seigneurie de *Gentilly* et celle de *Deschaillons*, avec les isles et batures qui sont dans le dit fleuve, au-devant du dit espace ; aussi l'isle appelée *Madame* située au Sud de l'isle et comté de *St. Laurent*, d'une lieue de tour ou environ.

    Régistre d'Intendance, Let. B. *folio* 38.

Acte du premier Avril, 1751, fixe la profondeur de la Seigneurie qui se trouve entre *Gentilly* et *Deschaillons* (*Levrard*) à quatre lieues.

    Régistre d'Intendance, No. 9, *folio* 78.

LIVAUDIERE.

Concession du 20me Septembre, 1734, faite par le Marquis *de Beauharnois*, Gouverneur, et *Gilles Hocquart*, Intendant, au Sieur *Péan de Livaudiere*, de trois quarts de lieue de front ou environ, sur trois lieues de profondeur ; bornée par devant au bout de la profondeur de la Seigneurie de *Vincennes*, d'un côté au Nord-est à la ligne de la Seigneurie de *Beaumont*, d'autre côté au Sud-ouest à la Seigneurie de *Mont-à-peine*, et par derrière aux terres non concédées, pour la présente concession ne faire néanmoins qu'une seule et même seigneurie avec la moitié de celle de la *Durantaie* dont le dit Sieur *Péan* est propriétaire.

    Régistre d'Intendance, N° 9, *folio* 25.

BARONIE DE LONGUEIL.

Lettres du 26me Janvier, 1700, faite par sa Majesté à Mr. *Lemoine de Longueil*, érigeant en Baronie la Seigneurie de *Longueil*, située dans le district de *Montréal*, contenant deux lieues ou environ de front sur le fleuve *St. Laurent*, sur trois lieues et demie de profondeur. Autre concession du 8me Juillet, 1710, faite par Mr. *de Vaudreuil*, Gouverneur, et *Raudot*, Intendant, au *Baron de Longueil*, de trois lieues de front, ayant profondeur jusqu'à la rivière *Chambly*, savoir, la continuation d'une lieue et demie de front au bout de la profondeur de la Baronie de *Longueil*, devant s'étendre jusqu'à la dite rivière *Chambly* avec une autre lieue et demie de même front au Sud-ouest de la première, s'étendant pareillement jusqu'à la rivière *Chambly*, sur le rumb de vent des autres Seigneuries du pays ; étant les dites concessions en augmentation de la *Baronie de Longueil*.

    Régistre des Foi et Hommage, N° 20, *folio* 99, 6me *Février*, 1781.

    Régistre d'Intendance, N° 5, *folio* 25.

    Insinuations du Conseil Supérieur, lettre B. *folio* 131.

    Cahiers d'Intend. N° 2 à 9, *folio* 210.

LOTBINIERE, PREMIERE PARTIE.

Concession du 3me Novembre, 1672, faite par *Jean Talon*, Intendant, au Sieur *Marsolet* d'une demi lieue de front sur une lieue et demi de profondeur, à prendre sur le fleuve *St. Laurent*, depuis la grande riviére *du Chéne*, jusqu'aux terres non concédées, tirant vers les terres de *St. Croix*.

Cahiers d'Intend. N° 10 à 17, *folio* 492.

LOTBINIERE, SECONDE PARTIE.

Concession du 3me Novembre, 1672, faite par *Jean Talon*, Intendant, au Sieur *de Lotbiniére*, de l'étendue de terre qui se trouve sur le fleuve *St. Laurent*, depuis la concession du Sieur *Marsolet* jusqu'à celle dés Religieuses Ursulines, (*Ste. Croix*) sur deux lieues de profondeur.

Cahiers d'Intend. N° 10 à 17, *folio* 494.

LOTBINIERE, TROISIEME PARTIE.

Concession du premier Avril, 1685, faite à Mr. *de Lotbiniere* de trois quarts de lieue ou environ de terre non concédée, à prendre d'un bout le long du fleuve *St. Laurent*, à la grande riviére *du Chéne*, joignant le commencement de la demi lieue de concession, faite au Sieur *Marsolet*, et de l'autre en remontant vers la petite riviere *du Chéne*, aux terres du Sieur *St. Ours*, avec deux lieues de profondeur.

Régistre des Foi et Hommage, N° 42, *Page* 183, *le* 23me *Février*, 1781.
Cahiers d'Intendance, N° 10 à 17, *folio* 502.

LOTBINIERE, QUATRIEME PARTIE, OU AUGMENTATION.

Concession du 25me Mars, 1693, faite par *Louis de Buade*, Gouverneur, et *Jean Bochart*, Intendant, au Sieur *de Lotbiniere*, de trois lieues et demie de front avec quatre lieues et demie de profondeur, à prendre au bout et où se termine la profondeur du fief de *Lotbiniere* et celui appelé la petite riviére *du Chéne* (les trois concessions précédentes à lui appartenante) ensemble tous les bois, prés, isles, riviéres et lacs qui s'y trouvent.

Cahiers d'Intendance, N° 9, 10, à 17, *folio* 510.

LOUIS GAGNIER, DIT BELLEAVANCE.

Concession du 3me Septembre, 1675, faite par le *Comte de Frontenac*, Gouverneur, à *Louis Gagnier, dit Belleavance*, de dix arpens de terre de front, à commencer depuis sa concession, en montant le fleuve *St. Laurent*, dans les terres non-concédées, séparant icelle et ce qui appartient au Sieur *Fournier*, avec une lieue de profondeur, pour être unie à sa part du fief *Lafrenay*, qui lui a été concédé conjointement avec le Sieur *Gamache*, part qui lui appartiendra.

Régistre d'Intendance, N° 2, *folio* 15.

LOUIS LEPAGE ET GABRIEL TIBIERGE.

Concession du 14me Novembre, 1696, faite aux Sieurs *Louis Lepage* et *Gabriel Tibierge*, d'un terrein qui se trouve entre la concession du Sieur *Pachot*, et celle du Sieur *Lessard*, située au lieu dit *Rimousky*, sur le fleuve *St. Laurent*, du côté du Sud, sur une lieue de profondeur.

Régistre d'Intendance, N° 5, *folio* 3.

AUGMENTATION A LA CONCESSION PRECEDENTE.

Concession du 7me Mai, 1697, faite par *Louis de Buade*, Gouverneur, et *Jean Bochart*, Intendant, au Sieur *Louis Lepage* et *Gabriel Tibierge*, de deux lieues en profondeur, joignant le derrière de la concession à eux déjà accordée, située au lieu dit *Rimousky*, sur le fleuve *St. Laurent*, du côté du Sud, tenant d'un côté à la terre du Sieur *Pachot*, et de l'autre à celle du Sieur *Lessard*, sur toute la largeur d'icelle, avec les isles et islets qui se trouveront dans la dite étendue.

Régistre d'Intendance, N° 5, *folio* 16.

LUSSAUDIERE.

Concession du 26me Juillet 1683, faite par Messrs. *Lefebvre de la Barre*, Gouverneur, et *de Meulles*, Intendant, au Sieur *de Lamotte de Luciére*, de la terre et seigneurie de la *Lussaudiere*, concédée par Mr. *Talon*, Intendant, le 22me Octobre, 1672, au Sieur *de la Lussaudiere*, et réunie au domaine de sa Majesté par l'Ordonnance du 26me Mai, 1683, consistant en une lieue de front sur une de profondeur, à prendre depuis les terres du Sieur *Crevier*, en descendant vers la rivière *Nicolet*, le chenail tardif y compris.

Cahiers d'Intendance, N°.2 à 9, *folio* 305.
Insinuations du Conseil Supérieur, *lettre* B. *folio* 125.
Régistre d'Intendance, N° 4, *folio* 22.

LUSSON.

Concession du 7me Novembre, 1672, faite par *Jean Talon*, Intendant, au Sieur de *St. Lusson*, d'une lieue de terre de front sur *(en blanc)* de profondeur, à prendre sur le fleuve *St. Laurent*, savoir, une demie lieue en deça de la petite riviere qui est entre l'*Echaffaud au Basque*, et le *Saguenay*, et une demie lieue au delà ; ensemble l'isle nommée l'isle au *Sieur*.

Régistre d'Intendance, N° 1, *folio* 45.

GROSBOIS OU MACHICHE.

Concession du 3me Novembre, 1672, faite par *Jean Talon*, Intendant, au Sieur *Pierre Boucher*, *de Grandpré*, d'une lieue et demie de terre de front, sur deux de profondeur, à prendre, savoir, trois quarts de lieue au dessus de la riviére à *Marcin*, *(Machiche)* et autant audessous de la dite riviére.

Régistre d'Intendance, N° 1, *folio* 39.

MAGDELAINE.

Concession du 28me Mars, 1689, faite par *Jacques de Brisay*, Gouverneur, et *Jean Bochart*, Intendant, au Sieur *Riverin*, de la riviére *de la Magdelaine*, étant au dessus des monts *Notre Dame*, du côté du Sud, ensemble demi lieue au dessus et demi lieue au dessous de la dite riviére, le long du fleuve *St. Laurent*, avec deux lieues de profondeur.

Régistre d'Intendance, N° 3, *folio* 26.

FIEF MARANDA PARTIE NORD-EST.

Concession faite au Sieur *Duquet*, Pere, le 3me Novembre, 1672, par *Jean Talon*, Intendant, de trente arpens de terre de front sur cinquante de profondeur, à prendre sur le fleuve *St. Laurent*, depuis la concession du Sieur *Duquet* son fils, jusqu'aux terres non-concédées.
Régistre d'Intendance, N° 1, *folio* 25.

FIEF MARANDA PARTIE SUD-OUEST.

Concession faite au Sieur *Duquet*, fils, le 3me Novembre, 1672, par *Jean Talon*, Intendant, de trente arpens de terre de front sur cinquante de profondeur, sur le fleuve *St. Laurent*, depuis la riviére *Vilieu* jusqu'aux terres non-concédées.
Régistre d'Intendance, N° 1, *folio* 25.

PARTIE NORD-EST DE MASQUINONGE.

Concession du 3me Novembre, 1672, faite par *Jean Talon*, Intendant, à *Pierre*, et *Jean Baptiste Legardeur*, Sieurs de *St. Michel*, d'une lieue et demi de terre de front sur pareille profondeur; à prendre sur le Chenail du Nord du fleuve *St. Laurent*, savoir : trois quarts de lieue au dessous de la riviére *Masquinongé*, et autant au dessus ; la dite riviére comprise.
Régistre d'Intendance, N° 1, *folio* 24.

PARTIE SUD-OUEST DE MASQUINONGE.

Concession du 3me Novembre, 1672, faite par *Jean Talon*, Intendant, au Sieur *Jean Baptiste Legardeur*, d'une lieue de terre de front sur une lieue de profondeur, à prendre sur le fleuve *St. Laurent*, depuis les trois quarts de lieues accordés au Sieur *Legardeur* de *St. Michel*, sur trois audessus de la riviére de *Masquinongé*.
Régistre d'Intendance, N° 1, *folio* 34.

MATANE.

Concession du 26me Juin, 1677, faite par *Jacques Duchesneau*, Intendant au Sieur *Damour*, d'une lieue et demie de terre de front, sur une lieue de profondeur, savoir, une demi lieue au deçà et une demi lieue au delà de la riviére *Matane*, et par augmentation une autre lieue de terre de front, aussi sur une lieue et demie de profondeur, y joignant, à prendre du côté de la riviére *Mitis*.
Insinuations du Conseil Superieur, Let. B. *folio* 9.

MILLE-ISLES.

Concession du 5me Mai, 1714, faite par *Philippe de Rigaud*, Gouverneur, et *Michel Bégon*, Intendant, aux Sieurs *de Langloiserie* et *Petit*, des terres qui sont à commencer où finit la Concession du Sieur *Dautier Deslandes*, dans la riviére *Jesus*, jusqu'à trois lieues au dessus, en montant la dite riviere, et trois lieues de profondeur, avec les isles, islets et batures qui se trouveront au devant des dites trois lieues de front ; en outre d'une augmentation des terres qui sont depuis la dite concession jusqu'à la *riviére du Chêne*, icelle comprise, qui est environ une lieue et demie de terre de front, sur pareille profondeur de trois lieues, pour être

la dite lieue et demie jointe à la dite concession, et les deux n'en faire
qu'une ; la première partie de cette concession faite au feu Sieur *Dugay*,
le 24me Septembre, 1688, mais réunie au Domaine du Roi, suivant
l'Ordonnance du 1er Mars, 1714.
Régistre d'Intendance, N° 6, *folio* 4.

AUGMENTATION DES MILLE-ISLES.

Concession du 20me Janvier, 1752, faite par le *Marquis de la
Jonquière*, Gouverneur, et *François Bigot*, Intendant, au Sieur *Dumont*,
de quatre lieues et demie de front sur la profondeur de trois lieues, à
prendre au bout de la profondeur, et sur le même front de la concession
accordée aux Sieurs *de Langloiserie* et *Petit*, située et bornée à commencer où finit la concession du Sieur *Dautier Deslandes*, dans la rivière
Jésus, jusqu'à la *rivière Duchêne*, icelle comprise.
Régistre d'Intendance, N° 10, *folio* 1.

MILLE VACHES.

Concession du 15me Novembre, 1653, faite par *Jean de Lauzon*,
Gouverneur pour la Compagnie, à *Robert Giffard*, Ecuyer, Seigneur de
Beauport, de trois lieues de front sur le fleuve *St. Laurent*, du côté du
Nord, audessous de *Tadoussac*, et de grandes et petites *Bergeronnes*, au
lieu dit *Mille Vaches*, avec quatre lieues de profondeur, tenant par devant
au dit fleuve et des trois autres côtés aux terres non-concédées.
Régistre des Foi et Hommage, N° 86, *folio* 31.
Cahiers d'Intendance, N° 10 à 17, *folio* 771.

TERRA FIRMA DE MINGAN.

Concession du 25me Février, 1661, faite par la Compagnie au Sieur
François Bissot de la Rivière de la terre ferme de *Mingan ;* à prendre
depuis le Cap *des Cormorans* à la côté du Nord, jusqu'à la grande ance
vers les Esquimaux, où les Espagnols font ordinairement la pêche, sur
deux lieues de profondeur.
Régistre des Foi et Hommage, N° 78, *folio* 355.

MONNOIR.

Concession du 25me Mars, 1708, faite par Messieurs *de Rigaud*,
Gouverneur, et *Raudot*, Intendant, au Sieur *de Ramzay*, de deux lieues de
front sur trois lieues de profondeur de terres non-concédées, le long de la
rivière des *Hurons*, joignant d'un côté la Seigneurie de *Chambly*, et de
l'autre côté aux terres non-concédées, courant du Nord-est au Sud-ouest,
avec les isles et islets qui pourroient se trouver dans la dite rivière, vis-
à-vis la dite concession, la dite concession portant le nom de *Monnoir*.
Régistre d'Intendance, N° 2 d 9, *folio* 355.

AUGMENTATION A MONNOIR.

Concession du 12me Juin, 1739, faite par le Marquis *de Beauharnois*,
Gouverneur, et *Gilles Hocquart*, Intendant, au Sieur *Jean Baptiste Nicolas
Roc de Ramzay*, de deux lieues de front sur trois lieues de profondeur, au
bout de la Seigneurie de *Monnoir*, concédée le 25me Mars, 1708, située
près *Chambly* le long de la rivière des *Hurons*, en courant Nord-est et
Sud-ouest le long de la continuation de la Seigneurie de *Rouville*,

joignant la dite Seigneurie au Nord-est et celle de *Sabrerois* au Sud-ouest.

Régistre d'Intendance, N° 8, *folio* 26.

MONT-A-PEINE.

Concession du 24me Septembre, 1683, faite à Mr. *Charles Denis*, Sieur *de Vitré*, de dix arpens de terre de front, sur quarante de profondeur, pour en jouir, lui ses hoirs et ayans-cause à titre de fief et Seigneurie à toujours.

N. B. Cet extrait ne mentionne nullement la situation de ce fief qui n'est connu que par son augmentation et la concession précédente.

Régistre des Foi et Hommage, N° 46, *folio* 207, 27me *Février*, 1781.

AUGMENTATION DE MONT-A-PEINE.

Concession du 18me Juin, 1749, faite par *Roland Michel Barrin*, Gouverneur, et *François Bigot*, Intendant, à *Claude Antoine de Berment*, Seigneur *de la Martiniére*, d'un restant de terre qui se trouve au bout de la profondeur du fief de *Vitré*, et qui est enclavé entre les fiefs de *Vincennes* et de *Lavaudiére* au Nord-est, et celui du dit *Berment de la Martiniere* au Sud-ouest, jusqu'à l'égale profondeur de six lieues que contient le fief du dit Sieur *Berment de la Martiniere*.

Régistre d'Intendance, N° 9, *folio* 41.

MONTARVILLE.

Concession du 17me Octobre, 1710, faite par Messrs. *de Vaudreuil*, Gouverneur, et *Raudot*, Intendant, au Sieur *Boucher*, d'une lieue et trente arpens de terre de front sur une lieue et demie de profondeur, à prendre dans les profondeurs entre les Seigneuries de *Boucherville* et de *Chambly*; joignant au Nord-est la Seigneurie de *Varennes*, et au Sud-ouest la Seigneurie de *Tremblay*.

Régistre d'Intendance, N° 2 d 9, *folio* 169.

MOUNT MURRAY.

Grant of the 27th day of April, 1762, by the Honorable *James Murray*, Esq. Governor of *Quebec*, to Lieutenant *Malcolm Fraser*, of His Majesty's 78th Regiment of Foot, of all that extent of land lying on the North shore of the river St. *Lawrence*, from the North-side of the River of *Malbay* to the River *Noire*, and for three leagues back, to be known hereafter, at the special request of the said Lieutenant *Malcolm Fraser*, by the name of *Mount Murray*, together with the woods and rivers or other appurtenances within the said extent, right of fishing or fowling, within the same, included. All kind of traffick with the Indians of the back country hereby specially excepted.

English Register, Letter E. *folio* 709.

MURRAY-BAY OR MALBAY.

Grant of the 27th day of April, 1762, by the Honorable *James Murray*, Esq. Governor of *Quebec*, to *John Nairn*, Captain of His Majesty's 78th Regiment of Foot, of all that extent of land lying on the North shore of the River St. *Lawrence*, from *Goose-Cape*, boundary of the Seigneurie of *Eboulemens*, to the River *Malbay*, and for three leagues back, to be known hereafter, at the special request of the said Captain *John Nairn*, by the name of *Murray Bay*, together with the woods and rivers or other appurtenances within the said extent, right of fishing and fowling on the same therein included. All kind of traffick with the Indians of the back country are hereby specially excepted.

English Register, Letter E, *page* 709.

NEUVILLE OU LA POINTE AUX TREMBLES.

Concession du 16me Décembre, 1653, faite par la Compagnie, à *Jean Bourdon,* contenant deux lieues trois quarts ou environ de front, sur quatre lieues de profondeur, tenant du côté du Nord-est au fief de *Desmure* et du côté du Sud-Ouest au fief de *Bélaire;* par devant le fleuve *St. Laurent,* et par derrière les terres non-concédées.

Régistre d'Intendance, N° 10 à 17, *folio* 660.

DERRIERE DAUTRE' ET LA NORAYE.

Concession du 4me Juillet, 1739, faite par *Charles, Marquis de Beauharnois,* Gouverneur, et *Gilles Hocquart,* Intendant, au Sieur *Jean Baptiste Neveu,* d'un terrein non-concédé, à prendre depuis la ligne qui borne la profondeur des fiefs de *La Noraye* et *Dautré,* jusqu'à la rivière de l'*Assomption,* et dans la même étendue en largeur que celle des dits fiefs ; c'est-à-dire, bornée du côté du Sud-Ouest par la ligne qui sépare la Seigneurie de *Lavaltrie,* et du côté du Nord-Est par une ligne parallele, tenant aux prolongations de la Seigneurie d'*Antaya;* lequel terrein ne fera avec chacun des dits fiefs de *La Noraye* et *Dautré* qu'une seule et même Seigneurie.

Régistre d'Intendance, N° 8, *folio* 29.

NICOLET.

Concession du 29me Octobre 1672, faite par *Jean Talon,* Intendant, au Sieur *de Laubia,* de deux lieues de front sur autant de profondeur, à prendre sur le lac *St. Pierre,* savoir ; une lieue au dessus et une lieue au dessous de la rivière *Nicolet,* icelle comprise.

Régistre d'Intendance, N° 1, *folio* 15.

L'ISLE DE LA FOURCHE, ET AUGMENTATION A NICOLET.

Concession du 4me Novembre, 1680, par le Comte de *Frontenac,* Gouverneur, et *Duchesneau,* Intendant, au Sieur *Cressé,* de l'isle de la *Fourche,* étant dans la rivière *Cressé,* ensemble les isles et islets qui sont dans la dite rivière, jusqu'au bout de la dite isle ; avec trois lieues d'augmentation dans la profondeur des terres qui sont au bout de toute la largeur de sa Seigneurie.

Régistre d'Intendance, N° 2, *folio* 21.

NOTRE DAME DES ANGES.

Concession du 10me Mars, 1626, faite par la Compagnie aux révérends peres Jésuites ; de la Seigneurie de *Notre Dame des Anges,* contenant une lieue de front sur quatre lieues de profondeur, joignant du côté du Nord-Est la Seigneurie de *Beauport,* et au Sud-Ouest le Comté d'*Orsainville;* par devant le fleuve *St. Laurent* et la petite rivière *St. Charles;* et par derrière au bout de la dite concession les terres non-concédées.

Cahiers d'Intendance, N° 2 d 9, *folio* 85.

F

NOUVELLE LONGUEIL.

Concession du 21me Avril, 1734, faite par *Charles Marquis de Beau-harnois*, Gouverneur, et *Gilles Hocquart*, Intendant, à *Joseph Lemoine*, Chevalier de *Longueil*, de l'étendue de terre qui se trouve sur le bord du fleuve *St. Laurent*, au lieu appelé *les Cascades*, depuis la borne de la Seigneurie de *Soulange* jusqu'à la *Pointe du Baudet* inclusivement ; faisant environ deux lieues de front sur trois lieues de profondeur ; avec les isles, islets et batures y adjacentes.

    Régistre d'Intendance, N° 7, *folio* 24.

NOYAN.

Concession du 8me Juillet, 1743, faite par *Charles Marquis de Beau-harnois*, Gouverneur, et *Gilles Hocquart*, Intendant, au Sieur *Chavois de Noyan*, de deux lieues de front le long de la rivière *Chambly*, sur trois lieues de profondeur, laquelle sera bornée du côté du Nord à un quart de lieue au Nord de la petite rivière du Sud, par une ligne courant Est et Ouest, du côté du Sud en remontant le lac *Champlain*, à une lieue trois quarts de la dite rivière, joignant par une ligne parallèle à celle ci-dessus au terrein concédé au Sieur *Foucault*, le premier Mai dernier, avec l'Isle aux *Têtes*, étant dans la dite rivière *Chambly*, avec les isles et islets qui se trouveront vis-à-vis le front de la dite concession.

    Régistre d'Intendance, N° 9, *folio* 19.

D'ORSAINVILLE.

Concession du mois de May, 1675, faite par Lettres Patentes de sa Majesté, aux Dames religieuses de l'Hôpital Général, du Comté d'*Orsain-ville*, contenant en superficie trois mille cinq cens soixant et quinze arpens, et de la profondeur de quatre lieues ; à prendre du bord de la rivière *St. Charles*, sur différentes largeurs, tenant par devant à la dite rivière et par derrière aux terres non-concédées, d'un côté, au Sud-Ouest à un fief appartenant au Sieur de l'*Epinay* par une ligne qui va au Nord-Ouest quart de Nord de la profondeur des dites quarte lieues, et du côté du Nord-Est au fief de *Notre Dame des Anges* ; le comté d'*Orsainville*, et la Seigneurie de *Notre Dame des Anges* étant séparés, à commencer par le front du dit Comté, par le ruisseau de *St. Michel*, suivant ses contours et serpentemens jusqu'à environ quinze arpens de profondeur, où le dit Comté d'*Orsainville* commence à être de onze arpens de front, jusqu'à la hauteur de trente cinq arpens du bord de la dite rivière *St. Charles* par une ligne qui court Nord-Ouest quart de Nord, au bout desquels trente-cinq arpens commence une autre ligne qui court au Nord-Ouest la longueur de quarante arpens, au bout desquels la dite ligne fait un tour d'équerre de trois arpens, au bout desquels reprend une nouvelle ligne laquelle forme la largeur des dits onze arpens, laquelle ligne va au Nord-Ouest quart de Nord, jusqu'au surplus de la profondeur des dites quatre lieues.

    Papier Terrier, N° 71, *folio* 324, *le* 24me *Avril*, 1781.
    Cahiers d'Intendance, 10 à 17, *folio* 730.

PACHOT.

Concession du 7me Janvier, 1689, faite par *Jacques de Brisay*, Gouverneur, et *Jean Bochart*, Intendant, au Sieur *Pachot*, de la rivière de *Mitis*, dans sa devanture, sur le fleuve *St. Laurent*, jusqu'à une lieue de profondeur et une lieue de terre sur le fleuve *St. Laurent*, moitié audessus et moitié audessous de la dite riviére sur semblable profondeur d'une lieue.

Régistre d'Intendance, N° 3, *folio* 21.

PASPEBIAC.

Concession du 10me Novembre, 1707, faite par *Rigaud*, Gouverneur, et *Raudot*, Intendant, au Sieur *Pierre Leymar*, de la pointe de *Paspébiac*, dans la *Baie des Chaleurs*, avec une lieue de front du côté de l'Est de la dite pointe et une lieue du côté de l'Ouest, avec les isles et islets qui se trouveront au devant de l'étendue de la dite concession, sur trois lieues de profondeur.

Insinuations du Conseil Supérieur, lettre C. folio 38.

PERTHUIS.

Concession du 11me Octobre, 1753, faite par le *Marquis Duquesne*, Gouverneur, et *François Bigot*, Intendant, au Sieur *Perthuis*, d'une lieue et demie de front, sur neuf lieues de profondeur, à prendre au bout des trois lieues de profondeur de *Portneuf.*

Régistre d'Intendance, N° 10, *folio* 17.

PETITE NATION.

Concession par la Compagnie des Indes du 16me Mai, 1674, à Messire *François de Laval*, Evêque de *Pétrée*, et premier Evêque de *Québec*, de cinq lieues de terre de front sur cinq lieues de profondeur, sur le fleuve *St. Laurent* dans la *Nouvelle France*, environ quarante deux lieues au dessus de *Montreal ;* à prendre depuis le Sault de la Chaudiére, vulgairement appelé *la Petite Nation* en descendant le fleuve sur le chemin des *Outawas.*

Cahiers d'Intendance, 10 à 17, *folio* 682.
Registre des Foi et Hommage, N° 142, *page* 238.

PIERREVILLE.

Concession du 3me Août, 1683, faite par *Lefebvre*, Gouverneur, et *de Meulles*, Intendant, au Sieur *Laurent Philippe*, d'une lieue et demie de terre de front sur une lieue de profondeur, joignant du côté du Sud-ouest les terres non-concédées, d'autre côté au Nord-ouest, d'un bout sur la Seigneurie du Sieur *Creviere*, d'autre aux terres non-concédées, avec les isles et islets qui se rencontreront dans la dite profondeur, la riviére *St. François* comprise dans icelle profondeur, ensorte qu'elle fut au milieu de la dite profondeur.

Cahiers d'Intendance, N° 2 d 9, *folio* 281.
Ins. Con. Sup. lettre B. *folio* 129.

TONNANCOUR OU POINTE DU LAC.

Concession du 3me Novembre, 1734, faite par *Charles Marquis de Beauharnois*, Gouverneur, et *Gilles Hocquart*, Intendant, au Sieur *René Godefroi de Tonnancour*, d'une demi lieue de terre de front sur une lieue de profondeur, à prendre le dit front au bout de la profondeur et

limite du fief ci-devant de *Normanville,* pour être la dite prolongation
en profondeur unie et jointe au dite fief de *Normanville* pour ne faire
ensemble avec le fief et Seigneurie de *Sauvaget* qu'une seule et même
Seigneurie, sous le nom de *Tonnancour,* laquelle se trouvera être d'une
lieue et quart de front sur deux lieues de profondeur : le rumb de vent
courant pour le front Nord-Est et Sud-Ouest, et pour la profondeur Nord-
Ouest et Sud-Est.

Régistre d'Intendance, N° 7, *folio* 29.

PORT DANIEL.

Concession du 12me Decembre, 1696, faite par *Louis de Buade,*
Gouverneur, et *Jean Bochart,* Intendant, au Sieur *Réne d'Encau,* de trois
lieues et demie de terre de front, au lieu dit le *Port Daniel,* dans la *Baie
des Chaleurs,* le dit front à commencer demi lieue à l'Est du cap qui fait
un des côtés de l'ance du dit *Port Daniel,* à continuer les dites trois lieues
et demie à l'Ouest, sur une lieue de profondeur ; avec les ruisseaux,
riviéres et étangs, si aucuns se trouvent dans la dite étendue.

Régistre d'Intendance, N° 5, *folio* 4.

BARONIE DE PORTNEUF.

Concession du 16me Avril, 1647, faite par la Compagnie au Sieur *de
Croisille,* située au bord du fleuve *St. Laurent,* du côté du Nord, conte-
nant une lieue et demie de front sur trois lieues de profondeur ; le front
joignant au Nord-Est au fief de *Monceau,* et du côté du Sud-Ouest au fief
Deschambault, dans laquelle se trouvent comprises les riviéres de *Jacques
Cartier* et de *Portneuf.*

Régistre d'Intendance, N° 2 à 9, *folio* 215.

DERRIERE LA CONCESSION DU SIEUR NEVEU, AU NORD-EST.

Concession du 7me Octobre, 1736, faite par *Charles Marquis de
Beauharnois,* Gouverneur, et *Gilles Hocquart,* Intendant, à Dame *Geneviéve de Ramzay,* veuve du feu Sieur de *Boishébert,* d'une lieue et demie
de terre de front sur quatre lieues de profondeur, bornée sur la devanture
par la rive du Nord de la rivière de l'*Assomption,* du côté du Sud-Ouest
par la ligne de la concession nouvellement accordée au Sieur d'*Argenteuil;*
d'autre, au Nord-Est par une ligne parallele, tenant aux prolongation de
la Seigneurie d'*Antaya* ; et dans la profondeur par une ligne paralléle à
la devanture, joignant aussi aux terres non-concédées.

Régistre d'Intendance, N° 8, *folio* 15.

RANDIN.

Concession faite au Sieur *Randin,* le 3me Novembre, 1672, par *Jean
Talon,* Intendant, d'une lieue de front sur le fleuve *St. Laurent,* sur
une demi lieue de profondeur, à prendre depuis le Sieur *de Comporté,*
jusqu'aux terres non-concédées ; avec l'isle nommée de son nom de
Randin.

N. B. Dans le Régistre du Sécrétariat le mot *une* a été sustitué à la
place du mot *demi* qui a été rayé.

Régistre d'Intendance, N° 1, *folio* 21.

AUGMENTATION DE RANDIN.

Concession faite au Sieur *Berthier*, le 27me Avril 1674, d'une demi lieue de terre de front sur une lieue de profondeur, à prendre derrière et joignant la concession du Sieur *Randin*, du 3me Novembre, 1672.

Régistre des Foi et Hommage, folio 38, *le* 26me *Janvier,* 1781.

REAUME.

Concession du 16me Mars, 1677, faite par *Jacques Duchesneau*, Intendant, à Demoiselle *de Lacombe*, d'une demi lieue de terre de front le long du fleuve *St. Laurent*, à prendre depuis celles qui appartiennent au Sieur *de St. Denis*, son père, en remontant le dit fleuve, avec deux lieues de profondeur.

Insinuations du Conseil Supérieur, lettre B. *folio* 16.

RIGAUD.

Concession du 29me Octobre, 1732, faite par *Charles Marquis de Beauharnois*, Gouverneur, et *Gilles Hocquart*, Intendant, aux Sieurs de *Cavagnal* et *Rigaud*, freres, d'un terrein le long du fleuve appelé *la Grande Rivière*, en tirant vers le *Long-sault*, de trois lieues de front sur trois lieues de profondeur, avec les isles, islets et batures adjacentes : le dit terrein, joignant la Seigneurie qui leur est échue par succession de feu le Marquis de *Vaudreuil*, située au lieu dit *la Pointe aux Tourtes*.

Régistre d'Intendance, Nº 7, *folio* 3.

RIMOUSKY.

Concession du 24me Avril, 1688, faite par *Jacques Réné de Brisay*, Gouverneur, au Sieur *de la Cardonière*, d'une étendue de deux lieues de terre, prés et bois, de front, sur le fleuve *St. Laurent ;* à prendre joignant et attenant la concession du *Bic*, appartenant au Sieur *de Vitré*, en descendant le dit fleuve, et de deux lieues de profondeur dans les terres, ensemble la rivière dite de *Rimousky* et autres riviéres et ruisseaux, si aucuns se trouvent dans la dite étendue, avec l'isle de *St. Barnabé* et les batures, isles et islets qui se pourront rencontrer entre les dites terres et la dite isle.

Régistre d'Intendance, Nº 2, B *folio* 24.

RIVIERE DU LOUP, AVEC AUGMENTATION.

Concession du 20me Avril, 1633, faite par Mr. *Lefebre*, Gouverneur, et *de Meulles*, Intendant, au Sieur *Lechasseur*, d'une lieue de terre de front sur quatre lieues de profondeur, sur le lac *St. Pierre*, demi lieue audessus et demi lieue audessous de la *Rivière du Loup*, icelle comprise.

Insinuations du Conseil Supérieur, Régistre B. *folio* 46.

RIVIERE DU LOUP ET L'ISLE VERTE.

Concession du 5me Avril, 1689, faite par *Jacques de Brisay*, Gouverneur, et *Jean Bochart*, Intendant, au Sieur *Villerai*, pour le Sieur *d'Artigny*, et au Sieur *Lachenaie*, de l'étendue de terre qui peut se rencontrer entre leurs concessions, avec deux lieues de profondeur; de laquelle ils jouiront moitié par moitié, et des isles et batures qui se

peuvent rencontrer vis-à-vis la dite étendue, à cause de la grande quantité
de terres inhabitables qui se rencontrent sur les concessions à eux ci-
devant faites, savoir, au Sieur *de Villerai* pour le dit Sieur *d'Artigny*,
depuis la riviére *Verte* jusqu'à deux lieues en descendant le fleuve *St.
Laurent ;* et au Sieur de *Lachenaie,* savoir trois lieues et demie, savoir,
une lieue au dessus de la rivière du *Loup,* et deux lieues audessous de la
dite riviére.
Régistre d'Intendance, N°. 3, *folio* 27.

RIVIÈRE DU SUD, AVEC LES ISLES AUX GRUES ET AUX OIES.

Concession du 5me Mai, 1646, faite par la Compagnie, au Sieur *de
Montmagny,* de la rivière appelée *du Sud,* à l'endroit où elle se décharge
dans le fleuve *St. Laurent,* avec une lieue de terre le long du dit fleuve
St. Laurent, en montant de la dite riviére vers *Québec,* et demi lieue le
long du dit fleuve, en descendant vers le golfe ; le tout sur la profondeur
de quatre lieues en avant dans les terres, en cotoyant la dite rivière de
part et d'autre, et icelle comprise dans la dite étendue ; et de plus les
deux isles situées dans le fleuve *St. Laurent,* proche du dit lieu, en
descendant le dit fleuve, l'une appelée l'isle *aux Oies,* et l'autre appelée
l'isle *aux Grues,* avec les batures qui sont entre les deux, le tout contenant quatre lieues ou environ de longueur sur le dit fleuve.
Régistre d'Intendance, N° 10 à 17, *folio* 572.

LA RIVIÈRE OUELLE.

Concession du 29me Octobre, 1672, faite par *Jean Talon,* Intendant,
au Sieur *de la Bouteillerie,* de deux lieues de front sur une lieue et demie de profondeur, à prendre sur le fleuve *St. Laurent,* savoir une lieue
audessus et une lieue au dessous de la rivière *Ouelle,* icelle comprise.
Régistre d'Intendance, N° 1, *folio* 6.

AUGMENTATION DE LA RIVIÈRE OUELLE.

Concession du 20me Octobre, 1750, faite par le Marquis *de la Jonquiere,*
et *François Bigot,* Intendant, à Demoiselle *Géneviéve de Ramzay,* veuve du
Sieur *de Boishebert,* de deux lieues de front sur deux lieues de profondeur,
à prendre au bout de la profondeur de la lieue et demie que contient la
Seigneurie *de la Bouteillerie,* pour faire, avec l'ancienne concession de
1672, une seule et même seigneurie, au lieu appelé la riviére *Ouelle.*
Régistre d'Intendance, N° 9, *folio* 70.

ROQUETAILLADE.

Concession en date du 22me Avril, 1675, faite au Sieur *Pierre
Godefroi de Roquetaillade,* par *Louis de Buade* Comte de *Frontenac,* des
terres qui sont le long du fleuve *St. Laurent;* contenant une demi lieue
ou environ de front, à prendre depuis ce qui est concédé au Sieur *de
Godefroi* son pere, au dessous des *Trois Riviéres,* en montant, jusqu'aux
terres de la Seigneurie de *Nicolet,* avec trois lieues de profondeur.
Cahier d'Intendance, N° 2 à 9, *folio* 152.

ROUVILLE.

Concession du 18me Janvier, 1694, faite par *Louis de Buade*, Gouverneur, et *Jean Bochart*, Intendant, au Sieur *Jean Baptiste Hertel*, Sieur *de Rouville*, de deux lieues de terre de front avec une lieue et demie de profondeur, joignant d'un côté la terre de la Seigneurie de *Chambly*, en descendant la rivière *Richelieu* ; de l'autre côté les térres non-concédées du côté du Sud de la dite rivière *Richelieu*.

Régistre d'Intendance, N° 4, *folio* 15.

SABREVOIS.

Concession du 1er Novembre, 1750, faite par le *Marquis de la Jonquiére*, Gouverneur, et *François Bigot*, Intendant, au Sieur *de Sabrevois*, de deux lieues ou environ de front, sur trois lieues de profondeur, bornée du coté du Nord par la Seigneurie concédée au Sieur *de Sabrevois de Bleuri*, le 30me, Octobre dernier, sur la même ligne ; du côté du Sud à deux lieues ou environ sur la dite Seigneurie par une ligne tirée Est et Ouest du monde, joignant aux terres non-concédées ; sur la devanture par la rivière *Chambly* et sur la profondeur à trois lieues joignant aussi aux terres non-concédées.

Régistre d'Intendance, N° 9, *folio* 73.

SAINTE ANNE.

Concession du 29me Octobre, 1672, faite par *Jean Talon*, Intendant, aux Sieurs *Sueur* et *Lanaudiere*, de l'étendue de la terre qui se trouve sur le fleuve *St. Laurent*, au lieu dit des *Grondines*, depuis celle appartenante aux Religieuses de l'Hôpital de *Québec*, jusqu'à la Riviére *Ste. Anne*, icelle comprise, sur une lieue de profondeur, avec la quantité de terre qu'ils ont acquis du Sieur *Hamelin*.

Régistre d'Intendance, N° 1, *folio* 15.

AUGMENTATION DE STE. ANNE.

Concession du 4me Mars, 1697, par *Louis de Buade*, Gouverneur, et *Jean Bochart*, Intendant, faite à *Marguerite Denis*, veuve du Sieur *de Lanaudiére*, de trois lieues de terre de profondeur derrière la terre et Seigneurie de *St. Anne*, sur toute la largeur d'icelle, et celle des Sieurs *de Sueur* et *Hamelin*, avec les isles, islets et batures non-concédées qui se trouvent dans la dite étendue ; la dite profondeur tenant d'un côté à la Seigneurie des *Grondines*, et d'autre côté à celle de *Batiscan*.

Régistre d'Intendance, N° 5, *folio* 5.

AUTRE AUGMENTATION DE STE. ANNE.

Concession du 30me Octobre, 1700, par *Hector de Calliére*, Gouverneur, et *Jean Bochart*, Intendant, au Sieur *Thomas Tarieu de la Perade*, de l'espace de terre qui se trouve au derriére de la Seigneurie de *Ste. Anne*, lequel espace contient environ deux lieues de front entre les lignes prolongées des Seigneuries de *St. Charles des roches (les Grondines)* et *Batiscan*, sur une lieue et demie de profondeur ; ensemble la rivière qui peut traverser le dit espace, et les islets qui peuvent s'y rencontrer.

Régistre d'Intendance, N° 5, *folio* 37.

TROISIEME AUGMENTATION DE STE. ANNE.

Concession du 20me Avril, 1735, faite par le *Marquis de Beauharnois*, Gouverneur, et *Gilles Hocquart*, Intendant, à Mr. *Thomas Tarieu*, Sieur *de la Perade*, d'une étendue de terre de trois lieues de profondeur, à prendre derriére et sur la même largeur de la Concession du 30me Octobre, 1700.

    Régistre d'Intendance, N° 7, *folio* 31.

STE. ANNE.

Concession du 28me Novembre, 1688, faite par *Jacques de Brisay*, Gouverneur, et *Jean Bochart*, Intendant, au Sieur *Riverin*, de la riviére *Ste. Anne*, située aux monts *Notre Dame*, dans le fleuve *St. Laurent*, avec une demi lieue de front sur le dit fleuve, moitié audessus et l'autre moitié audessous de la dite riviére, icelle non comprise dans la dite étendue, sur une lieue de profondeur dans les terres.

    Régistre d'Intendance, N° 3, *folio* 19.

STE. ANNE OU LA POCADIERE.

Concession du 29me Octobre, 1672, faite par *Jean Talon*, Intendant, à Demoiselle *Lacombe*, d'une lieue et demie de terre de front sur autant de profondeur, à prendre sur le fleuve *St. Laurent*, tenant d'un côté à la concession du Sieur de *St. Denis*; d'autre aux terres non concédées.

    Régistre d'Intendance, N° 1, *folio* 9.

TILLY OU ST. ANTOINE.

Concession du 29me Octobre, 1672, faite par *Jean Talon*, Intendant, au Sieur *de Villieu*, de l'étendue de terres qui se trouveront sur le fleuve *St. Laurent*, depuis les bornes de celles de Mr. *Lauzon*, jusqu'à la petite riviére dit *de Villieu*, icelle comprise, sur une lieue et demie de profondeur.

    Reg. Ins. Con. Sup. lettre B. *folio* 20.

ST. ARMAND.

Concession du 23me Septembre, 1748, faite par *Rolland Michel Barrin*, Gouverneur, et *François Bigot*, Intendant, au Sieur *Nicolas Réné Levasseur*, de six lieues de terre de front sur trois lieues de profondeur le long de la riviére de *Missisquoui*, dans le lac *Champlain*, les dites six lieues à prendre à huit arpens au dessous de la premiére chute qui se trouve à trois lieues de profondeur de la dite riviére, en remontant la susdite riviére de *Missisquoui*.

    Régistre d'Intendance, N° 9, *folio* 35.

ST. BARNABE.

Concession du 11me Mars, 1751, faite par le Marquis de *la Jonquiere*, Gouverneur, et *François Bigot*, Intendant, au Sieur *Lepage* de *St. Barnabé*, de cinq quarts de lieue de terre de front, sur deux lieues de profondeur, avec les riviéres, isles et islets qui se trouveront au devant du dit terrein, à prendre depuis la concession accordée au feu Sieur *Rouer de la Cardonière*, en descendant au Nord-est, jusques et compris à la pointe de l'Isle aux *Péres*, de manière qu'il se trouvera avoir trois lieues et un quart de front, sur deux lieues de profondeur, qui seront bornées en total à la concession des représentans de feu Sieur *de Vitré* au Sud-ouest, et au Nord-est à la pointe de l'Isle aux *Péres*.

Régistre d'Intendance, N° 9, *folio* 77.

ST. BLAIN.

Ce fief est une partie démembrée de la Seigneurie de *Verchéres*, comme il paroit par un acte de Foi et Hommage rendu devant Mr. *Begon*, alors Intendant, le 13me Février, 1723, fondé sur un acte de partage du 15me Septembre, 1686, suivant lequel le front de ce fief commence à la ligne de séparation entre les Seigneuries de *Vercheres* et de *St. Michel*, et contient vingt-trois arpens de front sur deux lieues de profondeur, sur le rumb de vent ordinaire des concessions de la Seigneurie de *Verchere*.

Régistre des Foi et Hommage, *folio* 3, *datée* 30me Janvier, 1723.

ST. CHARLES.

Concession du 1er. Mars, 1695, faite par *Louis de Buade*, Gouverneur, et *Jean Bochart*, Intendant, au Sieur *Hertel de la Fresnière*, de deux lieues de terre de front sur autant de profondeur, à commencer du côté du sud de la riviére *Richelieu* aux terres du Sieur *Rouville*, les dites deux lieues de front suivant et cotoyant la dite riviére, en descendant du côté de *Sorrel*, et les dites deux lieues de profondeur courant du côté du sud.

Régistre d'Intendance, N° 4, *folio* 20.

ST. CHARLES.

Concession du 14me Août, 1701, faite par *Hector de Callière*, Gouverneur, et *Jean Bochart*, Intendant, au Sieur *René Fezeret*, d'une lieue et demie de terre en superficie dans la riviére de *Yamaska*, icelle comprise, à prendre du côté du sud de la dite riviére, tirant sud-est, tenant d'un bout à la Concession du feu Sieur *Bourchemin*, et de l'autre aux terres non-concédées, avec les isles, islets, prairies et battures adjacentes.

Régistre d'Intendance, N° 5, *folio* 33.

STE. CLAIRE.

Concession du 17me Mars, 1693, faite par *Louis de Buade*, Gouverneur, et *Jean Bochart*, Intendant, à *Réné Lepage*, d'une lieue de terre de front à prendre à une ligne qui sera tirée au Nord-est et Sud-ouest, pour terminer la profondeur de la concession du Sieur *Couillard de l'Epinay*, située à la riviére du Sud, avec deux lieues de profondeur, joignant d'un côté au Nord-est la prolongation de la ligne qui fait la séparation des terres du dit Sieur de l'*Epinay*, d'avec celle du Sieur *Amiot de Vinçelot*; d'autre côté, au Sud-ouest, les terres non concédées; d'un bout, au Nord-ouest, la dite ligne qui termine la profondeur de la terre du dit Sieur de l'*Epinay*, et d'autre bout au Sud-est une autre ligne parallèle qui terminera les dites deux lieues de profondeur.

Régistre d'Intendance, Lettre D. N° 4, *folio* 12.

G

STE. CROIX.

Le titre de cette concession n'a pas été trouvé au Secrétariat; il paroit seulement par le Régistre des Foi et Hommage une déclaration faite par *Pierre Duquet*, Notaire Royal, au nom des Dames Religieuses Ursulines de *Québec*, propriétaires de la Seigneurie de *Ste. Croix* et autres lieux, devant Mr. *Duchesneau*, Intendant, qui dit, que les dites Dames possédent un fief et seigneurie au lieu nommé *Platon Ste. Croix*, contenant une lieue de front sur le fleuve *St. Laurent*, sur dix lieues de profondeur, borné d'un côté au Sieur de *Lotbiniére* et d'autre aux terres non encore habitées, aux dites Dames Religieuses appartenant par titre de l'ancienne Compagnie, en date du 16me Janvier, 1637, et confirmé par Mr. *de Lauzon*, Gouverneur, le 6me Mars, 1652.

Régistre des Foi et Hommage, N° 68, *folio* 312, *le* 24me *Avril*, 1781.

ST. DENIS.

Concession du 12me Mai, 1679, faite par le Comte *de Frontenac*, Gouverneur, au Sieur de *St. Denis* pour et au nom de *Joseph Juchereau*, son fils, des terres qui sont du côté du Sud, entre celles du Sieur *de Ladurantaie* et du Sieur *de la Bouteillerie*, le long du fleuve *St. Laurent*, contenant une lieue de front ou environ, sur quatre lieues dans la profondeur de la dite lieue.

Insinuations du Conseil Supérieur, Lettre B. *folio* 36.

ST. DENIS.

Concession du 20me Septembre, 1694, faite par *Louis de Buade*, Gouverneur, et *Jean Bochart*, Intendant, à *Louis de Ganne*, Sieur *de Falaise*, de deux lieues de terre de profondeur derriére la terre et Seigneurie de *Contrecœur*, sur toute la largeur d'icelle, qui est de deux lieues, laquelle profondeur passera en partie au delà de la riviére *Chambly*, et courra les mêmes rumbs de vent que la dite terre de *Contrecœur*; avec les isles et islets qui se trouveront dans la dite riviére *Chambly* par le travers de la dite profondeur.

Régistre d'Intendance, N° 4, *folio* 17.
Régistre d'Intendance, 9, *folio* 61.

ST. ETIENNE.

Concession du 7me Octobre, 1737, faite par le *Marquis de Beauharnois*, Gouverneur, et *Gilles Hocquart*, Intendant, au Sieur *François Etienne Cugnet*, d'un terrain restant à concéder vis-à-vis la Seigneurie appartenante aux héritiers *Jolliet*, sur la riviére du *Sault de la Chaudiére*, du côté du Sud-ouest, depuis le bout de la profondeur de la Seigneurie de *Lauzon* jusqu'à celle nouvellement concédée au Sieur *Taschereau*, contenant environ trois lieues de front sur la dite riviére du *Sault de la Chaudiere*, au Sud-ouest de la dite riviére, sur deux lieues de profondeur, ensemble les isles et islets qui se trouveront dans la dite riviére dans l'espace du dit terrein du côté du Sud-ouest, suivant qu'elles se trouveront situées au devant du dit terrein, et les lacs qui se trouveront situés sur les dites terres.

Régistre d'Intendance, N° 8, *folio* 20.

ST. FRANÇOIS.

Concession du 8me Octobre, 1678, faite par *Louis de Buade*, Gouverneur, au Sieur *Crevier*, de la Seigneurie de *St. François*, contenant une lieue de profondeur en montant dans la riviére de *St. François* ; ensemble les isles et islets qui sont dans la dite profondeur, et une lieue de large d'un côté de la dite riviére au Nord, à prendre au bout de la terre et Seigneurie du Sieur *de la Lussaudiere*, ensemble les terres qui se trouveront de l'autre côté de la dite riviére au Sud ; à commencer au bout de la terre et Seigneurie de *St. François* et jusqu'aux bornes du Sieur *de Lavaliere*.

Régistre d'Intendance, N° 2 à 9, *folio* 146.

ST. GABRIEL.

Concession du 16me Avril, 1647, faite par la Compagnie au Sieur *Giffard*, de la Seigneurie de *St. Gabriel*, à prendre au même endroit que sa présente concession, *(Beauport)* rangeant icelle de proche en proche, autant qu'il se pourra faire, sur dix lieues de profondeur dans les terres vers le Nord-Ouest.

Par le papier Terrier, Tome 2e, Folio 655, le susdit fief avoit originairement deux lieues de front. Cette concession ne joint pas *Beauport*, parce que la concession de *Notre Dame des Anges* qui est entre les deux est plus ancienne.

Cahiers d'Intendance, N° 2 à 9, *folio* 73.

ST. HYACINTHE.

Concession du 23me Septembre, 1748, faite par *Rolland Michel Barrin*, Gouverneur, et *François Bigot*, Intendant, au Sieur *François Rigaud*, Seigneur de *Vaudreuil*, de six lieues de front, le long de la riviére *Yamaska*, sur trois lieues de profondeur de chaque côté d'icelle ; les dites six lieues de front, à prendre à sept lieues de l'embouchure de la dite riviére, qui sont les derniéres terres concédées.

Régistre d'Intendance, N° 9, *folio* 36.

FIEF ST. IGNACE.

Concession du 20me Août, 1652, faite par Monsieur *de Lauzon*, Gouverneur, aux Dames de l'Hôtel Dieu, d'une demi lieue de terre de front sur la riviére *St. Charles*, sur dix lieues de profondeur ; démembré du fief *St. Gabriel*, par donation du Sieur *Robert Giffard*, Seigneur de *Beauport*, aux dites Dames ; à prendre d'un coté aux terres concédées sur la riviére *St. Charles* au Sieur *Guillaume Couillard*, d'autre part à la ligne qui fait la séparation des terres depuis peu accordées aux Sauvages, d'autre bout par derriére aux terres non-concédées, et par devant à la riviére *St. Charles*.

Papier Terrier, N° 64, *folio* 296, 19me *Mars*, 1781.

FIEF ST. JEAN.

Concession du 13me Octobre, 1701, faite par *Hector de Calliére*, Gouverneur, et *Jean Bochart*, Intendant, aux Dames *Religieuses Ursulines*, des *Trois Riviéres*, de l'espace de terre concédée, qui se trouvé dans le lac *St. Pierre* au fleuve *St. Laurent*, du côté du Nord ; consistant d'environ trois quarts de lieues de front entre le Sieur *Joseph Petit* dit

Bruno, Seigneur de *Masquinongé*, et le Sieur *Trotier de Beaubien*, Seigneur de la *Riviére du Loup*, sur la profondeur de deux lieues.
Régistre d'Intendance, N° 5, *folio* 34.

AUGMENTATION DU FIEF ST. JEAN.

Confirmation du 27me Mars, 1733, par sa Majesté, d'une concession faite le 10me Décembre 1727, aux Dames *Ursulines* des *Trois Riviéres*, d'un terrain joignant du côté du Nord-Est au fief de la *Riviére du Loup*, appartenant aux dites Religieuses, et du côté du Sud-Ouest au fief du Sieur *Sicard*, ayant environ trois quarts de lieue de front sur trois lieues de profondeur.
Insinuations du Conseil Supérieur, Régistre G. folio 42.

ST. JEAN DESCHAILLONS.

Concession du 25me Avril, 1674, au Sieur de *St. Ours*, de deux lieues de terre de front le long du fleuve *St. Laurent*, à commencer quatre arpens audessous de la *Riviére du Chêne* en montant le dit fleuve, avec deux lieues de profondeur dans les dites terres, nommée la Seigneurie *Deschaillons*.
Régistre des Foi et Hommage, folio 67.
Cahiers d'Intendance, 2 à 9, *folio* 243.

AUGMENTATION DE ST. JEAN DESCHAILLONS.

Concession du 25me Janvier 1752, faite par le Marquis *de La Jonquiere*, Gouverneur, et *François Bigot*, Intendant, à *Roc de St. Ours*, Sieur *Deschaillons*, dans la profondeur de la riviére *du Chêne* sur le méme front de la Seigneurie de la riviére *du Chêne* à lui déja concédée, avec quatre lieues et demie de profondeur à prendre au bout des deux lieues que contient sa dite Seigneurie.
Régistre d'Intendance, N° 10, *folio* 28.

By this concession of augmentation, and by the ratification of it, the first concession is said to contain only one league and a half, as per the *Régister* N° 10, *folio* 2, *et Ins. Con. Sup. Letter* K. *folio* 7.

ST. JEAN PORT JOLI.

Concession du 25me Mai, 1677, faite par *Louis de Buade*, Comte de *Frontenac*, Gouverneur, et *Jean Bochart*, Intendant, à *Noël l'Anglois*, de la consistence de deux lieues de terre de front, le long du fleuve *St. Laurent*, du côté du Sud, à commencer depuis les terres qui appartiennent à la Demoiselle *Lacombe*, en remontant le dit fleuve, jusqu'à la concession de la Demoiselle *Geneviéve Couillard*, avec deux lieues de profondeur.
Régistre des Foi et Hommage, N° 44, *Page* 194, *le 23me Sept.* 1781.
Cahiers d'Intend. N°. 2 à 9, *folio* 301.

ST. JOSEPH.

Concession du 23me Septembre, 1736, faite par *Charles Marquis de Beauharnois*, Gouverneur, et *Gilles Hocquart*, Intendant, au Sieur *Rigaud de Vaudreuil*, de trois lieues de terre de front et deux lieues de profondeur, des deux côtés de la riviére du *Sault de la Chaudiére*, en remontant, ensemble tous les lacs, isles et islets qui s'y trouvent, à commencer à la fin de la concession accordée aujourd'hui au Sieur *Taschereau*.

Régistre d'Intendance, N° 8, *folio* 8.

ST. JOSEPH OU L'EPINAY.

Concession du dernier jour de Fevrier, 1626, faite par Mr. le *Duc de Vantadour*, à *Louis Hebert*, d'une lieue de terre de front, près de la ville de *Québec*, sur la rivière *St. Charles* ; sur quatre lieues de profondeur.

Papier Terrier, N° 15. *folio* 75, 3 *Février*, 1781.

This fief is said to contain but one quarter of a league in front upon four in depth, by a certificate of examination of the title of Concession; as also by mention in the act of donation of this fief in marriage with Demoiselle Chavigny, to Sieur de l'Epinay.

N. B. This fief by actual measurement only eleven arpents in front.

Cahiers d'Intend. 10 *à* 17, *folio* 577.

STE. MARGUERITE.

Concession du 27mè Juillet, 1691, faite par *Louis de Buade, Comte de Frontenac*, Gouverneur, et *Jean Bochart*, Intendant, au Sieur *Jacques Dubois de Boguinet*, de trois quarts de lieues ou environ de front, étant au derrière des concessions qui sont le long du fleuve *St. Laurent*, audessus des *Trois Riviéres*, appartenantes aux Révérends Peres Jésuites et au Sieur de *St. Paul* ; joignant au côté du Sud-Ouest au fief *Vieupont* et au côté du Nord-Est au dit fleuve des *Trois Riviéres* ; ensemble la profondeur qui se trouvera jusqu'aux fiefs de *Tonnancour* et de *St. Maurice*.

Régistre d'Intendance, N° 4, *folio* 5.

SAINTE MARIE.

Concession du 3me Novembre, 1672, faite par *Jean Talon*, Intendant, au Sieur *Lemoine*, de trois quarts de lieue de terre sur demi lieue de profondeur, à prendre sur le fleuve *St. Laurent*, depuis l'habitation des péres Jésuites, jusqu'à la Riviére *Ste. Anne*, supposé que cette quantité y soit.

Régistre d'Intendance, N° 1, *folio* 32.

STE. MARIE.

Concession du 23me Septembre, 1736, faite par le *Marquis de Beauharnois*, Gouverneur, et *Gilles Hocquart* Intendant, au Sieur *Taschereau*, de trois lieues de terre de front sur deux lieues de profondeur, des côtes de la riviére dite *Sault de la Chaudiére*, en remontant, en commençant à l'endroit l'*Islet au Sapin*, icelui compris, ensemble les lacs isles et islets se qui trouveront dans la dite riviére dans la dite étendue de trois lieues.

Régistre d'Intendance, N° 8, *folio* 6.

ST. MAURICE.

Confirmation du 13me Avril, 1740, par le Roi de concession faite aux intéressés de la Compagnie des forges, établies à *St. Maurice*, du fief de *St. Etienne*, réuni au Domaine de sa Majesté, par ordre du 6me Avril précédent, et des terres qui sont depuis le dit fief de *St. Etienne*, à prendre le front sur la rivière des *Trois Riviéres*, en remontant jusqu'à une lieue audessus du Sault de la *Gabelle*, ci-devant dit le Sault de la *Verrauderie*, sur deux lieues de profondeur, pour être le dit fief et les terres qui sont audessus unis et incorporés au fief de *St. Maurice*.

Insinuations du Conseil Supérieur, Régistre H. folio 57.

ST. GERVAIS AJOUTÉ AUX SEIGNEURIES DE ST. MICHEL ET DE LIVAUDIERE.

Concession du 20me Septembre, 1752, faite au Sieur *Michel Jean Hugues Péan de Livaudière* d'un terrein non concédé derrière la Seigneurie de *Beaumont*, et qui se trouve enclavé entre les lignes des Seigneuries de *St. Michel* au Nord-est et de *Livaudiere* au Sud-ouest, ce qui compose deux lieues de front sur une lieue seulement de profondeur, laquelle lieue de profondeur joint la ligne du trait-quarré des profondeurs des dites Seigneuries de *St. Michel* et de *Livaudiere*, et en outre quatre lieues et un quart de front ou environ (ce qui est appelé *St. Gervais* sur la Carte) sur trois lieues de profondeur, à prendre au bout des profondeurs de *St. Michel* des deux lieues ci-dessus concédées et de la Seigneurie de *Livaudiere*, laquelle étendue de terrein de quatre lieues et un quart de front, ou environ, sera bornée par devant au trait-quarré des lignes de profondeurs de *St. Michel*, des deux lieues ci-dessus concédées, et de *Livaudiere* ; par derrière par une ligne droite et parallèle joignant aux terres non-concédées ; au Nord-est par la continuation de la ligne de séparation des dites Seigneuries de *St. Valier* et de *St. Michel*, et au Sud-ouest également par la continuation de la ligne de séparation de la dite Seigneurie de *Livaudiere*, à celle nouvellement concédée à Mr. *de la Martinière* ; lesquels terreins de deux lieues de front sur une lieue de profondeur et de quatre lieues et un quart de front ou environ sur trois lieues de profondeur ci-dessus désignés ne feront avec les Seigneuries de *St. Michel* et de *Livaudiere*, appartenant déja au Sieur *Pean* qu'une seule et même Seigneurie.

Régistre d'Intendance, N° 10, folio 9.

ST. OURS.

Concession du 29me Octobre, 1672, faite par *Jean Talon*, Intendant, au Sieur *de St. Ours*, d'un espace de terre de front qui se trouve sur le fleuve *St. Laurent*, depuis la borne de la concession de Mr. *de Contrecœur* jusqu'à celle de Mr. *de Saurel*, tenant pardevant le dit fleuve, et par derrière la rivière d'*Ouamaska.* Les isles qui sont vis-à-vis de cette concession, accordées par le Comte *de Frontenac*, Gouverneur, au dit Sieur *de St. Ours* le 25me Avril, 1674.

Régistre des Foi et Hommage, N° 80, folio 5, 28me Mai, 1781.
Cahiers d'Intendance, N°. 2 à 9, folio 244.

ST. PAUL.

Concession du 20me Mars 1706, faite par *Philippe de Rigaud*, Gouverneur, et *Jacques Raudot*, Intendant, à *Amador Godefroy*, Sieur de *St. Paul*, de la baie et rivière appelée *Quetzezaqui*, autrement dit la grande rivière, pays des *Esquimaux*, et de cinq lieues de terre de large de chaque côté le long de la dite rivière, sur dix lieues de profondeur; avec les isles, islets et battures qui se trouveront dans les dites baie et rivière audevant d'icelle.

Cahiers d'Intend. N°. 10 à 17, folio 746.

ST. ROC.

Concession du 1er Avril, 1656, faite par Mr. *de Lauzon*, Gouverneur pour la Compagnie, à *Nicholas Juchereau de St. Denis*, de trois lieues de terre de front sur deux lieues de profondeur, avec les isles et battures audevant de la dite Concession.

Cahiers d'Intendance, N° 10 à 17, *folio* 665.

SAINT SULPICE.

Concession du 17me Décembre, 1640, faite par la Compagnie aux Sieurs *Cherrier* et *Leroyer*, d'une grande partie de l'Isle de *Montréal*, &c. &c. Plus une étendue de terre de deux lieues de large le long du fleuve de *St. Laurent*, sur six lieues de profondeur dans les dites terres, à prendre du côté du Nord sur la même côte où se décharge la rivière de l'*Assomption* dans le dit fleuve *St. Laurent*, et à commencer à une borne qui sera mis sur cette même côte, à la distance de deux lieues de l'embouchure de la dite rivière de l'*Assomption*, le reste des dites deux lieues de front à prendre en descendant sur le dit fleuve *St. Laurent*; tout ce qui est de la rivière des *Prairies*, jusqu'à la rivière de l'*Assomption*, et depuis la dite rivière de l'*Assomption* jusqu'à la borne cidessus, réservée à la dite Compagnie.

Ins. Con. Sup. Pour le reste de la dite isle par titre 21 Avril, 1659; Voyez le même Registre, et pour les dites titres ratifications amortissement, Voyez Cahiers d'Intend.

SAULT ST. LOUIS.

Concession du 29me Mai, 1680, faite par sa Majesté aux révérends perès Jésuites, de la terre nommée *le Sault*, contenant deux lieues de païs de front; à commencer à une pointe qui est vis-à-vis le rapide *St. Louis*, en montant le long du lac, sur pareille profondeur, avec deux isles, islets et battures qui se trouvent au devant et joignant aux terres de la *Prairie de la Magdelaine*.

Régistre d'Intendance, N° 2 à 9, *folio* 122.

Augmentation du dit fief d'une lieue et demie vers la Seigneurie de *Chateaugay*.

Le même Régistre, folio 124.

SHOOLBRED.

Grant in Fief and Seigniory to *John Shoolbred*, Esquire, made on the fourth of July, 1788, by His Excellency the Right Honorable *Guy Lord Dorchester*, Governor General, of the following tracts and parcels of land in the *Bay of Chaleurs*, videlicet:

A certain lot or tract of land lying at *Bonaventure*, beginning at the South extremity of the public road, which leads from the harbour of *Bonaventure*, to the settlement on the North bank, thence running nearly North-east to the extreme point of the said bank, and bounded by the course of the harbour, thence still bounded by the course of the said harbour, nearly North-west, two hundred and sixty-four feet, thence South-west parallel to the first course to the public road, thence South-east two hundred and sixty-four feet to the first station: Also a lot of land and space of ground whereon was built a storehouse, situate four hundred and forty-four feet from the North-east point of the said bank,

and East of the public road, which with an allowance of fifteen feet on
each side and behind the space whereon the said store stood, containing
five thousand and thirty-five square links. · Also the lots of land and
space of ground whereon were built two other storehouses, with fifteen
feet on each side, and behind each of the spaces of ground whereon the
said storehouses stood, the one situate two hundred and forty feet from
the South end of the bank and one hundred and sixty feet West of the
public road, containing three thousand eight hundred and twenty-two
square links, and the other situate twenty feet distant from the North-
west corner of the last mentioned ground whereon the said store formerly
stood, containing five thousand and thirty-five square links, the said
several lots or parcels of land above mentioned containing in the whole
one acre, one rood, and twenty-one perches. Also a certain other tract
of land lying at *Percé*, between the *Bays of Chaleurs* and *Gaspé*,
adjacent to the Island of *Bonaventure*, being the last fishing post at present settled and established on the North bench, leading to *Mount Joli*,
at *Percé*, aforesaid, bounded on the West by a deep *grève* or ditch adjoining to a fresh water brook, thence running East seven chains of sixty-
six feet each along the bank, thence South ten chains, thence West seven chains, thence North parallel to the second course unto the first
station, containing seven acres. Also a certain other tract of land situate
on the Westernmost extremity of *Chaleurs Bay*, running up the river
Ristigouche, about fifteen miles to the first point of land below *Battery
Point*, beginning at a boundary line one hundred and fifty chains East
of the bottom of the Easternmost Bay of *Nouvel Bason*, running North,
twenty-two degrees East to the mountains, thence bounded by their
course at an average depth of forty chains from high water mark to their
base, round *Nouvel Bason* Westward to a small cove, three hundred
chains West of the said first mentioned Bay, bearing from the Northern-
most extremity of *Migoacha Point*, being a sand bank, South eighty-
four degrees North, eighty-four degrees West, the superficial content
of the said last described lands is two thousand and eighty acres. Also
a tract of land, beginning at the aforesaid cove, and running the several
courses of *Point Migoacha*, to the Western extremity of a salt marsh,
distant from a point, where the inaccessible coast begins, about eighty
chains, thence to the said point, containing one thousand six hundred
acres. Also a certain tract beginning at the first mentioned point, below
Battery Point, North nineteen degrees and a half East, eighty chains,
thence South, eighty-eight degrees East, eighty-nine chains, thence
North thirty-three degrees East, eighty chains, thence North eighty-
three degrees East, sixty-nine chains, thence North fifty six degrees
East, one hundred and seven chains, thence South eighty degrees East,
twenty-three chains, thence South fifty degrees East, fifty-eight chains,
thence South, sixty-seven degrees East, forty-nine chains, thence North
sixty-eight degrees East, eighty-eight chains, thence South sixty-six
degrees East fifty-seven chains, thence South sixty-five degrees East,
eighty-four chains, thence South seventy-three degrees East, one
hundred and fifty-six chains, thence South thirty-nine degrees East,
ninety-five chains, thence South twelve degrees East, one hundred and
seventy-five chains, thence South eleven degrees East fifty-five chains,
thence South, fifty-six degrees West, forty chains to *Yacta Point*, containing six thousand five hundred and fifty acres, more or less.

Book of Patents for lands, Vol. 1. *page* 1.

SILLERY.

Concession du 23me Octobre, 1699, faite par *Hector de Calliere*, Gouverneur, et *Jean Bochart*, Intendant, aux révérends peres Jésuites, de la Seigneurie de *Sillery*, d'une lieue de large sur le fleuve *St. Laurent*, et d'une lieue et demie ou environ de profondeur, jusqu'à la Seigneurie de *St. Gabriel* qui la termine par derrière, commençant du côté du Nord-Est à la pointe de *Puiseaux*, et du coté du Sud-Ouest à une ligne qui la sépare du fief de *Gaudarville*, lesquelles lignes ont été tirées l'une il y a environ vingt-cinq ans, et l'autre il y a quarante ans.

Régistre d'Intendance, N°. 5, *folio* 26.

SOREL.

Concession du 21me Octobre, 1672, faite par *Jean Talon*, Intendant, au Sieur de *Saurel*, de deux lieues et demie de terre de front sur le fleuve *St. Laurent*, savoir, une lieue et demie au dela de la riviére de *Richelieu* sur deux lieues de profondeur, et une lieue en deça sur une lieue de profondeur, avec les Isles *St. Ignace*, l'isle *Ronde* et l'isle *de Grace*.

Régistre d'Intendance, N°. 1, *folio* 13.

DERRIERE SOREL.

Concession du 18me Juin, 1739, faite par le Marquis de *Beauharnois*, Gouverneur, et *Gilles Hocquart*, Intendant, aux Demoiselles *Angélique Louise* et *Elisabeth de Ramzay*, d'un restant de terrein derriére la Seigneurie de *Sorel*, à prendre entre les lignes et bornes des Seigneuries de *Lavahiére* de *Fezeret* et *St. Ours* ; bornée du côté du Nord-est par la dite Seigneurie de *Lavaliere* ; du côté de l'Est par la dite Seigneurie de *Fezeret* ; du côté du Sud-ouest par la ligne de la dite Seigneurie de *St. Ours*, ce qui compose environ une lieue et demie en superficie.

Régistre d'Intendance, N° 8, *folio* 27.

SOULANGE.

Concession du 12me Octobre, 1702, faite par *Hector de Calliére*, Gouverneur, et *Jean Bochart*, Intendant, à *Pierre Jacques Marie de Joybert*, Chevalier de *Soulange*, de la moitié d'une langue de terre sise au lieu dit *les Cascades*, de quatre lieues de terre de front sur une lieue et demie de profondeur au plus large de la dite langue de terre, et une demi lieue au plus étroit ; à commencer à *la Pointe des Cascades*, en montant ; joignant la dite terre celle accordée aux enfans de Mr. *de Vaudreuil*.

Régistre d'Intendance, N° 5, *folio* 37.

TERREBOIS OU DEVERBOIS.

Cette Concession ne se trouve ni dans le bureau du Secrétaire ni dans le Régistre des Foi et Hommage : son front étant inconnu elle occupe sur la Carte l'espace qui se trouve entre les concessions de Messrs. *de Grandville* et *de Lachenaie*.

This concession was originally granted to Fran. Dionis Bourgeois, 15 Nov. 1673, and was to consist of three leagues by three.

See *Cahiers d'Intendance*, N° 2 à 9, *folio* 61.

H

1

TERREBONNE.

Concession du 23me Décembre, 1673, faite par la Compagnie à Mr.' *Dautier Deslandes*, de deux lieues de terre de front sur la riviere *Jésus* autrement appelée la riviere *des Prairies*; à prendre depuis les bornes de la *Chenaie*, en montant, vis-à-vis l'Isle *Jésus*, sur deux lieues de profondeur.

Régistre des Foi et Hommage, N°31, *folio* 143, *le* 13me *Février*, 1781.

AUGMENTATION DE TERREBONNE.

Confirmation du 10me Avril, 1731, de concession faite au Sieur *Louis Lepage* de *St. Claire*; d'un terrein de deux lieues, à prendre dans les terres non concédées dans la profondeur, et sur tout le front de la Seigneurie de *Terrébonne*.

Registre des Foi et Hommage, N° 31, *folio* 143. *le* 13me *Fevrier*, 1781.

AUTRE AUGMENTATION DE TERREBONNE.

Permission du 12me Avril, 1753, donnée par le *Marquis Duquesne*, Gouverneur, et *François Bigot*, Intendant, au Sieur *Louis de la Corne*, de continuer le défrichement dans la profondeur de deux lieues, au de là des fiefs de *Terrebonne* et *Desplaines*.

Régistre d'Intendance, N° 10, *folio* 13.

TREMBLAY ET VARENNES.

Concession du 29me Octobre, 1672, faite par *Jean Talon*, Intendant, au Sieur *de Varennes*, de vingt-huit arpens de terre de front sur une lieue de profondeur, à prendre sur le fleuve *St. Laurent*, bornée d'un côté à la concession du Sieur *St. Michel* et d'autre celle du Sieur *Boucher*; et la quantité de terre qui se trouvera depuis le Sieur *Boucher* jusqu'à la rivière *Notre Dame*, la moitié d'icelle comprise, sur pareille profondeur, avec deux isles qu'on appellé *Percées*, et trois islets qui sont audessous des isles.

Régistre d'Intendance, N° 1, *folio* 17.

TROIS PISTOLES.

Concession du 6me Janvier, 1687, faite par le Marquis *de Brisay*, Gouverneur, et *Jean Bochart*, Intendant, au Sieur *de Vitré*, de deux lieues de front le long du fleuve *St. Laurent*, du côté du Sud, à prendre depuis la concession du Sieur *Villerai*, et descendant le dit fleuve, la rivière des *Trois Pistoles* comprise, et les isles qui se trouveront dans les deux lieues de la présente concession, sur deux lieues de profondeur, même celle au *Basque*, si elle se trouve dans la quantité présentement concédée.

Régistre d'Intendance, N° 3, *folio* 2.

PARTIE DES TROIS PISTOLES.

Concession du 6me Avril, 1751, faite par le Marquis *de la Jonquiere*, Gouverneur, et *François Bigot*, Intendant, au Sieur *Nicholas Rioux*, du terrein qui se trouve non concédé entre la Seigneurie de *Trois Pistoles* et les terres appartenantes aux représentans de feu Mr. *de Lachenaie*, ce qui peut faire environ trois lieues de front sur quatre lieues de profondeur, avec les isles, islets et battures qui se trouvent au devant du dit terrein.

Régistre d'Intendance, N° 9, *folio* 81.

TROIS-RIVIERES.

Les Régistres qui concernent cette partie de la Province ne suffisant pas pour placer, sur la Carte, les différentes concessions, elles y sont posées d'après un plan du lieu, sur lequel, dit-on, les propriétaires se réglent quant à leurs limites. Ces limites en quelques cas ne sont pas les mêmes que celles indiquées dans les titres originaires, différence qui peut avoir été causée par des échanges ou cessions faites entre les concessionnaires primitifs ou leurs représentans.

La figure A contient la ville et la banlieue des *Trois Rivieres.*—B la Commune.—C suivant le susdit plan est un octroi fait aux Jésuites le 9me Juin, 1650.

VAUDREUIL.

Concession du 12me Octobre, 1702, faite par *Hector de Calliére*, Gouverneur, et *Jean Bochart*, Intendant, à Mr. *de Vaudreuil*, pour ses enfans nés et à naître, de la moitié d'une langue de terre, située au lieu dit *les Cascades*, contenant quatre lieues de front sur une lieue et demie de profondeur au plus large de la dite langue de terre, et une demi lieue au plus étroit, à commencer vis-à-vis l'*Isle aux Tourtes*; joignant icelle pareille Concession accordée au Sieur *de Soulange*.

Régistre d'Intendance, N° 5, *folio* 38.

VAUDREUIL.

Concession du 23me Septembre, 1736, faite par *Charles Marquis de Beauharnois*, Gouverneur, et *Gilles Hocquart*, Intendant, au Sieur *Fleury de la Gorgendiére*, de trois lieues de terre de front et de deux lieues de profondeur des deux côtés de la rivière du *Sault de la Chaudiére*, en remontant, à commencer à la fin de la concession accordée aujourd'hui au Sieur *Rigaud de Vaudreuil*, ensemble les isles, islets et lacs qui se trouvent dans la dite riviére, dans la dite étendue de trois lieues.

Régistre d'Intendance, N° 8, *folio* 9.

VERCHERES AVEC AUGMENTATIONS.

Concession du 29me Octobre, 1672, faite par *Jean Talon*, Intendant, au Sieur de *Vercheres*, d'une lieue de terre de front sur une lieue de profondeur, à prendre sur le fleuve *St. Laurent*, depuis la concession du Sieur *de Grandmaison*, en descendant vers les terres non concédées, jusqu'à celle du Sieur *de Vitré* ; et s'il y a plus que cette quantité [qui est la predite Seigneurie de *St. Blain,*] entre les dits Sieurs, *de Vercheres* et *de Vitré*, elle sera partagée également entr'eux.

Régistre d'Intendance, N° 1, *folio* 23.

Autre concession, par le Comte *de Frontenac*, Gouverneur, au Sieur *de Vercheres* le 8me Octobre, 1678, d'une lieue de terre d'augmentation dans la profondeur de sa Seigneurie de *Vercheres*, pour être unies et jointes ensemble.

Régistre d'Intendance, N° Let. B. *folio* 4.

VIEUPONT.

Concession du 23me Août, 1674, faite à Mr. *Joseph Godefroi* Sieur *de Vieupont*, d'une étendue de terre sur le fleuve *St. Laurent*, du côté du

Nord, à commencer depuis la rivière appelée la *troisième rivière* jusqu'à celle appelée la *quatrième rivière* ; contenant quinze arpens de front avec une lieue de profondeur. Par une Ordonnance du 15me Juin, 1723, il a été réglé que le fief cidessus auroit dixsept arpens de front sur une lieue de profondeur.

Cahiers d'Intendance, pour l'ancienne Concession.

Au plan plus haut cité un lopin de terre entre Vieupont et Labadie *est dit appartenir à Mr.* Tonnancour.

Régistre des Foi et Hommage, N° 95. folio 78.

VILLERAY OU DARTIGNY.

Cette Concession ne se trouve pas au Secrétariat, non plus que dans les Régistres des Foi et Hommage ; elle occupe sur la Carte l'espace qui reste entre les Seigneuries de *l'isle Verte* et des *trois Pistoles*.

VINCELOT.

Concession du 3me Novembre, 1672, faite par *Jean Talon*, Intendant, à Demoiselle Veuve *Amiot*, d'une lieue de terre sur autant de profondeur, à prendre sur le fleuve *St. Laurent*, depuis le Cap *St. Ignace*, icelui compris, jusqu'aux terres non-concédées.

Régistre d'Intendance, N° 1, folio 26.

AUGMENTATION DE VINCELOT.

Concession du 1er Février, 1693, faite par *Louis de Buade*, Gouverneur, et *Jean Bochart*, Intendant, au Sieur de *Vincelot*, d'une lieue de terre de front avec deux lieues de profondeur, derrière et au bout de son fief de *Vincelot*, au Cap *St. Ignace*, qui a pareillement une lieue de front seulement, sur une lieue de profondeur, suivant les alignemens généraux de ce pays.

Régistre d'Intendance, N° 4, folio 9.

VINCENNES.

Concession du 3me Novembre, 1672, faite par *Jean Talon*, Intendant, au Sieur *Bissot*, de soixante et dix arpens de terre de front, sur une lieue de profondeur, à prendre sur le fleuve *St. Laurent*, depuis les terres appartenantes au Sieur *de la Cisière*, jusqu'aux terres non concédées.

Régistre d'Intendance, N° 1, folio 30.

YAMASKA.

Concession du 24me Septembre, 1683, faite à Mr. *de Lavalière* des terres non concédées qui sont entre la Demoiselle *de Saurel* et le Sieur *Crevier*, vis-à-vis le lac *St. Pierre*, du côté du Sud, contenant une demi lieue de front ou environ, ensemble les isles et islets et battures au devant, jusqu'au Chenail des barques, comme aussi trois lieues de profondeur, à commencer dès l'entrée de la rivière des Savannes (*Yamaska.*)

Régistre des Foi et Hommage, N° 45, folio 197, 3me Février, 1781.
Cahiers d'Intendance, 2 à 9, folio 143.

FIN.

GENERAL STATEMENT of the Lands granted in free and common Soccage in the Province of Lower Canada, within the undermentioned Townships, which have been laid out and sub-divided since the Year 1795, shewing also the Proportional Reservations for Crown and Clergy.

No. of Grants	Townships	By whom granted	Leaders of Townships	Date of the Patent	Number of Acres granted	Reservations for the Crown.	Reservations for the Clergy.
1	Dunham	Lord Dorchester	Thomas Dunn, Esq.	Feb. 2, 1796	40,895	8400	8400
2	Brome	General Prescott	Asa Porter, Esq.	Aug. 18, 1797	46,200	9030	9030
3	Bolton	Ditto	Nicholas Austin	Ditto	62,621	12,190	12,400
4	Potton	Ditto	Lauchlan M'Lean	Oct. 31	6000	1260	1260
5	Farnham	Ditto	Samuel Gale, &c.	Oct. 22, 1798	23,000	4830	4830
6	Hinchinbrook	Ditto	Gilbert Muller	Jan. 3, 1799	5200	1040	1040
7	Hemmingford	Ditto	Robert Gordon	March 18	20,800	4160	4160
8	Clifton	Ditto	David Steward	June 13	12,600	2520	2520
9	Armagh	Ditto	Thompson and Blais	July 13	2400	410	630
10	Rawdon	Ditto	James Sawer	Do.	1900	400	400
11	Chatham	Ditto	P. L. Panet and Wm. Fortune	Nov. 27	2200	410	410
12	Buckingham	Sir R. S. Milnes	Capt. Robertson	Do.	2000	420	420
13	Dorset	Ditto	John Black	Dec. 30	53,000	10,710	10,710
14	Hunterstown	Ditto	John Jones	April 29, 1800	24,620	4600	4600
15	Stoneham	Ditto	Kenelm Chandler	May 14	24,000	3428	3428
16	Tewkesbury	Ditto	Capt. Wulf	Sept. 18	2000	400	400
17	Stanbridge	Ditto	Hugh Finlay, Esq.	Sept. 1	41,790	8890	8610
18	Grantham	Ditto	William Grant	May 14	27,000	5250	5250
19	Upton	Ditto	Dd. Alex. Grant	May 21	25,200	5210	5000
20	Tewkesbury	Ditto	Denis Letourneau	May 14	24,000	4610	4620
21	Stanstead	Ditto	Isaac Ogden	Sept. 27	27,790	5250	5040
22	Broughton	Ditto	H. Jenkin and Wm. Hall	Oct. 20	23,100	3140	5340

No.	Township	Grantor	Grantee	Date			
23	Stukeley	Sir R. S. Milnes	Samuel Willard	Nov. 3	23,625	4200	4650
24	Hereford	Ditto	James Rankin	Nov. 6	23,100	4620	4410
25	Eaton	Ditto	Josia Sawer	Dec. 4	25,620	5250	4620
26	Shefford	Ditto	John Savage	Feb. 10, 1801	35,490	7098	7098
27	Barnston	Ditto	Lester and Morrogh	April 11	23,100	4735	4693
28	Orford	Ditto	Luke Knoulton	May 5	14,280	2899	2487
29	Newport	Ditto	Edmund Heard	July 4	11,550	2310	2310
30	Stoke	Ditto	James Cowan	Feb. 13, 1802	43,620	10,542	3912
31	Barford	Ditto	J. W. Clarke, Esq.	April 15	27,720	5880	5670
32	Windsor	Ditto	Officers and Privates, Canadian Militia	July 14	50,900	10,641	10,665
33	Chester	Ditto	Simon M'Tavish, Esq.	July 17	11,550	2310	2310
34	Simpson	Ditto	Officers and Privates, Canadian Militia	Do.	42,135	9326	8387
35	Halifax	Ditto	Benjamin Jobert	August 7	11,550	2310	2310
36	Inverness	Ditto	Wm. M'Gillivray	August 9	11,550	2310	2310
37	Wolfstown	Ditto	Nicholas Montour	August 14	1',550	2310	2310
38	Leeds	Ditto	Isaac Todd	Do.	11,760	2420	2630
39	Stoke	Ditto	Minor Children of William Boutellier	August 28	1890*	378	378
40	Ireland	Ditto	Joseph Frobisher	August 20	11,550	2310	2310
41	Durham	Ditto	Thomas Scott	August 30	21,991	4410	4410
42	Sutton	Ditto	Sundry Persons	August 31	39,900	8000	7800
43	Compton	Ditto	Jesse Pennoyer	August 31	26,460	5250	5250
44	Wickham	Ditto	William Lindsay	August 31	23,753	5364	4439
45	Arthabaska	Ditto	John Gregory	Sept. 30	11,550	2730	2100
46	Thetford	Ditto	John Mervin Nooth	Nov. 10	23,100	4620	4410
47	Ely	Ditto	Amos Lay, Junior	Nov. 13	11,550	2310	2310
48	Roxton	Ditto	Sundry Persons	Jan. 8, 1803	24,784	4620	4620
49	Ixworth	Ditto	Matthew O'Mara	Nov. 22, 1802	1260	210	420
50	Buckingham	Ditto	Fortune and Hawley	Jan. 22, 1803	14,910	3570	3560
					1,088,844	221,421	216,118

No. of Grants.	Townships.	By whom granted.	Leaders of Townships.	Date of the Patent.	Number of Acres granted.	Reservations for the Crown.	Reservations for the Clergy.
			Amount brought over		1,088,844	221,421	216,118
51	Granby	Sir R. S. Milnes	Officers and Privates, British Militia	Jan. 8, 1803	38,152	7908	7977
52	Milton	Ditto	Ditto	Jan. 29	24,518	6090	6273
53	Clifton	Ditto	Sundry Persons	March 5	23,546	4914	5064
54	Bury	Ditto	Calvin May	March 15	11,550	2310	2310
55	Hatley	Ditto	Henry Cull	March 25	23,493	4890	4910
56	Ascot	Ditto	Gilbert Hyatt	April 21	20,188	4200	4200
57	Ditton	Ditto	M. H. Yeomans	May 13	11,550	2310	2310
58	Clinton	Ditto	J. F. Holland	May 24	11,550	2510	2100
59	Bulstrode	Ditto	Patrick Langan	May 27	24,463	4894	4894
60	Kingsey	Ditto	George Longmore	June 7	11,478	2448	2422
61	Hemmingford	Ditto	Sundry Persons	June 17	8596	1707	1707
62	Kildare	Ditto	P. M. De La Valtrie	June 24	11,486	1990	2520
63	Clifton	Ditto	Mary Barnet	July 23	7035	1594	1680
64	Potton	Ditto	Henry Ruiter	July 27	27,580	5516	5516
65	Newport	Ditto	N. Taylor	August 4	12,600	2400	2400
66	Brompton	Ditto	William Barnard	Nov. 27	40,753	7800	8000
67	Shipton	Ditto	Elmer Cushing	Dec. 4	58,692	11,725	11,739
68	Stanstead	Ditto	Richard Adams	Dec. 6	1976	210	173
69	Tingwick	Ditto	Sundry Persons	Jan. 23, 1804	23,730	5040	4620
70	Warwick	Ditto	Ditto	Do.	23,940	4830	4830
71	Eaton	Ditto	Isaac Ogden	March 1	6300	1680	1890
72	Westbury	Ditto	Henry Caldwell	March 13	12,262	2701	2462
73	Hemmingford	Ditto	Dn. M'Naught	March 27	420	84	84
74	Nelson	Ditto	Officers and Privates of the Canadian Militia	April 21	38,326	7561	7745
75	Somerset	Ditto	Ditto	Do.	38,790	7483	7619
76	Windsor	Ditto	Mary Charlotte de Castelle	May 17	420	84	84

No.	Township	Grantee	Names	Date			
77	Tring	Sir R. S. Milnes	Sundry Persons	July 20	22,995	4400	4400
78	Hemmingford	Ditto	Matthew Scott	Dec. 24	2520	504	504
79	Barnston	Ditto	Sundry Persons	Jan. 7, 1805	2310	152	152
80	Rawdon	Ditto	R. Henry Bruere and Selby	Jan. 14	3150	630	420
81	Kingsey	Ditto	Major Holland's family, &c.	Jan. 28	11,198	2132	1998
82	Hatley	Ditto	Moses Holt's family	Feb. 21	2304	374	384
83	Newton	Ditto	C. De Lotbiniere	March 6	12,961	2331	2526
84	Onslow	Ditto	Forsyth and Richardson	March 9	1073	210	210
85	Melborne	Ditto	Henry Caldwell	April 3	26,153	5092	6184
86	Chester	Ditto	Sundry Persons	April 11	11,707	2320	2320
87	Dudswell	Ditto	John Bishop	May 13	11,632	2247	2483
88	Wendover	Ditto	Sundry Persons	June 24	12,558	2739	2266
89	Halifax	Ditto	Matthew Scott	June 25	11,243	2210	2520
90	Durham	Ditto	St. François Indians	June 26	8150	1620	1365
91	Stanstead	Ditto	Sundry Persons	August 2	3578	511	511
92	Farnham	Hon. J. Dunn, President	Jane Cuyler, &c.	Sept. 9	5040	600	802
93	Hull	Ditto	Philemon Wright	Jan. 3, 1806	13,701	2482	2243
94	Aston	Ditto	Sundry Persons	Feb. 17	27,127	5454	4847
95	Auckland	Ditto	Poleury Deschambault & others	April 3	23,100	4400	4400
96	Aston	Ditto	John Nelson	June 27	1260		
97	Frampton	Ditto	P. F. Desbarat, &c. &c.	July 10	11,569	2212	2200
98	Granby	Ditto	Jn. Margaret Isabella Simpson	July 3	420		
99	Acton	Ditto	Gother Mann, &c. &c.	July 22	22,859	4800	4842
100	Eardley	Ditto	Sundry Persons	August 22	5250	1300	1275
101	Buckland	Ditto	Sundry Persons	Nov. 26	12,182	2433	2367
102	Chatham	Ditto	Col. Dl. Robertson and Dr. S. Fraser	Dec. 31	5250	800	800
103	Lingwick	Ditto	Sundry Grantees	March 7, 1807	13,650	2600	2400
104	Lochaber	Sir R. S. Milnes	Archd. McMillan, &c.	March 26	13,261	3313	3291
105	Templeton	Ditto	Ditto	Do.	8919	2052	1829
					1,908,628	387,148	381,193

No. of Grants	Townships.	By whom granted.	Leaders of Townships.	Date of the Patent.	Number of Acres granted.	Reservations for the Crown.	Reservations for the Clergy.
			Amount brought over ..		1,908,626	387,148	381,193
106	Grenville	His Excellency Sir J. H. Craig, K. B. Gov. General, &c.	Ditto				
107	Ham	Ditto	Partial grant........	Jan. 28, 1808 ...	1260	211	400
108	Stanfold	Ditto	Jenkin Williams, &c...	Feb. 6	1250		
109	Maddington......	Ditto	G. W. Allsopp......	July 8, 1807..	26,810	200	200
110	Ditto	Ditto	Sundry Persons	Dec. 24, 1808 ..	6005		
111	Acton	Thomas Dunn	Sundry Persons	Dec. 1........	6033		
112	Granby, Milton, and Simpson	Ditto	George Walters Allsopp ..	July 22, 1806 ..	24,004		
113	Hull............	Ditto	Sundry Persons	July 29........	2590		
114	Frampton........	Sir J. H. Craig..	Robert Randall	Sept. 21, 1807 ..	630		
115	Wendover........	Ditto	Sundry Grantees......	Sept. 9, 1808 ..	12,380		
116	Onslow..........	Ditto	Benj. and Alex. Hart ..	Sept. 26......	200		
117	Windsor, Simpson, Somerset, and Nelson	Ditto	Roswell Minor, &c. &c.......	Nov. 1?......	12,667¾		
			Sundry Persons	Dec. 27	3780		
118	Farnham	Ditto	John Allsopp, &c. &c. ..	Feb. 11, 1809 ..	10,176		
119	Sherrington	Ditto	Frs. Baby and others ..	Feb. 22......	19,278		
120	Upton	Ditto	Lewis Schmidt and family	May 27	678		
121	Sherrington......	Ditto	Susan and Margaret Finlay	May 29	8395		
122	Wentworth........	Ditto	Jane de Montmoulin, &c. ..	June 3........	12,390		
123	Templeton	Ditto	Sundry Grantees	Nov. 29	8620		
124	Stanstead	Ditto	Sir R. S. Milnes......	March 19, 1810.	21,406		
125	Coupton	Ditto	Ditto..............	Do............	13,110		
126	Barnston	Ditto	Ditto..............	Do............	13,546	58,512	58,512
127	Shenley	Ditto	James Glenny	May 1........	10,298		
128	Shipton..........	Ditto	James Barnard	July 10	210		
129	Potton..........	Ditto	Thomas Shepherd	July 18	210		
130	Grenville........	Ditto	Archibald Campbell....	Dec. 12	616		

131	Ely	Ditto	Doctcci Higgins	Jan. 21, 1811	630
132	Newton	Ditto	Saveuse de Beaujeu, &c.	April 25	1137
133	Godmanchester	Ditto	Robert Ellice, &c. &c.	May 10	25,592
134	Barnston	Ditto	William Somerville	June 18	3200
135	Inverness	Ditto	Robert Skinner	Do.	600
136	Kingsey	Ditto	Edward Bayncs	Do.	600
137	Hemmingford	Thomas Dunn, gent.	Stephen Sewell	Sept. 18	3200
138	Hinchinbrook	Sir Geo. Prevost	Lieut. Col. R. Ellice, &c.	Dec. 30	5719
139	Ham	Ditto	Martha Mitchell	Dec. 31	1200
140	Chatham	Ditto	Sundry Persons	Jan. 10, 1812	13,319
141	Leeds	Ditto	George Hamilton	Dec. 7	8002
142	Eaton	Ditto	Joseph Cummings	Dec. 17	200
143	Sherrington	Ditto	Hon. J. Young	Dec. 30	
144	Godmanchester	Ditto	John M'Kindlay and others	Jan. 4, 1814	
145	Kingsey	Ditto	Donald M'Lean and family	Jan. 11	
146	Durham	Ditto	Ditto	Do.	
147	Leeds	Ditto	John Palmer and Rich. Sheppard	March 3	
148	Hemmingford	Ditto	John Graves and others	March 16	
149	Lingwick	Ditto	Hon. John Young	March 21	17,000
150	Ascot	Ditto	James Bangs	March 26	200
				Total	2,203,709½

445,660

439,705

Statement of the English Naval Force on Lake Ontario, 1814.		Statement of the American Naval Force on Lake Ontario, 1814.	
Names of Ships.	No. of Guns.	Names of Ships.	No. of Guns.
Saint Lawrence	102	Superior	60
Prince Regent	58	Mohawk	44
Princess Charlotte	42	Pike	
Montreal	24	Maddison	33
Niagara	21	Jefferson	28
Star (brig)	16	Independence	28
Charwell	15	Sylph	24
Magnet (schooner)	12	Oneida	18
Netly	10	Lady of the Lake	2
GUN-BOATS.		Four small craft	8
Cleopatra		Ten gun-boats	10
Lais			
Ninon		Total	291
Nelly			
Regent			
Thunderer	11		
Wellington			
Retaliation			
Black Snake			
Prescott			
Dreadnought			
Total	311		

K

Statement of the English Naval Force on Lake Erie, 1813.		Statement of the American Naval Force on Lake Erie, 1813.	
Names of Ships.	No. of Guns.	Names of Ships.	No. of Guns.
Detroit	20	Laurence	20
Queen Charlotte	18	Niagara	20
Lady Prevost	12	Caledonia	3
General Hunter	6	Ariel	4
Erie	2	Summers	2
Little Belt	2	Porcupine	4
Chippawa (8-inch howitzers)	2	Tigress	1
		Scorpion	2
Total	62	Trippe	1
		Total	54

N. B. This squadron was captured and destroyed the same year by a superior American force. Although the English ships exceeded the Americans in the number of guns, yet the calibre on the side of the latter was so much larger, that on estimating the weight of metal thrown by one broadside from each squadron, the American was to the English as 3 is to 2. The number of men on board the Americans was nearly in a similar proportion.

Statement of the English Naval Force on Lake Champlain in Aug. 1814.		Statement of the American Force on Lake Champlain in Aug. 1814.	
Names of Ships.	No. of Guns.	Names of Ships.	No. of Guns.
Confiance . . .	28	Saratoga (ship) . .	28
Linnet (brig) .	16	A brig . . .	26
Chub (sloop) . .	13	Ticonderoga .	22
Finch (sloop) . .	11	Commodore Preble .	11
Icicle (sloop) . .	4	Montgomery . .	9
GUN-BOATS.		Ten gun-boats . .	20
Sir James Yeo . 2		Total	116
Sir George Prevost . 2			
Lord Wellington . 2			
General Simcoe . 2			
Marshal Beresford . 1			
Sir Home Popham . 1			
General Brock . 1 } 19			
Tecumseth . 1			
Lord Cochrane . 1			
Canada . 3			
Blucher . 2			
Sir Sydney Beckwith 1			
Total 91			

N. B. This flotilla was captured and destroyed by the American flotilla before Plattsburg.

TABLE OF LATITUDE AND LONGITUDE.

	Latitude.	Longitude.	
Anticosti Island, S. W. Point	49.23	63.44	North, West from
Quebec (City of)	46.48.49	71.11	Greenwich.
Montreal (City of)	45.31	73.35	—
Kingston (Upper Canada)	44. 8	76.40	—
York	43.33	79.20	—
The Grand Portage on } Lake Superior	47.58	89.52	—

Rates of Pilotage for the River St. Lawrence.

From Bic to Quebec.

	Per Foot.		
	l.	s.	d.
From the 2d to the 30th April, inclusive	1	0	6
From the 1st May to the 10th November, inclusive	0	18	0
From the 11th to the 19th November, inclusive	1	3	0
From the 20th November to the 1st March, inclusive	1	8	0

From Quebec to Bic.

	l.	s.	d.
From the 2d to the 30th April, inclusive	0	18	3
From the 1st May to the 10th November, inclusive	0	15	9
From the 11th to the 19th November, inclusive	1	0	9
From the 20th November to the 1st March, inclusive	1	5	9

Rates of pilot water and poundage on pilot money are payable at the Naval Office by masters and commanders of vessels.

For every foot of water for which masters and commanders of vessels are bound to pay their pilots from Bic to Quebec, and from Quebec to Bic, 2s. 6d. currency per foot.

For vessels going to Three Rivers or Montreal,
   Of 100 to 150 tons inclusive, 2*l.* currency.
   Of 151 to 200 tons inclusive, 3*l.* —
   Of 201 to 250 tons inclusive, 4*l.* —
   Of 251 tons and upwards,   5*l.* —

On settling with pilots, masters, or commanders of vessels, or the consignees of such vessels, are to deduct 1*s.* in the pound for the amount of the sums to be paid for pilotage, which will be exacted by the naval officer at clearing out, the same being funded by law, under the direction of the Trinity House, for the relief of decayed pilots, their widows and children.

Regulations for the Payment of Pilotage above Bic to Quebec.

At or above the anchorage of the Brandy Pots - - - -	⅔ds of the present rate for a full pilotage.
At above the Point of St. Roc -	½d Do. Do.
For above the Point aux Pins, on the Isle aux Grues, and below Patrick's Hole - -	¼th Do. Do.
And at and above Patrick's Hole	The rates already established by law for shifting a vessel from one place to another in the harbour of Quebec, viz. 1*l.* 3*s.* 4*d.*

Rates above the Harbour of Quebec.

From Quebec,	For vessels of register measurement,	To Quebec, From Port-Neuf,
To Port-Neuf,		
	not exceeding 200	
4*l.* currency.	tons.	2*l.* 10*s.* currency.
	If above 200 and not	
5*l.* . . .	exceeding 250 do.	3*l.* 10*s.* . . . .
6*l.* . . .	If above 250 tons.	4*l.* . . . . .
To Three Rivers,		From Three Rivers,
or above Port-Neuf,	For vessels not exceeding 200 do.	and above Port-Neuf,
6*l.* currency.		4*l.* . . currency.
	If above 200 and not	
7*l.* . . .	exceeding 250 do.	4*l.* 10*s.* . . . .
8*l.* . . .	If above 250 tons.	5*l.* 10*s.* . . . .
To Montreal,		From Montreal,
and above 3 Rivers,	For vessels not exceeding 200 do.	and above 3 Rivers,
11*l.* currency.		7*l.* 10*s.* currency.
	If above 200 and not	
13*l.* . . .	exceeding 250 do.	8*l.* 15*s.* . . .
16*l.* . . .	If above 250 tons.	10*l.* 15*s.* . . .

Pilots are at liberty to leave vessels forty-eight hours after they arrive at the place of their destination.

Duties payable in this Province under several Acts of the Parliament of Great Britain, viz.

25th CHARLES II. Chap. 7.

		Sterling. *l. s. d.*	
On Ginger - - -	per cwt.	0 1 0	Exported from this province to any other part than Great Britain.
Logwood - - -	do.	5 0 0	
Fustick and all dying wood	do.	0 0 6	
Tobacco - - -	per lb.	0 0 2	
Indigo - - -	do.	0 0 2	
Cocoa Nuts - - -	do.	0 0 1	

			Sterling.		
			l.	*s.*	*d.*

6th Geo. II. Ch. p. 13.

On foreign Sugars or Pannelles	-	per cwt.	0	5	0

4th Geo. III. Chap. 15.

On foreign white or clayed Sugars	-	per cwt.	0	22	0
Ditto Indigo - - -		per lb.	0	0	6
Ditto Coffee - - -		per cwt.	0	59	9
Madeira ⎫					
Fayal ⎬ Wines - - -		per tun	7	0	0
Teneriffe ⎭					
From Great ⎰ Portugal, Spanish, ⎱ Wines		do.	0	10	0
Britain ⎱ and other ⎰					

6th Geo. III. Chap. 52.

On British plantation Coffee -	-	per cwt.	0	7	0
Molasses - -	-	per gal.	0	0	1
British Pimento -	-	per lb.	0	0	0½

14th Geo. III. Chap. 88.

For every gallon of Brandy or other Spirits of the manufacture of Great Britain - - -	0	0	3
For every gallon of Rum or other Spirits which shall be imported or brought from any of his Majesty's sugar colonies in the West Indies - -	0	0	6
For every gallon of Rum or other Spirits which shall be imported or brought from any other of his Majesty's colonies or dominions in America -	0	0	9
For every gallon of foreign Brandy or other Spirits of foreign manufacture imported or brought from Great Britain - - - - -	0	1	0
For every gallon of Rum or Spirits of the produce or manufacture of any of the colonies or plantations in America, not in the possession or under the dominion of his Majesty, imported from any other place except Great Britain - - -	0	1	0
For every gallon of Molasses and Syrups which shall be imported or brought into the province in ships or vessels belonging to his Majesty's subjects in			

	Sterling. l. s. d.
Great Britain or Ireland, or to his Majesty's subjects in this province - - - -	0 0 3
For every gallon of Molasses and Syrups which shall be imported or brought into the province in any other ships or vessels in which the same may be legally imported - - - -	0 0 6

Additional Duties laid on by the Provincial Parliament; Acts 33d Geo. III. Cap. 8, 35th Geo. III. Cap. 9, and 41st Geo. III. Cap. 14.

	l. s. d.
For every gallon of foreign Brandy or other Spirits of foreign manufacture - - - -	0 0 3
For every gallon of Rum or other Spirits except British manufactured Spirits, imported from Great Britain or Ireland - - - - -	0 0 3
For every gallon of Molasses and Syrups - -	0 0 3
For every gallon of Madeira Wine, by one Act 4d. by another 2d. - - - - -	0 0 6
For every gallon of other Wine, by one Act 2d. by another 1d. - - - - -	0 0 3
For every pound of Loaf or Lump Sugar - -	0 0 1
For every pound of Muscovado or clayed Sugar -	0 0 0½
For every pound of Coffee - - - -	0 0 2
For every pound of Leaf Tobacco - - -	0 0 2
For every pack of Playing Cards - - -	0 0 2
For every minot of Salt - - - -	0 0 4
On Snuff or flour of Tobacco, per lb. - -	0 0 4
On Tobacco manufactured in any other way than into Snuff, or flour, or powder - - -	0 0 3

Deduction of Weight.

On Coffee Bags or Bales, 3 pounds for every 100lb.
———— in Casks, 12 pounds for every 100lb.
Muscovado and Clayed Sugar in Casks or Boxes, 12 pounds for every 100lb.
Loaf and Lump Sugar in Casks or Boxes, 15 pounds for every 100lb.
Leaf Tobacco in Casks or Boxes, 12 pounds for every 100lb.

Leakage on Wines, Spirituous Liquors, and Molasses.

Three gallons on every hundred gallons.

Waste of Articles subject to Duties by Weight.

An allowance of three pounds on every hundred pounds.
On Salt, an allowance of waste of three Minots on every 100 Minots.
Salt landed below the east bank of the River Saguenai, on the north side of the St. Lawrence, and below the east bank of the River of the Grand Mitis on the south side, is not subject to duty.

Drawback.

There shall be allowed by the collector four-pence on every bushel of salt exported from the port of Quebec to any place beyond the above limits.
Seven-pence on every tierce of salmon, and four-pence on every barrel of salted beef or pork, or salted fish of any sort, exported from this province.

New and additional Duties.

New and additional duties imposed by the Provincial Act 45th Geo. III. Cap. 13, intituled, " An Act to provide for the erecting of a Common Gaol in each of the Districts of Quebec and Montreal respectively, and the Means for defraying the Expenses thereof."

		l.	s.	d.
* On Bohea Tea, per lb. -		0	0	2
* Souchong, or other Black Teas		0	0	4
* Hyson Tea - -		0	0	6
* All other Green Teas -		0	0	4
Spirits, or other strong liquors, per English gallon -		0	0	3
Wines - do.		0	0	3
Molasses and Syrups do.		0	0	2

* All Goods, Wares, Merchandises, and Effects (with certain exceptions), that shall be put up to auction or outcry, 2½ per cent. on the value at which said goods, &c. shall be sold or adjudged.

* New Duties.—Those on Spirits, Wines, Molasses, and Syrups, are in addition to what is already imposed upon them.

The duties imposed by the above Act are to continue for six years from the passing thereof, viz. the 25th March, 1805; and are to be raised, levied, and collected, and paid in the same manner and form, and under the same rules and regulations, penalties and forfeitures, as are by law now established for the levying and collecting of other rates and duties, with the same allowance for leakage and for the waste of articles by weight, subject to the said duties.

By another act of Parliament these duties have been continued for a further term of years.

Additional Duties—1813.

			l.	*s.*	*d.*
Upon Madeira Wine, per gallon	-		0	1	0
Port do. do.	-	-	0	1	0
Rum do.	-		0	0	6
Foreign Brandies and Geneva	-		0	1	0
Salt, per minot	-		0	0	8
Refined Sugars, per lb.	-	-	0	0	1
Leaf Tobacco, do:	-	-	0	0	3
Manufactured do. and Snuff, per lb.			0	0	6

A duty of two and a half per cent. on the invoice value of *all goods imported*, not already subject to duty, excepting salted beef and pork, salt fish, fish oil, wheat and peas, furs and skins.

This duty is *five* per cent. when the goods are imported by persons who have not resided six months in the province.

Fees to be taken by the Officers of Customs at the Port of St. John's, according to the Order of the Governor and Council of the 7th July, 1796.

	l.	*s.*	*d.*
For every Report of the arrival of and permit to unload any Vessel, Boat, or Bateau under five tons burthen	0	1	3
For ditto of any Vessel, Boat, or Bateau of five tons or upwards, and not exceeding fifty tons burthen	0	2	6
For ditto of any Vessel exceeding fifty tons burthen	0	10	0
For ditto of any Waggon, Cart, Sleigh, or other Carriage	0	0	4

	l.	s.	d.

For every entry of Goods imported by water communication   -   -   -   - 0 1 3

For do. of do. subject to duty by any Cart, Sleigh, or
other Carriage   -   -   -   - 0 0 6

For every Certificate of Goods having paid duty and
protection for the same   -   -   - 0 0 6

For every Bond for payment of Duties   -   - 0 2 6

By a subsequent Order of the Governor in Council of the 22d August, 1797, the following Additional Fees are allowed at the Port of St. John's.

For every Report of the departure of any Vessel, Boat, or Bateau under five tons burthen, towards the United States of America, subject to be reported at the Custom-house of the Port of St. John's by the Order of His Excellency the Governor in Council, bearing date the 7th day of July, 1796   0 1 3

For ditto of any Vessel, Boat, or Bateau of five tons or upwards, and not exceeding fifty tons burthen - 0 2 6

For ditto of any Vessel exceeding fifty tons burthen - 0 10 0

For ditto of any Waggon, Cart, Sleigh, or other Carriage 0 0 4

For every entry of Goods exported by water communication   -   -   -   -   - 0 1 3

INDEX.

A.

B.

C.

D.

I.

K.

L.

N.

O.

P.

Q.

R.

S.

V, & U.

W.

Y.

THE END.

DIRECTIONS FOR PLACING THE PLATES.

ERRATA.

Page 12, line 2, *for* by roads, *read* by-roads.
—— 27, — 12, *for* tracks, *read* tracts.
—— 28, last *line*, dele the *comma* after *Canada.*
—— 48, *line* 22, *for* track *read* tract.
—— 59, last *line*, *for* their *read* its.
—— 111, *line* 24, *for* Ellis *read* Ellice.
—— 214, — 10, *for* beach, *read* beech.
—— 228, — 7, *for* acres, *read* arpents.
—— 264, — 10, *for* Scaswinepus, *read* Scaswaninepu
—— 267, — 4, *ibid.* *ibid.*
—— 285, — 22, *for* Deschaillors, *read* Deschaillons.
—— 423, — 10, *for* government, *read* parliament.
—— 485, — 19, *for* Beauliece, *read* Beaulieu.

$ 4 —

T. DAVISON, Lombard-street,
Whitefriars, London.

Bind Oldach.   '4 -
                 6.25
                 ————
                 10.25